Ski Pioneers

Ski Pioneers

Ernie Blake, His Friends, and the Making of Taos Ski Valley

PHOTO BY KEN GALLARD

**As Told to
Rick Richards**

To Wendy

Rick Richards

Library of Congress Catalog Card Number: 92-73483
ISBN: 1-56044-157-7

Published by Dry Gulch Publishing in cooperation with
SkyHouse Publishers, an imprint of Falcon Press
Publishing Co., Inc., Helena, Montana.

Design, typesetting, and other prepress work by
Falcon Graphics, Helena, Montana.

Printed and bound in Korea.

Photographs on the following pages by Ken Gallard:

Page 1   *Ed Baca in Walkyries Chute*
Page 36   *Dick Taylor in Walkyries Bowl*
Page 73   *Mike Kaplan in Cuervo Chute*
Page 114   *Ed Baca, Dana Brienza, & Doug DeCoursey*
           on Lorelei
Page 143   *Mike Kaplan & Dana Brienza in West Basin*
Page 183   *James Herrera on Kachina Peak*

Distributed by
Dry Gulch Publishing, P.O. Box 310,
Arroyo Seco, New Mexico 87514,
1-800-435-4742, and
Falcon Press Publishing Co., Inc.,
P.O. Box 1718, Helena, Montana 59624, or call
1-800-582-2665.

CONTENTS

PREFACE ix

ACKNOWLEDGMENTS x

INTRODUCTION xi

I The Making of Ernie Blake

CHAPTER 1 2

From St. Moritz to Aspen

• Ernie's Schooling in Zuoz • The Bloch Family Immigrates to America • André Roch's Aspen • Ernie's First Jobs • West with Lanz of Salzburg • Early Colorado Racing •

CHAPTER 2 14

The Pre-War Years

• Ernie Meets Rhoda • Early Sun Valley—Pfeifer, Iselin, Engen and Lang • Friedl Pfeifer in Jail •

CHAPTER 3 27

The War Years

• Ernie's View of Hitler • Ernie Joins the Army • Bloch to Blake • Ernie's Work in Intelligence •

II Skiing As a Way of Life

CHAPTER 4 37

Post-War

• Aspen and Buttermilk Development • Friedl Pfeifer • Fred Iselin •

CHAPTER 5 44

Early Santa Fe

• Santa Fe Gets a Lift • Kingsbury Pitcher • Help from a Texas Millionaire • Early Lifts and Ski Methods •

CHAPTER 6 50
A Look at Twining

• Twining Geology and History • Choosing Twining •
Pete Totemoff • Bob Nordhaus and the Sandia Tram •
Expert Opinions •

CHAPTER 7 64
Innovations That Changed Skiing

• Howard Head and the Head Ski • Bogner Ski Pants and
Monica Brown •

III Building The Mold For Taos Ski Valley

CHAPTER 8 74
Early Beginnings of TSV

• Pattison Family Land • The Hondo Lodge and Public
Relations • The First Ski Lifts •

CHAPTER 9 83
Skiing, A Way of Life

• The Trailer Years • Chilton Anderson Arrives • Hirings and
Firings • Threat of a Swindle •

CHAPTER 10 90
Poma Lift and Trail Cutting

• Building the Poma Lift • Cat Driver Bud Crary •
Burroughs Land Dispute • Cutting Trails • The Old Road •
Dr. Al Rosen •

CHAPTER 11 .102
The French Connection

• Jean Mayer Arrives • Papa, Mama, and Dadou Mayer Arrive
• The Hotel St. Bernard • A Chef Named Yvon • The Hotel
Edelweiss • Ernie and Jean Mayer •

IV Taos Ski Valley Becomes a Reality

CHAPTER 12 115

Ski School and Techniques of Skiing

• Jean and the Ski School • Max and Theresa Killinger Arrive
• Ernie's Teaching Ability •

CHAPTER 13 126

Early Instructors' Exams and National Races

• Early Instructors' Exams • National Veterans' Race • Ernie
and the 1960 Olympics • Ski Racing Today •

CHAPTER 14 135

The Chicago Connection

• Support from the Chicago Area • Importance of the Santa
Fe Railroad • The Power of Ernie's Personality •

V Men Of Vision

CHAPTER 15 144

Loyal Supporters Shape the Ski Valley

• Rhoda, the Woman Behind the Man • A Destination Resort
• Foundations of a Ski Patrol • Shovelling and Packing
Techniques • Avalanche Control • Georgia Hotton •

CHAPTER 16 161

Men With a Vision

• Early Thunderbird Lodge • An Amazing Letter-Writing
Technique • The Martini Tree • Dave McCoy's Success at
Mammoth •

CHAPTER 17 168

Competition Among the Pioneers

• The Texas Market • On the Road and in the Air • Good
Public Relations • Taos Steepness and Mystique •

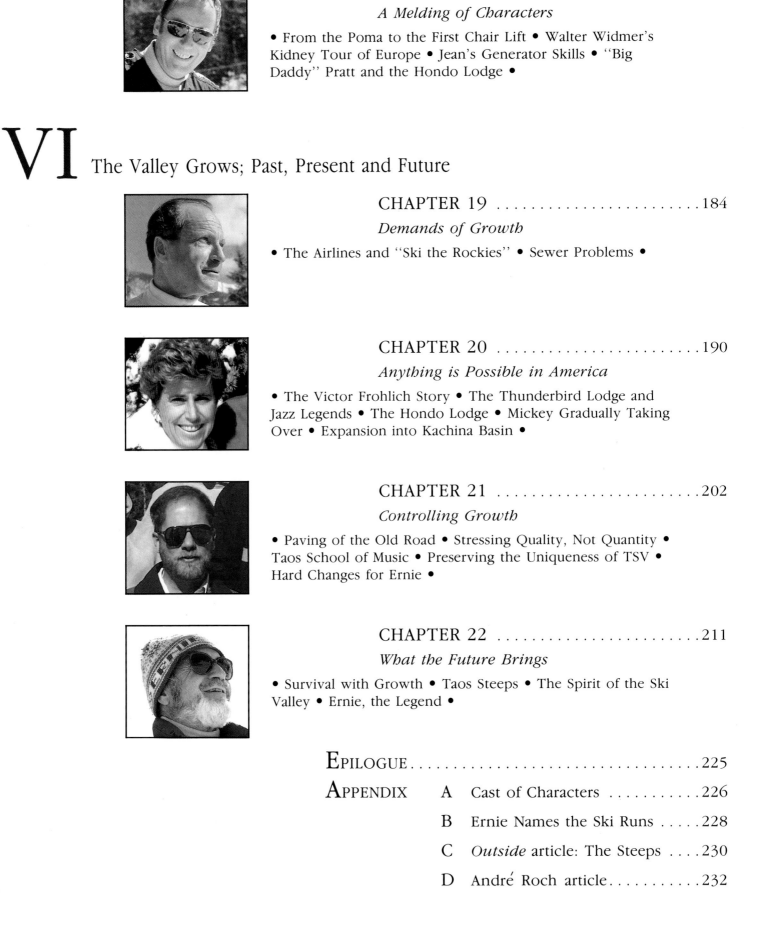

CHAPTER 18 174

A Melding of Characters

• From the Poma to the First Chair Lift • Walter Widmer's Kidney Tour of Europe • Jean's Generator Skills • "Big Daddy" Pratt and the Hondo Lodge •

VI The Valley Grows; Past, Present and Future

CHAPTER 19 184

Demands of Growth

• The Airlines and "Ski the Rockies" • Sewer Problems •

CHAPTER 20 190

Anything is Possible in America

• The Victor Frohlich Story • The Thunderbird Lodge and Jazz Legends • The Hondo Lodge • Mickey Gradually Taking Over • Expansion into Kachina Basin •

CHAPTER 21 202

Controlling Growth

• Paving of the Old Road • Stressing Quality, Not Quantity • Taos School of Music • Preserving the Uniqueness of TSV • Hard Changes for Ernie •

CHAPTER 22 211

What the Future Brings

• Survival with Growth • Taos Steeps • The Spirit of the Ski Valley • Ernie, the Legend •

EPILOGUE 225

APPENDIX   A   Cast of Characters 226

B   Ernie Names the Ski Runs 228

C   *Outside* article: The Steeps 230

D   André Roch article 232

PREFACE

A few years before Ernie Blake died we talked about doing this book. During those times I would walk up to the beaver pond with him; he was trying to keep his knees and mind as nimble as possible in those last years. Ernie wanted to do a book so I began taping his thoughts. We talked about war, world history, ski history, and how skiing started in Europe and America. We talked about how Taos Ski Valley came about, how it all happened—how he, Ernie Blake, happened. I taped many hours on many things, and then he died. It was a great loss. When we've known someone like Ernie and he goes, there's no way around it, we just plain miss him.

Dick Needham (editor of *Ski Magazine*) wrote, "The people interviewed in this book are/were themselves the most dynamic and colorful characters in the history of American skiing. Ernie Blake himself could easily be the subject of any book—a high-I.Q., Swiss-German bon vivant, Swiss fighter pilot, WWII interrogator (for the U.S.) of German rocket scientists (Himmler and Goering included), and hob-nobber with European royalty. He was the founder of New Mexico's Taos Ski Valley, builder of the ski sport in the U.S., and one of skiing's truly legendary characters. But most of all, Ernie represented to all who met him what was great and wonderful about the sport of skiing."

I had the "in" to all these wonderful characters because I have been around the ski business for a lot of years in many different places and was also the adopted son of Dr. Al Rosen of "Al's Run." I was in the kitchen that Sunday afternoon in 1955 when Ernie and Rhoda and Pete Totemoff came to Al's house—Ernie with his green Swiss hunting jacket with leather patches on the elbows, Pete with a red scarf, and Rhoda with her always smile. That was when Ernie announced, with his Swiss accent and those steel blue eyes, that he wanted to start a ski area up in Twining canyon and needed some help and advice.

I taught in the early days for Ernie. I was hired and fired more than most. I kept leaving and coming back. I'd have been the youngest ski instructor to make full certification on the first go, but Ernie didn't allow it. Chilton Anderson came and told me I passed, and it was a great celebration until the results were about to be announced. Chilton came back and told me that I could not be allowed my full certification my first time, no matter how good I was. That wasn't the way you did it under Ernie's rules; nothing good could be that easy.

I left Taos and went to Switzerland where I taught in Klosters-Davos, then back to Taos, then back to Switzerland for Hotel School in Lucerne, then back to Taos. I left again and went to Aspen where I taught skiing for Fred Iselin at Highlands. I ended up owning

Rick Richards.

Rick's Racks, (which followed Ed's Beds). I owned Montezuma Basin above Aspen where I ran summer racing camps for kids. Then I went back to Taos, then Hawaii, then to Stowe and back to Taos. It was always back to Taos. Over the years Ernie and I became very close; for some reason Ernie liked to talk with me.

When I was talking with Jean Mayer about this book he said, "You know, Rick, I was thinking that your book should go a little bit beyond Ernie. It should be not just a biography of Ernie Blake, but a means of expressing feelings about mountains and skiing, what skiing has done for America. Your book," he said, "could be a classic of the spirit of the mountain and skiing as it was intended originally. I wouldn't want it to be just the story of Ernie Blake; he was so much more than that."

My idea from the beginning was to interview Ernie's friends, the key players in Ernie's world of skiing, those who were involved in the pioneering of skiing in Taos Ski Valley as well as in the American West. My goal was to form a collage of what Ernie was through impressions, remembrances, and stories; how Ernie and his friends affected the things they created, what they dreamed, and what they left behind. It's not my story, it's theirs.

Rick Richards
Arroyo Seco, New Mexico, December 1992

EDITOR'S PREFACE

In this book, you will be taken on a journey through many of the lives of the key people in the ski industry of the West. The book is organized chronologically, beginning with the earliest years of Ernie Blake, and ending after Blake's death. He is the book's center. But spinning out and around Ernie Blake are the many others who make skiing what it is today. As a reader, you will enter into a roomful of these people. You will hear these people's voices rather than the voice of an omniscient author. Be willing to enter a kaleidoscope of voices and this book will wash over you like the deepest powder. I'm not a skier but when I finished the book I wanted to get right out onto those slopes. Enjoy this many-voiced journey.

Renée Gregorio
Santa Fe, New Mexico

ACKNOWLEDGMENTS

I want to thank Ernie for our walks; I miss those the most. I want to thank the mountains and the ocean and all the in-betweens. I want to thank Rhoda and Mickey for allowing me access to Ernie's papers and photographs. To all the people I interviewed, it was my joy. To all of you who were a part of all of this, but who I didn't talk to, you are still a part of it. Much appreciation goes to Nancy Halmstad who transcribed over sixty different people's tapes onto her computer so I could get them onto mine; to Bob Sturtcman who loves fiddling with computers and Ken Gallard for his help in gathering photographs and assisting with who knows how many "period-quotation marks," not "quotation mark-periods"; to Dick Needham who gave me first light that my wish for this book might be possible; to Lito Tejada-Flores, editor and publisher in Telluride, Colorado, for telling me that if I wanted my dream to come true, I needed to do some more work; to Renée Gregorio, editor; to Noelle Sullivan and SkyHouse Publishers; and my wife, Jean, who helped me do that work. Thanks to all the contributors of photographs; the Kit Carson Historic Museums; the Colorado Ski Museum and Ski Hall of Fame; the Aspen Historical Society; the Community Library, Ketchum, Idaho; Stowe Mountain Resort; the Aspen Skiing Company; Vail Associates; Mammoth Mountain; Winter Park; Sandia Peak Ski Area; Paul O'Connor, photographer, Taos, New Mexico, and to all the individuals who supplied their own photographs. Thanks also to Peter Shelton, for the article "The Steeps" in *Outside Magazine,* and to Clarke Dunnam, Taos artist, for drawing the skiing Taos Indian pin and the Taos logo. I couldn't have done it without my dogs and cat; they were a special help. But most of all, I thank my wife, Jean, for letting me chase the dream. And my children, David, Britt, and Tapley, for caring so much.

Namaste

"I pray there is no reincarnation. Nothing could equal the journey I've had, and everything else would be a boring encore."

Ernie Blake
1913-1989

Ernie Blake, Summer 1933. COURTESY BLAKE FAMILY COLLECTION.

Dick Needham: Ernie. The name mean anything to you? It has a kind of mischievous, malevolent ring to it, doesn't it? Ernie McCulloch, technical editor of *Ski Magazine* in the early sixties, was a fiery, fearless, redheaded Canuck who could beat the stretchies off any hotshot who challenged him on any North American hill—including the entire French Olympic team—then proceed to tell his hapless victim where he beat him, how he beat him, and why.

Another Ernie I know belongs to my boat club. He swears like a bosun's mate, swaggers like a pirate, and he calls you in the middle of the night to tell you your boat's been holed and is sinking, just for fun.

But my favorite Ernie...the ornery, irascible, lovable Ernie who built Taos Ski Valley but for some reason seemed always to transcend Taos...is gone.

Ernie Blake was 75 when he died on January 14, 1989, and I suppose someone of that age is entitled to cash in when he chooses, but I can say without being maudlin that I have never felt the loss of anyone in this sport so much in my life.

What Ernie did most was introduce me to his skiing friends, and the tapestry of their recollections of life with Ernie serve well as brush strokes in building his portrait. Ernie's life, after all, was the stuff of writers' dreams.

Herman Kretschmer: I first met Ernie in the fall of 1960, and that was a day that changed my life. I wonder how many of us can remember their first meeting with Ernie and how many lives were changed?

Max Killinger: I think Ernie has to be remembered for his history. I'm almost tempted to say that they don't make men like him anymore. It took that special time when he was brought up.

Buzz Bainbridge: Ernie had warmth in spite of it. You couldn't help but feel warm toward him. When you were mad at him, you felt good about him. He was just that kind of a personality. I used to be furious at him, and yet, if he smiled at you, you'd just roll over like a dog and wag your tail. You were so pleased that you pleased him.

When Ernie got in his little command post up there and got on that speaker and said, "You will enjoy the snow;" or "Get your skis off the fence, please," it was that voice from heaven.

Warren Miller: How do you talk about a guy that's left a real legacy? Ernie, he was really a crotchety old son-of-a-bitch. Crotchety is the wrong term—crusty is the best. He knew what he wanted. He knew instinctively what the skiers wanted, and he gave it to them.

Wolfie Lert: Ernie was able to meld the Hispanic and Indian, call it the Southwest, with American and European skiing and create a new mix, a new casserole. That's what Ernie succeeded in doing. Taos is so different.

Dick Needham: God bless you, Ernie. You were everything that was fun and wonderful and memorable about this sport. You made us feel special, if only because we made your acquaintance.

SECTION I

The Making of Ernie Blake

By chance, by birth, and by choice our characters are molded by the circumstances that surround us. Ernie Blake's character was formed by his deep roots in Switzerland and Germany. He went to a private school in the Engadine, in Switzerland, which shaped his youth. From an early age he excelled at sports and began downhill skiing in 1917 in St. Moritz. The Bloch family immigrated to New York in the thirties because Ernie's father believed that America was the land of choice and chance and Hitler's Germany was quickly becoming a place where that was not so, especially with a name like Bloch.

It was only a short time after Ernie immigrated to the United States in 1938 that he became connected with the beginning of the ski industry in America. His first real jobs were with Saks Fifth Avenue in its ski department and then later with Lanz of Austria in New York City. Mr. Lanz was Ernie's lift ticket West. Ernie was commandeered by Lanz to drive him West because Lanz had lost his driver's license for drunken driving. They set out on what Ernie called the "Thunderbolt Trip." It was on this trip that Ernie got a chance to see for real what he had only read about in André Roch's article on Aspen. The Rocky Mountains turned out to be more fantastic than Ernie had ever expected. He and Lanz sought out ski races on Loveland Pass, Pike's Peak, and anywhere else they could find a competition. It was on this trip that Ernie bumped into most of the early ski pioneers in America as he raced his way across the country.

It has always been said that behind every great man is a great woman, and for Ernie that became so when he had the good fortune to meet Rhoda Limburg in Stowe, Vermont, and romance her in New Mexico. Ernie and Rhoda spent their honeymoon in Sun Valley where Ernie met up with his old school chum Fred Iselin and other European ski greats like Friedl Pfeifer, who had the ski school in Sun Valley and was responsible for the laying out of the trails and lifts. After the war he did the same thing in Aspen. Alf Engen was there, too; he cut the Sun Valley trails and was later the man behind Alta. Ernie was quickly getting to know the main characters who pioneered skiing in the West.

That World War II was coming was certain to all the Europeans who had immigrated. Ernie enlisted in the U.S. Army, hoping to get into the 10th Mountain Division, but was branded a possible Nazi spy. By the time he was sent to Europe, the U.S. Army had targeted him for Intelligence. As happens with things in the army, Ernie wasn't trustworthy enough to enter the Mountain Troops, but he was plenty good enough for Intelligence. The army changed his name from Bloch to Blake and it became apparent how valuable he was with his insight into the German mentality. During the final year of the war, Ernie interrogated some of the most famous war criminals of the Nazi army, such as Goering, Speer, and Keitel.

There is, if we are fortunate, a time when we find out who and what we are. For Ernie this was his time, when he got a glimpse of what he could be.

CHAPTER 1
From St. Moritz to Aspen

Ernie: My mother, a Swiss, was the first to take me skiing. She wasn't much of a skier, but she was energetic. She was a sight with a big floppy hat the size of an automobile tire and long, tall ski poles. In St. Moritz in 1917, she took a disastrous fall in deep snow—it was all deep snow back then. Being four years old, I was afraid she was gone forever. It took two instructors to dig her out and carry her back home. At that point, I told her that she could save herself the trouble of buying me skis for my birthday, and if she had already, I told her I'd burn them.

I had been skiing since the winter of 1917-18, the last winter of the First War, when we took ski lessons in St. Moritz. When I went to school in the Engadine in Switzerland from 1923 to 1932, skiing was a mandatory sport. Our school took us three times a week, and we often went Saturdays and Sundays for fun. As for competition skiing, we could only do it if the area was absolutely free from avalanche danger. The school was worried about its business.

Walter Widmer: Downhill skiing, when Ernie started to go to school in Zuoz, was still in its infancy. The first downhill Olympics or alpine type of Olympic skiing was not until 1936. Ernie was skiing before the '20s.

Ernie: I grew up in a strange school, largely foreigners. The name of the school is the Lyceum Alpinum Zuoz, and the school motto is "Mens Sana in Corpore Sano": *A healthy mind in a healthy body.* Only ten percent of the kids were Swiss. Zuoz is a small village which dates back to the early 16th century. It's a beautiful village, one of the most beautiful in Switzerland. I was there from the age of ten to nineteen. My school was small, but quite famous, because it had most of the European nobility. The school was favored by a lot of people who weren't happy with the government of their country. It was a very tight group and a very sports-minded school, run on British principles. Boxing was an illegal sport; we did that in secret, but the English sports teachers fostered it.

E. J. Spencer was our sports coach and our English teacher. He played a tremendous role. He emphasized sportsmanship and team spirit. I made the school ice hockey team at the age of sixteen, the youngest ever. I was very proud of myself, but after the first game in which I shot five goals out of the eight we scored, I was fired from the team for selfishness because I had

shot with a trick wrist I had and had not passed the puck as Spencer wanted. So I was dropped from the team and had to wait two more months until I was called back.

Howard Head: Ernie talked about his high regard for E. J. Spencer. I could see the love and respect he had for that man. He was tough! He was tough and Ernie loved him; a lot of his sportsmanship and human growth came from that man. He was like a "good father" to Ernie.

Ernie: E. J. Spencer was a little more military than a father. He had another thing that cost us lots of lost games. When we knocked an opponent down in a hockey game, we were taught to stop and let the puck go and pick up the opponent from the ice and say "sorry, partner" in English and then play on, which did not work too well as far as scores were concerned. But it was a good education. E. J. Spencer was a great person. He played a tremendous role in the lives of many kids from many countries.

The friendships of the boys of that school were important; it's a small school of about 160 boys, and

Mother in Marienbad, 1904. COURTESY BLAKE FAMILY COLLECTION

Zuoz, 1931, hockey team (Ernie second from right). Courtesy Blake Family Collection.

Hockey in Davos, 1934. Courtesy Blake Family Collection.

we overcame the hatreds and the misery of the Second World War. We had each other to rely on during the Hitler years, and at the end of the Hitler years, we fed a lot of Germans including the grandsons of the German emperor who had been in the school and who were short on food and everything else.

Our school was full of very interesting people. For example, Albert Einstein was a part of our school orchestra. My father had given Einstein a dinner party, and I was asked to walk him home to make sure he got through the snowy slopes. Einstein lived there in the village in a chalet above the school. There was no path, so I walked him home. It was a great honor, but I wasn't aware of that then. I was merely struck by his long hair. I discussed with him not mathematics, but the upcoming second Tunney/Dempsey fight because I was very much involved in boxing.

Wolfie Lert: Ernie was kind of a hero in that school. He was captain of the ice hockey team. He would have been on the German Olympic team if he hadn't been Jewish. Ernie was really a sportsman, and it's typical that people keep saying that Jews are no good at sports.

Godie Schuetz: That was one of the most privileged boys' schools in Europe. Many Germans went there. That must have been one of the reasons why the army wanted Ernie to work at the Nuremberg trials as an interpreter. He was perfect in German and English, he knew the German mentality from A to Z, and he knew some classmates who were nobility in Germany.

Ernie: I was born in Frankfurt, Germany. I came to school in Switzerland because my mother's family was Swiss. I finally opted for Swiss citizenship, and served in the Swiss air force. I spent most of my life in Switzerland, from the age of one-and-a-half to nineteen. Then I went a year to a German university in Frankfurt and a year to a Swiss university in Geneva. In between, I served my periods in the Swiss air force.

Herman Kretschmer: My fascination with Ernie started out because of his intimate knowledge of royalty and nobility that previously I'd only read about in books. You'd mention the Kaiser or something like that, and he'd say, "Oh yeah, I remember the Kaiser's granddaughter, so-and-so, pulled me up by the ears one time." Later on, he produced one and had her living in Taos Ski Valley. I think that was one of the first things that intrigued us.

Ernie called me one day and said, "You'll never believe it. I am in *Burke's Peerage.*" The book showed Victoria and her daughter who was married to Frederick of Prussia, Kaiser Wilhelm II. He was the Emperor of Germany during the First World War and his son was Wilhelm Victor; his daughter was Victoria Marina. And the daughter's name was Countess Lingen; her true name was Princess Victoria Marina von

Countess Lingen (Princess Victoria Marina von Preusser) Taos Ski Valley, June 1976. COURTESY BLAKE FAMILY COLLECTION.

Ernie & Rhoda Blake with Jimmy & Rosalyn Carter, TSV, December 1986. COURTESY BLAKE FAMILY COLLECTION.

Preusser and her daughter's name was Dohna Maria Pearl. She worked for Ernie fitting boots. They lived in Taos Ski Valley. They bought a house up there which tickled the hell out of Ernie. She even taught in the German school with Ernie. That's the reason Ernie got the medal from the federal government of Germany. Let's face it; who else do you know has a direct descendent of Queen Victoria, or of the Kaiser, fitting boots in the ski shop at Taos Ski Valley?

Pete Totemoff: Ernie would throw out names of famous people as if he knew them; the funny thing was that he really did know them. Like old Jimmy Carter was even up there a year or so ago.

Ernie: I taught skiing to three girls who had just been introduced at court in England. One was the Honorable Pamela Digbee, and she had just married Randolph Churchill and divorced him. Their child was a son by the name of Winston Churchill and he became a highly acclaimed journalist and military expert. In her third marriage, she married Averell Harriman who was part of the Union Pacific Railroad which had built Sun Valley and created the design and construction of chair lifts. That was in 1935-36. I taught these three girls skiing in 1936-37 in Arosa, Switzerland, near Davos. These were my first students; I had all three at the same time. There were no lifts yet and they were not willing to climb, so we had a sleigh with two horses and a driver with icicles running out of his beard who drove us up every morning. Then we skied down. Once we went climbing, and I had to climb and carry their skis and them all the way up. Then it was too steep for them, and we had to carry them down again. They were not athletic, but they were very beautiful. They seemed very dull to me, but the girl who married Randolph Churchill and later Averell Harriman was not dull because she's a big wheel in the Democratic party now, and she's a great friend of the McKinneys who own *The Taos News* and the *Santa Fe New Mexican.*

Ernie: Our family immigrated to the United States because my father was smitten by America. He had lived in America for seven years during the very exciting time of the Spanish Civil War. New York was a charming place then. In Frankfurt we had a Murphy bed in our home, a Lazy Susan long before anybody else had one, and we had the first electric refrigerator in town. Everything was American. My brother brought back a typewriter from the United States; it was an Underwood. My mother had never been to this country until we immigrated in 1938.

My father wanted me to be a serious businessman. He was all for sports but not as a business, not as a way to make a living. That was not done. My father wasn't alive anymore when I started with the idea of a ski business. He objected to professionalism in sports. He liked me being a good hockey player. He came to every hockey game I played. He was pleased when I won ski jumping tournaments.

Vera Bloch: Our mother, Jenny Guggenheim, was born in Hofen, Switzerland but went through school in Basel. In her diary, they went to museums and concerts constantly which kept them busy with cultural things. In Frankfurt, we'd have a resident violinist, a Hungarian. My mother would have concerts, and my father said, "If she didn't have enough guests, she would go in the street and invite everybody over." He said it with such charm that my mother was not

Father in Frankfurt, 1935. COURTESY BLAKE FAMILY COLLECTION.

Marlo (sister), Mother, Ernie & Rudi (brother), Frankfurt, 1919. COURTESY BLAKE FAMILY COLLECTION.

Marlo & Ernie in Holland, September 1930.
COURTESY BLAKE FAMILY COLLECTION.

offended. He had a good sense of humor. My mother was wonderful. We were the first to have a bidet and corn flakes in Germany.

Rhoda Blake: My mother had a different attitude towards things; she didn't think it was proper to even mention the word "bidet," much less have one in your house. My sister had one in her house in England, and my mother tried to get her to take it out!

Ernie: Rhoda's mother was very much a Park Avenue woman. There is the famous story about Mickey right before he was born. I was in the army in Maryland, and Rhoda went home a week or so before the baby was due. Rhoda was very frail, sickness hampering her when she was a young girl. So, her mother should have known that Rhoda was not kidding when she said, "It's time for me to go to the hospital now." Her mother said, "Dinner is to be served now, and we will eat first." They ate and then went to the hospital.

My mother-in-law was the big reason I had to succeed, because I couldn't admit to her that I would carry on losing money. She didn't go for the ski business; she was upset. She sent the family lawyers to talk me out of it and told me to become a doctor or lawyer, especially if I had any sense of duty to my children.

Rhoda: My mother kind of indicated Ernest had a health problem when he came West since skiing wasn't a "business." Ernest's mother, however, was very tolerant of the ski business. You know, most people looked at it as if, well, that wasn't a real profession in those days. My mother definitely felt that this was not a serious way of making a living, and it really wasn't at that time.

Wolfie Lert: Rhoda's mother thought her daughter had married this nice kind of international banker, and that's what you wanted for your daughter, but he turned out to be a ski bum. It was a sad situation.

Rhoda: Ernest's mother was very determined. For years they wanted a house. Finally, Ernest's mother went to the bank to surprise Adolph for Christmas and gave him a house. She borrowed the money. The only problem was, he surprised her with a house also the same Christmas. It goes without saying, they kept the one his mother bought.

Vera Bloch: Our mother must have had some of the best decorators. The basement was like the dining car on a train. The upstairs was like a ship. The entrance was a railroad station. They had a wonderful party to celebrate its completion.

We did not take furniture when we immigrated. We brought silver, two tapestries and some paintings. Each one of us brought a certain number of books and some money. Living in America was not like living in Germany; here we lived very simply. My father's business, hatters' fur, was international enough that there were funds; there were partners in Holland and other places. One of my relatives said, "We immigrated, but the Blochs just moved." We did have an easier time, but it was not what we had in Germany by any means.

The span of children in our family goes like this. Margarete Louisa, or Marlo, came first. She became a doctor. Rudolph Ludwig, who became Rudi, came two years later. Ernest was born two years after Rudi. He was more like our mother and he was her favorite. Then there was a span of ten years until I was born.

Rhoda: Rudi was very laid back and casual; he had none of Ernest's energy and drive. Ernest was more conservative in his outlook while Rudi maintained a little of their background in the way he worked, the jobs he took, the way he lived. Had Rudi been younger, he would have been a hippie. He was a great physical therapist, because he was the type of person people would tell their troubles to while he was working with them. And where the doctors gave up, he didn't.

Ernest used to love to tell the story that when he and Rudi would go to the park to play, the other nannies would take their children away. This was because one day they were playing with Sandy Sanderson, and they were hanging him while playing cowboys, and their mother came just in time.

Adolph (father), Mother, Ernie & Vera (sister), Marienbad, 1934. Courtesy Blake Family Collection.

And then there was the story of the mattresses in the hotel, a very elegant hotel. It was built around a courtyard, and the first floor had a glass ceiling, and they had all their lovely teas and things there. In those days, it was customary for the maids to take the mattresses and air them on the balcony. Rudi and Ernest went around the balcony, flipping the mattresses, which then went through the glass. They were politely asked to leave.

Vera Bloch: They got along as brothers. We had a shooting range in the basement so you can imagine the size of the house. Ernest was close to Marlo; she came to Taos quite a bit. She would know things were wrong before I did. I almost learned by accident from her that Ernie had Parkinson's disease.

Ernie: Besides my father's love for America, the other major thing that influenced me to come to the United States and made me determined to explore the West was a story in the "Swiss Academic Ski Annal of 1937" about Aspen. I read it that year while being cared for with a broken leg in a hospital that was primarily for well-to-do ladies to come and have abortions. I broke my leg being very stupid. Like an idiot, I skied over a cliff in the fog after the Italians told me to wait until the sun came through. I called them a bunch of cowardly spaghetti-eaters, but I broke my leg and ended up in this abortion clinic. I was asked to translate Roch's story from the "Swiss Academic Ski Annal" from French into English, and my translation was published by the Colorado Historical Society. *(Ed. Note: A copy of this article is included in Appendix D.)*

The article had been written by André Roch, the famous man after whom the Roch Cup is named. He is the man who found Aspen. He had just come back from the exploration of Aspen together with a south Tyrolean-Italian by the name of Dr. Guenther Langes. They had been commissioned to come to Aspen to investigate how much potential there was for a ski resort.

They were commissioned by three young men with money; one was young Ted Ryan, who was the grandson of Thomas Fortune Ryan of Philadelphia. He inherited a vast fortune from his grandfather. Another was Billy Fiske, a wealthy American kid who was a star performer in the 1932 Olympics in bobsledding who was killed in the earliest part of the war while fighting in the Royal Air Force. The third one was Tom Flynn. They built a lodge between Aspen and Ashcroft, the Highland Bavarian Lodge on the lower part of Mt. Hayden.

Darcy Brown: Billy Fiske, Ted Ryan and Tom Flynn had built the Highland Bavarian Lodge. I was working in Denver at that time. What got Aspen started was André Roch going out and doing additional surveys for them.

Billy had been skiing in Europe, and they thought they could use that same height-above-timberline approach to skiing in Colorado without realizing there was a hell of a difference between 6,000 feet and 13,000 feet. They had a bill in the Colorado legislature to help finance the Mt. Hayden area tram. Then it fell through because of the war. I don't think it would have been a success, but if it hadn't been for the war, it might well have gone through.

Ernie: They hired André Roch and Dr. Guenther Langes, a famous slalom specialist, not a medical doctor but a doctor of law or philosophy. He came to Aspen and found that the lodge, already full of guests, was built in entirely the wrong place. Roch also told them the lodge was in the wrong place, but that it was nonetheless a fabulous situation because they had some great unexplored skiing around them.

Roch and Langes went and climbed all the surrounding mountains with seal skins. They spent a whole winter there under abysmal conditions, actually. But they were both rugged mountaineers. Roch had been to the Himalayas several times; he was a great adventurer. This story and knowing how my father felt about America left no question that I would go to the United States and explore the West for its skiing.

When I arrived in this country on August 28, 1938, I found that getting a job was much harder than I had anticipated. I arrived with $600, which was like $6,000 today, but it still didn't last very long. My father had brought me up on the idea that anybody who was willing to work and had a little brains would make a fortune very quickly in the United States because there were none of the handicaps that you had in Switzerland where people insisted that you have only one job your whole life, or, at the most, two. In America they didn't mind if you changed jobs if there was a better opportunity and so forth. I found that nobody had any jobs. It was the Great Depression. In 1936, there had been a boom that interrupted the depression, but in 1937, the stock market went straight down again.

I first tried to work for a Ford dealer and they had a big promotion. I went to the Italian section of New York because I spoke Italian. Every time I sold a car, which was a hell of a job then because nobody had any money, they told me that it was a relative or a friend of theirs, and it didn't count; I never got my commission.

My first real job was with Saks Fifth Avenue, beginning the 1st of December, 1938. I lived in the Duane Hotel, a comfortable, elegant hotel on Madison Avenue between 37th and 38th streets. I ended up being a ski instructor for Saks Fifth Avenue on their snow trains Friday night from

Grand Central Station to North Creek, New York. We came back Sunday night and we were back on the job on Monday morning. It was a sleeper train with two bar cars and a rental and purchase place car.

The main ski that we sold at that time was the wooden Attenhofer ski. The merchandise manager of Saks Fifth Avenue was a half-year older than I; I didn't like him because he didn't sell steel edges to people unless they could prove that they were top notch skiers. He didn't think beginners needed steel edges, which is the very opposite of what we felt. They also had Northland skis and Lund skis, and the ski clothing was mostly from Lanz of Salzburg where I had my second job.

Mr. Lanz took me away from Saks after I insulted Mr. Saks by telling him that his stuff was too gaudy and in bad taste, not knowing who he was. Even so, it took me a year-and-a-half before I got to Aspen and then only because Lanz, an Austrian and an avid skier, lost his driver's license for drunken driving and wanted to open a new ski store in San Francisco. I came along because he needed a driver; I was dying to get to Aspen. I always remembered the article by Roch.

Mr. Lanz and I took off for Denver on our "Thunderbolt Trip." It started with a hard drive from New York because it was all small roads. There was very little of the Pennsylvania Turnpike in operation yet. The worst part was from Pittsburgh on west through the hills of Pennsylvania and West Virginia. You endlessly saw the same scenery; the same farms seemed to come by. It took three days to get to Denver. We drove very hard.

In Denver, we thought we'd look at the skiing in Colorado, so we climbed up on Berthoud Pass and skied on Berthoud the first afternoon. Then we went and saw there was a race the first Saturday we were there. We went to the race on Loveland Pass in which you drove your car to the highest switchback and walked up from there with skins. There was a monstrous snowstorm that day.

Racing was important to me. It was the 7th of April, 1940, I remember that; it was the Zipfelberger Ski Race. Darcy Brown was there; I beat him. I met him there for the first time. The Schnackenberg brothers, Larry Jump, and Ralph Barr were there. The Zipfelberger brothers and the German-Bavarian cook from the Hilton Hotel in Albuquerque were there. I didn't know there was any skiing around Albuquerque. Bob Nordhaus, Max Dercum, and the people who formed Arapahoe were there. Everybody was there. That was a thrill to me. It was an unpacked course. There were guides to check our speed after we left, and to help us find our way through fog and snow. It was great fun.

Darcy Brown: We used to drive up back in the days when it was nice to have a non-skiing girlfriend

Ernie in Italian Alps. Courtesy Blake Family Collection.

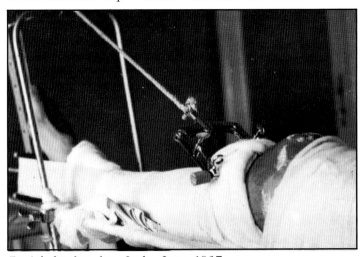

Ernie's broken leg, Italy, June 1937.
Courtesy Blake Family Collection.

Sepp Lanz, 1940. Photo By Ernie Blake,
Courtesy Blake Family Collection.

Ernie preparing for "Thunderbolt Trip," March 1941. COURTESY BLAKE FAMILY COLLECTION.

to drive the car around for you. I used to like those old races; that was when I first met Ernie, racing on Loveland Pass.

Bob Nordhaus: I met Darcy and Ernie racing back in 1940; we went up for a May Day race at Berthoud Pass, up at Fern Creek Headwaters. Everybody dressed up and had a good time. It wasn't too serious a race. I went up there with Blickenderfer and Darcy and three or four others.

A bunch of them had a little house at Empire which is right on the road; one road goes to Loveland and one goes to Berthoud. We always stayed up there overnight. Two of us drove from Albuquerque on a Friday night, skied Saturday and went to Empire and drank and sang. Henry Bradford who was from Denver would go crazy. He was playing records and dancing at two in the morning, and this race was the next day. It was in this little house right on a steep bank, and Darcy got up and threw all the records out the window and down the hill. So, we were not in good shape. I raced the next day, and it was a very steep course. Sunday night, we drove back to Albuquerque. In those days, you drove all night and skied and then drove all night the next night. Max Dercum used to go to those early races. He was a serious skier. Everybody else was having a good time.

Max Dercum: Racing was important to all of us back then. There were George Engle and Larry Johnson and some others who were involved; but Loveland Ski Area was just a rope-tow hill in the earliest days. They'd had a CCC (Civilian Conservation Corps) camp there and a temporary shelter which was for the CCC, and a dorm and bunkhouse. That turned into the first day shelter for Loveland Basin.

Arapahoe was among the earliest ski areas in Colorado; in fact, we all started the same year: Aspen with their single chair lift, Berthoud with the first double chair lift in 1946-47, and Arapahoe. We formed the Corporation of Arapahoe in 1946 and started assembling the old mining cables and the old equipment from the 10th Mountain Division, some of the cable trams that they used there for evacuation for supplies in Italy. We put some of that material together. The same engineers from Denver designed Aspen's first chair lift, the double chair lift at Berthoud, and the Arapahoe Basin lift.

Ernie was up here for those old races. There was a race on an almost annual basis. The Zipfelbergers put on this race on the top of Loveland Pass down towards the Zipfelberger Hut. It wasn't in the actual ski area, but they had a trail and they also assembled some people there, those who were very influential in developing skiing in Colorado in those days. That was back in 1945.

Berthoud Pass, Colorado, March 1940. Photo By Ernie Blake, Courtesy Blake Family Collection.

Loveland Pass, Colorado, April 1940. Photo By Ernie Blake, Courtesy Blake Family Collection.

Ernie Blake, March 1941. Courtesy Blake Family Collection.

Edna Dercum. COURTESY COLORADO SKI MUSEUM, VAIL.

Darcy Brown & Ruth Prase, Independence Pass, Colorado, June 1941. COURTESY BLAKE FAMILY COLLECTION.

George Engle: I raced with Ernie and Darcy Brown and Max Dercum in the late 1940s when we were up there on Loveland Pass. But the biggest recollection I have of Ernie was he came down here with a friend of his from Santa Fe, and they were driving a jeep with side curtains on it. They stayed at Miller's Idlewild Inn which has since burned. A funny old lodge. It happened that a girl working there, who is now my wife, was making beds and waiting on tables. Ernie got acquainted with her and we all went out and partied a little bit. Ernie kept taking Joyce off in the evening to Adolph's Bar, and I wasn't very happy with this. He finally said, "Well, you better marry that girl." So I did. That was my first real recollection of Ernie. I then got to know him better from racing.

I knew nothing of the ski business; I went into it because I wanted the life it offered. I'd always heard about Colorado and the snow. I had skied a lot in New England over the years from 1935 until 1943. When I ended up in Denver, I had to get a job right away, and I went to work for an oil drilling company in their accounting office. After a while, I didn't like the city and asked to be put out in the field. They kept promising me, and we kept working more and more until finally I was working six days

and five nights a week. So, the week before Christmas, I told the office manager I was taking a week off. He said I couldn't do that because they were too busy, and I said, "Either I get a week off or I'm gone." He let me go for a week.

I came up to Winter Park. I ran into some people, and they found out I could ski, and they needed a patrolman. They were dependent upon just a small group, the beginning of the National Ski Patrol—the Denver branch. There were just a few guys in it, but they only came on Saturdays and Sundays and sometimes not then. So, I was hired to be the first paid ski patrol. I didn't ask how much it paid or anything. I went back to Denver and packed up my gear and went in to the office and said, "I quit." I was making probably $200-$250 a week, and I moved to Winter Park for $5 a day and never regretted it. It's a great life. It was fun, and it was tough going in those days, but it was worth it, never a question.

Max Dercum: Ernie had great experiences in Switzerland, in Italy and in Europe when he was growing up. He was experienced in alpine skiing before any of us. He loved to race and he set up many races in New Mexico including some of the old Masters' Races and the Veterans' Races. They called one the Senior Olympics. Then, more recently, we had the Taos Cup. Ernie thrived on competition. I'm still racing in the old International Masters, and my wife Edna is too.

Wolfie Lert: The thing that I cannot ever forget is that I went racing and Edna Dercum beat me.

Max Dercum: I was not able to compete in the Internationals as I had planned, but Edna won the Gold Medal in Giant Slalom in the International Masters in Winter Park this year, 1991, at the age of seventy-seven. Edna was just elected to the Ski Hall of Fame which makes us the third husband and wife in that group.

Otto Lang: Ernie was such an enthusiastic racer. The thing that pleased me very much was that I sponsored him for the Ski Hall of Fame.

George Engle: I can remember the first race that I went to at Sandia when Ernie had that National Veterans' Race, the first one down there. Poor Ernie. He was beside himself because the night before the downhill, the winds came from the west and covered that whole mountain with so much red dirt that you could not move. I can remember how disappointed he was, but we side-slipped most of the dirt off of the snow, and we had a race. It wasn't much of a race, but Ernie and Rhoda were just great. Ernie wanted his own ski area; he talked about it even then.

Ernie: Mr. Lanz and I left Loveland, and from there, we went to Colorado Springs. We went up on Pike's Peak where there was another competition. They had a rope tow in Glencove, and they had a chef who had fought in the Boer War which seemed awfully long ago, forty years earlier. From there, we went to Salt Lake. We skied at Alta. Then we went on to California and skied at the Sugar Bowl, and we took part in the Silver Belt Races. That was when I met Joern Gerdts who became one of the famous *Life Magazine* photographers, who did many ski photos early on.

Joern Gerdts: I met Ernie in 1940 in Los Angeles while Ernie was on his trip with Sepp Lanz. Then the Scharfs at Sugar Bowl put in a ski shop in 1941 after Hans Hagemeister had left, and I ran the ski shop for Lanz. Ernie bought all the sweaters and ski boots and skis for the store. He was the advisor of what to get because the Scharfs were not very good at ski equipment. They were boyhood friends of mine, and had started with Lanz. They came over from Europe and met Lanz on the boat, and they started the Lanz Ski Shop of California in Los Angeles. It was in 1941, the first time Ernie was there.

I started skiing in Garmisch-Partenkirchen early on. I left from Germany, in 1939, and came to California and skied first in Mammoth. We had skis

on top of the car, and when we stopped for the red light, people kind of looked.

Ernie: A year later, after my first trip out West, I went back to Aspen in 1941 and visited and skied with Darcy Brown. The war was obviously coming, and there was no sense in a ski area. Besides, I had nowhere near the financial means.

Darcy Brown: I was one of the original investors in the Aspen Ski Company. I owned some of the land that they were using to ski on, and I was director of the company right from the start, although I didn't take over active management of it until 1956-57. I was born in Aspen in 1912. My

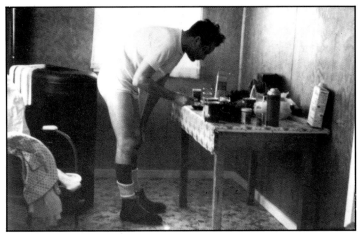

Ernie travelling in 1941. COURTESY BLAKE FAMILY COLLECTION.

Joern Gerdts. COURTESY JOERN GERDTS.

father came to Aspen in 1880 and was in the mining business there and later got into ranching and other business interests.

Warren Miller: Darcy's father came over Independence Pass when it wasn't done. It took him two weeks to go ten miles with their wagons. They were in the timber and hardware lumber business in Aspen. He and a partner loaned a guy $132 worth of shoring timbers for one-third interest in a mine. His one-third interest on $132 turned out to be three million dollars in the 1880s. What would that be worth today? If any of us had gone to Aspen in 1947, we could have also bought $20 lots, but we didn't have the $20.

CHAPTER 2
The Pre-War Years

Ernie: I met Rhoda Limburg the Christmas of 1940 on the top of Mt. Mansfield in Stowe, Vermont. I was skiing with Count Haugwitz-Reventlow and a gang of young skiers who had skied with him as I had in St. Moritz when we were schoolboys. Count Reventlow had just been divorced from Barbara Hutton, and every afternoon he wept into his martini. We were supposed to cheer him up. He had a beautiful British girlfriend, and his British butler was along. The butler pressed our pants; this was a long time before stretch pants. We looked very elegant every morning.

Rhoda and I met on top of the chair lift at the Octagon, Christmas, 1940-New Year's 1941. They had these duck cloth covers over the chairs that kept the cold in, and you really froze your balls on that lift. It was the coldest chair lift I have ever experienced.

My eyes focused on Rhoda because she wore Langer pants. She bought them at Lanz, or maybe someplace else, and we got acquainted. But, I had no time for Rhoda, and she had no interest in me because I read *The New York Times* on the lift when I got bored riding. Then when I'd get to the top I would stuff the Sunday edition into my chest and stomach when I was done reading it, so I looked pretty ridiculous. We didn't make a great impression on each other.

Rhoda: Ernest looked like a dumpy penguin with those papers stuffed in his pants.

Ernie: Five months later, I was invited to a tennis party at Rhoda's mother's house in the country in Westchester, and that's when Rhoda and I became friendly. I told Rhoda I was going skiing at Alta in June. Every sensible New York girl would have sneered at that, but she thought that was a great idea. We decided to meet at Alta, and that was the beginning of the end.

Rhoda brought me to New Mexico and the Santa Fe-Taos area. Rhoda had gone to Mexico with two girl friends, and when they finally came back, we met in Santa Fe. We spent a week together there horseback riding and doing other things. That was the end of the summer of 1941. I drove down from Sun Valley after I toured around selling clothing and ski accessories to everybody in the West. Rhoda and I traveled back to New York together. She had a Buick, and I drove my Ford. Rhoda and I became engaged on that trip across the country and we decided we'd live in northern New Mexico somewhere between Santa Fe and Taos.

Vera Bloch: It was an engagement party that my relatives certainly remembered as the first really big and happy affair for those who had immigrated to New York. That engagement party is still talked about in memory.

Ernie: I became a citizen on the 27th of June, 1943, in the army. I married Rhoda on the basis that she would make me a citizen, but she became a citizen on the basis of my citizenship.

Rhoda: We thought I was an American citizen; it was only when Ernest went to get his citizenship that we discovered I wasn't. I was adopted when I was about three. It was assumed that I also became a citizen, having been adopted by American parents at such a young age, but I wasn't.

Ernie: Rhoda was a war orphan from England. Her father was a New York State Supreme Court judge, but the judge, as judges will do sometimes, forgot to check her citizenship. Rhoda's father was like the shoemaker whose kids never have good shoes.

Rhoda has the same integrity as her father. He was a first-class man, a truly honorable man. I don't say that easily about people. I don't know many men who hold onto and have this straightforward, honest character. Rhoda has it. Mickey has inherited much of that.

Rhoda: Ernest was made a citizen very simply. One morning, the army took all the guys at the camp down to Fredericksburg and made them all citizens, without question. I remember there were a bunch of people sitting outside the courthouse, "Did you hear that? Those guys in uniform are all foreigners!" They were all there to be sworn in.

Ernest and I went to Sun Valley on our honeymoon. And we almost got divorced on our honeymoon. Ernest could ski, and I couldn't; he was not about to stay on the beginner's hill, and I didn't want to go down the steep runs. So we ended up compromising. He went skiing on the big mountain, and I went skiing on the baby slope, and we met at the end of the day.

Walter Widmer: I never saw Ernie and Rhoda ski together ever; not one single time.

Ernie: While Rhoda and I spent our honeymoon in Sun Valley, Friedl Pfeifer was there then, and that's where Friedl and I met. Fred Iselin was also there; we were old school friends from Zuoz. Friedl was running the ski school for Averell Harriman, and he did a great job in laying out the trails and getting Sun Valley started. Friedl does not get enough credit for all he

Old single chair & "Octagon" Restaurant top of Mt. Mansfield, Stowe, Vermont, 1940s. PHOTO BY DERICK STUDIO, COURTESY STOWE MOUNTAIN RESORT.

did. Alf Engen was also involved with getting Sun Valley started; he worked for Friedl.

Friedl, Alf, Fred Iselin, and Otto Lang were all in Sun Valley at that time. It was a tremendous group of characters. They were all pioneering, and they all did a fantastic job in Sun Valley and with skiing itself. Harriman liked Friedl's ideas. Friedl was a magnificent skier and very strong like Fred; they made skiing a beautiful sport.

Joern Gerdts: Of all the skiers, I always thought Friedl was about the most graceful skier I ever saw. Alf Engen was great and so was Fred Iselin, but Friedl was something else. Friedl knew skiing like Ernie; they were raised with it very early on.

Friedl Pfeifer: I started skiing about 1915 when I was four years old in St. Anton, Austria. St. Anton was the birthplace of alpine skiing through Hannes Schneider. After World War I, skiing was just beginning to make it. Skiing was, of course, thousands of years old in Scandinavia and Austria for transportation, cross-country. Alpine skiing came after the First World War, and it got popular very quick. Before, I was sledding and cross-country skiing. We had to because that's the way we went to school.

In 1925 Hannes Schneider tapped me on the

Count Haugwitz-Reventlow & Jean Model, Stowe, Vermont, January 1941. COURTESY BLAKE FAMILY COLLECTION.

Ernie & Rhoda, honeymoon, Sun Valley, Idaho, February/March 1942. Courtesy Blake Family Collection.

Rhoda Blake, Alta, Utah, June 1941. Photo By Ernie Blake,
Courtesy Blake Family Collection.

shoulder as a kid of fourteen and asked me if I would want to be a ski instructor some day. He discovered me through our school races. I won almost all the races, and he saw me as a natural. I have memories when we would all race down together. You could compare yourself halfway down and one-third down or two-thirds down; it was great. Racing the clock was so lonesome. You're up on this huge mountain and have to go down all by yourself, and there's no one to compare with.

One race I raced in Italy on a huge mountain, and again I got very bored. Every minute, somebody went off. About two-thirds down, and I thought I was doing pretty good, and here comes this guy right by me. I was about to throw in the sponge, but thank goodness I finished it, because the bottom slope being springtime was cut up with frozen ski tracks. Most of the other racers had a lot of problems with it because when you turned and got into one of those frozen grooves, you'd bury it. So, I went slower because I knew that. I finished up and went to my hotel and started packing, thinking I must be nearly last with close to one hundred racers. I went back to see who won it, and the people started clapping; they were clapping for me. The guy had fallen and didn't get up. I'll never forget that.

Otto Lang: Friedl saw Sun Valley, and then he went to New York where he was hired by Alice Kiaer, sort of the godmother of the American Olympic Ski Team, to coach the American Ski Team. Through her, he met Averell Harriman, and they talked about Sun Valley.

Harriman and Friedl immediately had a great rapport. Harriman liked his ideas, and Friedl was very savvy. He knew exactly what had to be done. He said, "What you have now is nothing. This is for beginners and intermediates. You won't attract any of the better skiers. You have to develop Baldy. We could cut trails and open the slopes and have a lift up the mountain."

Harriman liked the idea, and so when he heard Friedl was going to coach the American Ski Team, he said, "Take them to Sun Valley, and they'll be our guests." That's the way Friedl came to Sun Valley. The brass of the Union Pacific Railroad wasn't happy with having Sun Valley, but Harriman was the boss so they had to go along with it. Ultimately, Friedl became the head of the ski school, taking over from Hans Hauser.

Friedl Pfeifer: I was trying to get the first trails cut at Sun Valley. It was a miserable job. I knew I was getting the lift up, but there were all these trees you had to cut. So somebody suggested to get the CCC. I thought, what the hell is CCC? It was after the war, and Roosevelt started it for kids who had never seen a blade of grass. They were taken out in the country to do some manual work. When somebody suggested getting the CCC, I asked, "What about those big trees?" They said they had a guy leading these troops in Ketchum, Idaho who could do it. There was a Norwegian, Alf Engen. I didn't know then who he was.

So, here Alf came with about fifteen or twenty of them. The first day I saw him, I thought he was fabulous, and of course, he turned out to be a skier too. I didn't know his history at that time, but he came, and he had jumped at Salt Lake City, the longest jump ever in the world.

The CCC workers were great. Great young people. They were so happy out of the town; they had an axe, and they felt like heroes to see a tree fall down. And Alf Engen did it all. Alf knew how to work with people; he always had a special way with people. He is a fabulous human being.

Alf Engen: I got a crew of men, about one hundred men, which is what they gave me to do the clearing of the trails. So, we went up and cut all of River Run. Then we went over on Warm Springs, and we set up a run at Warm Springs from the bottom to the top through all that woods. It was very difficult to get these guys to get down on their knees and cut them low enough. Friedl would get after them saying we couldn't have stumps left that way.

Roosevelt took these people who hadn't gone to school or anything and they came from the South and

Count Felix Schaffgotsch surveying Sun Valley potential.
COURTESY UNION PACIFIC COLLECTION, P 2331, REGIONAL HISTORY DEPARTMENT OF THE COMMUNITY LIBRARY, KETCHUM, IDAHO.

from the North. They came from New York and all over. They were actually still fighting a war, these young kids, even on the job. So, you had that to contend with. I was in tremendous shape at that time, and I wanted to see the work done, and Friedl was on me to get it done.

One day, I had one really big guy from the South. In camp, they were all scared of him. So when he'd sit down, they'd all sit down, and I couldn't get them to get up until he started to go. On this particular day, I said to him, "I think I have come to the end of the rope for me. Now you are going to go to work, and you're going to tell these guys to come and go to work." I said, "It's either you or me. It's just as simple as that because if you are big enough to take me, you can have the job. Come and get it."

And he came towards me. He was a little bit bigger than I was, but he wasn't as quick. I dropped down low, and I got him by both legs and gave him a heave, back to the hill, and he went down at least twenty or thirty feet. So, I said, "Do you want the job or do you want me to handle it? Are you going to do as I say?" He didn't say anything, but he went over to the boys and said, "You guys go to work."

When we got down to the camp that night, I said, "You got a little beat up on top. Do you want to try here on the ground?" He said, "Okay." So we did. We put on a good exhibition, and he put on a real good fight; they all liked it. So I asked him into my place to see if he'd like to be my leader. He said he would like to very much, and from then on, I never had any trouble with that camp.

I worked for the Forest Service in Hayward, Utah. But, when they started to build Sun Valley, Count Felix Schaffgotsch was the one who picked out Sun Valley; he was a friend of Averell Harriman. Felix knew about skiing. He was a skier, not a racer like Friedl, but probably one who was the most knowledgeable about resorts. He saw this place in Sun Valley, and it was a big snowy year in 1936 with all these rolling hills over there just like Austria. Right after that, Harriman asked me to come, to see if the Forest Service would let me come.

At that time, there was mostly ski jumping. We had to have a ski jumping hill. So, I went up, and I supervised building the ski jump in Sun Valley. After that, we got into a little bit more of the downhill trails.

Friedl was there, running everything for Harriman including running the ski school. The first to run the ski school was Hans Hauser, then Friedl Pfeifer, then Otto Lang, and so on. Friedl was in charge of laying out all of these trails. We started right down at the bottom of the River Run and went all the way to the top of Baldy. We cut up all of Canyon Run, Prospector and Warm Springs; we did it all with the CCC boys.

Harriman invited me to come to Sun Valley for my honeymoon; my wife and I got married in 1937. I had been at Sun Valley all during the summer of 1936-37, until just before Christmas with the CCC boys. When my wife and I arrived, the orchestra was playing, and Harriman came out to meet us at the lodge. Somehow, right then, my wife and I stayed for ten years. He hired me right then. That was before the work on Baldy. My wife was secretary/treasurer of the ski club, and practically all the movie stars in Hollywood had been there, and the senators and big politicians and big doctors were all there at that time.

Harriman gave us a room at the lodge which we stayed in all the time we were there. Across the hall, Gary Cooper had hired that room for the year with his wife. All the stars were there, just like we talked to anybody here. They were just all good friends. I skied with guys like Clark Gable and Hemingway.

Oh, I knew Hemingway very well. I fished with him and Clark Gable too. Hemingway was writing one day; he lived in the lodge then. There was a pond out there, and the ducks came in and quack, quack, quack, and he didn't like that, so he would shoot through the window. He got reprimanded for that, though. Hemingway was the only one who could have done that and gotten away with it, or maybe Fred Iselin, or his dog Bingo.

Rhoda, honeymoon in Sun Valley, February 1942.
PHOTO BY ERNIE BLAKE, COURTESY BLAKE FAMILY COLLECTION.

Ernie: Fred Iselin was in Sun Valley then already with Friedl. I knew Freddie from way back, from 1925. He was a schoolmate of mine. Fred did things different; he did them his way. Fred was in Sun Valley from the beginning with Friedl; then they both went to Aspen after the war. Friedl I knew from before the war from my days with Lanz of Salzburg. They were both in Sun Valley, actually, when Rhoda and I were there on our honeymoon. Fred was a famous character; what a showman!

In school, in Zuoz, Fred was in a parallel class as he took a different major, but we were together. We skied together. He was a far superior skier from the time that we were small boys. He was the first one of any of our schoolmates who could do the forward flip. He was a great athlete, but he did not conform to the school. I was the school captain and responsible for creating hockey teams, both ice hockey and field hockey, and cricket teams. Freddie didn't cooperate. He was a single operator who did things his own way. But we were tremendous friends.

Fred won many, many more important races than I did. He was all his life long an incredible skier. He was, incidentally, the son of the man who brought skiing to Switzerland and was very important in the structure of ski history in the world, Colonel Christof Iselin from Glarus, Switzerland. Freddy was the only son. There were three daughters besides him.

Friedl Pfeifer: I met Fred in the FIS (International Ski Federation) in Chamonix in 1937. Then when I took over Sun Valley Ski School, I was looking for ski instructors. There were seven the first year, and I built it up to over fifty. Somebody told me that Fred was in Los Angeles. So, I traveled to Los Angeles and contacted him.

When I left Sun Valley, I wanted Fred to take over after me, but it didn't work out because the management didn't like it—the Swiss so to speak. Fred was one of the classic characters; Fred and his dogs and dogs stories. He could sure make you laugh; he was very disruptive, a free spirit.

Gary Cooper & Averell Harriman, Sun Valley. Courtesy Union Pacific Collection, P 3278, Regional History Department Of The Community Library Ketchum, Idaho.

Friedl Pfeifer. COURTESY UNION PACIFIC COLLECTION, P 2785, REGIONAL HISTORY DEPARTMENT OF THE COMMUNITY LIBRARY, KETCHUM, IDAHO.

Sun Valley, Dollar Mt. COURTESY UNION PACIFIC COLLECTION, P 2931, REGIONAL HISTORY DEPARTMENT OF THE COMMUNITY LIBRARY, KETCHUM, IDAHO.

Fred Iselin at Sun Valley. COURTESY UNION PACIFIC COLLECTION, P 2945, REGIONAL HISTORY DEPARTMENT OF THE COMMUNITY LIBRARY, KETCHUM, IDAHO.

Fred Iselin racing the Harriman Cup, 1942. COURTESY ARRIAGA COLLECTION, P 3496, REGIONAL HISTORY DEPARMENT OF THE COMMUNITY LIBRARY, KETCHUM, IDAHO.

Alf Engen: Fred and Elli had a big St. Bernard dog named Bingo. And you could always see Bingo coming out there with a Brandy cask under his collar. Bingo got to know his way around Sun Valley, and he had a lot of freedom to walk around when Fred wasn't there.

So, Bingo started to go down to Ketchum to the pool halls, and at that time, those guys were making home brew. They were making this home brew on the outside, and Bingo would go down and see this thing, and he would get drunk. And every day, he would make his trip down to Ketchum, and if Fred couldn't find him anywhere, he would get on the telephone and ask if Bingo was there. "No, I haven't seen Bingo today." So he'd call up another pool hall and another one, "Is Bingo there?" "Oh, yeah, Bingo is here." "Put him on the phone," Fred said, "and let him hear me." Then he'd say, "Bingo, you come home." And Bingo would go right home. That's a true story, and it happened time and time again. I used to see Bingo in the flower beds, standing there on all four feet kind of weaving around; he had a little too much of that stuff, see.

Bingo was a showman like Fred. If you had a camera with you and tried to shoot Bingo's picture, he would sit there and pose—just like Fred. He would do that until you walked away.

It was a famous group of men who were in Sun Valley then; look what they all did for skiing. I always said, when Sun Valley is right, with the right snow and the right combination, there's no place in the world like that to ski. It doesn't happen too often because the snow conditions aren't all that good. It's tough in Sun Valley, but it has a wonderful feeling.

Alf Engen: I was born in 1909 and I started skiing when I was about two years old at home in Norway. I came to America in 1929, and I didn't even know they had snow in this country. When I came here, I hunted for a soccer field and when I found one, I stayed there until someone came to play. That's how I came here, and I used my life savings to get here. They paid me to play soccer in Chicago where I had relatives. I played for Chicago, and we played Milwaukee just before Christmas. It was a cold day, and I heard that someone was ski jumping out in the park there. So I told my manager after the game, "You've got to take me out and see what it's like." I went out there, and sure enough, they were jumping with a scaffold jump.

21

Alf Engen as a young boxer. COURTESY ALF ENGEN.

Alf Engen arrives in the U.S. as a professional soccer player. COURTESY ALF ENGEN.

So I went up and asked one if I could borrow his skis and jump once, and he looked at me and said, "No, because you haven't got ski poles or boots or anything." I said I didn't mind because I could see what kind of bindings he had—they were long thongs. I said I could do it with long thongs and I'd make out. So, I went up and jumped. When I went back up again I said, "Boy that was fun. Mind if I try once more?" He said, "I don't know who you are, but the way you jump, you can have them all afternoon." I must have jumped eight or nine times, and I had broken all the records.

Right after Christmas, the professional jumpers had their first tournament in Wisconsin. I told them I didn't have any skis or anything. They gave me skis and said they'd get clothes for me for this tournament. This was the biggest scaffold hill set in the world. I borrowed some skis from Hans Haugen. They were two grooves, and I was used to three grooves. They were not the best skis. When the tournament was over, I had won it, and I set the new world's record for scaffold hills. I jumped 187 feet; I remember that. That set me up for a while. Then it was week after week after week for five years; we were professionals, and we made good money.

I had people come over here from Norway in ski jumping, and I was setting the pace, the records, and they didn't know how I did it. I developed another form, too, for one thing. We were jumping for money; we jumped everywhere. The Haugen brothers started it, and they got all the best ski jumpers in America together.

We went out to California, the East, Midwest. By our rules, there was no form. It was just distance, but you had to stand up. The more trouble you had in the air, the better the people liked it, so we were acrobats too. We jumped for everything we had, and everyone on the team was for that because there were twenty of us; half of the money we took in was split between all of us. So, you always got something. The other half was in three prizes, so we had to go for it.

Everyone pressed me to go too far down into the transition, the place where the hill flattens out. They wanted more speed all the time. I could out-jump them, but if we had a sailing contest, I could miss and hit the flat. So, I had to learn how to ski fast or slow. There's a way to do that, too. If I was really concerned and I had too much speed and we had to start from the same place, I would be very far forward and press on my tips. And I had my heels up, and that slowed me up. Then I could let them go. But now, if I wanted more speed, I would pull the tips up. Then I developed a form. I couldn't figure out how I could go so close to the transition all the time. If I went past the transition, I ould be dead, see. In the air, I looked like a jackknife. If I went too far, all I did was open up.

I was a professional ski jumper for many years, and believe it or not, I was the first man to jump the length of a football field on that kind of equipment—311 feet. Friedl and I did double jumps more than once. Oh, Friedl, he could jump, and he had jumped back in Europe. To do a double jump with Friedl, that was a thrill.

Friedl Pfeifer: I've got a picture of Alf at Sun Valley way up in the air. He had sort of accused me that I wouldn't have the guts to double jump, and I said, "Yes, let's go."

We were quite a group in those days. Otto Lang took over the ski school after I was put in jail and went to the war camp. I asked Otto to come to Sun Valley because Rockefeller always brought Otto as his private instructor. After this happened a couple of times, Harriman wanted to know why Rockefeller always brought Otto out as his private instructor; he wanted him to come to Sun Valley on a permanent basis.

Otto Lang: It was a sheer fluke that I came to Sun Valley. I had opened my ski schools in Mount Rainier and Mount Baker and Mount Hood, but Nelson Rockefeller, who I had met my first week in the East, took a liking to me. While I was at Mt. Rainier and Averell opened Sun Valley, he wanted to attract all the celebrities and all the movie stars. Nelson was an avid skier and had a great following of friends. Harriman invited Rockefeller to Sun Valley and said he'd give him his private railroad car if he'd come. Nelson said he'd come but he wanted Otto Lang to come to Sun Valley also, and Averell said fine. Hans Hauser didn't have any objection, and I came and spent eight days with them and then went back.

The next year, the same thing happened again. Rockefeller went to Sun Valley and he wanted me. By that time, Friedl was already in charge. Averell asked Friedl, "Why is it that Nelson always has us send to Mt. Rainier for Otto? Why don't you try to get Otto to come to Sun Valley?" Friedl said that I had my own ski school, I just got married and he didn't think I'd want to. Friedl wrote to me, and I was ready to go. The weather in the Northwest in the winter drove me bananas with snowstorms and roads closed, and half the time you couldn't go out. It was rough. So I started there with Friedl, and the war broke out; he was interned first.

I started the first ski school at Mt. Rainier; that's the one I left when I went to Sun Valley. There is still Mt. Baker and Mt. Hood, and they opened the other side of Mt. Rainier, Crystal Mountain, which is much better with more protection. Mt. Rainier was impossible; every storm would really hit it. The lodge was not constructed for winter use. Alf Engen was in

Alf Engen, ski jumper. COURTESY ALF ENGEN.

Alf Engen, Forest Service trail cutter. COURTESY ALF ENGEN.

The Engen Brothers, Sun Valley. COURTESY BOYLE COLLECTION, COMMUNITY LIBRARY, KETCHUM, IDAHO

Alf Engen & family, Ski Hall of Fame. COURTESY ALF ENGEN.

Otto Lang, Sun Valley. COURTESY UNION PACIFIC COLLECTION, P 2886, REGIONAL HISTORY DEPARTMENT OF THE COMMUNITY LIBRARY, KETCHUM, IDAHO.

The Shah of Iran & Otto Lang. COURTESY BOYLE COLLECTION, P 1459, REGIONAL HISTORY DEPARTMENT OF THE COMMUNITY LIBRARY, KETCHUM, IDAHO.

Otto Lang, Ski Hall of Fame. COURTESY OTTO LANG.

Sun Valley then, and Fred Iselin was there too; it was a great group of pioneers. I took over the ski school after they took Friedl away.

Ernie: While we were in Sun Valley on our honeymoon, Friedl had just been arrested. The FBI had put him in a jail in Salt Lake City.

Kingsbury Pitcher: Friedl was running the ski school in Sun Valley in the last pre-war year which was 1941-'42. In the middle of the winter, the FBI came right into The Challenger Inn and bagged Friedl up and walked him out of there as a dangerous enemy alien. So, Fred Iselin and Otto Lang were running the Sun Valley Ski School in Friedl's absence.

Alf Engen: I remember Friedl was put in jail because he was an Austrian, which he couldn't help. He had done nothing wrong, and of course, he got out because he hadn't done anything wrong. He volunteered for the army, the 10th Mountain Division, and he was sent to Europe where he got wounded.

Ernie: There was the famous story about Millicent Rogers bringing gourmet meals to the jail because she was married at that time to Seth Furlich, a fat, balding, middle-aged Austrian ski instructor, who was also put in jail. They were all arrested. The FBI didn't have a place to put them, so they put them in jail. Millicent was a very wealthy woman; her father was Colonel Rogers, the first partner of Rockefeller. And her husband from her first marriage, Peter Sanders, was in the same school as I was in Switzerland. He was an Austrian.

Millicent Rogers went to the warden of the jail in Salt Lake and said, "I'm unhappy that my husband has to eat jail food. I would like to have good food brought in." The warden said, "That's all right, but you can only do it if you do that for everybody." She said okay and they ate like kings for several months.

Joern Gerdts: I didn't know who it was who brought the food, I just knew that someone brought this very elegant caviar and all kinds of stuff to the boys in jail.

Friedl Pfeifer: The Millicent Rogers tale, I'm afraid that's not the story. That went around but, no, it wasn't true. They arrested me right after Pearl Harbor, and I got out in February. I went back to Sun Valley and finished that season, and then Sun Valley closed. In March, I volunteered for the 10th Mountain Division; they had a flyer out for ski instructors. I taught skiing and mountain climbing in the army and how to live out in twenty degrees below zero. I was an expert because I was trained well.

I had applied for citizenship in the U.S., but you had to wait five years at that time. Also, each country had a quota on how many Austrians could immigrate. But the first thing that happens when a war breaks out is a huge hysteria. That's what happened to me. So I sort of understood it, but luckily I had tremendous backing by Averell Harriman. And then of course I did get into the Mountain Troops and fought in Italy.

Alf Engen: I could cry every time I think of how difficult it must have been for Friedl. He was with the Americans on the Brenner Pass. His brothers could have been with the German army on top of the pass skiing slalom. Every day the Americans watched them and wished they were up there skiing with them. They had their guns on them, but they said they couldn't shoot anyone on a slalom course up there, and they didn't. Then one day, the Americans were sitting having lunch, when suddenly a big bazooka went off, and there was a direct hit on Torger Tokle who was blown to bits. Torger was one of our famous ski jumpers. From then on, the Americans had no qualms about hitting them. They went in after them. There were more than Torger who were killed, but he was a hero.

Friedl Pfeifer: To understand how I got to Sun Valley, you must understand why I came to America, and first we have to go through what got me out of Austria. It was a very famous guy whose first name is Adolf. I had to go out immediately because I was a German overnight and a soldier. I had to go illegally. I had some pretty good connections to get a stamp on my passport and to be allowed to go into a foreign country. I went to Italy on the pretense that I was officiating in a very important ski race there—the Marmolada. I had another prop. I broke my leg at the FIS that year, and I still had on a cast; it was very handy to have. The day after the entrance, the 14th, was a forced march. Everybody had to go into the street. If you didn't come out, they went in and got you.

I knew things were happening. All of the officials, like the mayor, were thrown out immediately and replaced by the Nazis. A good friend of mine, a ski instructor, was appointed mayor. I didn't have to march because I had a cast on. I hobbled up to the restaurant, and he came towards me. I greeted him in the usual way, and he screamed at me, "One says Heil Hitler," and that sort of did it. You can tell stories for ten hours, but you cannot tell the right story of what Hitler did to all of Austria. You were just completely nothing overnight. He had total control over everything. Hannes Schneider was thrown in jail because he was too popular. Anybody who had any kind of influence over more than one person got put away.

I got onto a boat in Venice and traveled to Australia where I started a ski school, the first one in Mount Kosciusko. That's the highest point in Australia, and it's named after a Polish hero. I knew I would come to America eventually, and I arrived here the first of October after the winter season in Australia. When Hitler came to power in Austria, it was a place to go away from.

Ernie at Sun Valley, March 1942.
COURTESY BLAKE FAMILY COLLECTION.

Sun Valley Lodge under construction, 1936.
COURTESY UNION PACIFIC COLLECTION, P 2287, REGIONAL HISTORY DEPARTMENT OF THE COMMUNITY LIBRARY, KETCHUM, IDAHO.

Friedl Pfeifer at Sun Valley. COURTESY UNION PACIFIC COLLECTION, P 2785, REGIONAL HISTORY DEPARTMENT OF THE COMMUNITY LIBRARY, KETCHUM, IDAHO.

CHAPTER 3
The War Years

Ernie: I met Hitler in January of 1933, just before he became chancellor, and I went to one of his meetings in Frankfurt with my fellow pilots from the academic glider flying club. We were not impressed by his speech, but it impressed the masses greatly. It was run on ideas of the Roman Empire, the Napoleonic times with the golden eagle and the flags and some ceremonial ideas they had stolen from the Communists and the party in the Catholic church. It was a mixture of things.

It turned out that he had a god-given gift, an incredible gift to speak. He spoke for hours; he sweated; he was exhausted when he came home. He spoke for two to three hours. He had the masses with him. He knew how to maneuver them; he learned very quickly, but it was basically a gift he had by nature, unlike anybody I have ever met.

But it didn't seem possible for Hitler to become a real dictator. We discussed that very much in detail, if such a thing were possible in Germany as Mussolini in Italy. Mussolini had gotten to power eleven years earlier and everybody said it was impossible; the land of Göethe will never go for this kind of bullshit.

I was sure there would be another war. When we were being brought up as small kids, our German relatives were already dreaming of their revenge on the French. They wanted us to be rough and tough boys. They wanted us to be fighters. It was very much bred into the Germans and into their thinking process. I was shocked when I came to school in Switzerland that they didn't appreciate me fighting with other kids. That was not done. It was like the attitude in America, that you don't fight, that you try to get along with everybody.

Wolfie Lert: I remember too, our teachers in Germany, the French teachers, starting the French lessons in our school saying it's our duty to learn French so we are able to take care of them when we "get them."

Elisabeth Brownell: Germans, well, we always pushed the other one down. Ernie was so German, and I am very German. I grew up there; it was my life. The young years, when you are learning, make the biggest impression on a person. Later you have it more under your control.

Max Killinger: The amazing part is, I could say being a German, I have this guilt complex of what happened during the Nazi era. But me, personally, I don't feel like I have this communal complex because I am a German, so therefore I have to be ashamed because some of my countrymen did it. It took me eight years before I even found out that Ernie was Jewish. Then I asked him once what his feelings were against Germans. He said, "What do you mean? I am a German too." So it wasn't like he was a Jew, and I was a German; he never felt that way.

Harry Franzgen: I went skiing with Ernie and sitting on the chair lift we talked about how it was for us as children. I recall Ernie said, "I know how you grew up and about our educations. We did not get understanding. So, we feel at a loss." I do not know how to relate to my sons. I am constantly afraid I am making a mistake; yet, I find that I try to be as hard as I was treated. It is not because hard is good. We really don't know any better. There is a definite void in our upbringing and in our character. It is very hard for people like us who come out of that era to show love and understanding.

The era Ernie comes out of is one where you have to address your parents with the proper German "Sie"; you don't have it in the English language, so it's hard to understand what that means. But you treated your parents like an authority. You knew them, but they weren't something you loved; if you did, it was great, but that was not required. It was strictly on a respect basis. Love and discipline went hand in hand.

We had the fencing, the dueling in my fraternity, even though it was illegal to duel. There was a very strong honor code, and if you didn't abide by that, you were socially totally unacceptable at home. Ernie understood that, and he knew there was no give in me. Over the years, I've learned that's silly, but I am fifty-one years old. I had a good woman on my side, and she taught me a lot. I married an American who was pretty much totally opposite of me, and she has molded me. You learn from others.

Ernie: The masses of Germans didn't give a damn about the Jews. It's hard to blame everybody because the first five years of Hitler's government did away with unemployment. They'd had tremendous unemployment, six-and-a-half million unemployed in a country that small. That was more than 10% of the total population out of work at that time, a vast percentage of the work force. Hitler did away with that in a very short time. They needed to import labor from other countries after five years. He bluffed his way into great victories. They got things back that had been taken from them after the first war. So, the great

Official Nazi/Third Reich documents.
COURTESY BLAKE FAMILY COLLECTION.

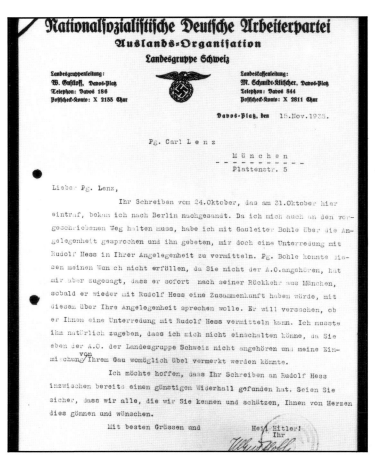

Official Nazi/Third Reich documents.
COURTESY BLAKE FAMILY COLLECTION.

masses of Germans were thoroughly imbued with the wonders that Hitler had achieved for them. If he had died that year, he would be a saint to them today.

The German people felt that the persecution of the Jews was a terrible thing, but it was a minor thing compared to the benefits that they were reaping. Everything was changing. In a revolution, there are always things that are not desirable, but you have to overlook those "trouble spots."

Ernie: I knew another war was coming. It was inevitable. I volunteered for the Mountain Troops which is how I got into the army. I volunteered on the basis of being active in racing in 1939, '40, '41. I was a Class A racer in the East, and we got the letters from the director of the National Ski Patrol asking us to join before the war broke out. The National Ski Patrol was organizing the volunteers for the Mountain Troops. They took me with glee, and I had orders from General Julio who was the adjutant general of the U.S. Army.

When I got to the reception, they were very nervous because I was born in Germany even though I was a Swiss citizen. I had served three different ser-

vice periods in the Swiss air force: 1933, '34 and '35. I wanted badly to get in the Mountain Troops, but they wouldn't accept me; they didn't trust me. The army thought I was a spy. I don't know what damage I could have done if I had been a Nazi spy in the Mountain Troops.

Rhoda: Ernest's brother Rudi got into the 10th Mountain Division with no problem, but because Ernest was German-born and volunteered, and his brother was drafted, they decided Ernie must be a spy. And what's more Rudi was German-born but not a Swiss citizen. So, it made absolutely no sense. It made even less sense when on that basis, they did not take him in the Mountain Infantry, and then put him in Intelligence. That's the way the army works.

Alf Engen: I didn't get into the 10th Mountain Division either; my brother did, but I was a little bit old. I was working for the government in the Forest Service. The day after Pearl Harbor, they came to me and asked if I knew there was a war on, and I said yes. They said they'd like to have me and they needed me. I told them I couldn't go because I had a job with the Forest Service. They said they'd take care of it. So, we went up to the regional office, and that afternoon I was in the army, but I was put into research and development.

The first time I went to Camp Hale I wondered what they were sending us all that crap for. We brought all the ski stuff that was in the basement of the Northland Ski Company; that's how we started. But we knew that we were not just going to have two guys getting over there to fight; we had to move an army. We had to turn up with an army. We made white skis with holes in the tips so they could fasten ropes to them and make them into sleds. We didn't have ice axes, crampons, pitons, climbing ropes. We didn't have any of that stuff. But, little by little, we ended up having good equipment with great guys; it was a great army, the 10th Mountain Division.

Bob Nordhaus: Ernie was made an honorary member of the 10th Mountain Division of our Southwest Chapter. We did the citation; it was read at his funeral by Bob Parker.

Ernie: My father was German, and my mother was Swiss. I went to school in Switzerland, and I opted for Swiss citizenship long before Hitler; he had nothing to do with it. I had the choice because of my mother; I served in the Swiss air force. Being Swiss I had a great advantage in Germany because I could go there and be untouchable.

Rhoda: Ernest's mother smuggled money into Switzerland. They used old style wooden skis to hide the money in. They took the bindings off, hollowed out the skis underneath, and then put the money in, put the binding back on, and they shipped them to Switzerland with no name. So, all they had to do when they got to Switzerland was to pick the skis up. And if they'd been picked up by the authorities, they wouldn't know who had shipped them.

Herman Kretschmer: Ernie was far from being pro-German, except in his love for Porsches and Volkswagens, which is strange because he never made any bones about the fact that he was half-German. But he emphasized the fact that he was Swiss. There was always a Swiss flag outside Ernie's apartment and he loved his Swiss postman's hat that Walter Widmer gave him. He preferred being Swiss.

Ernie was doing his service in the Swiss air force. He had many amusing accidents. They had fabric fuselages and wooden floorboards. So, he got in the plane, and it was wet and snowy and his boots were slippery, and he slipped and slid and both feet came out of the sides of the airplane. I think at that time, the Swiss air force had about four planes, so Ernie demolished one quarter of the Swiss air force; at least, that's the way he told it. He talked mostly of the fun part of the war.

Ernie: So it was great disappointment that I didn't get into the Mountain Troops. It took me a year longer than I thought to get the army to take me. When I finally was taken, I was sent to Camp Upton on the far end of New York, off Long Island. It was bitter cold, in January. They kept me five weeks under observation, and then they sent me to basic infantry in Georgia. I went to Georgia and Rhoda had a long time getting all of our equipment, catching up with me. I found the U.S. Army to be very easy compared to the Swiss service I had been in ten years earlier. The generosity of the equipment and the treatment we got while there seemed incredible by European standards.

They gave us I.Q. tests and aptitude tests as I was

Ernie Blake in the Swiss Air Force, 1933. COURTESY BLAKE FAMILY COLLECTION.

in a battalion of mentally deficient and foreigners. I did relatively well, so the battalion commander wanted to see me. He asked what I wanted to do. I had read about the French resistance in *The New York Times*. I told him I wanted to be dropped in the Haut Savoie in France where I had been skiing during my student days in 1934-35 near Geneva. I spoke French almost perfectly. I thought I could help the uprising they had planned. That was the dumbest thing I ever did.

10th Mountain Division, Camp Hale, Colorado, 1943. <small>COURTESY COLORADO SKI MUSEUM, VAIL.</small>

Luckily, it didn't work out because it would have been with the OSS and many of the OSS people who were dropped were sold by the French to the Germans immediately, because the French Resistance, to a large degree, was bought by the Germans. The only reliable Resistance fighters were the French Communists; they wouldn't take bribes from the Germans. That's a sad thing to admit, but that's the way it was. The Communists were the only ones who you could rely on in the resistance business. The bourgeois outfits were apt to be infiltrated by the Secret Police.

I got secret orders to report to Military Intelligence School in Camp Ritchie, Maryland. Rhoda had just caught up with me with all of our ski equipment and clothing we'd had in Glenwood Springs. We had a hotel room rented near Camp Hale in order to be well prepared for the war. My wax machine, my wife's cooking things, my climbing skins, big steamer trunks, everything arrived in Georgia. Just when it arrived, poor Rhoda had to wait to find out where I had been sent now. The secret was not very secret except between Rhoda and me.

First, I had all sorts of language tests, and they put me in the Italian section on the basis of that. I went

through the Italian section, and I got through just before the invasion of Sicily. I figured I'd make the invasion of Sicily which would have suited me fine, because I spoke Italian reasonably well. I couldn't write it at all. I had traveled all over Italy. I knew Sicily, the parts where they planned to land. I had taken photographs of Italian cruisers in my earlier days at school and had sent them to the army before I got in. Anyway, in the Intelligence School, I was a private. I went through the school. I had the highest grade in the Italian section because the others were kids of gangsters. As a result, I got K.P. which is like punishment for five days in succession.

Then I was sent to a college in Blacksburg, Virginia when Rhoda was very pregnant with Mickey. I spent three months there angry as hell because I wanted to get into the war. I didn't want to hang around the United States for $75.00 per month. I had a very naive idea. I was damned lucky in actual fact.

I came back to Camp Ritchie after three months of German in Blacksburgh. I told them that I spoke better German than the instructors they had, so they used me as an instructor for three months, teaching German. They sent me with secret orders again to a place they couldn't tell me. I said, ''I know that's Camp Ritchie,

Ernie, November 1943. COURTESY BLAKE FAMILY COLLECTION

Ernie & Mickey, August 1944. COURTESY BLAKE FAMILY COLLECTION.

Ernie & brother, Rudi, May 1943. COURTESY BLAKE FAMILY COLLECTION.

don't give me that bullshit. I don't want to go there; I've been there.'' They sent me back and I ran into a captain I knew socially from Long Island who had been a dueling student in Germany and had dueling scars all over his face. He was an instructor in the German section, and he asked me if I could handle the German section; I said yes.

That's how I became an instructor in the German section. I taught everything from privates to colonels. Then they looked at our I.Q. tests, and Eisenhower needed officers for the invasion of Europe. So, I was one of the first ones who they commissioned of fifty. I got a straight commission without going to officers' school, which I had applied for twice before. When I was in Switzerland, it was very important that you were an officer. In this country, it is nothing, but in Switzerland, it's a very important distinction.

Ernie: My change of name from Bloch to Blake was initiated by the army. For obvious reasons, it was best to have an English, non-Jewish name. After the war, I didn't go back to the name Bloch, because I feel it's not fair to be marked, to wave a flag and allow others to make judgments before they know who and what you are. There has always been great prejudice in this world. I oppose anything that gives people the chance to make a judgment because of a name or some other superficial thing.

Herman Kretschmer: He never regretted changing his name. It allowed him a freedom that he wouldn't have had if his name would have been Bloch. ''Blake'' gave him an entrance into the world that he understood and appreciated.

I've heard him talk about the anti-Semitism of the Swiss. I also heard him talk, and he told me at least a half-dozen times, the Nazis made a terrible mistake in persecuting the Jews. He felt that the Jews were the greatest German patriots of all. They were highly nationalistic, and Hitler really was goofed up on that.

Wolfie Lert: There might not have been as much anti-Semitism as in America, that's quite possible. German Jews, especially from a nice family, were easily assimilated. These guys were more German than the Germans, extremely non-Jewish. We had certain words that had gone into the German language which we used like *mischugge,* but I never heard Yiddish until I came to America. It didn't exist in Germany. The anti-Semitism was there, but it came out, and it was partly poorer against richer, and you have this in this country too. The anti-Semitism of "No Jew in my golf club" and all this did not exist so much.

Ernie: I didn't feel there was much anti-Semitism in Germany when I was there. I didn't go through the terrible period which people forget . . . the Reichstag, or the persecution of the Jews, which was much worse actually than when they finally began murdering them in large quantities. The mistreatment, the killing of their ability to make a living. They were not permitted to sit on benches. They couldn't ride the street car. They couldn't go to the movies. They couldn't go to beaches or to swimming pools. Everything was forbidden to them. They couldn't have any gentile household employees.

You know when you chop wood, there are pieces that fly away. They are negative things. But it's minor in comparison to the whole. That's what they felt about the Jewish problem in Germany. The Germans felt that it was none of their business. It was between Hitler and the Jews. The great majority were not for it, and they were very much upset when it got to the brutality. The wealthy Jews had all fled by that time. It could be said that by the beginning of 1939, the people who had a way of getting out of Germany had left.

All of this I missed completely because I was a Swiss citizen, so it didn't affect me directly. We were never bothered by the police, but we had a lot of property in Germany, and we had a beautiful house, a very large house, opposite the university. I was in Germany until 1936, off and on. We had one factory in the southern part of Frankfurt, just over the Main River. We made the raw material for expensive felt hats called Hatters' fur (Huthaar). We sold to companies in Italy and Stetson in this country and Hochel in Austria and Czechoslovakia. One factory was half in Switzerland and half in Germany.

Our house was totally bombed out. From the outside, you couldn't see that. I found this out through a strange coincidence in England. I was doing a job on the Oxford Movement, which is a religious and pacifist movement, very strong in England and on the continent. The leader of the German Oxford Movement was a master sergeant of the German post

10th Mountain Division Troops.
Courtesy Colorado Ski Museum, Vail.

10th Mountain Division Troops.
Courtesy Colorado Ski Museum, Vail.

artillery. He was taken prisoner with the British; they gave him to me to interrogate. He came from Frankfurt, one block away from where we lived. He showed me pictures his son had taken after the big air raid of March 23rd-24th, 1944; his son had sent him pictures of what the region looked like, how all the houses were. And there was a beautiful picture that the kid had taken of our house, showing it in perfect condition. What I didn't realize, or I wasn't experienced enough to catch, was that the windows didn't reflect any light which meant the floors all were in the cellar. But, from the outside, it looked perfect.

Max Killinger: Ernie used to always say that real estate was not a good investment. I talked to him once about this, and he said to me that he was so indoctrinated by his father, ever since they had to leave a hundred-room mansion in Frankfurt and the land around it when they fled Germany. They never could sell it. His father at that time said to him, "Make a business so that you can pack it up and leave." Real estate is definitely not a part of it. And like with a lot of Jewish people, they still have this persecution complex in them, justifiably so. Maybe there's another Hitler lurking around the corner, and you have to pack up and leave. After two thousand years, you get conditioned to that.

Ernie: On the day of the invasion of Normandy, I was ordered to be flown to Europe. I was a second lieutenant by that time. I was sent to England in mid-summer of 1944, to Birmingham which was a dreadful place. It was all shot up by the German aerial attacks; it was depressing. We nearly froze to death living in workers' settlements without any heat. They had a fireplace, but we had nothing to burn. Rhoda had shipped me a brand new sleeping bag from Abercrombie and Fitch in New York, and I was very comfortable from then on. I spent the rest of the war sleeping in a sleeping bag, not dependent on any source of heat. The food in England was ghastly. It all tasted as if saw meal had been dumped on it, and the people all looked shabby. We had a lot of people in that camp who had been in the invasion and who had nerve damage. They had nervous breakdowns; shell shock is what they called it in the first war. In this war, they had more exciting names for it, but it was the same.

Rhoda: Ernest loved the military and he was embarrassed to say so, but he loved every inch of the war. He interviewed bigwigs and various Nazis and thoroughly enjoyed it. He interviewed people like Goering, Himmler and Speer, and it was fascinating. They were thrilling years—his interest in history, and having lived through the Nazi times, then coming back on the other side of it, in the Intelligence side!

Ernie: I had the good fortune to be appreciated by the British, and they gave me a general to interrogate which was very rare in those days for someone of my ranking. He was about fifty-one, a believer in Hitler, but a believer who saw the weak spots and the horrors. He told us about the shooting of Jews. That's the first time I heard of those things. At night, we listened to the prisoners talking about what we had talked about in daytime. That was the trick in the thing. We had listening devices built into the lighting device. He was the only one of all our prisoners who suspected that. He knocked against the wall to find the holes where our listening devices were. He didn't find them, then he talked freely. He told them about what went on in Russia, how the Germans preyed upon the civilians living in the area, how they had deteriorated, how they had become dishonest and stolen things from the Russians. He spoke very highly of the morality of Russian women, of the cleanliness of the Russian people, of the excellent school system and

Ernie at a strategy session. COURTESY BLAKE FAMILY COLLECTION.

kindergarten system they had. He spoke of the fantastic armored vehicles they had, superior to anything the Allies had. He was a great source of information.

During our interrogations we had very few prisoners who refused to talk. We never used brutality or anything like the gestapo did on the German side. We used the threat of delivering them to the Russians. That was the main threat used, that the Russians were looking for labor to rebuild their cities and their highways, their bridges, and that we'd ship them there if they didn't cooperate.

Besides, the Germans had a weakness which works very well in interrogation. They love to educate you. They want to tell you how they do everything better, how they know everything better. It was easy to get them by telling them that we knew nothing about a certain subject. They would talk for hours and tell me how it was done. Germans like to tell you what they think you don't know. It's just a question of steering them on a narrow track so they don't go off on tangents too far and lose a lot of time with that. We had limited time. We had to get results fast.

We interrogated Speer in this British castle which had been left undamaged on the north side of the Thames. He was only thirty-eight years old at the time. He had a beautiful lady friend secretary that worked for him. He was very well informed and gave us a lot of detailed information. He knew the production schedules of each and every item. He knew what was in development and what had gone to Japan, which was virtually nothing. We never discussed any philosophical questions about the atrocities.

General F. M. Wilhelm Keitel, who I interrogated, told in detail about the shooting and gassing of the Jews during the Polish campaign. He also told the story to three generals who shared the prison room with him, and they were shaken by what they heard. They had no idea of the persecution of the Jews, the murdering. And one of them said, "If that's true, then it would be fair if the good Lord takes my son who is fighting on such and such a front"; they had no idea what was really going on, these three generals. They knew that the Jews were being rounded up and transported to Poland from Germany; but, they didn't know what went on with them.

Keitel knew everything. He was very well informed. He told of the night clubs where they showed Ukrainian girls dancing and being whipped and things like that, blatant sex entertainment, pornographic. It was a great education for these other generals who didn't know anything.

Once with General Keitel, I made a terrible faux pas. He wore his army tunic open. There were two hooks on the collar that were supposed to be closed. He apologized for it and told us he had a sore neck, and before thinking what I was saying, I said, "I hope your neck will not be any sorer," which was not very thoughtful. He was very good looking but very dumb. I had to make him a chart to show him how the German army was organized. He was a "yes man" to Hitler. He was executed erroneously, I think, because he was too dumb to know what documents he signed.

The army wanted me to get these prisoners lined up for the Nuremberg trials, but I refused to. I didn't want to get involved in that. I didn't think it would be successful. The laws by which they were tried were made after the case had happened. It was not a good law, and it looked like revenge. I thought it would have been much simpler to put these people against the wall and shoot them after a military tribunal, but to make a big public affair out of it, I didn't think was worth very much.

I thought that we should have shot Goering when we took him as prisoner, that it was silly to drag it out. We should have spared him the nonsense. Goering was very knowledgeable. He had been shot in the groin during the putsch in Munich on the 9th of November. He was saved by two Jewish sisters who took care of him, and then he fled over the Austrian border. But, he suffered from this wound; it was very painful, and he became an addict to morphine.

The American army idiotically insisted on breaking him of his habit. Goering knew they were going to execute him in the long run; he was very clear on that. He was much shorter than I had thought. He was pale; he looked greenish actually, and his skin hung down in folds. His mind functioned perfectly. He was much brighter than he had been for the last few years.

He admitted the errors he had made, how he had let down Hitler by not doing his job, by getting involved in collecting paintings and sculpture and jewelry, generally not doing his job and running the air force effectively.

I was always interested in history. I knew a good deal about the personalities involved in the war, more than the average American officer. I had the enjoyment of getting things uncovered. I would guess that I interrogated about two hundred prisoners. Most of them made you understand that they were never Nazis, that they had been forced into that and that their oath forced them to stick to it.

Because of a crazy incident, I was asked to explain to General Patton about the information I had gotten out of prisoners about the A-bomb. I knew that something was going on, but what, how far we were or anything, I had no idea. In fact, I knew nothing until a year later in the summer of 1945 when we dropped our atomic bomb on the 6th of August 1945 on Hiroshima and three days later on Nagasaki. I gave Patton a briefing with about two dozen high ranking officers with him, generals and colonels. I was the lowest ranking, a first lieutenant by that time. I had ten minutes to explain that some German scientists who were prisoners of ours were on to a secret weapon. I was not permitted to say anything about radiation.

I found out about the atomic bomb quite by accident. It was really very comical. In the course of these interrogations and these questions, this general mentioned one night to his three general friends that the Germans had an uranium bomb which, if it were put in the V-1 or the V-2, both of which carried one ton of explosives, and if the Germans put that uranium bomb into the nose cone where the wire was, the whole city of London was only one shot away. I reported that in my daily file. We had no idea what was going on.

Then all hell broke loose, and I was isolated. My roommate, who was a British officer, was moved out. I had no idea that I had said something of importance. Then two civilian-clothed men and another five men came to visit me from British Intelligence in this secret camp of ours, giving me a list of questions I had to ask the German generals and what I couldn't talk about. It was very strict, and I couldn't have the list with me. I had to memorize it.

I knew nothing about the bomb except that an American friend, who came with me to the United States in 1938, had just finished two years working with an atomic scientist, a famous British scientist who was a professor of physics who had been smashing atoms. But, nothing qualified me in any way. I had no idea that I had hit on something so important. I had simply turned in my report after a regular day of interrogation and suddenly these civilians came to me,

Ernie in Germany, December 1945.
Courtesy Blake Family Collection.

Ernie, 1st Reserve meeting ORC, September 1946. Courtesy
Blake Family Collection.

my butler was exchanged, I couldn't go to regular
mess and eat with the other officers. I couldn't talk to
anyone. I was completely isolated and insulated. I had
to be. I was asked to explain this to General Patton.
Patton thought I was very funny, he patted me on the
shoulder, and that was that.

Mickey Blake: It was impressive, but my father
knew nothing really about the atomic bomb. My father
said Patton started laughing with the description of the
atomic bomb and said, "Any questions, please? Thank
you very much." The answer should have been, "I'm
sorry sir, I don't know, but I'll find out." But Ernie
wasn't going to expose himself to that with General
Patton. The old soldier had no problems with my
father. He may have been simply a first lieutenant, but
the ribbons on his uniform went from here to there,
because he'd been all the way across Europe in the
European Campaign.

Remember, for those guys, it was the absolute
highlight of their lives. No matter what they did later,
for ninety-nine percent, those war years were the
highlight of their lives. No one ever did anything that
matched it. My father was coming home on the train,
finally headed home, and the ribbons went so far
across his chest that two little kids who were sitting
across from him in those old train seats that face each

other asked him, "Did you fight in both wars, sir?"

Harry Franzgen: Once you have a sense of
history, you're not that idealistic any more. I think
Ernie looked at idealism as a weakness. I watched him
sometimes when people would come with an idea to
him, and Ernie could get pretty brutal. He turned a lot
of young kids off who thought they had an idea. Ernie
was very much a realist with a sense of history; he
could say he knew how this was going to end. Those
are invaluable lessons in life.

Rhoda: It was the military that really changed
Ernest. Ernest wasn't always outgoing. He used to be
very shy, and at the time we were married, didn't
automatically draw people to him. He had to know
them first. The war changed that.

Herman Kretschmer: The war was the biggest
thing for Ernie until his skiing career, which of course
was his greatest achievement. And, there's no question
about it, Taos Ski Valley, what better monument could
a man have? Up until then, the war was the greatest
thing that ever happened to him. He loved it.

SECTION II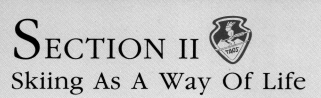
Skiing As A Way Of Life

After the war, Ernie was marooned in New York trying desperately to convince Rhoda's mother to relinquish her hold on Rhoda and allow them to come West. The Rocky Mountains were calling and Ernie knew that his friends Freidl Pfeifer and Fred Iselin were just beginning to start the Aspen ski area. Even then he was dreaming of a ski area somewhere in Colorado or New Mexico. It was a passion Ernie hooked onto when he was young, and he never let it go.

After Rhoda was allowed to leave New York, Ernie and the family came to Santa Fe where by luck and chance, he became involved with the Santa Fe Ski Basin and started what became a long friendship with Kingsbury Pitcher. Then he found ''the proverbial Texas millionaire'' who he hoped would become his lift ticket into the ski business.

In the end, though, Santa Fe provided too little cooperation, too few skiers, and not enough money, so Ernie continued his search for the perfect ski mountain. During this period, Ernie and Bob Nordhaus became good friends. Bob pioneered skiing in New Mexico with La Madera Ski Area in 1936. Later on, he built the Sandia Tram, now the longest single span in the world and the biggest tourist attraction in the state of New Mexico. And to think, the bankers pulled his credit because they thought it was a harebrained scheme.

Ernie got advice from ski experts Otto Lang, Pete Totemoff, and Wolfie Lert about his choice of Twining. All the experts told Ernie that he was crazy; the mountain was unskiable, it was too steep, and too remote. But Ernie was not one who listened to others' advice very readily and he had fallen in love with Twining. Further, he had great faith that his old friend Howard Head was going to revolutionize the ski industry with his new invention, the metal ski. The Head Ski was going to allow more and more people to ski, and they would be able to handle his tough mountain. He was sure of it.

CHAPTER 4
Post-War

Ernie: I did not get back from Europe until the summer of 1946, but the idea of a ski area came back as something that was again possible. During the war, I thought about the west and that famous story by Roch about Aspen, and I wanted to go west again, but Rhoda's mother could not allow her daughter to go away yet. It took three more years before we were able to move to Santa Fe.

Friedl Pfeifer had fallen totally in love with Aspen while he was at Camp Hale, so after the war he never went back to Sun Valley. He said once that was one of the hardest choices he ever had to make, as he was very close to Harriman. Fred Iselin went along with Friedl to Aspen, but Friedl is the one responsible for getting Aspen going. They had that old boat lift before Friedl came, but he knew about lifts and ski areas; he had already done Sun Valley. And he knew the snow was much better in Aspen. Sun Valley is a wonderful place, but the snow is not always good.

Friedl Pfeifer: I discovered Aspen while I was at Camp Hale, before we went to Italy. At the end of 1943, we went on a maneuver through the Rocky Mountains for a seventy-two mile hike. We came out above Aspen, and I looked over across Aspen and that was it. Right there. I was addicted at first sight—you can only say that with a woman—love at first sight. I'm positive God had skiing in mind when He made Aspen. I set up a good rapport with God before the last Pope was appointed because he was a skier.

I went from Camp Hale to Aspen; when the others went to Denver to chase girls, I went to Aspen to chase the mountain. It was very easy for me and natural. It was not a strain that I climb up the mountain. I learned while growing up how St. Anton grew from nothing to a ski resort; so I had quite the natural knowledge. There were only very few people in Aspen. The town was totally abandoned, a real ghost town. I told the townspeople that when I got out of the war, I would come and turn their town into a ski resort. They supported it; they were all wonderful people.

I knew about Andre Roch immediately. The local people in Aspen told me. Roch had the same handicap as Ernie and Fred Iselin; he was Swiss. The Swiss ski above timberline, and Roch wanted to ski above timberline and that's out. The air is too thin. And in Colorado, there's no body in this snow, no moisture. People go off the trail, and they choke; they go right

down. I saw that right away that they couldn't go any higher. People would find they couldn't do it with the difference in elevation, from 8,000 to 11,500 feet.

Ernie: Roch had laid out a run, Roch's Run, which was a very steep, narrow trail in the aspen trees next to Ruthie's; it was like eastern trails, and that was for a long time the standard run. At the bottom where the #1 lift is, they had two giant sleds with benches on them and a motor winch high up the mountain. It was called the boat lift. It made tremendous grooves in the snow. You paid a dime for a ride, and got a 300-foot vertical lift. There was always the danger that it would turn over. It was not without risk, but it was fun.

Friedl Pfeifer: There were two terrible things in my life. One was the day I had to tell Harriman that I would not return to Sun Valley. He wanted me to have Sun Valley, and he gave me a contract into my grave, I had to tell him I was addicted to Aspen, and I couldn't do it anymore. And the second worst thing was that I lost my family when I came to Aspen. I had a beautiful wife and family and everything going for us at Sun Valley, and I gave it up to go to Aspen. It was really rough for a wealthy woman like my wife in Aspen in the 1940s, a woman who's been used to the luxuries of life and doesn't know how to do without her friends or family; then add the war on top of it. But that's only part of her lifetime.

Another thing that I am sensitive to is that I gave in on the community in Aspen. I gave in because I didn't have the power to do anything else. You needed money; that's the only real power in the world. If you are around wealthy people, your worth is just a noise, that's all. There is nothing you can do about it. I begged them for two years to build Buttermilk. Finally I had to build it and then give it to them. I didn't give it; I made them pay for it. Those are the things that you can't shake totally. And moral help is sometimes better than financial help. Equally as bad as leaving Sun Valley was leaving Aspen. But of course, I really never left Aspen. I love those mountains and that valley, and the community was so good.

Joern Gerdts: Friedl Pfeifer is the person who got less credit than anybody for developing Aspen and the Buttermilk ski areas and skiing in general; he deserves a lot. I don't know why he never got his due. To me, Buttermilk is still one of the best laid out ski areas. Friedl did that. It looks perfectly natural. I think it was beautiful. People talk about Aspen all the time, and they mention Walter Paepcke and everybody else but hardly ever Friedl. He had lots to do with it. Maybe it

Friedl Pfeifer in the Old Aspen Boat Tow. COURTESY ASPEN HISTORICAL SOCIETY.

Old Aspen single chair. COURTESY ASPEN HISTORICAL SOCIETY.

was his personality; some people think he was unfriendly, but he wasn't. He was not a show-off; he was quiet. Fred Iselin was the one who was the showman.

Friedl Pfeifer: I formed the Aspen Ski Club in 1945 right after I got out of the army after six months in the hospital. I had an attorney in Denver form the Aspen Ski Corporation. Then I had a good contact with American Steel and Wire because I had ordered the first lifts at Sun Valley. I ordered the #1 lift for Aspen with no idea how to pay for it. I had friends in Aspen, and I talked everybody's ear off about how great this was going to be. I got some money together. Then Walter Paepcke came on the scene and he had to sort of stand behind it. The whole thing arrived the first of October in Aspen and American Steel never asked for any money.

I put that first lift in, the old #1 lift in Aspen. Everyone wanted to build a lift on the bottom slope only, and I simply said, "Absolutely not. This is going to go to the top." Nobody had enough faith in skiing to go to the top. I insisted on it. It was pretty incredible that I got it done because I had opposition from left and right, but I got it done.

Joern Gerdts: Friedl cared so much for the

people of Aspen. I met Friedl in 1946 or 1947 just when they were building the first lift on Ajax. I was going to do photography in Aspen that year. There was just the Hotel Jerome. Friedl was like Ernie; he had the eye for making ski mountains like Ajax and then Buttermilk, and Ernie with Taos and Dave McCoy with Mammoth. Those guys had the eye, they were the pioneers.

Friedl Pfeifer: After Ajax was going, I started Buttermilk. I bought the land; I bought a ranch, I had no money but I bought it. Then I went to the Aspen Ski Corporation and said I need a beginners' slope because we cannot go on teaching on the bottom of Ajax. There were hundreds of people skiing down through Little Nell. They said, "No, we don't want to go out of town," or something like that. So, I decided to do it myself. I needed Art Pfister as a partner because he owned the land above mine. I had very good rapport with the Forest Service. I started Buttermilk and it took off right away.

Two years later, Pfister got a little nervous about the future of Buttermilk, so I bought him out. I got another partner who had a little more money than I did, Robert O. Anderson, chairman of the board of

Atlantic Richfield. I also went down to Ruidoso, N.M. and laid out Sierra Blanca for Anderson. I did that with Kingsbury Pitcher and the Alaskan, Pete Totemoff.

Art Pfister: Friedl and I started Buttermilk in 1958. Then we sold it four years later in 1962 to the Aspen Ski Corporation. It was fun; it was an adventure working with Friedl. I'd go out and work during the week and come home on Friday or Saturday. I had an airplane and I was flying, working Texas and Oklahoma. Every week we'd need another $5,000 or $10,000, and every week I came home. It was hand-to-mouth but it worked fine. Buttermilk had to be built; at that time our teaching slope was Little Nell, and that's the steepest part of Aspen Mountain.

Nobody made any money back then. The Aspen Ski Corporation started making a little bit back in 1958. A lot of years were pretty slim, and you did the best you could with nothing. It's amazing how much equipment they need now compared with what they did with nothing before. They used to haul the towers up the mountain with an old 6x6 army surplus truck and put them up with a pulley. Nowadays, they use helicopters, or they have a big crane on the project to lift them up and set them in place. One thing about the way they do it now, you don't have to build all those lousy roads into the towers because they never seem to go away. Highlands still has theirs. I think we've wiped most of them out on Aspen Mountain.

I met Ernie here in Aspen, probably in 1948 or 1949. He always stayed with us. When they had the FIS he was interpreting, and that was a wild week. We skied every day, all day, except when he took a little time off when they were announcing. The FIS is the one they had late here in April. The instructors from Europe thought they were in heaven. Ernie told them they were. Every night it snowed about a foot, and he made it sound as though it did that every night during the season. We were open two weeks longer than we had ever been open before or since. If it had been a normal year, they couldn't have even gotten past mid-mountain. Ernie held the position he held because he was all those nationalities, Swiss, German and American. Even back then he charmed everybody.

I was on the board of directors for Aspen for over twenty-five years and on Taos's board for about the same amount of time. I was able to help a lot because everything that happened in Aspen, I knew was going to happen in Taos about eight or nine years later. So Taos missed a lot of the bad things that we had to live with here.

I'm not on the board here in Aspen anymore. When the board survived Marvin Davis buying it from 20th Century Fox, that was the end of the line. He sent us our gold watch and our "Dear John" letter, and we were out. I think it was run better before. You can't run a ski area out of a real estate office in Chicago.

Friedl Pfeifer: As Buttermilk became a success, the Ski Corporation accused me of conflict of interest because I had all the people going into ski school at Buttermilk because there was no beginner's hill at Ajax. They, of course, made it up. I saw things deteriorate left and right with the community, so through Robert O. Anderson, we made the Ski Corporation a proposition that I would give up Buttermilk for so much money and I did. I just couldn't take any more because it hurt. I felt very strong about Aspen, and it just got worse and worse. Making Aspen a ski town was my main idea, to have a ski community. But it didn't work the way I had planned, so I lost interest, and I got older too.

Warren Miller: There's a story about Friedl not knowing what to do, and Paepcke said, "You gotta buy land," and Friedl didn't know what to buy. It turned out he had $200, and so he bought eleven lots in Aspen. When I asked Dick Durrance about it, Durrance said, "Shhh! Hell, I only had enough money for seven of them." You know those lots today are a million dollars.

When Friedl opened the school at Buttermilk, everybody thought he was insane. God, who's going to go down to that wimpy little hill? He was smart enough to know there was no intermediate skiing on Ajax. Whoever changed the name from Ajax to Aspen Mountain ought to be shot. I liked it much better as it was.

Pete Totemoff: I quit going to Aspen a long time ago. When they changed Ajax to Aspen Mountain, that was a bad sign. The jet-set moved in and I moved out.

Ernie: Aspen was tremendous back then. Fred Iselin was one of the few classmates I had that stayed in the ski business. Friedl and Fred were two of the best skiers there ever were; their personalities matched their skiing ability. Freddie was an old friend from our school days in Zuoz, and an independent, happy soul. Fred could fly on skis; and a true hippie before there were hippies. He was a free spirit.

Pete Totemoff: Fred Iselin was a kind and gentle man. He skied like me, loosey-goosey; he used to fly like a bird. He was crazy though. I figured he'd kill himself skiing. Once we came down Spar Gulch, and that bastard hardly ever turned, and we were doing 1,000 mph by the time we hit bottom. He liked to go fast. We did all right together, but I never got in front of him because he would run over me.

Warren Miller: The marriage between Fred and Friedl was a very interesting one because of the Swiss-Austrian mixture. They were both in Sun Valley when I was living in the parking lot the first year. Then after the war they went to Aspen. They had a mutual respect. They were by far the two best skiers on the

Aspen pioneer Friedl Pfeifer. COURTESY SUN VALLEY CO.

Art Pfister—Aspen/Taos Board Member. COURTESY ART PFISTER.

mountain. It was their love of passing on problems that brought them together.

Friedl Pfeifer: I think that if Fred had been alive during the Roman Empire, he would have ended up in a marble statue. Often I had to restrain him because I wanted to have a serious discussion, but he always blew it. Fred with his many stories always disrupted our meetings. At the meeting places, there'd be one hundred and fifty instructors, and he'd tell a story, and they'd be on the ground rolling. That was something for a Swiss; the Swiss have the least sensitivity of any country.

One of Fred's great stories was that he never liked dogs. He loved dogs actually, but the story was better that way. His parents had a dachshund and sometimes his father was gone or tired so Fred had to take it for a walk. He always took a long leash because he hated being close to the dog. He had to go across a railroad to the other side, and on the way back the dog didn't want to walk, so he had to half pull him. A train came, so he hurried up a little bit and dragged him across the track, and after he got across, he looked back, and there was only half the dog!

Pete Seibert: Ernie had the same kind of approach as Fred Iselin. They had the capability to

41

Aspen ski runs. Courtesy Aspen Ski Corpporation.

kind of put everything in perspective and say, "We're here to have a good time." I can remember looking out the window over at Aspen, late November, early ski season, and he'd look out and say, "We don't need snow; we just need people." That was one of Fred's great comments, and Ernie understood that very well. If you gave Ernie a lodge full of people, he could entertain them. They were good at getting people to entertain themselves. They were the catalysts.

Alf Engen: Fred was one of them who, like Ernie, made the room light up. Fred and his wife Elli were good friends of mine. I raced with him. Fred was a Swiss and a marvelous man, and Friedl was a good Austrian with quite a sense of humor himself.

We were invited to a big party over at Harriman's cottage in Sun Valley. Friedl was there, and he was a real comic. He had a flare for it, like Fred, but not too many saw it. Harriman's house was full of all the right people, the movie stars and rich and famous, and they asked Friedl to do something, I forget what it was. He took his hair and he brushed it forward, and it came down right above his eyes. Then he had a black comb, and he put the comb right under his nose. He looked just exactly like Hitler, he went through there talking just like the führer with the

Buttermilk ski runs. Courtesy Aspen Ski Corporation.

same tune as he could speak the same language.

Fred was at the party, too. Something else happened that night that I will always remember. They said to clear the floor so they could dance. Then they started this music, a waltz. We used to call it the window dance; it's also called the kissing waltz. Here comes Fred with Elli and a hat on and never a smile or anything. He comes in, and he starts to dance real smooth, like silk over the floor, and Elli was a marvelous dancer. It went on and on and on, and of course, he tried to kiss her all the way through this dance. He goes on and on, but can't quite make it. It was so beautiful, what an evening.

Friedl Pfeifer: There was also a story about a hotelier named Walter from Davos. We always teased him. He had a wax ear, and that's how he became a character. He always followed me around with my girls. One time he came down the slope, and he was about one hundred yards above me, the snow was all packed down and he fell. I knew about it, that he'd lost it before, and here came this ear hopping down the slope, and I caught it. You couldn't notice it, but he did wear a cap most of the time.

Warren Miller: In the early years of Aspen, Fred used to ride up after they sorted out the classes. The ski patrol kept a bucket of wax at the top of old #1. Fred would always come up and wax his skis, but he never contributed to the pot. So one day, they filled that thing up with bacon grease, bubble gum, peanut butter and a whole lot of stuff. He had a pretty nice private lesson set up. He came out on his skis, and he had about five inches of powder stuck to him. He was a great guy and a hell of a skier.

Max Dercum: Fred always came up with a funny way of saying things. He said, "Back in the early days, my pants were baggy and my face was smooth, and now my pants are smooth and my face is baggy."

Kingsbury Pitcher: I can remember a time with Fred up in Spar Gulch. They used to have the FIS course up there, and there was a big fly-away bump. If you have a pre-jump if you're racing, they shape it a little bit, so ski school went up there to see if it was shaped right, and Fred went up an impossibly high distance and just took off and landed like a shot duck because he landed right on the flat. He bounced a couple of times and stood up, looked around and then skied off rather slowly. Elli Iselin was up there, and she said he was hurt. He just ruined himself. He couldn't do a thing for a month, but that was his fate you know. He always had to say he could fly farther and land harder.

Fred was a truly kind person. I miss Fred more than anybody really. The way he died was kind of a needless thing, like out of a novel. You say your character is your fate; Fred's character was to die the way he died. I was around a number of times when

they were taping movies, and Fred would always over-perform. *(Ed. Note: Fred died of an embolism after a ski accident while shooting a movie.)*

Friedl Pfeifer: It was good for us in Aspen in those early years. Fred and I did okay together. We did it the way we knew would work, but it changed. There was a camaraderie there that isn't anymore; the locals are all gone. There were a lot of characters back then like Ralph Jackson, the original ski bum. He never paid for a lift ticket. But then it changed.

CHAPTER 5
Early Santa Fe

Ernie: While Friedl and Fred were in Aspen getting that area going, I was still in New York; I couldn't get out of there. After the war, I came back to the States in May of 1946, and I got out of the army in July of 1946. But, we had to stay in the East because my mother-in-law couldn't separate herself from Rhoda.

It was 1949 before we managed to get out of New York to Santa Fe. Rhoda had been crazy about a home; the owner was in the war when we were there before. But he was in Santa Fe in 1949 when we came back. While she was negotiating with him, I talked to the Chamber of Commerce. They told me there was no interest in industries or anything. But then, when I left the Chamber of Commerce angrily, someone said that there was a crazy group of people who wanted to build a ski area at Santa Fe Basin to which the Forest Service had just built a road. I gave the ski people a $1,000 check, which was a lot of money in those days, and helped them take down the lift they were going to transfer to Santa Fe.

Kingsbury Pitcher: Some people in Santa Fe had been trying for years to get from Hyde Park up to Santa Fe Ski Basin, and it was a big problem because of the road. There was a guy here named LeFever who had an old rope tow in Hyde Park. Finally, Eleanor Roosevelt intervened in the road controversy because the Indians didn't want a road up there, and she actually got the road which was finished sometime after the war. LeFever then moved his rope tow up to the Basin.

There was no skiing the winter of 1945-'46. Everything was down. Sun Valley was still a hospital. The rumor was that the rope tow would operate up at the Santa Fe Ski Basin, but it was difficult. Nobody could get anything done. Back then, all the members of the ski club would get together and go up there to work. But, you find yourself, like all volunteer efforts, nailing a tin roof on some shack and wondering why everybody else was standing around looking at you, two people working and twenty of them drinking. It sort of got ripe.

Ernie: There were no real ski bums in this region. In Santa Fe, it was Kingsbury Pitcher and Buzz Bainbridge, Dr. Lord, Sr., and Dr. Lord, Jr., Mrs. McKinney, Watson, the five Brennans, and John Dendahl, who later made the Olympic team.

Kingsbury Pitcher: Ernie was very interested in doing something, and he said, "What do you think

about Santa Fe?" I was totally negative. At some point they started talking about this homemade double chair lift they wanted to move to Santa Fe.

Ernie: It was a broken-down, old mining lift that Santa Fe was trying to get started with; it came from the Eureka Mine near Silverton, Colorado. It wasn't meant for chairs; it was meant for metal, wagons, heavy things riding on the cable with a detaching grip. It was a bi-cable lift, and it worked for skiing which was our intent. It gave us a 630-foot vertical rise and that was plenty for the skiers back then when there was virtually no skiing.

Mickey Blake: I was there the first time they ran the Santa Fe chair lift. Old man Page was the lift engineer, very similar to Walter Ruegg here at Taos. My father would try to explain to them that the skiers were a necessary evil. They went to the Eureka Mine in Silverton and picked up all this junk which was basically an abandoned old mine lift. The track cable was built in Sheffield, England in 1888, and they used that track cable until the day they took it down.

That old bi-cable lift was the original detaching lift

Ernie skiing back East, 1948-49.
COURTESY BLAKE FAMILY COLLECTION

because the old mine cars detached. The old Weber clutch was the nightmare of that lift. Normally that clutch worked fine and if a mine car fell off the line once in a while, it was no big deal, but it was a problem when the chairs would fall off with the people in them. That finally did happen when one of the clutches let loose and came rolling back. It was empty and rolled back on a navy pilot, and he jumped out and was okay. Ordinarily, somebody would have gotten squashed.

It was primitive in those days. We used those crank phones for everything. Before radios, I can recall ski patrolmen having one on the shoulder, and they would hook on to the call line. The Santa Fe ski patrolmen also carried a hatchet and a shovel. When the chairs would fall off the line, it would look bad when you're riding up the lift with all these chairs lying on the ground. So, they would dig a hole with the little shovels like they have today, they'd roll the chair into it, and then the hatchets were very important because they would cut pine boughs—and that whole lift line was surrounded by evergreens—and they would lay the boughs over the chair and then pack it tightly with snow. It looked like little igloos going up. This was in the days before moguls.

Kingsbury Pitcher: Right after the war, there was lots of talk about skiing and not much action. It was very difficult because the community was full of people who claimed to know something about skiing. They didn't know anything. They wanted to have a word in it; they wanted to ride free; nobody wanted to pay. It was a terrible situation.

Ernie: Most of the winters of 1949, '50, and '51, the snow didn't come until mid-February. The previous years, the snows had been so high that they had cut the trees all at waist level which was easier to chain saw. We had a monstrous time getting enough snow to cover those stumps. We grossed $4,200 approximately each of the first two years in Santa Fe which was not enough to pay the wages. But we did develop an interest from the Texas market, particularly Amarillo, Lubbock and communities around that part of Texas.

Kingsbury Pitcher: After watching Santa Fe stumble around, I went back to Sun Valley because I had been there as an instructor in 1941. After the war they opened up again, and they invited everybody who was alive who wanted to come back and work to do so. I thought that's where the real skiing was so I went up there. I completely checked out for a year. I then decided that maybe teaching wasn't quite as good as it had been pre-war. They had paid a lot and all your expenses, and it was a very lush kind of clientele, and so most instructors were European and hardly any Americans were

Santa Fe Ski Area, March 1954. Courtesy Blake Family Collection.

working there. I was the first American in the Sun Valley Ski School. The rest of the "Krauts" wouldn't speak to me for half the winter.

A little time passed, and we bought a ranch in Arroyo Seco, the one that I sold to Chilton Anderson, and moved to Taos about 1951. But the school system was awful. Then we went up to Aspen once in the fall just on a camping trip, and my wife Jane asked what would be wrong with trying to go to Aspen in the winter. I could get a job with Friedl again, so we went up asking for a job, and he said "Sure." Friedl was a straight shooter. He said I would have to start at the bottom again, even though I had been with him in Sun Valley. I stayed in Aspen with Friedl and Fred until about 1961.

While I was there, I got interested in Snowmass with my old friend Bill Janss, but it looked like that was never going to go. Janss bought the land. I did the pioneering. I climbed that mountain a few times in a very sneaky way because we didn't want Johnny Hougland and those farmers out there to know that anybody was looking at it. We went through a long period of deception. I used to get somebody to drop me off on some odd day of the week and go up entirely through the timber, not leaving any tracks and go up on the divide someplace and climb up to the top and look around.

I had a hard time convincing anybody that

Snowmass had any future. Everybody was against it. They said, "It won't work and it's too flat," but by comparing the mountains, you could see that Ajax and Snowmass weren't a whole hell of a lot different. I had a kind of revenge because my friend Jim Snobble said it will never go, and some years after, I was up there at Sam's Nob just about 4:00, and Jim was up there with all these grooming cats and swarms of skiers, and he's trying to get on the hill; he can't get the skiers out of his way. I went up to him and said, "Hey, Jim, I hear it'll never go."

Max Dercum: Pete Seibert got his financing for Vail at the Ski Tip Ranch in the early 1950s. He was driving an old Pontiac or something, owned by his mother. I had some guests in here from Milwaukee, one of whom was Fitzhugh Scott and a few other people who were involved. They were all sitting around this fire and here comes Pete and he said, "There's something I'd like to show you here. I've got a model out there in my car. Can I bring it in?"

He brought in this model of Vail, of the mountain and what he had hoped for there. He had been working on this thing secretively, had purchased this land and ranch down there in the valley as some sort of hunting property for shooting rabbits or whatever. Pete showed all this potential area to Fitzhugh, the architect, and all these other people who we had been working with on the idea that we were going to form a corporation interested in building a ski lodge at Arapahoe. Pete instead talked these people into going to Vail and investing with him.

Kingsbury Pitcher: Ernie struggled with Santa Fe for a few winters and then moved on. When we bought Santa Fe Ski Basin years later, all these old records were still around, and I saw the best thing that Ernie did was that he took it on himself personally to pay all the suppliers like the Propane Company at the end of the winter, though the operation was essentially broke. He didn't leave anybody holding the sack. He said, "It's no good and I want to tiptoe away from it," but he treated them very well; he could have just walked away. The history up until then had been a history of flakes like the people who built the lift; when they saw it wouldn't work, they took some notes and left and created a mountain of debt. Ernie didn't do that at all; he paid everybody off.

Ernie: The Santa Fe area was running out of money, and we had an explosion in which the upper terminal blew up because I couldn't make the lift operator stop smoking; we had learned that butane leaked out of the bottles. He always insisted on smoking. The first time it had blown up with us both in the operator's cabin. We were pushed out with a soft hand. It was not bad, but it was enough

Unloading Sno-Cat near top of Snowmass. L to R: Bill Mason, Don Rayburn, Hal Hartman, Art Bowles. Courtesy Aspen Historical Society.

Stein Eriksen with wife & Colorado Governor Love at Snowmass. Courtesy Aspen Historical Society.

Kingsbury Pitcher & Bill Janss, Snowmass founders, December 1988 (21st Anniversary). Courtesy Aspen Historical Society.

to teach us not to permit smoking. But he didn't stick to it; and one day it blew up and burned, and we had a monstrous situation. Pete Totemoff was helping me then; he was the snow ranger.

Pete Totemoff: Ernie and I, we got along pretty good up there in Santa Fe Ski Basin. There wasn't a whole lot of business back then, and we got to skiing together and playing hockey. He made a little ice rink in the back. We did it all; if he needed help fixing the lifts, I'd help him fix the lifts, groom the slopes. It was sort of a casual thing in the beginning. Ernie and I did a lot of the clearing up in Santa Fe Basin by ourselves. The part where the lift used to be was a rock garden. We spent one summer just shooting rocks. Ernie liked that; he liked to play with powder. We shot rocks for a whole month and got them out of the way. Otherwise, you had them stick up through the snow. Then we had the leak in the propane system, and it blew the propane tank up, and the lift shack went skyrocketing.

Ernie: After Santa Fe blew up, I went and found the proverbial Texas millionaire, Mr. Joe T. Juhan, a man who had made his fortune late in life in the oil shale properties in the vicinity of Rifle, Colorado. It was Juhan that was the rich man who, as a tax gimmick, had bought the chair lift in Glenwood Springs, Colorado. I was hired to run that chair lift and also the one in Santa Fe. On that basis, he came into Santa Fe and told us he would give us any amount of money we needed to rebuild the lift that had exploded and burned and wanted to give us facilities to build an additional restaurant and possibly housing space. Juhan didn't give a damn about skiing. He was not an outdoor man at all in that respect. He had never been on skis, but he wanted to do something for the community of Glenwood Springs, and tax-wise, it gave him a lot of write-offs which was what he wanted.

Ernie: Skiing in this country was nowhere near as well-developed as in Europe. There was a big difference. At that time, the average European skier was far superior to the average American skier; the opposite is true today. I realize we still don't do very well in racing since the Mahre brothers have retired. The percentage of Americans who can handle deep snow efficiently and elegantly is way above that in Europe, partly because in the Rockies the snow is so much lighter and easier to ski. But also, it's the enterprising spirit of Americans who don't stay in tracks as Europeans are apt to do.

In this country, when I first came here, there were no lifts to speak of in the East. The cable car up Cannon Mountain was already functioning, but that was it. You walked up the mountains. The snow was quite wet, and you could form substantial steps and paths that were usually already well-packed. You walked up and carried your skis. It was rare that we used our climbing skins. But then, by the last two years before the war, the chair lift came along which was an invention of the Union Pacific engineers when they started building Sun Valley. They spread all over, first to Alta, then to Sugar Bowl, then to Stowe, and to Glenwood Springs. Everywhere, there were chair lifts coming. The chair lift is strictly an American invention which came to Europe only after the war. It was developed from a banana unloading device on a cable, claws that hung from an endless cable that the Union Pacific used to unload the fruit shipped from the United Fruit Company. It became the lift that made American skiing.

The T-bar is a Swiss invention. The first one was built in St. Moritz in 1934 above the Suvretta House. They spread like wildfire. There were several built before the war; at Pico Peak, there were a series of them and Winter Park also had T-bars. North Conway had something called the ski mobile, which I think still exists. They were little mini-sized railroad cars that held one person and went up a steep hill.

The rope tow is an American invention. The first one was built in Canada in 1932, and I think in 1935, Woodstock, Vermont, had the second one. It was a terrible invention. I never allowed their operation wherever I was in charge because I felt it was much too difficult for a beginner to learn to ski with a rope tow. It was much better to force them to learn to climb, which Americans don't like to do. The clutch effect of your hand and the flexibility of your knees was something that the expert skier had and caught onto easily. But for a beginner, that was very difficult unless they were exceptionally gifted. So, the rope tow was not the ideal uphill device.

The skins we used for climbing when we started skiing in 1917 were made out of sealskin; they lasted only two or three winters if you skied all winter as we did. That was our major expense; they cost fifteen francs a pair, which was about $3 at that time, but a dollar bought a lot more than it does today. Then around 1930, they were replaced by plush skins which were much cheaper but actually better. They were constructed precisely the same way, but they were made from synthetic textiles, and they permitted you to climb a little steeper than you could with regular sealskins. The sealskin climbing meant that skiing was a much healthier sport then, but you got only one or two runs a day. You couldn't build up to endless ski runs as you do today and ski 102,000 feet as Jean Mayer did in 1965. I did 87,000 feet in that same day.

Godie Schuetz: In 1927-28, my first skiing experience was on barrel staves. I'll never forget that. My father had one of those big wine barrels with a leather strap. You just stepped in and no ski-shoe

Early days at Santa Fe Ski Area. Courtesy Kingsbury Pitcher.

boots, nothing like that. I went up to the top of this hill, which was only like our beginners' slope in Taos after the snow came, and then I came straight down. You just hoped that you wouldn't fall down. If you fell down, then you had to worry about those barrel staves hitting your head. My next ski was an ash ski. There were no edges, just old bear-trap style leather bindings. The ski poles were hazelnut sticks, you put the string through the top. Those were the real beginnings of skiing.

It was just skiing around your house. There were no ski slopes, and no real ski resorts at that time. They came later, about five or six years later; then the first skis came out with partial pieces of edges screwed on to the skis, but no tips. The tips still didn't have any edges. Then the Attenhofer binding came. Then some clumsy ski boots were manufactured. For ski pants, you still skied with socks and knickers.

Pete Totemoff: We'd climb all day for one run. That's why I laugh at these new skiers bitching about waiting in line. We didn't climb just a little hill; we climbed mountains. Back and forth, back and forth, just for one stinking run. I used to ski on skis made by the Northland Ski Company. When you bought a pair of skis from that company, they gave you a little book on it with all the turns and how to do them.

The telemark was the old Norwegian turn. That was one of the first turns that everybody used. There are old pictures of Twining with those miners using those big, long skis. They used this big, long pole which was like an outrigger to turn one way or the other. It took a quarter-mile to turn. Then right after the war, it was all white army surplus skis with no edges. You had to put edges on yourself.

George Engle: Skiing back in the old days was something to behold. I can remember seeing the first people make turns; that is what got me, watching them make turns on the side of a mountain on skis in snow. I started skiing when I was a kid. I'm from Massachusetts originally, and I had always played around in the backyard when I was a boy with pine skis and toe straps and all that. But I never had seen anything like modern skiing or turning; I never was able to turn.

One Sunday in March, my dad wanted to go on a picnic, and we went to Mt. Grace which is a mountain just south of Brattleboro, Vermont and north of our town about eighteen miles. Mt. Grace had these CCC boys who had cut a ski trail on that mountain before there were lifts or anything else. The picnic spot was right at the foot of that trail.

I wandered over to the foot of this trail, and I could see tracks on it, but I couldn't figure out who could have made them because there were turns. All of a sudden, I looked up, and three guys came down, one behind the other, forty to fifty feet apart making turns. Down near the bottom, there were two benches, and then you came down a 150-200-foot drop after each bench to a brook. One after the other, they came down, and they'd jump off one landing and halfway down jump off the next landing, then jump the brook and turn and stop in the parking lot where I was. Wow! It was incredible. It turned out to be the Chivers brothers from Dartmouth. I got talking with them, and I had to get a look at their equipment. And that just did it. That's how I started skiing. I was fifteen at the time in 1935.

Ernie: During those early years, while I was running Santa Fe and Sunlight in Glenwood Springs, I was exploring different areas. I always was searching for the perfect spot for a ski area. I had looked at Mt. Sopris between Aspen and Glenwood Springs and Crested Butte. Of course we knew of Wolf Creek, Colorado. The third area I looked at for my ski resort was Twining, near Taos, which was inaccessible as far as a road went. It was merely a question of finding the perfect spot and then finding a way of buying it.

Wendy Blake (Stagg), Santa Fe Ski Area, January 1952.
PHOTO BY ERNIE BLAKE, COURTESY BLAKE FAMILY COLLECTION.

Ernie with Peter & Wendy, Santa Fe Ski Area.
COURTESY BLAKE FAMILY COLLECTION.

Peter Blake, Santa Fe Ski Area, January 1954.
COURTESY BLAKE FAMILY COLLECTION.

CHAPTER 6
A Look At Twining

Ernie: I looked at Twining casually from 1951 on. In October of 1953, I started running Santa Fe Basin and Glenwood Springs; I had to commute regularly. I had my own plane. I got bored flying a straight line between Santa Fe Airport and Glenwood Springs, so I took a detour to the west and the east, and the east turned out to be the interesting area.

Pete Totemoff: That flight that Ernie keeps publicizing, that one when we went over Twining with Red Lang in that "172" or whatever it was, Ernie embellished it so much that you'd think we flew over the South Pole or something. It was one of the worst flights I'd ever been on, and I've flown a lot of miles. I started flying way back in the 1930s with bush pilots and air attack officers in the Forest Service.

I did a lot of mountain flying. Ernie was very apprehensive when we got up in there. I'd move around from one side of the plane to the other to look at where the trails might be, where they should go. Ernie turned around and said, "Quit moving around in back." He thought I was making the plane bounce around, but you know in mountain flying, you get a lot of turbulence anyway. He was the most nervous pilot I've ever been with. It's a good thing he got rid of that plane or he would have crashed it.

Max Killinger: For being in a ski area, Ernie had very little knowledge of physics and mechanics. Once I drove with him to Santa Fe in his Porsche, and it hurt my feelings so badly for a good machine because he didn't know when to switch gears or anything like this. I'm still surprised to this day that he could fly an airplane.

Ernie: I looked at a vast area, but my eyes were attracted to the big snow basin north of Wheeler Peak in La Cal Basin. There was a tremendous snow basin which took until July or August to melt. I thought it was an optical illusion. At first, I thought it was maybe a calcium deposit because the color would indicate that. That's what attracted me. But Twining hadn't nearly as much snow as Wolf Creek Pass; we knew that from the beginning. The fact that it was so hard to reach was an asset to me because it made it like a destination resort, not a weekend or in-and-out resort, which I didn't want it to be.

Ed Pratt: Some of the old remnants of Twining were still visible when I first went to the Ski Valley in 1961. In the big parking lot you could still see the old concrete foundations for the one general store, and the

old hotel and the cabins. Those foundations were still there, but since that parking lot has been built up, they're gone now.

Of course those early years, in the summertime, we spent a lot of time horseback riding and walking through those mountains up in there and running across many of those mining caves, where they had found a little gold, but mostly copper. I recall up towards Williams Lake and that area, there were still remnants of some miners' cabins.

Ernie: There was minimal gold taken out of Twining, mainly copper. There was a functioning, money-making gold mine at Elizabethtown which was just over the hill. They didn't get any gold out of Twining; it was a lot of work for very little.

Robert Hooper: In 1866, the Gold Rush was on. The amount of gold taken from Twining has to do with the geology of the area, and that makes the history and geology of the Taos Ski Valley area necessarily intertwined. The Taos region is one of the most unique geological areas in the world. The town of Taos is situated in the Rio Grande Rift Valley extending about 600 miles from Poncha Pass in Colorado in the north, to near El Paso, Texas in the south. No rift valley in the world is larger, save the one in eastern Africa. The rift started to develop about twenty-six million years ago, producing the large volcanic center around Questa, north of Taos. In Taos, to the west, we see Tres Orejas and a whole series of small volcanic cones, but the only volcanic products from the Questa caldera still in evidence are ash sheets in Amalia, in the Rio Costilla Valley. The rift's actual master fault runs almost dead north and south, very close to the break between the flatish mesa and the Sangre de Cristo Mountains. Thus it runs perpendicular to the mouth of the narrow valley leading up to the Taos Ski Valley. The Sangre de Cristo Range borders this immense rift valley on the east for three hundred kilometers from southern Colorado to an area east of Santa Fe.

The Taos Ski Valley and the peaks surrounding it, including the highest point in New Mexico, Wheeler Peak, at 13,161 feet, are composed of Precambrian granite and metamorphic rocks, basement rocks that are 1.8 billion years old, some of the oldest rocks in the lower forty-eight states. As you drive up along the Rio Hondo Canyon to the Ski Valley, you will see dikes along the first part of this canyon that represent the densest felsic dikes swarm known in the world. In terms of a volume percentage of this material, it is

Ernie Blake and his commuter plane, early 1950s. COURTESY BLAKE FAMILY COLLECTION.

phenomenally high. Then you will cross a major fault around Amizette and the Gavilan Canyon that separates the younger rocks of the Hondo pluton which are around twenty-four million years old, (and associated with the Questa volcanic period), from the basement rocks of the Taos Ski Valley and Wheeler Peak area. The uniqueness of the Taos area is that it encompasses an enormous spectrum of time from the 1.8 billion-year-old Ski Valley to the Questa volcanic period of twenty-five million years ago to the Jemez area active "only" one million years ago.

Glaciers probably formed many of the big valleys surrounding the Rio Hondo Canyon, like the meadows above Gavilan and Italianos Canyons, the Williams Lake area and La Cal Basin on the way to Wheeler Peak. The big rounded boulders in the river valley are probably of glacial origin. The profile of this valley, however, is very V-shaped, narrow, steep-sided and sinuous. This is not typical of glacial origin, so this Rio Hondo Canyon is more a result of river action than it is of ice.

Philip Reno: During the Gold Rush, miners crossed the westward mountains and moved down the Rio Colorado del Norte (now the Red River) and Rio Hondo, the Taos Ski Valley's river, to Twining

Flight over Twining (Taos Ski Valley).
COURTESY BLAKE FAMILY COLLECTION.

Canyon, prospecting the hills and streams along the way. William Fraser was one of the first, and he settled in the Valdez Valley at the mouth of the Hondo Canyon and set up a toll gate to let wagons up to the valley beyond.

About six miles up, there were soon scores of miner's tents above Gavilan Canyon. The prospectors were attracted by the fault caused by the uplift of mountains as the great rift pushed against the

Miners' town of Amizette. Courtesy Kit Carson Historic Museums.

Hotel Twining (TSV). Courtesy Kit Carson Historic Museums.

Mining company officials at the Twining Mine (TSV). Courtesy Kit Carson Historic Museums.

rocks. It's on the face of this fault that early miners in the late 1880s looked for minerals, hoping to strike it rich with gold. They were prospecting here on the presence of a quartz vein which, under some conditions, is indicative of gold and other minerals. The rocks in this area show abundant evidence of faulting demonstrated by the little black lines in the Gavilan Canyon rocks. These fractures, if temperatures and other variables are present, allow the later fluids containing minerals, thus gold, to infiltrate the older rock faults, and the early miners saw this mineral scar and the iron staining on the rocks. But not much gold was ever found, perhaps because the temperatures were too low for gold ore to form in any amount, and the mines in the Taos area only yielded in total around $100,000.

Al Helphenstine and his wife Amizette settled at the base of the Gavilan Canyon and built a log cabin which served both as a hotel and post office. The name Amizette was given to the suddenly appearing town, which soon after housed two thousand people.

Gerson Gusdorf opened a store selling everything from flour to dynamite and prospecting equipment. A stage ran daily from the Denver and Rio Grande railway station at Tres Piedras to Amizette. For

entertainment, dances were held regularly at the store. The best known mines were the Shoshone and the Jackpot. The Gusdorfs were offered $20,000 for the Shoshone, but turned it down, and never later got a penny for it. Gold was scarce, and the only men to make anything much from Amizette were the real estate men from Denver who sold lots.

William Fraser found copper further up the canyon when the gold petered out. He sold stock in the Fraser Mountain Copper Company, and the largest investor was a Mr. Albert Twining, a banker from New Jersey. The growing town further up the valley was named for him. Around 1900, mining operations here began in earnest, and a huge copper smelting mill was built at the site of the Taos Ski Valley basin. Electricity was generated by a Pelton water wheel, run by water piped in from the Lake Fork and Hondo streams. Many cabins sprung up, and Twining had electricity fifteen years before the town of Taos. "Tenderfoot Katie" ran the kitchen in the large hotel built for officials and guests, hence the name of the today's restaurant at the base of the ski hill. Juan Concha, later to be governor of the Taos Pueblo, worked in Katie's kitchen. There was a livery stable, and bunkhouses for the miners who worked a nine-hour shift every day including

Early dwellers in Twining (TSV). Courtesy Kit Carson Historic Museums.

Sundays and holidays. On paydays, Gerson Gusdorf would drive up from his Amizette store with cash for their checks, and a wagon filled with things that the miners needed.

By 1900, Jesse Young, of the Brigham Young family, was finishing his sawmill at the head of the pass between Twining and Red River. From this mill, lumber for cabins and cordwood for the smelter were brought down to Twining.

In 1903, the mine failed, as the metal in the smelter "froze." Mr. Twining lost all of his money, later embezzled some, went to jail, and finally left the Taos area. William Fraser, still living in Valdez, and Jack Bidwell, who prospected for years in the hills around Twining, formed a partnership which soon ripened into open hostility. Bidwell later died in poverty in a Raton hospital.

Bert Phillips, Oscar Berninghaus and the Taos Society of Artists painted often in the canyon. Bert even worked a claim on Gold Hill and fitted out a pair of skis from barrel staves on which he would ski down from the mine, with Indian snowshoes strapped on his back for the return trip up. When the mountain area around Taos was taken into the National Forest system in 1906, Bert Phillips became the first forest ranger and

named the forests for Kit Carson. Much later, Taos banker and flour mill owner Ben Randall took over the Twining property. He let the artists and their families stay in the hotel and cabins for which he was given sketches from time to time to settle accounts.

Louis Cottam was named forest ranger in 1917. He watched over the timber and grazing, and laid out many of the trails and roads. The road to Twining came into Forest Service management, and the toll road ended. Gerson Gusdorf took the first automobile up the road, but "pushers" were needed, as the road crossed the Rio Hondo incessantly. An axe was also needed to cut the many logs the beavers felled across the road.

When Twining's mines were humming with activity, game rapidly disappeared in these mountains. In the 1930s, however, Tom Holder, Jr. became the Taos game warden, and by his retirement, game was again plentiful. Beaver, grouse, deer, elk, bear, bobcat and mountain lions all called this valley home. With the advent of the Ski Valley, game once again became scarce.

By 1930, the towns of Amizette and Twining were all but gone. Ben Randall sold the machinery for scrap and the hotel and cabins for the lumber in them.

Miners tobogganing in Twining. Courtesy Taos Ski Valley.

Mabel Dodge Luhan bought the mill's great beams for use in the building she gave to Taos for a hospital. Aspen filled in the slopes that had been denuded of their trees.

In 1946, Mr. and Mrs. Orville Pattison purchased the land that had been the Fraser Mountain Copper Company. The Pattisons built a rock house from the stone foundations of the old mill, and another dwelling for their son, Buell. Some years later, Orville Pattison built his own generator, and Buell built the Thunderbird Lodge. Ernie Blake and Pete Totemoff came in the early 1950s, and the Twining valley once again became populated, this time for the grand winter sport of skiing.

Ed. Note: Twining History from: Reno, Philip. And Farther on was Gold. Denver: Sage Books, 1962.

Ernie: Twining had the combination of snow and vertical differential. I wanted to have potentially a three-thousand-foot vertical drop, equal to a thousand-meter differential, so we could go in for big races if we needed to, something that's not as important today anymore, but it was very important to me then. And we wanted a place with mostly north to northeast slopes, because that's the side of the mountain that will hold snow when you're this far south. The idea of a ski area in Twining was a completely crazy idea. I was convinced that I would succeed from the beginning on, but I was foolish for there was no reason to think so.

Georgia Hotton: Ernie cut out for himself an

San Geronimo Day at old Taos Pueblo. Courtesy Kit Carson Historic Museums.

incredible job when he decided that he could sell skiing in northern New Mexico. But he chose a very excellent spot. Twining is one of the great ski areas of the world, not just because of what Ernie Blake was able to accomplish, because in fact he discovered a magical place where the snow does come and where the mountains are steep and yet we were able to find some easy ways down the mountain for beginners and intermediates. It became a lot of fun for everybody, although in the first days it was all straight down.

Wolfie Lert: One day it was raining like hell, and Ernie said, "Come up, I'll show you where I'm going to have my ski area." I drove up because I was looking at every new ski area for *Ski Magazine*.

I drove up Twining canyon which was just a dirt road then, and I came to where the stream went across the road about a mile-and-a-half below the base area and that was the end of the road, because we had just had a big rainstorm, and that stream was full of water and there was no bridge and no way for me to drive over it. Ernie was waiting for me on the other side with his jeep. I waded across and went into his jeep, and he drove me up and he showed me this mountain. Everything was solid trees and he said, "I have decided

Entrance to the Ski Valley Canyon.
Courtesy Pattison Family Collection.

56

this is where I'm going to have a ski area." I told him, "Ernie, you are nuts. You're out of your mind." So much for the good advice. Ernie didn't take much advice from anybody. Ernie was an extremely stubborn man who knew what he wanted when he wanted it, and he was going to go and do it. And he did it.

Ernie: Pete Totemoff came with me the first time on foot on the 15th of May in 1954. We climbed up carrying our skis and then the snow became deep and we put on our skins part of the way to Bull-of-the-Woods and then went on up to Fraser Peak. Then we came down the west face of the mountain behind the mine tunnel of the rock slide that faces us here and skied down the rock slide. There were three-and-one-half feet of fresh powder snow which was very light in the morning, but when we came down later on, was very heavy. But skiing for both of us was great. We decided that this was a place worth investigating.

Pete thought it was too steep to be of any interest commercially. I was of the idea that Americans were learning to ski so fast, and the standard of the American skiing was improving so rapidly that it seemed to me that wouldn't be a handicap.

Pete Totemoff: Oh, I knew how to ski, and I knew how to make a long splice. On the rope tow, you have to know how to make a long splice. Being somebody from the sea, I knew all of the knots and the splices already. Nobody else knew how to splice.

I've walked every one of these damn mountains and checked them out for the Forest Service—in the whole Southwest, not just here, summer and winter. You name it, I've climbed it.

I'm an Aleut Indian, from the Aleutian Islands. My tribe is the one Michener writes about in his book *Alaska*. I was born in a small village, and then we moved to Cordova, Alaska where I was raised. We were out in the "boonies" about five miles from town. I went to a naval radio school. Back then, the only communication to anywhere was through the naval stations. That was my schooling, from grades one to ten. I had to ski to go to school, two miles a day. That's where I learned to ski; snowshoeing was too hard work. The coast snow is heavier than shit. It would pile up on top of the snowshoe about a foot high, and you could hardly lift it. So I learned to ski.

I came to New Mexico for my health because of bad lungs. I spent two years in the hospital in Albuquerque. I'm not cured but, you know, nobody, when I skied and I was short of breath, ever knew that I only had a lung-and-a-half.

I helped to start the Sandia Ski Area in New Mexico and made it work. They had a lift and couldn't make it run. I got that thing operating. I got started in the ski business because Bob Nordhaus put an ad in the Albuquerque paper for a manager of the ski area, and I applied. It was crazy. I always had a lot of good friends, and they helped me; it's been going ever since.

Pete Totemoff. Courtesy Jean Mayer.

Undeveloped Taos Ski Valley with Hondo Lodge.
Courtesy Pattison Family Collection.

Bob Nordhaus: Pete came up in 1946 to the ski area and said he wanted to help out, and he taught and ran the rope tow and ran the little cafe down in the base of the lodge; Pete could do everything. He stayed with us for quite a while. Then he went around to various places through the Forest Service. But he was also here with the Forest Service when we built the Sandia Tram and was one of the inspecting people of the tramway. He taught skiing and taught my kids how to ski. Pete was just great.

Buzz Bainbridge: Pete, Bob Nordhaus, and I were racing in Telluride a few years back. Because of our age, we were supposed to get a handicap, and the president of Telluride came to me after the first day and he said, "We didn't give you a handicap because

Pete Totemoff skiing. COURTESY BLAKE FAMILY COLLECTION.

you've made the cut without it. We figure it'll save us a lot of arguments if we don't give you guys your handicap." They were supposed to handicap us 1/30th of a second or something for every year over fifty. But we ended up racing head to head.

Governor Lamm was there racing, and Pete says to Governor Lamm, "Governor, you could have been an Aleut. We take our old people and we put them on an ice flow to get rid of them." This was just after Lamm had made that statement that the old people ought to move aside and let the young kids have a chance. Lamm says, "For God's sake, won't you let me forget that?"

Pete Totemoff: Chilton Anderson has a really good picture of me racing at Taos; perfect form, position. I won this race, and Dr. Pond didn't want to give me the trophy. It was a national race, and here's this Indian that came up and beat the shit out of everybody. He made an announcement. He said, "I don't think I'll give Totemoff the trophy." All through my career it's been like that. It was a national race, and they didn't want to give the trophy to "this Indian."

I won the Governor's Cup about fifteen years ago in Albuquerque, and Harold Brooks didn't want to give me the trophy—a big one. He just didn't think I deserved it, I guess, but I beat everybody. They made a big deal out of it just like Dr. Pond did. It was the same thing in Telluride when I first won the race up there. They said, "You don't look like a skier; I don't know if we should give you this trophy." What's a skier supposed to look like?

In a way, Ernie and all of them trusted me, but they were always wary. Even the Forest Service was wary about me. They never knew what the hell I was going to do. When you're an individual, what the hell? Especially a guy like me who came down here from Alaska to die. I figure I had it made, and I don't have to depend on anybody or anything to keep going.

It's a different situation with me being an Indian. You're never really one on one; you have to overcome a lot of prejudice with people, especially gringos. Whether you like it or not, you better show them you can do things just as well as they can, and probably better. That's the way it's always been, especially in skiing. Skiing has gotten to be a macho thing.

When I was passing the ski instructor exam, Ernie was behind them giving me the full certification. They were prejudiced; they couldn't see an Indian skiing better than they did. I always had to beat them in a race in order to prove myself, and they didn't like that either. I'm proud to be Indian. I can trace my ancestry way back. Most of these guys can't go back more than a generation, and their father was probably a bootlegger.

George Engle: Peter Totemoff, now there's another character. I remember when Peter took the exam at Arapahoe Basin. He was strong enough, but not in his free skiing at that time; we did not pass him the first time around. He was as disappointed a man as there ever was. But, he came back and did it again, and passed.

Pete Totemoff: I got it coming and going. People like Willy Schaeffler, those guys were superior, silver spoon from the East, or Willy was a proud Kraut. Willy Schaeffler made it quite obvious that I wasn't an Anglo, a German or a blue-eyed whatever. He was a real asshole. He was one of the worst of all of them. It's in their race. I've worked with a lot of the lift operators that built all those lifts in the country, and if you're working with a Kraut, you've got to let him know that he can't run over you; they'll try, and if you don't let them, then they're your friends.

Ernie and Harold Brooks, the photographer from Albuquerque, skied together a lot. When Brooks died, I saw in his obituary that he was a good friend of Ernie Blake's, and that he skied with Ernie Blake. I would want mine to say "Ernie Blake skied with Pete Totemoff."

I still ski once in a while. But I'm burned out. I've got skier burnout. Shit, I've been skiing over sixty years. I'm still in one piece, sort of. I had to choose sex or skiing, and women are such tactile beasts.

Bob Nordhaus: It was sad Pete died. At the funeral, it was interesting to have champagne at the grave side. That was really honoring Peter. He would have liked that. He was looking down, and I'm sure he approved. I've never seen that before. *The Albuquerque Journal* quoted him as saying, "A good powder run was better than an orgasm"—and they published that!

Louie Bernal: There's somebody in this world that looks after Ernie, that takes care of him thinking about this place. That man from Alaska, Pete Totemoff. I know him. I know him when I started working here.

This man told me he was an Aleutian Indian from up there in Alaska, and that may have helped him understand the way of the nature of God too. He had somebody take care of him, a Spirit that take care of him. We don't see them, but they're the ones who lead us where we can go.

Bob Nordhaus: I never thought Ernie was nuts, I never thought anybody was nuts; they all thought I was nuts to start skiing in the Sandias; and they really thought I was nuts when I started the tram. They cut off my credit on everything else I was doing. They figured I had gone to far this time with this tramway idea. But, we had a lot of local support. We raised a million dollars locally. It's the longest single span in the world.

I think having skiing and the tram is nice for Albuquerque. I think if Ernie and I and all the rest that started these ski areas, hadn't enjoyed it, none of us would have gotten into the ski business for the money. The Sandia Tram is the largest tourist attraction in New Mexico now. And when I said I was going to do the tram, every bank ran from me.

I started the first ski area in New Mexico. I grew up in Albuquerque. I was born in Las Vegas, New Mexico, and we moved to Albuquerque where I went to junior high school. I got back from law school in 1935; I didn't ski until after that. When we came back here, there was nobody using the mountain, and we decided well, we have a nice mountain, so we started skiing with groups. We began skiing on a road up above Doc Long's cabin in the Sandias.

Then in 1937, Graham McGowan came down from Colorado. He surveyed the Sangre de Cristos and this mountain for possible ski areas. He was working for the Forest Service. On a map, he looked over all of the Sandias, and he picked the spot that we now use. He laid out on paper the major trails that we now have. He laid out the Santa Fe Ski Basin also.

In 1936, we cleared a little area at Tree Springs just below the present Sandia Peak area. In 1937, we put in our first rope tow, a 1,500-foot rope tow. In 1938, we built the log cabin. In 1939, we extended the rope tow to a 3,000-foot rope tow in two sections. Then at that time we were exploring and climbing up to the Crest.

Ben Abruzzo became a partner and we started La Madera Ski Area. Ben was the American Eagle Balloon Pilot along with Maxie Anderson and Larry Newman; Ben and Maxie started the Balloon Fiesta. We started the Albuquerque Ski Club and ran the area until World War II. Then after the war, Ben and I bought it from the ski club with the idea of expanding the ski area. We started the ski area because we decided that the Sandias were just too pretty to leave alone all winter.

Years later we began building the Sandia Tram; the construction started in 1964. We got bids from Bell Engineering, Monroe, and Pomagalski, and Bell was much cheaper. At first they said they couldn't build a single span with only one tower. They said it was impossible. Then finally we persuaded them that they could, and they said it was the toughest construction job they had ever done. As a matter of fact, their chief engineer came out here, and we were looking over the plans together, and all of a sudden I saw beads of perspiration coming down his face, and he said, "My God, I've forgotten two cables!" So, he'd been on two track cables instead of four. They had under-designed.

Early Sandia Peak Ski Area.
Photo By Caplin & Thompson, Courtesy Sandia Peak Ski Area.

The Ben Abruzzo Family, Sandia Peak.
Courtesy Sandia Peak Ski Area.

Early Madera/Sandia Peak. Courtesy Sandia Peak Ski Area.

Bell supervised the construction, but we had our own people like George Boyden who is probably the best there is. It was tough. The cable pull took six months. We got a winch that had been used for hauling transmission lines across the Mississippi and it had three big reels. There was only one crane in town that was big enough to load it, so they'd go unload it and bring it up and then go back and get another one. They needed scaffolding to support the cable so it wouldn't scrape on the rocks. To pull that cable took six months!

Pete Totemoff: It was quite an experience to build the Sandia Tram in Albuquerque. Those guys that built that were like Walter Ruegg; they were builders, not engineers. The most beer it took to build anything was that tram in Albuquerque. Those Germans drank beer like it was going out of style. They drank cases every day. It's just like water to them. See, the guys in this country are required to be certified as engineers to do all this stuff. These guys were builders, not engineers, but they knew engineering, too. Right away, the ones who were working there started recalculating some of this stuff on that tram, and they descovered it wasn't sturdy enough, so we had to modify a lot. Then the design engineer came over from Switzerland, and he put a rubber stamp on it.

George Boyden is the technical manager, and Jay Blackwood is the manager. George wasn't an engineer, but he could build trams, and knew more than most of those highly educated, so-called engineers. A lot of these lifts that they put in were put in by these guys who had the experience, and they didn't have the engineering degree, but they could do it; they put in lifts all over the world, not just here. After so many years of doing that, they got a feel of what should be done; they did the recalculations later, but they knew by looking what would work. These guys didn't just build ski lifts;

*Santa Fe Ski Area, 1959, Ernie, Pete & Blanche Totemoff,
Ben Abruzzo & Bob Nordhaus (front).*
COURTESY KINGSBURY PITCHER.

*Dedication of Sandia Tram. Ben Abruzzo, Governor
Campbell, Bob Nordhaus.* PHOTO BY JIM BOYER, COURTESY SANDIA
PEAK.

George Boyden servicing Sandia Tram. COURTESY SANDIA PEAK.

Sandia Tram. PHOTO BY JAY BLACKWOOD, COURTESY SANDIA PEAK.

they built mining trams and all that kind of shit all over the world.

Bob Nordhaus: To me, the tram seemed the logical thing to do summer and winter to connect Albuquerque with a ski area. For instance, I saw the tram on the Zugspitze in Germany; it was then the longest single span in the world. My dream was to connect Albuquerque and the top of the Sandia Mountains and have a year-round operation.

It was the same for Ernie; he had a dream from very early on. He wanted his own ski area. Ernie was a pioneer of skiing along with a few others that really were the founders of American skiing.

Pete Totemoff: Ernie wanted a ski area so bad he could taste it. When I told him about Twining, he really jumped at it. He took off like a sky rocket. First, I took him up towards Gold Hill; that's where I thought the ski area should be. He didn't like that. He wanted to put it where he could use the Hondo Lodge for cheap and clear that hill. We tried to talk him out of it, some of us like Wolfie Lert and Otto Lang, by saying it was too steep, and the skiers couldn't handle it. But, he went ahead anyway and proved us wrong.

Wolfie Lert: Ernie brought in Otto Lang, who was the first ambassador of the St. Anton Ski School of Hannes Schneider, ran the Sun Valley Ski School and started several ski areas in the Northwest. Then he was in the movie business for a long time. He still skis actively and lives in Seattle.

Ernie: Otto Lang thought it was impossible also, that you couldn't build on so steep a mountain and so wooded a mountain. But, he also saw the advantages of the twice as high tree line that there is in Europe. It protected the snow from sun and wind. You didn't have so many crusted, miserable surfaces that you had in Europe. This was all before packing machines became standard equipment.

Otto Lang: I was working in the film business, and I was looking for some locations in the New Mexico area. I stopped off in Santa Fe, and I knew that Ernie was there, and he was a skier, so I said I'd like to ask him over. We started to talk, and he told me what his plans were. He had just come back from the war. The only area that was functioning in Santa Fe was this funny little hill, just an open meadow. It was nothing. He said to me that he had the choice to take over that ski area or else to look for a new ski area. He asked, "Would you mind coming with me and help me look around a little bit?"

Ernie had a plane, and I said I would love to. So, we got into his plane which was held together with baling wire and chewing gum. We flew over the area of Santa Fe Ski Basin. I told him, "Ernie, this is nothing. There is nothing to develop there." So, he

Wolfgang Lert, April 1975, Taos Ski Valley.
PHOTO BY ERNIE BLAKE, COURTESY BLAKE FAMILY COLLECTION.

Ernie Blake and his "Search Plane," Taos, August 1956.
COURTESY BLAKE FAMILY COLLECTION.

flew me towards Taos, and I saw Wheeler Peak and the Blue Lake area, and we sort of circled around and saw an area, and I asked if we could get in there.

We landed in Taos, got in Ernie's jeep that he used for an airport car, and there was a logging road, and we drove to the end of this old road and I said, "Ernie, this is it?" Actually, I sort of had my eye on Wheeler Peak which I thought would offer more of an opportunity for skiers, but it was pretty inaccessible. Ernie said that he thought that's where he'd start out. So, it just happened. Taos wasn't ideal; it was too steep, but it was one of the best areas. Ernie did an excellent job with that mountain.

Max Dercum: Edna and I were staying in Santa Fe with Ernie, and we drove up to Taos from Santa Fe. Ernie had a jeep in Taos. We drove up the very old logging road to Twining and on beyond to the junction of two main streams. We drove up through the draw and parked the jeep. We saw a black bear cut across the valley. Ernie stood there and pointed out his dreams. I knew what Ernie was dreaming. He was dreaming of something better than anything that existed at the time.

Ernie: The two Schwarzenbach boys, Robert and Chris, were there looking with us when we found the Hondo Lodge the first time. They were four and five years younger than I, but they went to the same school in Switzerland. They were optimistic about the area. The Schwarzenbachs were the first ones to take a positive outlook. They had built a very similar area in the East, which I never skied, called Mad River; that was built by them and Roland Palmedo.

"Pitch" (Kingsbury Pitcher) was back and forth back then. He had gone back to Sun Valley and Santa Fe. At one point he came to Taos. He had Chilton Anderson's property and was going to be a rancher or something.

Kingsbury Pitcher: Ernie showed up that first summer and said, "Would you be interested in coming in as a partner in Taos Ski Valley?" And I said, "Well, there's a couple of things. Number one, I don't have any money because it's all tied up in this piece of property. Number two, I think it's impossible." Having seen it then, and seeing what Ernie did, made me realize what his real ability was in communication and marketing and making people accept something because at the start, nobody could ski at Taos. Nobody was good enough; the equipment was terrible. Everybody kind of floundered around at the bottom; they had some tough years. For the second time I gave Ernie a very negative opinion. I said I didn't really think Taos Ski Valley would work.

Pete Totemoff: Ernie wanted me to come in with him on Taos. I said we couldn't get along; one of us would kill the other in a year's time. I told him it was all his and that I would help him but otherwise I didn't want any part of it. It had to be his alone because nobody could work with him. He was too opinionated and hardheaded with his tunnel vision. He was going to do it, and he was going to do it his way and don't get in the road. He made a lot of mistakes, but he survived them because he was so damn determined to make it go.

CHAPTER 7
Innovations That Changed Skiing

Ernie: I was convinced we could teach people to ski our steep mountains and that the equipment was changing so rapidly that more and more people would be able to ski. Head skis were just coming in, and that was going to make a big change. I felt they would revolutionize the industry.

Pete Totemoff: You know what really made skiing? The Head ski really is what made it work. Nowadays, with the new equipment, any damn fool can ski. And the other thing is Bogner pants, stretch pants, because it got the ladies' styles. Wherever the ladies are, the guys follow.

Ernie: I met Howard Head at Tuckerman's Ravine in the spring of 1948. Howard was there with his sandwich experimental ski.

Howard Head: I made my first skis in 1947; they all broke that winter at Stowe. I made a better ski, and took it up to Tuckerman's in the spring of 1948 where Ernie and I met. But I had not made my first successful ski yet; I was still experimenting. In 1950, I went back to Tuckerman's Ravine with what turned out to be the first successful Head ski. That was demonstrated by Cliff Taylor who brought my first ski that really worked over the headwall at Tuckerman's and came up to me with a smile. He'd found just a superlative experience.

I wound up making thirty-nine unsuccessful models, and the fortieth one was the one. So in the spring of 1950, I went into the production on that first pair that had worked, and it really was a success. I could sell every pair I could make because the word was going around.

Warren Miller: I met Howard when I was teaching skiing in Sun Valley in 1949. Howard was out there in front of the ski school dorm, as it was called, with five or six pairs of these funny looking metal skis, and everybody just laughed. He talked some guys into using them, and of course, they broke them right away. They were aluminum colored, almost like polished aluminum. In 1946 or 1947 he'd go up to Bromley and get Neil Robinson to spend all day Saturday and Sunday breaking one pair after the other.

Then he'd go back and work at his aircraft factory and try different glues and different things. In those days, you used fiberglass, which was still a powder that you had to mix. That's how antiquated it was, and there just wasn't good bonding resins for metal to wood. Of course, Howard was always dedicated to

metal and never accepted the fact that fiberglass had a different property.

I think that of the four or five guys who have contributed the most to skiing, Howard is at the top of the list, along with Ernie, Dave McCoy, Everett Kircher of Big Sky and Boyne, Ed Scott with his pole and Bob Lange with his boots.

Howard Head: I went out to Sun Valley in 1949, and I got real enthusiasm and fascination from the instructors, but Pete Lane bought twenty pairs of skis and then sent them back. He knew they were no good, and he wasn't interested in the feeling he got from the skis; he was interested in whether they really were good enough and stood up. They weren't good enough for him, and he ruthlessly sent them back to me. He did me a great favor.

Alf Engen: Head skis changed skiing, they sure did. I was one of those who skied with the first pairs he brought up on Baldy in Sun Valley. They were white, snow white, no color at all. He brought four pairs up there right into the round house, and he asked me if I wanted to ski with them, and I said sure, so we skied down the Canyon Run. I skied down on them, and of course, they were very flimsy. I don't think he had the right glue at the time because they came apart. But he came back the next year with some better skis and the next year even better.

I admire Howard Head more than anyone in the ski business. He's the one who really put skiing to where we all love it; to where everyone could ski, with his limber ski. I could see it, the Head ski was going to make a difference. I have never turned down anyone for anything new. I've always tried it. Then for years I was always on Head skis. I hardly used anything else. Three kinds—the Standard, the Flexible and the Vector. I think that Howard Head is one of the great geniuses of our time.

Howard Head: I took the skis all over the country in the early years. We all did; it was the only way back then. I took a ski trip, for example, in 1952, from Baltimore to Pittsburgh, to Detroit, to Chicago, to Minneapolis-St. Paul, showing, trying to sell, but also asking for suggestions and comments with the idea to learn something to improve it still further. And then up into Canada, across Canada to Vancouver and down—Jim Whittaker met me in Vancouver and escorted me down to Seattle and then down to Oregon, to San Francisco. Then, to Utah, and then south to Colorado Springs and Aspen where I spent about three or four days. Then on to Winter Park, Arapahoe, Denver, and

Tuckerman's Ravine, Mt. Washington, New Hampshire, April 1939. PHOTO BY ERNIE BLAKE, COURTESY BLAKE FAMILY COLLECTION.

Ernie at Tuckerman's Ravine, April 1939. COURTESY BLAKE FAMILY COLLECTION.

finally home. Those were whirlwind trips. I did that trip in six weeks.

George Engle: I had a boy teaching for me then who had been on the U.S. "A" Team. So, Howard brought all these skis, but he wouldn't let us see them. They were all black, and he never let us see the bottoms. He'd put them down in the snow and adjust the bindings to us and say, "Now go and do this or that." Then we'd come down and write down our feelings about this pair of skis and what it was.

Howard was some kind of a guy. He'd try some of the damndest skis. He brought some 7-foot-3-inch skis, and they were the forerunner of the Competition model, and he got three pairs—one pair we found out later had a center groove that was rounded like they are now and that skied fine; the next pair had a square groove, square edges and you couldn't turn that ski very easily. You had to tilt it on the edge to get it loose to turn. The third ski had three or four little narrow, square grooves. I didn't start at the top; I came down about one-third of the way and turned them loose, but they wouldn't turn at all. I ended halfway down to the practice hill before I could get those things stopped; it scared me to death.

Dave McCoy: Howard furnished skis for some of my family while they were racing. Pancho skied on Head skis all through the British Championships and the Olympics, and I think that the famous poster that was made of him on skis was a big boost for Head. Howard wasn't that athletic, but he enjoyed seeing his product being used by the kids. Out on the hill, he would talk to me once in a while about how I thought the skis were working.

Ernie: The Head ski, however, was enormously more expensive than any other ski, and it took a major decision to consider it. I tried it on Howard's suggestion in Aspen. I found it wonderful. I went way out on the financial limb and bought twelve pair to retail. That was the minimum that you had to take to retail in Santa Fe Basin. We hit a snowless Christmas, but I had a lot of well-known Texan families skiing with me, respectively, waiting patiently for the snow. I sold all twelve pair before there was any snow on the strength of their price and big black good looks. We sold them all. There was no choice of bindings. If they didn't want Cubco bindings, we didn't sell them. There was no discounting. We took the Head franchise with us from Santa Fe to Taos. It sustained us financially in the early years in Taos.

Howard Head. Courtesy Howard & Martha Head.

Howard Head & Karl Pfeiffer in Vermont.
Courtesy Howard & Martha Head.

Howard Head, designer. Courtesy Howard & Martha Head.

Howard Head: I think one of the successes of Head skis was because dealers would buy as many as I told them to. They knew they were like money in the bank. If they didn't sell them one year, they'd sell them the next. Then we had something called the Authorized Head Ski Dealer.

At first, the Head ski was metal color, no color. Then it was black and we had to put a color in it. For me, white was best at first. There are subtle changes you can see from year to year. For true skiers, their only interest was the way it skied, not the color.

Ernie: And I had the wisdom to state that no skier would ever ski on an artificial metallic ski that didn't smell of tar and ski wax!

Howard Head: All the people of good judgment agreed with Ernie.

Ernie: Well, I've eaten my words ever since then. I met Head again in Aspen in 1951 when I had already heard of the Head ski being marketed in small numbers. There was a lot of talk about the Head ski, and how Howard Head got into this crazy business.

Howard Head: I skied once or twice when I was in college, you know, 800-foot hill skiing and just go down it once, and gee that was fun. That was literally once or twice. Then I got busy and got out of Harvard, went bumming around to see what I wanted to do. This was in 1936. I wanted to be a "creative writer." I got a job with *The March of Time* movies to be a writer, but I never wrote anything. I wound up haunted by their film cutting machine, so I sort of became a maintenance man and copy boy. After nine months, they very quietly fired me. I got a second job with Pathé News. The same story. I went there to be a reporter, and I must have told a good story because they hired me. But, after five weeks there, they found out that all I wanted to do was study all the machinery. Then I found a company called The Motion Picture Corporation of America which was a one-man movie producer, and again, I must have talked well because I got a job as his office manager. After a month, he found out that I always lost the keys to the office. I never shut it up on time. That was a general characteristic; I didn't know where I was going.

Back at Harvard, by the end of my sophomore year, I was doing very badly. I had terrible marks. I remember I had to drop a course with a great creative writing teacher. When I entered in the fall, I found that I had entered Engineering Sciences. I could no longer take creative writing because I was in the wrong school. I got an AB in Engineering Sciences, and suddenly my marks jumped up to As and Bs, and I was on the Dean's List and everything.

I got through college on that run. I got out of college and totally ignored it. I just went to New York to be a creative writer.

Having been fired from three jobs in New York, I retreated to Philadelphia, which was my home town, and got a job with *The Philadelphia Record* as a reporter; I'm a very stubborn guy, four in a row. After a whole year, I woke up to the fact that after three years out of Harvard on the Dean's List, I was making $20 a week as a copy boy.

I woke up to the fact that something was not going right in my life. I took a formal aptitude test at Stevens Institute, and sure enough, my creative writing study was the lowest they had ever had. At the time, I was angered by the fact that their test was: *You are on the moon, it turns out to be made of green cheese; write about that for ten minutes.* I sat there and in ten minutes wrote a line and a half because I couldn't find anything logical or creative to say, and nothing flowed at all. Later I was told they never even read what you wrote. All they did was count the number of words as to your possibility as a creative writer. I was afraid to put down something illogical or irrational.

Then they gave me a test called "Structural Visual Ovation," and I supposedly got the best result on that that they had ever recorded. That finally got my attention. So, I decided, well I guess I better get a job with a name mechanic. I lived in Philadelphia, but I found a job in Baltimore. I wanted to get down there and be an engineer, but I couldn't make a drawing, and I couldn't read a blueprint. But, I did talk them into a job as a riveter out in the factory, and I was very good, and within six months they made me a rivet boss.

Within a month, I'd gotten into such conflict with the manager that I got demoted again, made a mechanic. I shrugged my shoulders; that wasn't really what I wanted to do. For about two weeks, I'd go and change into a dress suit and every day at lunch, I would go over to the engineering office. After two weeks, they gave up and invented a job for me called administrative engineer, which means the guy who makes studies for a project engineer, writes letters, and does research. In between jobs, I went out on the floor and looked over the engineers' shoulders and presently learned how to draw. Within three or four weeks, I maneuvered a move onto the drawing board which is what I really liked.

Normally, it takes five years to become a layout man, and I did it in nine months. So, I was settled in. I was satisfied with the life of drawing parts of airplanes, like wing tips and ribs and small parts; I had nothing to do with the design of the whole airplane.

I got the ideas for the Head ski from stuff I had learned in college. I designed strut structure, and I had a very good sense of strength and weight and how to get from here to there. I would have been intuitively good at making diving boards. I rapidly found out I was a very good layout man, and at one point, they made me a checker which means someone who checks other peoples' drawings. I was so good at that that it was unpleasant. There was one guy almost in tears saying, "What did you do that to my drawing for?" There were errors in it that I saw but he couldn't. Then the same thing happened as in riveting. I got to be a project engineer.

Then they made me assistant project engineer, and I was a disaster; I couldn't create anything and all I could do was look over other peoples' shoulders. I was supposed to teach them, and I couldn't teach. Then the war ended—this was all through World War II, 1939 to 1945. The company got bored with what it was doing but continued designing airplanes, but only for something to do. They didn't care if they were good or not. I just emotionally withdrew from them.

In 1946, I was alone one March-April and decided to go skiing for a week up at Stowe. I simply loved the sport again. I got much more kick out of it than the first time, but the skis were so clumsy, so I thought this was going to be tougher than I thought. I went back again after six months for a week in 1947 and had an even better time. I remember getting a little tight coming down somewhere around on Mt. Mansfield, but I was still clumsy as hell—or the damn skis were clumsy.

I was going home on an all-night train; there was a guy sitting beside me, and we were talking and I heard myself say, "I think I can make a better ski out of aircraft material than out of that bloody, sloppy hickory." I assumed the idea would go away like all ideas do, but when I got back to Baltimore, I found that it hadn't gone away. It kept me awake at night.

So, within a week, I had bought a band saw and some kind of mechanical equipment, rented a shop for $20/month and went to work and made a Head ski consisting of thin aluminum top sheet, very elastic, high-strength aluminum. The trouble was that the wood had to be bonded to metal, and it wasn't generally done then. To bond, you have to coat the parts with glue and then apply two things: heat and pressure simultaneously. But you couldn't go to a hardware store and order a ski press; there weren't any then, and I couldn't afford an elaborate hydraulic press. So I had to attack it by building an aluminum shell mold in the shape of a ski with the top open—a floatable top, with a layer on top, another one. You put the skis in, and then you could put the top down, and if you could squeeze it, you'd have the pressure. And if somehow you could get heat, you had the heat.

The way I did that was to cut out all the parts; the parts consisted of honeycomb and an eight-inch

Howard Head cutting honeycomb core material.
COURTESY HOWARD & MARTHA HEAD.

Howard Head running early laminating press.
COURTESY HOWARD & MARTHA HEAD.

plywood wall and two layers of aluminum—one on top and one on bottom, all super light. When it was finished, it only weighed two pounds as opposed to the five pounds of hickory.

So what I did was cut out a top skin and a bottom skin and didn't bother to put a groove in. I got the shape pretty good. I still have the first ski I ever made. Then I cut out fibered plywood pieces that were the right contour, and I cut out a honeycomb slab for the middle and put glue on all these pieces separately and let them dry.

The mold had two side walls that would hold these parts and the top had the contour of the sidewall. Then, the thing on which the parts set was this quarter-inch aluminum band, a plate, that held the two side walls apart. So when you packed the parts, and then there was a top, you packed the parts into the mold and applied pressure. In order to apply pressure at the top, I made a neoprene bag that I applied this whole mold full of parts in and sucked the air out of the bag with 15 pounds per square inch of pressure. Then all that was left was that you needed pressure. I built a tank and this mold in the bag with the suction running which could be dropped into a tank of 350-degree crank case oil—all kinds of smell. But half-an-

hour later, sure enough, out came the first Head ski, and I didn't test it because it was so precious to me. Then I made several more and did test them and found they were construction-wise weak. Hickory is much stronger than I had been told.

I just used aluminum alloy. I wasn't building a ski, I was building a structure. I wanted to prove I could build a lighter, better ski, and at that point I wasn't good at finding out what a ski should be like. I just assumed I knew it all. If I built it lighter, it would be better. It turned out not to be true. That was July and of course there was nowhere to test it. But I made six pairs in the fall and took them up to Stowe and showed them to the instructors.

The first episode was in front of the fireplace before we went up on the slope. They examined them really excitedly. These skis only weighed two pounds. Well, they'd gone up to two-and-a-half by then. And Bud Phillips in his excitement grabbed the ski and put the heel on the floor and flexed it, and the heel split off on my first ski.

In the next week, the instructors broke every ski in that group, but the feedback wasn't that these skis were ridiculous; the feedback was there was something magical in these skis. I came back to Baltimore in January, walked into my engineering boss's office and said, "I quit. I'm going into the ski business."

So I went to a shop that must have cost $25 a month and looked around for scrap aluminum, still looking around to make it stronger. I wasn't smart enough yet to try and make a thing that skied well. I had to make something that was strong enough so it wouldn't break. By the next winter, I had one that was strong enough and weighed maybe three-and-a-half pounds. In the meantime, I've got three or four guys helping me on credit because they were excited about it, too. I couldn't pay them, and the material was all scrap so I could do a lot on very little money. I knew that the molding process was too absurd, so I built a pants press mold which you could clamp down loosely but then have a floating flexible head that pushed the parts into place with a fire hose as the pushing member.

I wish I still had those original molds. Other parts of the machinery were rapidly improved and so that year I must have made forty or fifty pairs, still being stubborn about not complicating my perfect structure with things like steel edges and plastic bottoms. So I moved through the next winter testing those. These were grooved but still no steel edges or plastic bottoms. I found out that winter there was a real enthusiasm for the ski, but too many people just said, "These are great, but you slide all over the hill on them and the bottoms freeze." So in 1949, I finally accepted the fact that I had to put on steel edges and plastic bottoms.

Howard Head with first ski. Courtesy Howard & Martha Head.

That really was the first successful ski. It was the same as the later Head Standard except for the no-plastic top, so it really was the first successful ski. I think it was first called the Head Expert, and then I didn't like that name. Then it was called just Head. Then I realized I was going to have to make room for more models, so I just invented the word Head Standard. There was a later period when there was the Head Vector; that was the first ski around 1952 along with the Head soft, medium and hard, totally descriptive titles. There was a period when there was the Head Flexible, the Head Standard and the Head Racing. There were about three degrees of stiffness. We sold 300 pairs the first year, which was all I could make, and 1,100 the second. I wasn't the type to go out and get financing. I didn't think about it. I just made what I could make—2,500 the third year and 4,500 the fourth, then 8,000, then 18,000, then 27,000.

We had the Head Competition; to get the racer was very important. That's when they were beginning. It was that year that Pete Seibert won, or placed second in the Roch Cup at Aspen. Once the ski was right, it went. Until it was right, it was no good.

Our big break with Europe came really from the Swiss guy, Walter Haensli, who was at Sun Valley in

1949-'50. I gave him the dealership for all of Europe and sixty pairs. He very quickly sold one-third of my total production. His volume went up to 15,000-20,000 pairs very quickly, and then he got the racing team.

Getting the racers was very important. There were amazing coincidences. I owned the ski world in 1955-'58 for everybody but one class of skier, and that was the racer; the racer wouldn't touch them. At first I thought that was because they were prejudiced, but I found out pretty soon that nobody is ever prejudiced about anything; if it works, they'll go for it. I realized the ski was obtuse and vibratory. So, I put a rubber layer on the top skin and eventually came to the Competition Series, and then the racers just flooded to them. So, in 1964, Head really did own the whole ski world.

Then I began to get very tired, and I made some mistakes. I couldn't direct groups. If I'm watching the process, I will see that no mistakes get made in manufacturing, but if I have to hire a director of manufacturing, and he lets the glue heating slip or something, you can have a desperate time all winter. The company ran into some trouble, and I could sense that very well. The skis themselves were having trouble around 1956-'57 when everybody would have said was the top of our career. I could see bad skis coming in

Ernie and Howard Head at Pioneers of Skiing dinner in Telluride, 1986. PHOTO BY KEN GALLARD.

too fast. I could see those, and I didn't close my eyes to them. If those skis had remained substantially perfect structurally, we would have just gone onward and upward. Just about that same time, someone decided to try the same thing in fiberglass. I fought it, of course, because I didn't want to believe that anybody's ski was as good as mine, but it turned out to be better.

So, fiberglass edged in on us, that was it. I had to hire a president who didn't know anything about skis. All he knew about was merchandise. Alex Schuster came to me personally, though, and said that he'd made up his mind to start a strictly clothing business, based on his skill as a designer, and would I like to do it? At that point, I was blind-tired and just shrugged my shoulders and said, "Yes." That's the total thinking with which Head Ski Wear got started.

If I'd been able to administer as well as I could create, I don't know where we would have gone. I think there are all kinds of inventors as good as I am who weren't even as good at seeing; I could see the whole mechanical picture without missing anything. That's the story of Head skis.

Ernie: Then Howard invented the oversized Prince tennis racket. Those were two major sports that Howard made much easier and more fun to do. The racket made it easier for everyone to play tennis and enjoy it, like with his skis. No one had thought to change the size. Howard was a genius when it came to

that sort of thing. Unbelievable that he invented the Head ski and the Prince tennis racket. A real genius.

Howard Head: I retired in 1968 from the Head company, but then found that I was restless and took up tennis. I found I couldn't play; the racket twisted in my hand and very quickly concluded it wasn't me; it was the clumsy racket. Then in 1974, I had one of these real breakthroughs in the middle of the night; don't make the racket heavier because it's got to have a light balance. Make it wider. With the tennis racket, I just took a classic tennis racket and arbitrarily made it wider and then expanded the hitting surface down into what was the throat about three inches. The thing was extraordinarily successful right straight from the start.

Ernie: Howard Head changed the ski world and the tennis game as much as Bogner stretch pants did skiing.

Howard Head: I love it! Head skis and Bogner. That's right. And of course, other things like good ski boots—buckle boots—and of course Lange boots; that was another breakthrough.

Ernie: We learned about Bogner fashion and the introduction of sex into skiing in the spring of 1956 when we had fled to Europe because the situation here was very primitive. We studied the European ski areas. Bogner had just come out with stretch pants. It was an interesting year to be in Europe, and we came back with lots of ideas and went ahead building the area from the summer of 1956 on, based to a large extent on experience we had gained in Europe. Tight pants for the ladies, sex and skiing, an easy ski for everyone; a remarkable achievement along with the tennis thing. Wolfie Lert was with Bogner in the beginning along with Hans Hagemeister as Bogner importers to the United States.

Wolfie Lert: Monica Brown was really the number one Bogner model.

Monica Brown: Ernie was an Intelligence Officer in the war in Germany. After the war, he looked up some mutual friends and asked them if they needed anything. He would come in his jeep with his officer, and they would shoot wild boar in the forests and then bring the meat to his friend in Frankfurt. And this friend became an editor-in-chief of one of the leading German magazines. When I went to New York to visit my mother, they gave a good-bye party for me, and they said, "If you go to the States, you must visit our good friend Ernie Blake. You like to ski, and he owns a ski area, and you'll just love it."

They wrote me a letter of introduction to Ernie, and Ernie answered that letter to my address in New York, and in case he would miss me in New York, he sent a copy to Munich. So, when I arrived in New York, I had this fabulous invitation to come to Taos Ski Valley, and I looked it up on the map. I saw that New Mexico was way out nowhere and Munich was right there, so I flew back to Munich instead. And when I was in Munich, I was kind of heartbroken, and I thought, darn it. I saw his second letter, and I had been there with Bogner that night and told them about it, and Willy Bogner said, "Oh, I know Ernie. Ernie was the starter at the Olympics, and he started little Billy. Monica, pack your bags and go back." That's exactly what I did.

People were always kidding Willy Bogner; they would say, "Why do you put this un-sportive girl into your ski clothes?" And he would say, "You won't believe it, but she does ski." But I really learned in Taos because I did not ski that much in Europe on a regular basis. I was not the first model for Bogner; there were a group of us, but I think I was the only one who skied. When I came from Munich to Taos, I felt in a way like coming home because I escaped after the war from the Russians. We had lived in the mountains. I grew up in Silesia, Poland and during the war the soldiers had surrounded the mountains so you could not be evacuated the regular way. You had to go up the mountains and ski down on the other side. So we put all our belongings on big sleds, mother and three children, and an aunt waited on the other side of the mountains with a car. That's the way we got out.

Ernie introduced me as the Bogner model and the fashion consultant, but all I did was straighten out a few ski pants and hang a sign on the door in the morning, "Out to ski, leave a message." After every run, we would check for messages, but everybody very much accepted that skiing was it. From 8:00 to 10:00 was in the shop, and then you went out, either to teach or to ski, and the best was to ski before everybody else.

When I came to Taos, I could not believe it because here is this America where you throw a garment away if the zipper doesn't work, where you never put up a hem or darn a hole; you throw the dress out. You buy everything new. Everybody told me this. Here I am coming to this remote little place where everybody does everything themselves from scratch. So, I felt perfectly at home, and I learned skiing from scratch. Ernie stuck me in a class with the Mayers for two weeks and said, "Just listen to what they say."

When I came to Taos from an overcrowded Europe, St. Anton, people actually greeted you on the mountains! Those guests that have been there and keep coming back know one another. It's a big, happy family. It reminded me of growing up in the mountains. Everybody knew everybody and it was like the stories I heard from my grandmother who was the

Monica Brown, Bogner model. PHOTO BY WILLY BOGNER, JR., COURTESY MONICA BROWN.

Monica Brown, Bogner model. PHOTO BY WILLY BOGNER, JR., COURTESY MONICA BROWN.

Monica Brown, Taos Ski Valley, 1964. COURTESY BLAKE FAMILY COLLECTION.

Pete Totemoff kissing Monica. Courtesy Blake Family Collection.

only woman (and alone) skiing in the mountains and everybody would say hello; everybody would know who she was.

And then to come to America which I thought was slick, high-rises, consume and consume, a throwaway society, and you come into this little village where you don't need a car and basically don't need anything, everybody helps everyone. When it is dark and the skiing is over, you sit together on long tables and spin stories. Ernie was the greatest at that, he just was overflowing with them.

SECTION III
Building The Mold For Taos Ski Valley

Ernie stumbled onto the Hondo Lodge on one of his early trips to investigate the Twining valley. He had already spent time scouting with Orville Pattison who owned the east side of the Hondo River, but he knew that land was the wrong exposure to hold snow. The west side was the proper exposure and, as he found, it had the beginnings of a lodge.

The first lift was only 300 feet long. Ernie and Rhoda and three kids lived in a 16-foot trailer under rough and claustrophobic conditions. Chilton Anderson arrived on the scene and got his job because he was tall enough to put the cable back on the towers of the second lift which was a 1000-foot, home-made job moved over from Tres Ritos and built by Indians for the second year of operation. Soon there were enough employees that Ernie could show one of his famous traits: how quick he was to fire and then rehire them. Further, he made it clear that he had a phobia about being swindled. A tough man for a tough mountain.

Twining really started to look as if it was going to be something different when Ernie put in the big Poma lift. To ride that lift up was far harder then skiing down. Al's Run was as narrow as the old road up Twining canyon. The Poma was built totally by manpower; everything was carried up the mountain. Then Ernie got lucky when Bud Crary came with his bulldozing ability and cut the first roads under impossible conditions. Ernie seemed to always need a challenge going on, whether it was a land dispute over boundaries or a fight with his "compadre," Dr. Al Rosen. It was always something to keep his blood pumping and the stress factor high.

Ernie had the ability to charm people, to give them a view of his dream and to pull them along and make them believe. He had an extraordinary gift for public relations. Jean Mayer sensed from Ernie's first letter that Ernie's dream was also the same dream burning in himself. Jean arrived in the ski valley on Christmas Eve, 1957. He and Ernie fought on many levels, but underneath they had great understanding and they shared the same hopes for their mountain. The following year Jean's parents came over from France with his brother Dadou and the crazy chef, Yvon. The French connection had begun and the nucleus of the ski valley was in place.

CHAPTER 8
The Early Beginnings of Taos Ski Valley

Ernie: We met Orville Pattison when we first investigated Twining as a possible site for a ski area. After the ski trip with Pete Totemoff in March of 1954, I came up three or four times with Rhoda and Mickey and marched with Mr. Pattison, Sr.; who was then sixty-seven years old, which seemed fantastically old to me. He climbed very well.

During 1954-'55, we explored all different possibilities. Pete and I climbed all over the Pattison property, but quickly learned that was the worst exposure for holding snow. We knew the other side was best but frightfully steep.

Mickey Blake: Orville could hike like a son-of-a-gun. He knew Twining, he had more than 1,500 acres up there, and he'd hiked all over. He really knew the country and knew a lot about the old mines and history.

Buell Pattison: Dad's parents, my grandparents, used to go to Red River back in the late 1920s and 1930s; they always wanted a place in the mountains. Dad didn't like Red River, because in the 1940s Red River was wide open, bars and gambling, and he didn't think that was a good atmosphere for us kids.

My dad bought the place in 1946. That first summer, we camped on the old Twining Hotel site in tents and built the old rock house up there. We bought it originally because my dad wanted to get out of the hot country around Clovis, New Mexico, and come up where it was cool after all the farm work was done.

We owned the land on the east side of the Hondo River, which was roughly 1,500 acres. The west side where the ski area is now located was roughly a quarter section; it was called the Randall Lewis tract. At roughly the same time two guys by the name of Taylor McCasland and Paul Riding bought the south portion of that quarter section. Then John Burroughs,

Pattison cabin. COURTESY PATTISON FAMILY.

the ex-governor, bought Taylor McCasland's share, long before the Ski Valley ever went in.

Mickey Blake: Orville was a farmer from Clovis and always wore bib overalls. He had a cow and some chickens at the valley; he built his house there and had an organ. I remember my father once went on a jeep trip with Orville. Luciester, Orville's wife, went along and on the way up they were going up near Bull-of-the-Woods. It was a World War II jeep that they had to push start. My father thought there was something wrong with the differential because it made a high whining noise, but when they stopped, the high whining noise continued. It turned out that Luciester was singing her hymns.

Buell Pattison: The first time I met Ernie was in the summer of 1955. There wasn't much up there except we had built the rock house, which Tony Bryan owns now. In 1950, we built a log house which is above the Thunderbird.

Ernie: Pattison leased me all his land for a dollar a year in November of 1955, all of the 1,500 acres on the other side of the Rio Hondo, save the land at the bottom. Then he decided he didn't want to do it. Years later, before he died, he came and gave me a check for $900 and told me that he regretted having reneged, and wanted to make up for it before he was called by his Maker. I told him it wasn't necessary, but he insisted. He was a good man.

Buell Pattison: Dad got along with Ernie all right. I can't remember any big disputes or anything like that between Ernie and him. Everybody gets, or has, a different point in their life where they have conflicts with their neighbors once in a while. Everything always ironed out for the better.

I feel today that my strength has not been my own, but the good Lord's. In fact, I witnessed to Ernie one time. I gave him a Bible, and I even wrote something inside the cover of it. I said, "You've always said you liked history. Let me give you one of the greatest history books ever written." And he kind of took it, not very seriously, until he read what I wrote inside it, and his whole attitude about it changed; and he appreciated it. I know one thing, he said that if he ever did believe, he would want to believe the way my mother did after my little brother Lane got hurt up there. He said that was the kind of faith that he wanted to have, a God like that.

Ernie: Back then when we were first getting started, it was all forest, a tremendously dense forest; nothing was visible. The only thing there was the beginnings of the Hondo Lodge, and there were two cabins in the trees which were just being built, but we didn't know about them. The Chalet Alpina, the raw building, which I later bought for $900 total, was there in the woods. You couldn't see it at all. We found it much later on.

Pattison family in front of Hondo fireplace.
COURTESY PATTISON FAMILY.

Early Hondo Lodge, October 1957. BLAKE FAMILY COLLECTION.

The Hondo Lodge had been started by Ben Harker and John Zagava but they ran out of money ten years before we rediscovered it. They they were living in Dallas and they had a job making matchbook covers. The Hondo Lodge was meant to be a summer lodge for wealthy Texans who wanted to take their secretaries to a place of sex, drinking and gambling. They had a hideout for liquor. It was walled in and had no door in or out. It was a brilliant idea. They had built the lodge being very "spendthrifty" and methodical; they made sure that each wooden beam from the tree trunks had to match with the others in color and in shape. That took them forever, and they ran out of money before they had anything completed.

I met Harker and Zagava on our third or fourth visit, quite by accident. They came out of the dark inside of the Hondo Lodge, beer in hand, quite high, not coherent, unshaven. We told them that we were thinking of a small compact ski area with one little T-bar. I told these two matchbook people that we would build a small lift if they would let us use their land. They told us their land went up to the top of the mountain, and I foolishly believed that. I didn't know about land in New Mexico, and it cost me a fortune later and my first experience in court to straighten that out.

Hondo Lodge buried in snow, March 1970. PHOTO BY DAVE MARLOW, COURTESY BLAKE FAMILY COLLECTION.

They showed me fancy matchboxes they'd made with a painting of the Hondo Lodge on them. They had printed an expensive brochure. It told people how little black slaves would bring their luggage in, and they would ride from Taos to the Ski Valley in a sleigh pulled by four horses with silver bells and all of that which was nonsense. Sleighs are fine for a half- or quarter-mile, not for twenty miles. The Hondo at that time had four rooms; that's all they had. They didn't think of winter at all. They were thrilled to hear my idea.

With that idea, they went to Dallas and formed the Rancho Hondo, Inc. with Doak Walker who was the famous football player. He was playing with the Detroit Lions and had been, as an amateur, the star at SMU. He was number 37. That was a holy number for them. He was only just divorcing his first wife at the time. He came the first Christmas; he was the core of the ski idea in Dallas.

Harker and Zagava printed a brochure for us, a fabulous, very expensive folder that was prepared in Dallas. It told you about howling wolves here at night, and that we'd pick up your luggage in Tyrolean jackets. It showed Wendy, my daughter, with red cheeks and people skiing on the T-bar lift. But it was mostly the lurid fantasy of Dallas advertising persons. The first winter we had thirty

kids from SMU come for Christmas with a chaperon, and we gave them ski lessons.

We quickly started getting good publicity; there were stories in *The New York Times,* and we traveled vastly through Texas and gave movie shows and fashion shows and got the Lubbock-Amarillo-Midland-Waco and later Dallas-Ft. Worth groups together to lure them up here.

Our first lucky break with publicity was a story that *Sports Illustrated* did in December of 1956. That gave us a big boost when they told people about the outrageous area we were building. It was a one-page story which mentioned Doak Walker and Longhorn trail and the crazy Texans who had no fear of anything and broke their legs trying to learn to ski in two days. They showed a sketch of the runs. It got us a lot of attention. *Sports Illustrated* was only three or four years old then and it had a tremendous readership. It was very ski-minded and it has lost that, unfortunately.

Georgia Hotton: Another important thing Ernie did with his public relations early on was to get Ezra Bowen, who was one of the editors of *Sports Illustrated,* to come out and see for himself what Taos had to offer. Ezra put together a very special book called *The Book of American Skiing* in 1963. That first article and the book did a whole lot for Taos.

The front cover of that book had a picture of Longhorn. Chilton was in the picture and so were Ernie and Mickey, also a fellow by the name of Hans, a ski instructor, Jean and Dadou. It shows this group of colorful skiers coming down this beautiful mountain; it just happens to be Longhorn at Taos Ski Valley, and it gets credited for being that in this book of American skiing.

But also in that book, in the very early pages where Ezra Bowen is talking about the history of skiing, you have a picture of Ernie, a picture taken back when he was a Swiss ski guide; he's waxing his skis, a handsome young man. Then he is written up in the early part as being one of the people who took skiers from New York on what Ezra Bowen described as a horrible rattler, a train from New York up into New England to ski.

At the very end of the book, Ezra has a section on "The Best": Aspen is the best for chic, and Taos gets two mentions under the best, one for ambiance and the other for snow. Two places mentioned for snow— Alta, Utah, and Taos. What more could you ask in terms of PR? Taos got an incredible amount of mileage out of that book, and Ernie gets the credit for that, no question.

Joern Gerdts: I was working for *Sports Illustrated* and *Ski Magazine* as a photographer. When I went to Taos, I did some photographs for *The Book of American Skiing.* That may have been my picture on the cover of Jean and Dadou Mayer and Chilton Anderson, and there were some others.

Godie Schuetz: Ernie's personality was unique; it was something new, something different. It was not a stereotype. I think most ski areas lack a personality. You think of Ernie and there's a real, big, strong personality all in one. There was the skier and the entrepreneur; he was well-versed in the English language as well as German and Swiss; he was witty, and he had this gift of creating interest by being controversial. He called the Texans "turkeys," and then he turned around and said, "Well, that wasn't meant to be an insult." It was reverse publicity that was his forte. He created controversy that gave him publicity which he didn't have to pay for. Writers who were looking for a good story for their magazine said, "Ah, Ernie's an interesting subject. I'll go and see him."

Ernie was the best PR man, not only for TSV, but for the state of New Mexico. Nobody who's up there now can come close to that standard or that type of publicity. It is a gift. Some people have it; they are quick. I would think of him as Churchill, for instance. When you read about Churchill, you read that he was a big raconteur. He was very intelligent when it comes to the English language and an example of quick wit. I think that's Ernie's talent. He could do it in a subtle way, if he wanted to be sort of nice, or he could be very rude and just let you have it, bang. And you felt

that you just better not open your mouth again. In the book *Churchill,* there was this lady friend of his, and she was married to somebody else and didn't even care for Churchill. So, at a big dinner party, she was sitting next to him and she says, "Winston, if I would be your wife, I would cook a good soup, and I would poison it and make you eat it." And Churchill said, "Well, dear lady, if I would be your husband, I would eat it."

Ernie was the same way. Some people have a gift of coming right back and making you feel really dumb. He just ignored most of the criticism; he said it wasn't even worth it to think about it. You need pioneers like him.

Warren Miller: Ernie knew instinctively what the skiers wanted, and he gave it to them. I know that most of the people who skied there were extremely loyal. He was doing this thing long before snow compaction and all that sort of stuff, and he really believed in the ski sport. He donated his life to it.

Art Pfister: If you introduced Ernie to someone he'd just fascinate that person. People would talk about it for a long time. And he didn't go out of his way to do that. He was just dynamic. And not only that, Ernie would remember them. I've seen newspaper and magazine people when he's done an interview, and they couldn't wait to write the best things in the world and they did.

Another thing that Ernie always did that no other owner of a ski area in the damn world would ever do: he got up and made that 6:00 or 7:00 weather report to the radio station in Albuquerque and all over, every morning. Do you see Bob Maynard doing that here in Aspen? Or me? Not me. No, but Ernie did it. He got more free publicity than the other major ski areas paid for combined.

Pete Totemoff: Whatever Ernie was marketing, bullshit or a ski area, he could do it.

Georgia Hotton: Ernie got publicity not just in ski magazines, but Taos Ski Valley has gotten full-length articles in the *Wall Street Journal* and *The New York Times* and in newspapers all over the country and in magazines all over the world. In any story that is written about American skiing, Taos is always mentioned. In many cases, it's mentioned as the standard against which others are measured. This was not only about Ernie Blake, but also about Rhoda Blake who had major input into keeping this a very special kind of place.

Ernie was this charismatic character, but there was also a modesty about him, a sense of humor about him which gave him the ego strength, if you will, when he picked up the telephone to say, "This is the janitor speaking." They'd call and want information, and he'd say, "Well, I'm only the janitor, but perhaps I can answer your question." A lot of the calls came in at really weird hours like 10:00 at night, midnight, and worse than that, right into Ernie's own home. He would answer, and he would give them all this incredible information about Taos Ski Valley. People were impressed; they thought if even the janitor knew all this, it must be a fabulous place.

Alice Galanka: I knitted him a hat with "Janitor" in big letters knitted into the design on the front, and he loved that hat. He came back from Vail one time and called me in a panic saying that he had taken the hat with him and had lost it, and he was sure the maids in his hotel had stolen it, and he had called the management and told them so—and would I please get to work immediately on making another one, which I did; then he found the first one in his suitcase. I also made him hats saying, "Ernie" and "Ernie Who?" which appear in a lot of the pictures of him.

Georgia Hotton: I've said before that Ernie was like Victor Borge in what he did when he went to talk to these Texas ski clubs to get them started. Ernie introduced them to the idea of skiing. A lot of the wealth behind the Colorado ski resorts and in the investment capital in Colorado and in Utah came out of Texas, and it came out of Texas in large part, I believe, because Ernie turned these people on to skiing.

In the early days, it was interesting to note how many of our guests came back year after year. There weren't that many choices in terms of ski areas at that time, but again, everybody was made to feel part of the family because of the way the lodges and packages were set up. You came for a whole week. You shared a table with several other people. Ernie and Rhoda, the Blake children, the ski instructors—we all sat with the guests. We were not off in our own little separate places. So, everybody got to know Ernie, and they felt they knew him on a first-name basis. When you came you were treated not just as another tourist. You were treated as a guest of Taos Ski Valley, and your host and hostess were Ernie and Rhoda. That made people have the feeling that they were coming home. Selling the fact that you could come to New Mexico and ski in the lightest of powder, in conditions often comparable to those in Alta, Utah, was a big selling job. Ernie was able to do that. That was part of his magic.

Ernie: Taos was considered too steep, too remote, and then most people said of New Mexico that there was no snow, everybody knew that; it was a desert state full of snakes and such things, but not snow. There was always a problem for Taos Ski Valley in the early days, of convincing people that, yes, New Mexico was part of the United States, you didn't need a passport to get there; and yes, New Mexico had lots of snow in certain parts of the state.

The Murchisons from Texas were our students at

Ernie in his "janitor hat." PHOTO BY KEN GALLARD, COURTESY BLAKE FAMILY COLLECTION.

Santa Fe Ski Basin. She took lessons from me, but he didn't because he already skied quite well. He had gone to school in the East. He didn't speak like a Texan at all; he spoke like a college boy from Boston or thereabouts. We developed the idea of getting a ski club started in Dallas and bringing them here which is one of my great failures.

I started the club successfully enough, that was in 1955-'56, and it very quickly became the biggest ski club in the country, thanks to the money the Bass boys stuck into it. John Murchison invited me to come to Dallas, to that official opening of the ski club, to start that as the representative of the Southern Rocky Mountain Division of the U.S. Ski Association. That's what it was called in those days. I have been the director of it since 1953.

I flew down there, and when I arrived at the airport, I met the Murchisons, and they told me they unfortunately couldn't keep their commitment because an uncle of theirs had died somewhere in a remote part of Texas, and they had to leave. They told me to spot the Bass boys, both of whose wives were very pregnant at the time, and they would do everything I needed. They had all the money needed to start the club and the energy, both husbands and wives all being very enthusiastic skiers.

Early promotional picture, March 1969. PHOTO BY ERNIE BLAKE, COURTESY BLAKE FAMILY COLLECTION.

Now I did find them, and they were fantastic, and the club was a great success, and I thought I had an automatic source of money to finance Taos and a source of skiers to fill the hotels. But it ended in a terrible flop because the Hondo Lodge, which was operated out of Dallas with the football star Doak Walker being the president, was really run by people under him who were incompetent. Walker was a very nice guy and a very quick learner of skiing. But the people who ran the Hondo Lodge did a terrible job.

That is when it was so primitive, when everybody slept in one room with a pot-bellied stove. There was no electricity, no running water, no flush toilets; the toilets were outside.

The Bass boys were coming, so I had called them before Rhoda and I fled to Switzerland in February. I told them not to come and to wait until there were better accommodations. They insisted on coming anyway. They came, and the ladies had to go to the bathroom in the middle of the night. They put on their mink coats and walked out—it was an outdoor facility where the #1 terminal is now—and it was 35 degrees below zero, and that spoiled their enthusiasm for Taos totally.

The operators of the Hondo Lodge were inexperienced, inept, lazy people who made a terrible mess of it. Until Jean Mayer came, the Hondo Lodge was a disaster. We had a nice cook, Amelia, a Hispanic lady, and we had the Indian Pete Concha who now is one of the religious leaders of the Pueblo. But, he was just a young man then. That was in 1956. It was being run by Zagava and a guy by the name of Joe Dyer who was a creep and an idiot who thought he was going to be the great organizer, a friend of Doak Walker. Harker and Zagava went broke in 1957, and Taos Ski Valley bought them out and brought the Hondo Lodge into the Twining Ski Corporation.

We knew the Hondo Lodge was terrible. That's why Rhoda and I left the first winter. Bob Nordhaus went with us, but his children cried all the time so we left him. In February, we went to Davos, to St. Anton and to Zuoz, the village where I grew up. Bob Nordhaus was back with us. We looked at ski operations there.

While we were in Davos, I raced in the Parsenn Derby in the old man's class. I was one of the few people who had Head skis; I had Head Standards. We didn't race all the way to Kublis; we stopped at the Schwendi to have a schnapps, but it was plenty far enough; it was a long race. I won it by a minute or something because I was in good shape, obviously, and had skied all winter. I would have won by a larger margin, but I made the error of having my skis hot waxed before the race, and it peeled off on the long flat part after the steep section. You come in at this tremendous speed, and the speed was too much for it. I could feel it, and I was sure I would lose the race, but I continued and won.

I was one of the few, if not the only one, who had Head skis in Europe then. They were still a rarity and a very much desired object. Before leaving Europe, I gave those Head skis to E. J. Spencer, from my old school, to make his remaining years of skiing more pleasurable and permit him to learn to ski European powder snow, which is like mashed potatoes and needs a ski that helps and is not a hindrance.

Georgia Hotton: That first year, Ernie and Rhoda very wisely were not in Taos. They went to Europe to learn as much as they could about skiing and ski resorts. Ernie already knew a whole lot, but he wanted as much as anything else to find out what was the best equipment, not only for skiing, but also for ski lifts.

Ernie asked the Swiss government not which was the most popular lift, but the safest lift. He did not like heights, and so at first he wasn't even going to consider a chair lift, but when he did consider a chair lift, he went through and got the Swiss records on which were the safest. That was why he went with Stadeli lifts.

Buell Pattison: Ernie and I skied together a lot, and through the years, I finally found out he was scared to death of heights. When he rode on a chair lift, Ernie would wrap his arm around a chair. He'd never climb up on the tower of a lift. The only thing he would mention to me, if I remember right, is that he went over a cliff skiing one time in Italy, and that's what made him scared of heights, because of that fall.

Ernie: The ski-kuli was the first lift we had which I built in January, 1956. It went up 300 vertical feet and was 1,000 feet long and was driven by a 12-horsepower, air-cooled, single-cylinder diesel engine. It ran hot even in the winter. The ski-kuli arrived late from Germany, so instead of having it up in November, we had it up in late January. It didn't go up very far, only just to the bottom of the steep part of Al's Run. We bought it for $2,700 from Erich Konstam in Munich. He was the inventor of the T-bar.

Wolfie Lert: I looked at what Ernie had that first time, and he had this tiny little wire—it wasn't even a rope tow—you know this little wire lift, the ski-kuli. I looked at that and said, "Man, there's nothing here yet."

Ernie: Mickey has been involved in the Ski Valley from the beginning. Mickey knows mechanics and electrical things much better than I ever did. He worked from the very start. The first Christmas he drove the snow cat, the Weasel, and he couldn't see over the dashboard.

Mickey Blake: I used to tow skiers up to the Burroughs' trail. You couldn't get through there now; I don't know how the hell we got through there then. That damn snow cat with skis on the front was just ridiculous. Al Rosen got very sick on that Weasel one time. It leaked exhaust; we were going up toward Bull-of-the-Woods.

Pete Totemoff: Ernie had absolutely no idea why the wheel turned. Mickey was good, but Ernie didn't know the first thing about lifts or any of that stuff.

Max Killinger: There is so much mechanical stuff going on up there that Ernie can be more than glad that there was somebody in the family like Mickey that showed an interest in it. I don't think Ernie had a lack of interest or a lack of aptitude; it was just not his cup of tea. I remember when Dan Kraybill,

"Zap" as we all know him, started working there and Ernie said, "I understand you are a mechanical hot shot." And Dan said, "It depends what you mean by that." He said, "Well, do you know anything about Porsches?" And Dan said, "I know a little bit." And Ernie said, "Okay, take off my ski rack."

Ernie: It was the summer of 1956 that we put in the lift from Tres Ritos to replace the ski-kuli. The Tres Ritos Ski Club sold the lift to us. Actually, it was Al Rosen who arranged it. We put $2,000 in cash and $1,500 in tickets, if I remember right. It was a thousand vertical feet to the top of Showdown, and that was plenty of skiing.

After Tres Ritos shut down, the Bolanders who ran it moved to a better location and built a bigger ski resort and ski lodge at Sipapu which was a great attraction, especially for religious groups. Old man Bolander was a great competitor.

Pete Totemoff: I had to come over there and fix that Platter lift many times when it went haywire in order to help Ernie keep it running. It was never designed to be put on a damn steep hill like that; it was a baby lift. Al Rosen would call and say, "We can't get this dumb lift running," and he wanted me to come up, and he'd pay my expenses and a salary.

We moved that lift from Tres Ritos to Taos because back then, everybody liked Taos. We were trying to do something economically worthwhile, and it's carried on to this day. When I started working for the Forest Service, we made every effort to create an industry of some kind to help the people in depressed areas. Like with the Forest Service, we went to Tres Ritos and other places and started fire fighting crews so that in the summertime, they could get a few bucks. It was the same way with this skiing.

So, when Ernie decided he wanted a lift, I told him to move the Tres Ritos lift over to Twining because Twining always had good snow, and it's got the right exposure. Tres Ritos was too low. Taos had the elevation, the exposure and good snow, all in one. When Tres Ritos was done and there was no more snow, there was still three to four feet of snow up in the Twining Canyon. So, we decided to move it over there. That way Taos would get the benefit of this revenue coming in and employ people; now it's one of the biggest employers in the county.

In a way, we really created an industry that is one of the biggest in New Mexico. We did it to bring in tourist dollars. And the state is not even aware of the fact that it brings in so much money. We started a business that really helped the communities when they didn't have any business at all; winters were dead.

Ernie: Until 1963, we had no electricity, and not until 1964 did we have telephones. It was very primitive in the beginning. We had people in Taos help us. Dr. Pond took reservations with the help of a ham

Susan Rosen & friends Sno-Cat skiing.
Courtesy Blake Family Collection.

radio system. And then we had Herman Kretschmer who was supposed to take our telephone calls. It was very romantic, but not practical. But in the beginning, nothing about this ski area was practical, except that it was done with hardly any indebtedness. It was sweat equity.

We came back from that trip to Europe in 1956 and built the T-Bar lift from Tres Ritos. With Al Rosen's help, we got the REA, the electric company in Taos, to move the lift from Tres Ritos to here. They did the work; we paid them for gas and actual working hours on Saturday and Sunday. It was a fantastic situation that we owe entirely to Al Rosen. They didn't charge me overtime, they charged us regular labor rates, and they took the lift down with their equipment which was nothing for them. We then built it with eighteen Indians from the Pueblo under Tom Castellano, and Pete Totemoff helped. By December, we had it ready.

The lift from Tres Ritos served us beautifully because we got nearly 1,000 vertical feet out of it instead of the 300 we had the first winter with the ski-kuli. So that second winter we operated, we had a lift that rose 900 feet which was as high as anything in New Mexico at that time.

During our second year, the only year the old Tres Ritos lift was in operation, we were a very small

Sno-Cat skiing, Taos Ski Valley. COURTESY BLAKE FAMILY COLLECTION.

operation. There were only a few of us teaching. Pete Totemoff and Tony Perry from Santa Fe taught. Chilton Anderson was here right away, but he did not become an instructor until the second or third winter.

I remember that idiot scientist from Los Alamos who did the hat trick; he did the best of all. He skied right into the upper bull wheel and derailed the Tres Ritos lift which meant we had to let up the counterweights and release the tension, a monstrous job. I told him in very unkind terms that I thought this was too stupid even for a scientist. He said, "Well, I have a principle to leave nothing unskied," which meant he wanted ski those few feet. I don't think he ever came back. Chilton was very useful because when we built the T-bar lift, it always

Towed by Sno-Cat. COURTESY BLAKE FAMILY COLLECTION.

derailed and because of his height, he was able to go with one movement and put it up, whereas Mickey and I needed a ladder to get the cable back on the sheaves.

Chilton Anderson: Once in a while, I had to climb up to the top of the mountain with Ernie to fix the lift. This is something that I never could have stood doing by myself or with somebody else. But with

Ernie, it was always fun because he would talk all the way up, and it was always fascination. You got his life in the army, his life before the army, his life after the army, and all this sort of thing. He used to say, "I'm building the ski area for my family, so we have a family ski area and a place to enjoy skiing." So I enjoyed my walks with Ernie, because he had such an interesting background and stories.

CHAPTER 9
Skiing, A Way of Life

George Engle: Skiing was a way of life, money was not important, and we never really cared as long as we could get along and we were eating. I remember when we finished that first season at Winter Park with the ski school and the ski shop, we ended up with about $800 above expenses and everything was paid for. But that was the total wages we would get for the year. Instead of dividing it up—there were only four of us since one had already dropped out—we decided we'd take a trip to California. We had an old station wagon, and we spent the $800 and came back broke and went to work on the summer program.

Linda Meyers: It was fun because it was a culture. I bet every single one of these old-timers has said that skiing was a way of life. It isn't today; it's a recreation, and it's a business.

Ernie: The total gross income for the first winter was $1,600. The second winter was $8,000. Those first years we lived in a sixteen-foot, second-hand trailer, bought for $1,020, that we moved up here from Santa Fe. It was a mini-trailer, but we lived with three children in there. The first winter, it was parked over near the post office where the Bryan house is now, where the shower building was that the Pattisons had built, a very crude, one-room shower cabin. We had 800 skier days the whole season which didn't lead to a large profit. We had no tax problems. Those first years were very rough.

Rhoda: First we lived in the sixteen-foot trailer, five of us; and on weekends, it was seven. We'd all get to bed. Wendy and Peter slept on the table that we pulled out, which was about forty-five inches wide. Ernest and I had the bed at the other end, and I built a bunk above that bed for Mickey. Then on weekends, we had the people who helped run this place. If every room was rented, we'd put a cot right down the middle of the hallway, and the weekend help would sleep there. Nobody could move until they got out.

Lee Varoz, Sr.: You know, when Ernie started over here at Taos Ski Valley, they used to eat K-rations. They used to eat the K-rations and C-rations to prevent spending money because they wanted all the money they could have to build that Taos Ski Valley. He used to do other things to prevent from spending money just on little things. There had to be something that would be worthwhile spending for.

Walter Widmer: I don't know of anybody, including myself, who would have wanted to live like

they did. That trailer they lived in, I got claustrophobia just being in there all by myself, and there was the whole family. It was quite amazing, and they always lived very frugally, very simply. Ernie did what he loved to do. Money didn't worry him. They had enough to eat and to live. When you think about his and Rhoda's background, then what they did here is much more amazing.

Wolfie Lert: I think hardly anybody gives enough credit to Rhoda for going along with it because of the way they lived up there; that was something. The trailer camp was really unbelievable! Those first years they lived like Okies. For Rhoda, with her background, to live that way was incredible. Rhoda was a nice Jewish society girl from New York City, living like the worst pioneer from the old sod roof days. It was quite amazing that she took it and bore him all those children in the meantime.

Ernie and Rhoda never lived lavishly. They always had everybody and anybody dropping in at the most inopportune times. It didn't matter if the linoleum was pulling up or the cupboards never closed, or if the rug had a hole in it; it was unimportant. Important was that the lift ran right and that the lift lines weren't too long.

Jean Mayer: Ernie lived his whole life where I don't think he ever had more than $25 in his pocket. The money never went through his pockets or his hands. Whatever was made was put back into the Ski Valley. All the people would talk about money, their finances, their financial well-being; you can never find anything in Ernie's life that would demonstrate that. Yet he had taste, the very high class of a king. That's what I felt. He also had the common touch, the grace.

Max Killinger: Beside the little green Porsche that he had, Ernie was never into luxuries. His personal tastes were very, very simple. As a matter of fact, I thought they were rather poor. When I went up to his apartment, and here he had entertained ambassadors and a lot of VIPs, the plaster was hanging from the ceiling and the carpet was worn out where you went in; the kitchen had very dinky cabinet work and stuff like this. It never bothered him, and he never tried to pretend that he was somebody.

Chilton Anderson: The very first year Taos was open, I packed up my skis and went up there one day to go skiing. That was the year Ernie had his little ski-kuli. There were no trails cut or anything. But, here was some guy up there teaching two people, and he asked if he could help me, and I said, "Yes, sort of thought I'd go skiing." And he said, "You'll have to wait until I've finished with my lesson with these two people," because he couldn't run the lift and teach at the same time.

Ernie wasn't there; Ernie was off in Europe touring with Rhoda. The road up the valley was terrible; that was when it went back and forth across the river, and had the little wooden bridges. And I got stuck in my truck. I just said, "The hell with it," and turned around and went out and didn't go back again that year. There was no point. Then the next year, Ernie put in the Tres Ritos lift, and that was the one that kept breaking down. That really was the first year of skiing in Taos Ski Valley; that's the one I count as the first year.

That year at Christmas Ernie asked me if I would I teach. "Teach? I don't even ski." "You snowplow better than they do." "Well, how do I teach?" "Don't worry about it; you'll figure it out," and that kind of thing and off we went. And, God, this was great. Ernie talked me into teaching, and I said, "Gee, this is good for the ego." People thought I skied great because I just snowplowed down Snakedance, or what there was of it. Before I started teaching, Ernie had given me a free lift pass, because the fact was, I could reach up and put the cable back on that little lift. So, Ernie said, "Well, I'll make you honorary ski patrol, but don't try to bring anybody down because you don't ski well enough."

I skied some in Putney, Vermont, where I went to school as a boy. I was not a skier; I had done it a few times. It was Al Rosen who talked me into it. You know, going up and kind of coming down. Ernie would stick his head out of the window and holler, "No! Bend the knees," and we'd bend the knees, and then he'd say, "Good," and then he'd go back into his office, and we'd go on having fun.

John Koch: Chilton was something, he sure was. He said to me one time, "I'm not having a good time skiing powder. How do you do it?" I said, "Chilton, you gotta smile. I can't tell you how to do it. Jean or Dadou can tell you how to do it. I can't tell you how to do it, but I know you have to smile."

Chilton Anderson: I've been honorary ski patrol and elected sheriff, and have been here over thirty some years. Hey, I've gone from being the assistant ski school director to nothing, and from being hired to fired; and assistant ski school director and nothing again. And then back and forth, and the supervisor and senior supervisor because of my age, what the hell! I was hired and fired probably more than anyone or at least as many times as anyone up there. Things had to go Ernie's way, and if they didn't,

Chilton with students in front of old Al's Run Poma Lift.
Courtesy Pattison Family Collection.

Chilton Anderson, April 1975. Courtesy Blake Family Collection.

Judy & Chilton Anderson. COURTESY ANDERSON FAMILY.

James Herrera & Gina Nelson—Looking to get fired.
PHOTO BY KEN GALLARD.

you were fired. The thing about being fired, at least on my part, was that you were only fired until you showed up for work the next morning.

Ernie: Oh, I fired Chilton many times, but he would never leave; he always came back, and we were fortunate for that.

Rhoda: Anybody who was here for any number of years has been fired many times. It's interesting that so many of the people Ernest fired turned up again. He and Jean used to really go at it. I remember when they had a fist fight on Snakedance. But they were still good friends. They really cared about each other, and they fought, but fighting was a part of Ernest. He was very

military, very Germanic in ways, but you can't run this place by committee.

Walter Widmer: As long as I knew him, Ernie would literally give you the shirt off his back. But, if you took advantage of him, he would hunt you to the ends of the earth for ten cents. That was just his way. Ernie was always the soft one around here. He sounded tough, and he'd fire people, but anybody he ever fired just kept on working. On the other hand, if you ever got in wrong with Rhoda, that would be too bad because she would follow it up.

Lee Varoz, Sr.: When we first came, me and some of the others, we didn't like Ernie, but now we do. I only needed one chance. I done my work and that was all I needed. One thing though, Ernie, he would tell you off. And then he would turn around and he'd be very friendly. He used to get a lot of guys in their goats, I would say, but he would turn around and forget everything; he had to be that way. You know, dealing with a lot of people, it's hard.

Pete Totemoff: When Ernie wanted to, he made people feel pretty important. And he would make them feel like shit, too.

Max Killinger: It was hard for him to forget some things. You could apologize and say, "I'm really sorry, Ernie." He forgave you, but he never forgot. Wendy once said to me, "The problem with most of the people in relation to my father is that they don't see his sense of humor." After she said that to me, I actually looked at Ernie in a different way. He could tell you something with the straightest face, and a lot of people didn't know him and thought he meant it, and he was just pulling your leg. He could keep a straight face. That helped me a lot to understand Ernie because after a while, when he rubbed me the wrong way, I always could say to myself, maybe he was just joking. Sometimes it would help when he said something, and I said, "You're not serious," and then he started smiling. My stand about Ernie is clear, but in the beginning, he was a mean son-of-a-gun.

I also felt that he expected perfection from everybody. Rather than feeling that this was something outstanding, he felt that this was the standard. He didn't say, "You did a good job," when you did a good job. You knew that's what you had to do when you worked for Ernie.

Walter Ruegg: I think most people knew that he didn't really mean to be that serious, that he was joking when he said he fired you. Even if you had disagreements with him, you still had to respect the guy. I was never fired by Ernie. I was fired by Mickey, but I think Ernie knew me well enough that if he fired me, I would have gone. I wouldn't have stuck around. Mickey fired me. But at that time, Mickey was pretty hot-tempered, and I'm sure a few days later, he wouldn't have done it. Discipline was Ernie's strong point, being Swiss and German combined he was strict, but fair. I had many clashes with him, but I still had to admire him for what he was doing.

Theresa Killinger: In order to be a great man, he had to have his principles and his ideas. He had to bring them about, but the outcome, whether he was mean or super strict, was quality. You could feel that there was quality behind all he did, and that's why you went along. You got bawled out and things went wrong, but after all, the quality in the end was the plateau you were going for. I think that this was his strength. I had my run-ins with Ernie, and I would say "Humph," and I would go on.

Elisabeth Brownell: Ernie never showed a weak side. When he was weak, and I lived very close with him, he never showed that side. He turned it into anger when things didn't work out. Then he found a scapegoat who he put down all the time, put them on the black list. That was his way out. He was covering up. That is German; you don't show any weakness and you remain stern. He looked so much like a Prussian general. Unjust, he was unjust. He needed somebody to be the whipping boy.

Monica Brown: I did not see him as being afraid. In retrospect I would think for him being afraid would be his bullying out. When you are that far towards the wall, you have nowhere to go backwards, you can only go forward and be aggressive and that's what he was. Then he would just bully.

Herman Kretchmer: There's a famous story that Ernie used very frequently. It originally came from Kaiser Wilhelm. He would say, "This guy reminds me of a story my father told me of a fellow who was standing by, walking around with his mouth open, waiting for a roast pigeon to fly in." Ernie used to use that very frequently when he was talking to me about people who were useless and lazy. I was only fired once, and that stuck. Ernie wasn't always nice.

Tom Brownell: When he fired Herman Kretchmer, he did it over the bull horn. He shouted, "Herman, get out of here," and Mickey got so upset they had a fight, and that's when Mickey gave Ernie a black eye. Ernie could be mean and vicious. It takes somebody who's been around in the early days to know he could be nasty and really vindictive. Later on, he became the nice old man. Ernie and I had mutual respect, and he knew I wasn't beholden to him. I had my own thing, so it didn't really matter; I think that was the big difference. Everybody else, the Mayers included, had to get along with him. He never fired me; he didn't have anything to fire me from.

Ernie: John Koch I fired many times. I liked John; he would do anything we asked him, but he could never stay clean. He also liked to blow things up with dynamite, and he was somewhat crazy.

John Koch: My biggest running constant battle with Ernie was he was always on me about not having clean pants. Heck, I never knew from minute to minute what we were going to do. One day I went up to the shop and I bought a new pair of Bogners; it was the biggest purchase I think I'd ever made in my life. It cost me more than my car did. The very next morning, it was right into the mess again, so what could I do? If there was something no one else would do, it became my job; grease the bull wheel, fix the sewer, all the dirty jobs were for Koch, and I loved it. But I couldn't stay clean.

I would say Ernie and I had a love/hate relationship. We had our share of discussions. I can't really sit here and say hate with a straight face. I had way too much respect for the man and for what was there. The disagreements, I think, were cockiness-induced. I was a smart-ass kid: "I've done this for two years; now I certainly know exactly what I'm doing" attitude. Then you'd run into the proverbial, "Well, we didn't do it that way in Switzerland." Well, come on, you know, this is 1967 in America.

The last day I was there, I had my stuff loaded up in my van, and there was snow, more snow than you could stand, and Ernie kept Al's closed. Since I was doing all the avalanche stuff, I never really skied the lower part of the mountain that much when there was much snow on it. I kept skiing wherever I could, and I kept looking at it, and it said "closed." Standing there were George Brooks and Jean Mayer, and they were looking at it, too. The top part was getting trashed out. I was standing there and saw lower Al's Run, no tracks, and I'm talking a lot of snow. I looked at Jean and George, and they said, "No, we have to work here." I said, "I'm on my way to new adventures; I'll see you," and I think I did Al's in ten or twelve turns; that's how deep the snow was. It was everything the brochure said it was supposed to be and more.

Suddenly toward the middle of Al's, there was Ernie riding the lift up, and on his radio I could hear him screaming, "Where is the ski patrol? There is somebody skiing Al's Run. I want him." I just waved. I got down, took my skis off, got in the van and drove off. With all the good and all the bad, I couldn't have ended it any better.

Bud Crary: Ernie fired me every time he paid me. He'd say, "Hell, I can't afford that. You just quit." I'd say okay; it didn't make a difference. I could get a job anywhere. "Oh, well, maybe you'd better come back." He did that for seventeen years.

I only got cross-wise with Ernie once. He didn't pay me the whole summer. He didn't have the money, I guess. Anyway, I forget how much he owed me, but I had worksheets with my time. I don't know how many sheets there was, but it was a summer's work at $10 per hour.

The first of October, he said, "Bring me your

hours." I got up there with my hours, and he looked at my time cards. He added it all up on an adding machine. "Hell," he says, "you're not right by no means." And, oh man, I flew off the handle because I knew I'd been giving twenty minutes every day more than what I really put down. I'd stop and eat a snack and drink a cup of coffee and same way in the afternoon about two or three o'clock. He kept on saying, "That's not right," and I was getting madder by the minute. He says, "I know what you worked because I was up every day you worked there this summer; I was up there with a stop watch, and I was keeping your time. When the tractor wasn't running, I didn't count it." That's what he told me, and I don't doubt that's what he did. He didn't like nobody to steal from him. Anyway, the whole summer was a lot of hours and working sometimes on Saturday too. He never did say how much was wrong or which way. He was really getting a bang out of it, but I didn't at all after a summer like that.

Well, he seen I was about ready to come over the desk at him, and he said, "Well, I've added this up and you're sure not right because I've got thirty minutes more than you've got." He was just trying to get my goat. And he paid me the thirty minutes over what I had, but he didn't tell me that for thirty-five to forty minutes. But you know after that, he never questioned me. I'd go up there on the first of the month and take him my bill or send it up, and he never questioned it.

Monica Brown: The first time I came to Vail it was in 1963, and that was the first time Ernie fired me. I went to Vail with Larry Mullin who was instructing in Taos at the time. He ended up in Vail also as the ski school director for a number of years. We were just looking around; Vail had just started. Then we came back to Taos and Ernie fired everybody again because we had taken off for a weekend. He was furious because he had an incredible storm, and it knocked out the power, and he didn't have any lifts running and the snow was covering everything. We were on our legitimate day off, but he found out that we went to the competition; "You are fired. None of my staff goes to Vail."

Papa Mayer: He was absurd the way he was, you know, when the German in him came through. He put everybody on the attention. He was a king. That was the atmosphere of Taos Ski Valley that made everybody kiss the ass of Ernie.

Harry Franzgen: How did I get on with Ernie? That's a very tender question. I felt hot and cold. At times I didn't know why I got hit over the head. I had guilt feelings because I thought, "What does the great man have against me? What did I do?" Then,

on the next moment I didn't know why I was treated so nice. But that was Ernie.

Tony Bryan: I would say that I was only seriously fired about three times, and I was kind of threatened with firing generally a couple times a year. It got to the point that if you weren't threatened with being fired, you kind of felt you probably weren't doing a particularly good job. It was kind of a status symbol in its own way.

In Taos in the beginning, I was a mere ski instructor and as such quickly learned that I was one of the lowest forms of animal life. I learned also that nepotism played a far greater role in advancement within TSV, Inc. than performance; I left for Vail. I learned to avoid Ernie when he was on a rampage, fearing that he would fire me just for coming into his view. I firmly believe that if the guillotine had been an acceptable form of punishment for the 20th century, Ernie would have erected one and put it to frequent use. I would probably have been one of the chosen.

One of my many jobs was to haul garbage for the Ski Valley at the rate of $40 per month. I can remember billing Ernie for one-third of a month on one occasion. That would be $13.33 and one third cents. Because there was an extraordinary amount of garbage, and because it was before the advent of the calculator, I rounded the figure to $14 and sent Ernie a bill for that amount. I will never forget the phone call I received and the outrage expressed by Ernie feeling that I had cheated him out of sixty-seven cents. As a result, for the next week, "Big Daddy" Sarge Pratt had orders to let me teach skiing only if all other instructors had been used.

Godie Schuetz: I was one of the very few he never fired, but as I say, I knew my place. I was an employee and Ernie was really a good, close friend, but it was with a certain distance. I was able to get along with Ernie; I think it was coming from the same background, the Swiss military; discipline wasn't anything strange to me. Discipline was written in capital letters; being on time was written in capital letters. That went for everybody, not just the ski school. Leave out the discipline Ernie emphasized so much, and I don't think Taos Ski Valley would be what it is today.

Godie Scheutz: Also, Ernie really had a fear of being taken advantage of. If he labeled someone a swindler, or if he said someone was sabotaging him, they were finished. Walter Widmer told me this story after it happened. Around noontime, Rhoda had done some shopping in Taos, and she got out of her car up there by the ticket office. A lady in her mid-thirties came up to her and Rhoda had ski clothes on. She asked Rhoda, "Would you be interested in having this lift ticket for the rest of the afternoon? My husband is not skiing this afternoon, and I wondered if you would like to buy it for the rest of the day." Rhoda said, "Yeah, I am interested, but I don't have any money on me; let me go and get my husband." This was the time when Ernie was really untrusting of everybody, and one of the worst things you could do was to cheat him out of a dollar. So, Ernie came down and said, "My wife said you have a ticket. Let me see it." Anyway, he bawled this lady out. He told her she was trying to cheat him, the Ski Valley, and really let her have it. He took the ticket away from her.

So then the lady was in tears. She goes to the next worst soul she could have gone to, Walter Widmer, and tells Walter about this: "I just met the rudest man in my life. I was just trying to give the ticket to this lady because my husband didn't feel like skiing. This man comes to me, and he told me off and made me feel really bad. I think I know this man. I think he's that Swiss who owns the Casa Cordova down there, and I'm never going to go back to his restaurant ever." It all happened because of the accent. A lot of people thought I was Ernie. I went to Ernie and said, "Ernie, I think you owe me a couple of thousand dollars or so." He said, "Why?" I told him the story and said, "This is a loss of business and bad advertising as far as I'm concerned, and I had nothing to do with it."

Henry Hornberger: Ernie was a tough man. I got fired seriously, severely fired several times; he just reacted violently when he was pushed. And most of the time when he would fire somebody was when he felt somebody was swindling him. "Swindling" was his universal word.

The tip jar swindle, that's the one that I got fired for one time very seriously. The second year I was here I was working in the rental shop and Kay, Walter's old girlfriend, came in looking for a pair of skis. They had a deal where people brought in their skis to be adjusted or minor stuff like that, and they put money in the tip jar because the work was too insignificant to charge for it.

That day, Ernie was going to go skiing with Kay, and he waited for her up at the lift. There was a new guy in the rental shop, and she came to pick up her skis; he didn't know who she was, gave her her skis and said, "That'll be $5 in the tip jar." She said "I don't have any money, can you put it on my account?" Of course that didn't ring any bells with him either. And Ernie's waiting, getting pissed. Kay asked, "Is Henry around?" I happened to hear something going on and caught the tail end of it and said, "No, Kay, that's fine, go."

So, Ernie's pissed, and he's standing there waiting while she's trying to get her shit together. He asked

Tony Bryan, Vail instructor. COURTESY TONY BRYAN.

Henry Hornberger, perpetrator of the "tip jar swindle." PHOTO BY KEN GALLARD.

where she'd been, and she told him the guys in the rental shop needed money for adjusting her bindings. She said, "You're supposed to put the money in the tip jar and Henry..." Well, Ernie had heard enough, and my name was tacked on to the end of it.

So, I hear on the radio, "Anybody seeing Henry Hornberger? He's fired, get his pass, he's out of here." I didn't turn in my pass, but I left.

It was starting to snow and the next day I wandered up to the lift, and was putting on my skis when Ernie skied up to me. He stood there, and oh, shit, what can I do? I stood up, and he said, "What are you doing?" And I said, "Going skiing." He said, "You're not supposed to go skiing." "It's a good powder day though," I said. I didn't feel apologetic even though I knew by this time what had happened because Kay had come up and said "Henry, I am so sorry," and she wasn't able to calm him down and mellow him out at all. He felt as though I was ripping him off.

In the meantime, of course, Mickey had charged in there and grabbed the tip jar and got about a hundred bucks, which they didn't realize had just been emptied. Those guys were making big bucks. I wasn't even part of the split.

Ernie said to get on the lift, so I jumped on the chair with him, and I started explaining the story. I got off at the top of #1, and he said, "Go to chair #2." We skied over to chair #2, and we talked about it some more. So, on those two lift rides, I told my story. We got to the top, and he never said anything; we got off and he said, "You want to go ski Longhorn or Lorelei?" because he was going to open them. I said, "Longhorn," so we skied over to Longhorn, and he said, "It's all yours; go for it." And that was it; I never heard another word on it. There was no "I'm sorry," or "We better get those guys," or anything like that. He let me have first crack at the mountain. That's where he was pretty amazing.

Fred Fair: I was fired at what I thought was the height of our relationship. I was not working full-time anymore. I had kind of set myself up to be the pilot instructor and charter pilot, so Ernie, in one of his many moments of graciousness, suggested I take two of these people up and teach them how to ski powder. As I left, he admonished me by saying, "Don't break their legs." Everybody smiled and chuckled, and we went up Al's and were skiing Inferno. It was snowing very heavily and about eighteen inches of fresh snow was on the ground.

My method of teaching was to show them and try and break my rhythm at some point where I could still see them and coach them down the hill. As it was not the best of visibility, it was hard to break one's rhythm, so I actually skied out of their sight, but we were in voice contact. So, I said, "One at a time, come on down and remember down, up, down, up and float like a bird. The first guy came down and there was a crash, and I still couldn't see anything. Then trickling up to my feet, this little bolt in the snow came right down to my feet. This guy had broken his leg and was all doubled up in a fetal position, howling with pain and right behind him came Ernie. Ernie had come up to check on them. He took one look at this guest and said something like, "Get down and get off my mountain and on the way down, tell the ski patrol, but I don't want to see you again."

Theresa Voller: Ernie was a good friend. You know, business was business, but friendship was something else. He yelled and screamed and a few minutes later, there he was again, smiling.

Franz Voller: Did you know that all of us at Taos Ski Valley are Aries, including Ernie? All the lodge owners—Ernie, Franz, Jean, Tom—everybody. That's why they're all stubborn and hard-headed. Maybe that's why we understood each other. We were born under the same sign, and we understand how our brains work. Sometimes we get a little stubborn.

Tony Mitchell: Ernie fired for effect from time to time and there were some fundamentals that you didn't break. There was the thing about haircuts and dirty pants and that kind of stuff, or those skis on the fence, but loyalty, honesty, and integrity were things you didn't transgress.

Bob Brierley: Everybody thought Ernie was a tiger that would eat you, but many a kid would come up here, and they didn't have any money. Ernie would tell them to get a shovel from so-and-so. In about half an hour, he'd go get the shovel and tell them to go ski. Ernie had an iron shell, but was a pussycat at heart. Those cold blue eyes would look at you, and all at once, he'd get a twinkle and start to grin and it was all gone.

Theresa Killinger: He was much more mellow as he got older. It was just wonderful the last few years; they were actually delightful. Then you began to understand him more and you could tune into him, and he wasn't so rough on you anymore.

Kevin Beardsley: Deciding to quit was the hardest decision I ever made in my life so far. To turn back at 23,000 or 24,000 feet after three months of killing ourselves in the Himalayas, we sat and debated that for days, and it was a hard decision. But that was nothing compared to the month or two of back and forth in my mind that it took to get me to quit at Taos Ski Valley. The hardest thing was telling Ernie, and we both started to cry. He sent me the most amazing letter a little later saying of all the people he'd had working there, that he couldn't imagine doing it without me. He made me feel great; it was just his way of doing things.

CHAPTER 10
Poma Lifts and Trail Cutting

Ernie: Those early years were very difficult; it was all pioneering back then. In May of 1957, we laid down the lines for the big Poma lift. We invested $5,000, a vast amount of money, and bought two Poma lifts; one was for the beginners' hill which we had to clear first, and one was to go to the top of Al's Run. The Poma went to the top of where the #1 chair goes now. In total, the Poma lift cost about $30,000 including access roads and cutting the trails. That was a lot of money for me in those days.

It was May when we started cutting the lift line along Al's Run all the way to the top. We came out in the right place on that perfectly chosen plateau, which permitted us to go on to Longhorn, an avalanche area that needed very little cutting. We got our first two-man chain saw which was easier and lighter to handle than our earlier saws. The Poma was built with eighteen Indians from the Pueblo under the leadership of Tommy Castellano.

We carried everything on our backs; we had no way to get a road up. We had contracted with somebody to build the road, but they didn't manage to get it done. By the time we got ready to build the lift, there were three feet of snow. We had a mule that went on strike right on the first day. He told us he wasn't going up that steep thing. So we carried everything—the cable, the tower parts, the pads for the towers—by manpower.

We had everything organized in the parking lot of the Hondo Lodge, and then we had a tremendous snowstorm the 13th of October, followed by another one on the 15th of October, and it buried everything. We had signs, number 1, number 2, number 3, but this was all buried. We had to carry everything into the Hondo Lodge and melt it out and get it up. It was a monstrous job.

Mickey Blake: The Indians stayed with it and did an unbelievable job except for various religious holidays that drove my father wild because he wasn't used to that. They carried every last piece of that lift up there by hand. The Poma lift was a B-20, detachable lift that Pomagalski himself came to build. He was concerned about it because at the time it was the steepest Poma lift anywhere in the world. The old guy was in his sixties and could shinny right up those towers. They had those goof-ball ladders, those skinny things that looked like a piece of spaghetti. The Poma

had no safety system at first. I can't believe that now that I think back on it!

Ernie: The big Poma was the best lift we ever could have had for the beginning of Taos. It was terribly steep and difficult to ride, but I liked it. As the Poma lift was being built by the Indians, then we began to clear the trails, and that's when I engaged my first Hispanics; there were Lee Varoz, Sr. and Andres Montoya. I hired them for a dollar an hour. Lee was great; he helped me out with everything up here. I could trust him to get things done; he was a big help to me and a good friend.

Lee Varoz, Sr.: Ernie, he trust me with everything. He trust me with the keys, the whole works at the Ski Valley. He wrote a lot of magazines which I was in. A lot of people would come from the East, a skier from Chicago, New York or whatever, and they would say, "We know you, Lee. You don't know us, but we know you." And I told them, "How in the world do you know me?" And, "Well, I seen you in the magazine," which I guess was all over the country.

When I was already growing up, my father told me, "Lee, whenever you are on your own, I'm going to give you three advices." First, he said, "Don't kill or rob. And whenever you work for a person, no matter what your wages are, give all you have in what you doing for this man because he's paying his money." So, that's what I did with Ernie. I was very interested in my job and I loved the mountain. I still do love my mountain.

It was in May, 1956, when I started to work over there at Taos Ski Valley. I used to weigh 210 pounds. When I went over there, and I met Ernie, he said, "I don't know if we can carry all that fat up to the mountain." Because we didn't have no roads at that time, and we have to take everything on our backs, you know, chain saws, gasoline, lunch and water and everything. Ernie told me, "Well, I'm going to try you two weeks; if you make it, well it's okay. But I'll try you two weeks." So I worked there maybe three or four months, and then I told Ernie, "Ernie, this is the longest two weeks I ever lived, because you said you were going to try me for two weeks, and here I am already three months." I worked for him maybe twenty years. Ernie was very good with me.

Ernie, he only gave me orders, and I would carry them out, and he was very well satisfied with my work. He told me, "Chilton said you don't need a boss," and he told me that he didn't know how in the world I didn't need no boss. But he found out later that I didn't. I came to be his right-hand man for a long time. He liked me. Yeah, he used to like me very much. My son Lee, Jr. is up there now with Walter Ruegg, and they take care of everything; they do a good job.

Walter Ruegg: Lee, Sr. was a good man. Things have changed a lot since he was there. When he was running the #1 lift, one time a guy fell off four times when he was loading on the lift, and he never shut the lift off. He said, "Why should I shut the lift off? The guy has fallen off already." Today you couldn't do that anymore. You'd get in trouble with the insurance company. He was real good at checking tickets. He only had one eye, but he could see more than most people with both eyes. He would see if someone had a suntan; he knew he was there for a while, and somebody that had white skin, he would check a lot closer. Ernie told him he could have some money for each ticket that he caught.

Chilton Anderson: Back then Snakedance had great snow and no bumps. We didn't have enough skiers to cause bumps. That's when the speed record was set; a minute and twenty seconds from the top of the #1 chair lift to the bottom. You can't do that now. You came straight down Porcupine, you came through an area that we don't use anymore to get into Snakedance, made two turns, went into Chicken Alley, got into the gully, and came right straight down. There was no road at the bottom to jump off. It was all smooth, and there was plenty of room to stop at the Burroughs' cabin. It was done in a minute and twenty seconds by Max Baer. Nobody believes that. He prepared his line for weeks. He could take a week preparing it, because there weren't enough skiers to make bumps in it to ruin his line.

After the Poma lift went in, Ernie opened up Al's Run, which was so narrow then. It was just all trees. I mean, it was less than half as wide as it is now. You had to stop when you were skiing down Al's Run if anybody was using the Poma lift, and then make two quick turns in the Poma lift track.

John Koch: Not many people know about this; I think the time is good for not getting into any serious trouble about it or causing too many heart stoppages. But, one summer, we had to work on the Poma; the top of the concrete on some of the towers was cracking. We went up there carrying an eighty-pound electric hammer up and down Al's and we chiseled all the concrete off, then I had to form it up and pour new concrete around it. I'd drive up as close as I could in the old jeep and let all of the equipment off and start dropping concrete as close as I could.

I came up there one afternoon to start dropping off 55-gallon barrels of water, half-filled, which was all I

Lee Varoz, Sr., April 1975. PHOTO BY ERNIE BLAKE, COURTESY BLAKE FAMILY COLLECTION.

Rhoda with Peter & Wendy, 1957. COURTESY BLAKE FAMILY COLLECTION.

could handle. I got up there and rolled them off. The first break over on Al's, where you can still see right down into the base, there was a little knoll there, and I unloaded this last barrel of water. There wasn't anybody around, and the barrel took off, this sucker was about one-half of a 55-gallon drum. It started rolling, and it bounced higher and higher. All I could do was just sit down and watch. I mean, there was Ernie's house at the bottom, and the barrel was going straight for his house. I couldn't do anything but sit down, and my eyes were getting bigger and bigger, and this barrel was just going crazy. There used to be that rock right at that first pitch, and off to the side was a bunch of willows where I spent about two weeks one winter trying to figure out how to get to that rock so I could jump off it. The barrel got to that rock and hit something just right, and it took off into the trees. You talk about somebody that had the cold shivers and shakes. I sat there for a good hour before I even got in the jeep, drove down, shut everything down and went away. It would have taken the whole place out in one fell swoop.

Chilton Anderson: Longhorn was open from the top of the Poma lift, and that's the one that slid with Chris Schwarzenbach. Chris came in and said, "Hey, I just went down Longhorn in an avalanche," and that's when Ernie blanched. Ernie just said, "UGH! It doesn't avalanche in February. Now what the hell do we do? Let's get out some shovels and things and go look," and suddenly the other group that Chris had seen appeared. Ernie didn't worry about anybody else because nobody else was missing. That was the first major avalanche, and that was his introduction to one.

Ernie: Longhorn we knew from the beginning we would do because it was a natural avalanche path. We needed the provision of the avalanche forming part, and it needed cleaning up of the debris that the avalanches had left. We did that very early.

John Koch: Longhorn always fascinated me. The year of the big slide, as I remember people referring to it, was before I got there. I think back now, Ernie and Totemoff went up there after that happened and took those silly-ass snow fences and went up to about 150-200 feet from the top. They got these snow fences in Europe, these "retention fences," and it's in the book the Forest Service put out. But they're talking about concrete and steel, not snow fences. We used to think that snow fences did something. And they didn't!

Ernie: We didn't have roads to assist in our lift building in the early days. We were damn lucky we found Bud Crary; he built the access road to the top. He was the best goddamn cat operator I ever saw; a good man. Bud did the road building. When we started we didn't have all the complications with the Forest Service. We just built the roads with an eye level, which was a $15 optical instrument. We came

into that tremendous rock outcropping on the east side of the Camino Sinuoso where it meets with what is now Bambi. That last place nearly killed us because it took us endless dynamite and cat work to get it done. We had only a D-6 which is not a very big cat. If we had had a D-9, we would have ripped that rock out much faster. It took us about two weeks to get through that one rock outcropping, working Saturdays and Sundays.

Rhoda: To watch Bud on his caterpillar used to scare me to death. He'd take that cat out over a pile until half the cat was out over the top, and he'd bring it back just before it teetered and went down. He was incredible.

Ed Pratt: Bud was the best Ernie ever had. He was a super individual, with his expertise on the bulldozer, and was responsible for a lot of that ski area up there being skiable for other than super experts. He took that cat places where other operators wouldn't even look at, let alone go. I saw him put his life on the line three or four times with that bulldozer.

Bud Crary: 'Dozing was what I did. It was five years before I ever started working in the ski shop. Then I started pushing snow, sold skis, boots and poles, mounted them, but back then 'dozing is what I did.

At first Ernie had Bill Martin trying to build that road; he was the Holsum Bread man. He was up there workin' for Ernie; he was up there with an old, worn-out D-6. Bill was digging in that rock trying to get through it. He'd just got started good, trying to pick more dirt out, when a big rock rolled up under his belly pan. He'd come in there to load and turned, switched, and the rock rolled up and just flipped him off that road. He slid straight down 800 feet and wound up right in the creek. He froze on the levers, never turned over, just went down pushing rocks and trees as he went. Well, Ernie watched him a-sliding, and he just tore down behind him, slipping and sliding, steeper then hell. He got down there, and Bill was just sitting there just froze, looking straight ahead.

His hands were on the levers where Ernie couldn't get him loose. You know, he's gripping it so bad. The tractor had killed itself for some reason, I don't know. I guess maybe he hit the throttle. Bill doesn't know whether he shut it down or not. I guess he did, because it didn't kill him. You usually do that once. Anyway, Ernie slapped his face. Slapped him, I mean hard, both sides. Finally old Bill kind of come to, and Ernie got his hands off the steering clutches and got him off the tractor and took his hands and put some creek water on him because he was sitting in the creek, shaking and white as a sheet. Bill just walked over to his old truck and backed her over there, loaded that thing up, and he headed for Taos.

Right after that Ernie called me, and said, "I've got a

job for you." I said okay because I wasn't doing anything. I charged ten dollars an hour for a 'dozer which was about the average price. You worked ten hours, you made $100 bucks. Back then it was pretty good wages. So, I went up there, and Ernie took me up in that little old green jeep and looked it over and asked, "Can you get through there?" And I said, "I don't know; I can if anybody can."

So, I went up there, and I worked a-week-and-a-half, I guess, getting through that. I'd have to back up, haul dirt in on it and get up and knock some of those big rocks off above me and kind of make a road. Then I had the same trouble up at that Gold Mine curve. That was pretty narrow when you went around there and that 'dozer was just about right to stay on it. That angle blade when you hit a rock with the back end, it'll kick off see, so you have to watch; it can knock you off going down backwards, and I didn't want to do that at all.

I done all the roads and all the runs. I made twenty-one switchbacks up Al's Run. It was rough; all the turns are pretty well smoothed off now. They were just as wide as a D-6 blade, so it didn't tear up the ground out there to make a switch-back; I'd drive up one and then back up the other one. Of course, I could turn my cat around anywhere, just whirl it. It wasn't really a switchback road; they were cat tracks, that's all they were.

Later, I was in the ski shop twelve years. Bill Whaley came in one time looking for some new skis, and I traded this pair of skis that were good skis. Somebody from Chicago had come in and bought new skis and traded in their old ones, and Bill came in and said, "Sure would like that pair of skis," and I said, "I sure would like to sell them to you." He wanted to give $50 for them on trade-in. I said, "I've got to have $100 bucks out of them, to get my money back." He said he didn't have it, so I told him to go borrow from somebody. So he comes back about two hours later. He had $99.20. I said, "I can't do that at all. You just go borrow another eighty cents." He goes out again. He got it in dollars. I had to give him twenty cents back. And I didn't care. I was going to let him have them, but he didn't know. I go up and tell old Walter Widmer that, and it about killed that old bastard he was laughing so hard.

Rhoda: Bud could sell anything. We would have a pair of skis and stuff and maybe the whole thing was worth $20-$25, and he'd sell the damn thing for $70 or $80. He was doing it for us. We finally had to tell him, "You can't do this."

Bud was a great practical joker. We had a secretary whom he loved to bait. He did it by talking about his wife. One day he came up here with a flat tire. "Call my wife." So he gets on the phone and he says, "Tacky, I've got a flat tire. Get your ass up here and

Bud Crary with his grandson. PHOTO BY DAVE WIEST, COURTESY BUD CRARY.

Bud Crary, March 1970. PHOTO BY ERNIE BLAKE, COURTESY BLAKE FAMILY COLLECTION.

Bud Crary and his 'dozer. COURTESY BUD CRARY.

change it. What do you mean you've got the flu? You can get out of bed though, can't you? You come on up here and change that tire." And our secretary, she says, "That's the meanest man I've ever seen in my life."

He loved to tell the stories of the games he played on his wife. He'd say, "Well, today is our anniversary, and I told Tacky she could go anywhere she wanted, even McDonald's or A&W," this sort of thing and you

Powder tracks down Snakedance/Showdown, early years. Courtesy Blake Family Collection.

could just see this secretary getting madder and madder, feeling so sorry for the wife.

Bud Crary: You know, that gal hated me the whole time she was there. She didn't stay too long. She hated my guts because I'd done my wife that way.

Another time, I had to take peoples' driver's licenses when they rented skis and boots. Well, they didn't take mine when I let Tacky ski, but Yolanda Blake knew Tacky was there, and wantin' to go skiing. Yolanda was up there working in the clothing department, and she came in and said, "I came up to ski; I'm looking for Tacky," and I said, "Well, she's laying down there on the bench crying because she forgot to bring her driver's license, and I wouldn't let her have her ski gear unless she went and got it." I'd climbed down the ladder, from where Walter was, down to the ski shop, and she'd gotten Tacky and kneeled down there beside her; she was just resting was what she was doing, she wasn't crying. Yolanda told her to get a hold of herself, and oh, did she ever let me have it. I had her skis already fitted just leaning up against the wall. Yolanda, oh she "ate me out"—wouldn't let Tacky have skis 'cause she forgot her driver's license!

Rhoda: We had lots of fun in the early years. Then we worked hard, and we put in long hours. The crew that was here was basically a small congenial group, and there weren't all the hassles and problems you have today.

Ernie: It was the summer of 1957, while we were starting to build the Poma lift, when we got the papers signed by our neighbors, the Burroughs. They gave us the right to build the lift even though we didn't know the exact location of the boundary. Then they claimed that they had never signed it, that it was faked. They had to retract that, and then we won the case, but we ended up with having to pay them a lease fee agreement. It was the first time I was ever in court, and I learned about New Mexico land deals.

Herman Kretchmer: One of the great periods in Ernie's life, in retrospect, was the property fight with the Burroughs. I will never ever forget how Ernie referred to himself as the poor little immigrant boy.

When Ernie got ready to go to court which was in the old Taos Court House, he made sure that he looked like a poor foreigner. He took a wide tie and he tied the thing so that the wide part was way up and the narrow part hung down practically between his legs and just looked ridiculous. He went in there, and he testified. Tony Mitchell was the lawyer; he led him through the thing. Something in the testimony came out about good faith, and Ernie sort of implied that he was basically just a poor foreigner that came over to this country, and he just took people at their word, and he never thought that people would treat other people the way this governor was treating him. He did what he did on good faith, and he was very surprised. He pulled this poor immigrant thing until hell won't have it. He practically had everybody in tears. Here's Ernie with this ridiculous necktie hanging down and wearing that camel's hair jacket that he wore for years and years. It was his favorite jacket, and it was something that Rhoda wanted him to get rid of, but he couldn't part with it.

Buell Pattison: Ernie had a peculiar method of doing some things at different times. He would go ahead and do things without really getting the proper clearance or permission to do it. He put a trail through there down from the Kachina area which ran through the Burroughs' and Riding's land without, as far as I know, asking any permission. It all ended up in a lawsuit. It's hard to find boundary lines up there in the woods, unless you actually get out and have them surveyed and actually cut a line of sight through the woods.

Bob Nordhaus: Originally, there was a boundary dispute, and Burroughs gave Ernie a quitclaim deed, and there was an agreement that if the boundary was not correct, Burroughs would give the Blakes a ninety-nine year lease. Then it turned out that there was a mistake in the boundaries, so the deed was not valid, as I recall. So, the Burroughs filed suit to cancel the declaratory judgment to hold that the ninety-nine year lease was not valid. They claimed first that they hadn't signed it, that it was a forgery. Then they claimed that they didn't know what they were signing. The judge held 100% for Ernie and held that they had signed it, and that they were bound by the ninety-nine year lease, and he set a reasonable rental for them.

Georgia Hotton: It was like an old western feud, the conflict with the neighbors, Burroughs and Riding. Later, when the Burroughs and Ridings people realized that maybe Taos Ski Valley was a gold mine sitting on their doorstep, they decided to sue to stop lift operations, and they put through a court order on this right before Christmas. I remember sitting in the courtroom as an observer on that particular occasion and Burroughs, who was a former governor of the state, was saying he didn't know what he had signed. I thought, this is interesting; the former governor of the state signing something and now admitting that he didn't know what he had signed. But the judge ruled

Early days at Taos Ski Valley with Al's Run & Poma lift, March 1960. COURTESY BLAKE FAMILY COLLECTION.

The Burroughses' cabin. COURTESY PATTISON FAMILY.

that the contract was not valid and binding, and therefore, there had to be some further negotiations.

Bob Nordhaus: Burroughs was just a skunk, saying that it wasn't his signature, and that was a damn lie. I did some legal work for Ernie. Tony Mitchell did a wonderful job with his affairs, as he did with that Burroughs affair.

Harry Franzgen: Talking about land disputes with Ernie, one day I came up in the summer and there was a deep trench dug halfway around my lodge. I asked what was going on. Nobody knew anything or wouldn't say anything. I called the power company because it looked like they were putting in a new line; no, nothing. Yet, there was this deep trench, and I couldn't get to the lodge.

I found out finally that Ernie had started "Fly-by-Night," which was his television cable company. Nobody ever said anything. Eventually the trench was gone and filled in. So, one day, I brought a television up here and turned it on, and it worked; wow, this was great!

Zap Kraybill came over one day and said, "Do you want to be hooked up to the television?" I said, "Well, I have this thing in here, and it works just great." Zap kind of looked a little funny and said, "Oh." The next thing, we get a bill for television hook-up, so I go over and find Zap and ask, "What is this bill?" He said, "Well, you've got television, don't you?" "Well, yes, but I never hooked up to anything." "Well, this is just the way it works right now."

Finally, one day, Zap came over, and he gave me this electronic bullshit because of the reflection of the antenna and said, "So, you're getting good reception, but Ernie ordered me to change that. If you want to be hooked up, you have to pay for it." So one day, there was no television reception, and I asked Zap, "What's it going to cost to hook me up?" So, they hooked me up, and one day I got a bill and it was a few hundred bucks, and I said that's all right. So, I sent him a bill back for rental of the land. I thought that was fair. They used my land for the TV cable, and I just sent him a bill back. I heard Ernie was so upset; he just threw a fit, but nothing more happened.

Then in January during the Super Bowl, the bar was open, my restaurant was full and everybody was watching. It was the Dallas Cowboys who were great then. After halftime the television went out. I called Zap and asked, "What's the matter?" He said, "Well, I got the order to turn it off." I said, "What?" He said, "Yeah, I have to turn you off because haven't paid your bill." I said, "Don't do it!" and he said he couldn't do anything. So, I went out with an axe; I knew where the cable was and whacked right into the ground, and the whole thing was off. Five minutes later, I saw Ernie storm out, so I went out because I didn't want to see him inside the Lodge. So we had a hell of a fight outside.

Ernie: There have been many feuds over boundary lines; they are always a problem especially in the mountains and forests. We did all our own marking of trails ourselves. Pete Totemoff helped; Rhoda was always along. Lee Varoz, Sr. ran the cutting crews. After the Poma lift was in and the bottom part of the mountain was open, then we went on to explore the upper regions very slowly and cautiously equipped with spray cans with yellow paint and pink and purple ribbons. The first objective was to make Taos more accessible to skiers who were not capable of skiing extreme steepness.

Georgia Hotton: Rhoda was constantly out, and I would often go with her, designing easier ways down the mountain. We'd take orange strips and mark the trail of where it should be, and we'd spot: "Rhoda, you're a little bit lower than I am so that's okay; Rhoda, you're too much lower than I am, better come back up a few steps to mark that tree so that we don't have something here that's steeper than what we want." Rhoda was a good skier at that point. I was not. But she fully appreciated the fact that some people might like an easier way down the mountain.

Ernie: We laid out the trails with tape and a spray can, and we stuck to the furrows, the concave shape, that's the trick. We stayed on the north, northeast and east slopes when we could. We tried not to have them too abysmally steep, but we ended up with a very steep mountain anyway. By self-defense, in order to survive, we had to force everybody into ski school because they wouldn't have lasted a day without learning to ski right and being able to handle that steep a mountain. That's how we got into the ski school business. Now it's paying off, by reputation, at least, if not in dollars. We added run after run.

Walter Widmer: I remember very well, we used to climb to the upper mountain with skins in the springtime, and then go up Kachina. That was such a cliff; you know it was all trees, of course. And Ernie one day said, "Oh, I think I'm going to put a lift in here." I said, "What the heck; you going to get the people up on the lift—how the hell you going to get them down? There's no way. You have to let them down on ropes."

Ernie: We didn't admit that it was too steep; we didn't admit it to anybody but ourselves. We began to search for easier ways down the mountain. The first easy runs we built were Powderhorn and Porcupine.

To clear the slopes, we had to burn the logs. We ended up buying all the second-hand, used-up tires in the county, using them to keep the fires going. It made big clouds of black smoke. It was ugly, but it was very efficient. We cut pretty flush with the ground, but you could only do that to a point because the flushness also ruined the chain saws because they got lots of dirt and rock in the teeth. It was an expensive business; we burned a lot of wood which hurt me, having been brought up in a country where trees are very sanctified because they are the protection from avalanches, and where firewood is very valuable. I couldn't see burning stuff, but it was the only way. Nobody would pick it up for you, regardless of the quality of the wood.

You have to keep in mind that in the early years, you skied in deep powder most of the time because we had a capacity of about forty bodies at the area. The road was so bad that people didn't come just for a weekend or a Sunday. Having hardly any skiers, the

High mountain ski touring, Al's Run & Showdown below. Courtesy Blake Family Collection.

steepness was not that much of a problem as it seems and the snow wasn't skied off.

Chilton Anderson: When I think of what we brought up our people on; it's scary now to think back. I mean, Zagava, which is already steep the way it looks now; it scares people. That first year, it was just there, winding down through there. It was four to ten feet wide, and it hooked and curved and turned.

Ernie: Porcupine was cut in the summer of 1958. Mickey, Rhoda and I went to Alaska, and Jay Vaughn was in charge of the job. He erased much too much of the forest and took the protection from the wind away. The trees were supposed to stand and create a wind break and make the wind drop its snow load on the slopes. We had a terrible wind problem by the time I came back, but it was too late. You can't grow trees once they're cut. So, we had to revamp that trail extensively.

As we were leaving the parking lot on our trip to Alaska, there was a very good looking, older gentleman with a young son checking in to the Hondo Lodge. He asked me how I liked the Rambler. I said, "It's a terrible car. My wife has trouble getting around because every time she wants to shift gears, she has to stop and open the hood and go in with her arm to do it. It's not very convenient. For God's sake, if you are

Early T-bar, Taos Ski Valley. Courtesy Blake Family Collection.

Georgia Hotton heading down old Al's Run Poma lift line.
COURTESY BLAKE FAMILY COLLECTION.

Old Al's Run Poma lift, 1958, Hondo Lodge in background.
COURTESY BLAKE FAMILY COLLECTION.

Dr. Al Rosen in front of Al's Run. COURTESY BLAKE FAMILY COLLECTION.

a skier buy a Volkswagen; don't buy a Rambler." He said, "That's very interesting," and he took my name and address. His name was Roy Chapman. I had no idea who he was.

When I came back from Alaska, there were two telegrams on my desk, one from Detroit and one from Denver from American Motors. That was the firm that bought Nash-Rambler, they wanted to come and fix my car because Roy Chapman, the president of the company, told them to. I found he was listed with the highest wages in the United States; he made $102,000 base salary, which in 1958 was an enormous sum. They sent a man by train who brought out all the tools to fix the machine. Nice gesture, but it was a lousy car.

Ernie: In the beginning, the road up Twining was just a mule trail. It crossed the river at least twenty times over those old wooden bridges, the old bogs and the swamp near the top. It was one lane most of the winter. A tough proposition. Dr. Al Rosen made this Ski Valley with his ability to get things done. He got the state to help keep the road open in the winter and finally got a new road in 1971. Al got the Forest Service to divert funds to build bridges and to get the road smoothed out and widened so that by the second or third winter, we had a road, even if it was a rocky road full of chuck holes. Al Rosen created the area more than we did. He didn't have much time because of his patients who never paid their bills. He had a good sense of humor; he was the king of Taos; everybody loved him.

The Ski Valley was a crazy idea in the beginning, and if it hadn't been for Al Rosen, I would never have done it, but he talked me into it. He is the guilty party. It was his push that got us into this wild adventure. I remember, it was a Sunday afternoon the first time I went to Al's house with Pete Totemoff.

Tom Brownell: Ernie and Al, their relationship, what's to say? There's no other major run named for anybody else, except Al's Run, for Al Rosen.

Myrt Rosen: When Ernie wanted to get the road paved, he asked Al because Al was a politician. Al called George Lavender who was then the state highway commissioner. He lived in Taos and we knew him. He asked George if there was any possibility of paving the road to the ski area because it was still a Forest Service road. We were using the University of New Mexico snow blower to blow the snow off of it. George said to Al, "You're a registered Republican. I can't get you a road paved." And Al said, "As of this minute, I'm a Democrat. I'm going right down and change it." And he did. George said, "Okay, we'll get the road paved." That's New Mexico politics.

George was also responsible for the bridge going over the Rio Grande. The people who knew him called it "The Great George Bridge."

The Old Road to Twining (Taos Ski Valley). COURTESY KIT CARSON HISTORIC MUSEUM

Lee Varoz, Sr.: I want to tell you that it was very tough to go up there in the wintertime because in those days, it used to snow. Man, we used to have a lot of snow! We didn't have no road; it was just a wagon trail. It was very hard for a vehicle to go up when we had that kind of snow. We had to walk a lot of times maybe halfway up to the Ski Valley.

I remember one time we started to go up there to work, and we got there at four o'clock in the evening because of the snow. I had my pickup half loaded with rocks to have traction enough to just barely go a little bit. And then we would back up and then go forwards and bump into the snow again until we got there. When we got there, why Ernie put us to shovel a little snow on the ramp on the beginners' slope. Then we come home. But he paid us a full day, which it wasn't.

Mickey Blake: The old road was a one-lane road which crossed the river back and forth and back and forth. You can still see a little piece of it just below Taos East on the hillside there. Some of the Taos families drove up there in the summertime to picnic, and that was about the extent of the use of the road. With Al Rosen's influence as we grew, the Forest Service began to straighten it out and move it to the north side of the river and took out all the bridges.

The Rio Grande Gorge Bridge. PHOTO BY ULLI SEER COURTESY BLAKE FAMILY COLLECTION.

They must have done that in the late 1950s. There used to be a song, "If You Want to Go to Taos Ski Valley, You Have to Bring Along Your Rand McNally." Finding your way up there was a joke. Getting from Taos to Arroyo Seco was an adventure in itself.

Vidal Sisneros from the highway department finally took it over from the Forest Service. When we were first plowing it, they cleared it with an open bulldozer. He'd come in all frozen, and my mother would give him hot coffee and a shot of whiskey; in those days no one thought anything of giving him a shot of whiskey even though he was on the job.

Georgia Hotton: I remember driving down to town one day in the Blake's station wagon and coming down, I hit a car coming up. The car coming up belonged to a Texan, and fortunately we didn't do each other very much harm. I came on down and was running errands in town, and I ran into Ernie; he had come down because, there being no telephone, there was no way for him to get a message to me and he needed to pick something up. When I saw him I said I was really sorry that I'd hit a Texan coming down, and he said it was all right because he'd hit one too, the same day.

Walter Widmer: Many a time, people would drive out of here in the early morning to go to Albuquerque to catch a flight, or whatever, and then they came back up and said that the road is blocked; there's a tree down across the road. Ernie would get into that open jeep that always had chains on all four wheels, and he'd drive down to the bottom, cut up the tree and make it possible to go through again. It happened so many times, you wouldn't believe it. I used to be all bundled up with big gloves and so on, and Ernie would be driving without any gloves, as usual.

Pete Seibert: Ernie started down there in Taos before we did here in Vail. We went down in the early days when he was just getting going because I remember driving up that road. He had problems with the drainage, and he'd throw logs in there, and we'd bounce across in an old station wagon. He had a sign down there that said, "Now leaving the American Sector."

Ilse Mayer: Back then, we had young children and had to take them to school every day. There was not even a trace of a school bus to get up there and no snow plow half of the time. I felt like living in a newly discovered land. It was fierce.

Ernie: Al Rosen was a real character. He was remarkable how he skied with his oxygen tank. He was a pioneer in what heart patients could or couldn't do on the ski slope. It took great guts to ski with his bad heart. He was a country doctor of the old type who had tremendous compassion for his patients.

Dr. Al Rosen skiing with his oxygen tank.
COURTESY MYRTLE ROSEN.

Dr. Al Rosen, March 1968.
PHOTO COURTESY BLAKE FAMILY COLLECTION.

Myrt Rosen: We came in 1941; Al was the only doctor in the county during the war. When we first arrived, we could have bought anything we wanted in Arroyo Seco for $25 an acre, but we didn't have $25. Al was paid in paintings, poetry and chickens. He took care of D.H. Lawrence, Frieda Lawrence, F. Scott Fitzgerald, and Tennessee Williams.

Godie Schuetz: Al Rosen was a crazy character. I had an accident in Red River one time when I was over there. Ernie, Herman and I were skiing down this slope; we didn't have safety bindings at that time, and came into a sharp transition. I just went in there and the tip went down, and I fell forward and the binding didn't release. I yelled, "Ernie, I really think I hurt my foot. I can't stand on my foot. I think I broke it." "Aw, come on Godie, that's all right. You've been in the Swiss army; you can ski on down now. Don't be a weakling." So I skied down as good as I could and went home. They came up and we had a cheese fondue and my foot swelled up. I took some aspirins, but I finished the dinner and everything was fine.

Next, I go to see Al Rosen, the famous Dr. Al. He says, "Well, you have a fracture in your right ankle; I see something else in there—a chip." Well, that was after my first accident, my bad accident when I was in a cast for fourteen months with two operations. So, he said he'd put on a cast, and we'll see. I was not really very happy about that. "You don't think I need to have an operation on that?" He said, "Don't worry. We'll find out in about six to eight weeks." Al had a sense of humor too. I was unhappy, so I called up my friend in Dallas who was an orthopedic surgeon and told him about it. He said to come on down. So, they took the cast off and checked it out and said, "No, this will be all right," and so they put another cast on. I went back up. Al was a little bit upset with me.

Another time, I broke my nose up on a run, and I skied down. Dr. Rey Deveaux saw me first on the slope and said, "Godie, you look like hell." "How come?" "Well, because your nose is way over here." Then the nurse, Pam, said, "Eh, Godie, you look like hell." I said that I'd already been told. "You better go and see the doctor." Rey Deveaux was my doctor and I called him up. No, he was still on the slope, so I called Al. Okay. And the nurse says, "Dr. Rosen, Godie's nose looks real bad; I think he needs plastic surgery." "Send him down, I'll look at it." So I go into the hospital and am waiting for him to come. He comes and says, "Ah, Godie, your nose looks like hell." They put me down, and I'm laying down there and he tells his nurse Mary, "Mary, let me have an eight." And she says, "Don't you think, Dr. Rosen, that we need a ten?" (For numbing it). I'm the one they're talking about, and she's questioning him. He says, "Oh, no, no, eight is good enough. He's going to yell anyway, and I'm used to that." So he put this stuff in,

and he said here we go; he picks up my nose and you can hear it cracking awful. He says, "Okay, get up." I said, "Al, don't you think I need some kind of a protection for this nose?" Al says, "No. If you are dumb enough to go out there and break your nose again, that's your tough luck."

Chilton Anderson: Years ago, Al Rosen and I were in Aspen. He and I went up for a week in a big old Dodge power wagon. We skied a day or so, then put a sign in the window that said, "Tired of flat slopes? Come to Taos." People looked and said, "What?"

Dadou Mayer: For me, if it hadn't been for Al and Myrt Rosen, I wouldn't be here. It was not my parents, it was not Jean, it was not Ernie; it was Al and Myrt that saw in me a possibility and they wanted to help me and get me going. They were outside supports that really saw something in Taos Ski Valley, and they wanted to see it grow.

CHAPTER 11
The French Connection

Ernie: To start Taos Ski Valley wasn't guts; it was foolishness. Like I've said Al Rosen is responsible; he talked us into it but next to Al, Jean Mayer was the one we were lucky to find. Jean came by way of a good friend who was the president of the National Ski Patrol, Bill Judd. He sent us this cheaply done little booklet with job applications by a national ski patrolman for jobs and industry, and there was Jean Mayer's name. He was just finishing his two years with the American army. He was the chief of the American army ski patrol in Garmisch.

I ignored Judd's letter because Jean had so many capabilities that I knew we couldn't afford him with the limited amount of money we had. I didn't answer at all. So, a few weeks later, Bill Judd called me, and he got mad as hell when he found out that I hadn't picked up on this thing which he had circled, and he was very upset that I hadn't at least written to Jean Mayer.

So, I wrote Jean and said that this was a great place for skiing, and it was a pioneering effort, but there was no money in it, that we should have no false notions that we'd get rich here; nobody would get rich for many, many years, if ever. He wrote back that that was just the kind of adventure he was looking for, and he came the 24th of December of 1957.

Jean Mayer: When I came here in 1957, Al Rosen picked me up at the La Fonda Hotel. I had arrived by bus. Al started giving me hell for being late. He had no idea all I had gone through just to get there. "Oh you little French bastard, what are you doing coming late? We expected you way before." God, I was ready to turn right back around. He brought me up to the Hondo Lodge; it was the day before Christmas, and that was when I met Ernie.

I think our friendship came through the years. It didn't start with friendship but with competition; I remember it well. Because either way, Ernie wanted to challenge me. We had to have a ski race the next day, and I didn't have my skis yet, and Ernie, he skied very quick against me using a type of form which we didn't have yet. I couldn't believe it; I thought, "Who is this guy?" That's when I was hot, right out of the army. I had to kind of establish myself that way; I mean, he was always challenging.

Ernie was a tough cookie at the beginning. I really appreciated his competitiveness; I liked that. He was tough and mean and rugged, and that was his macho

thing; he had to be. But I remember that was a shock to me. You know, I was a little guy and just arrived, and he gave me hell.

Mickey Blake: Jean's one of the original people at Taos Ski Valley that has the basic understanding of what Taos is all about. My father was certainly the spirit of Taos Ski Valley as Jean is in many ways today. They had their fights, and a number of fistfights, but over time, they were able to establish a special relationship that certainly benefited the whole community. They were able to make it work.

Walter Widmer: Jean and Ernie were very similar characters. Very similar. I think Ernie enjoyed a fight basically; he was not mean. Ernie just enjoyed being challenged and challenging back. That was just part of him. He was rather aggressive; otherwise, he would have never built this place.

Tom Brownell: Obviously, Jean was extremely instrumental in building this area. After Ernie, it would be Jean with the St. Bernard and the technique of skiing, the teaching, the dedication that made the area.

Jean Mayer. PHOTO BY KEN GALLARD.

Charles "Papa" Mayer: Jean and Ernie had understanding with the people. Being caring and kind, that's the most important. Jean is very funny; he is like Ernie that way. He likes to have people to the St. Bernard. He likes the power. Padrino. In English, how do you say that? The biggest piece? Everybody kiss his hand. He is the chief of all the Mafia.

Warren Miller: I remember the first time I came to Taos. Jean Mayer had just opened the Hotel St. Bernard, and in those days it was more European than Europe. They had all French dishes, and silverware and the service was exactly like a small place in Chamonix or Val d'Isere. Ernie kept that flavor, and the Mayer brothers were a big part of that. They were big contributors with the ambiance and the ski school.

Myrt Rosen: Jean came that Christmas, in 1957, and the upstairs of the Hondo was just one big room. Jean quickly made it dormitory style. He put a curtain down the middle with girls on one side and boys on the other, and when he didn't have any more boys' beds, he'd put them on the girls' side. I said, "You can't do that," and he said, "What's the difference? After the lights are out, they're going to switch anyhow." That was the beginning of the French connection.

Chilton Anderson: Space was so scarce; extra space was nonexistent. Jean was going to manage the Hondo Lodge and also be ski school director. When he got there, there wasn't any place for him to stay because they didn't have any rooms. If he stayed in a room, he'd take up a place where a guest could stay. So he built a little log cabin in the corner of the main room and that was his private room. Then out in another part, he built his brother a room and one for Yvon Silve, the chef.

Ilse Mayer: I slept in this cubbyhole in the old Hondo Lodge. My God, it was terrible! There was a room for staff, and I had to share my room with another girl also named Ilse. It was a log cabin, and the plaster between the logs wasn't very tight and was falling out, and the wind was howling through the room. It was terrible. There was no electricity, maybe one little light bulb dangling from somewhere. But actually, we had a good time.

Myrt Rosen: My ski shop was in the Hondo, which was not finished. Between the logs, there used to be mice coming in, and I don't mind mice, but I resent their reading my book over my shoulder. I started the ski shop in the Hondo Lodge in 1956-'57 and opened that season. That first year when Jean built the St. Bernard, he only had the restaurant. I moved my ski shop into Jean's office. I had my little room in the back with a desk, a roll-away bed, and a bathroom. I remember it snowed every night those first years, and the sun came out every morning.

Papa Mayer: Jean was never against Ernie. He took a position and you know, generally, Americans don't

take positions. Ernie lived for work. Taos Ski Valley was more important for him than his son and maybe even than his wife. He was even involved when they had the Olympic games. He was on top; he wanted to be on top of all the people. Taos Ski Valley, that was his life. For Jean too, it is his life. Ernie had done everything else. For me, if I cannot ski tomorrow, I know I am not going to cry. There is a time for other things, like Mama.

Ernie: The St. Bernard Restaurant was built with the Mayer money. The Twining Ski Corporation gave them the land where the restaurant lies now. When they built in 1958, they just built the lowest floor, which was a restaurant. That reduced the insurance burden tremendously at the Hondo Lodge because the fire insurance was monstrous on having a commercial kitchen in this wooden building. I also bought a liquor license. There was no money in the corporation, so I bought out of pocket for $1,500, a license which today costs between $50,000 and $75,000. That is Jean's present license.

Chilton Anderson: Jean built that first part of the St. Bernard and that first little section of the bar. He used some of that wood from Malcolm Brown who had just cut some of the trails, that lovely wood with the uneven bark on the edge. Malcolm also built the fireplace in the St. Bernard. He used to bring up his ukulele, and Jean and I used to do the nighttime entertainment with him. We'd get together and I'd play the gut bucket.

Ernie: The hotel part of the St. Bernard started in the winter of 1959-60 with eight rooms above the restaurant which had been built in the fall of 1958. The next year, 1960, they built the A-frames, and then 1961-'62, they built the Alpenhof.

The Twining Ski Corporation, of which Al Rosen was the president, was the stockholder who bought the Hondo Lodge from Hondo, Inc. We gave them a $35,000 mortgage, loan on the debts that the Dallas corporation had made. They had bought blankets and millions of matchboxes with the picture of the Hondo Lodge; they were beautiful, but not the most essential thing. They had all sorts of luxurious things combined with terrible basic needs that were not fulfilled.

As Jean came in, by the second winter, we had the Santa Fe Railroad business picking up, so we did all right that winter. We all lost money, but we were at least in the position where we could see the thing growing.

Chilton was very generous and very enthusiastic about Jean. He helped Jean a great deal. Jean thinks Chilton has a great business sense; I don't think that's true. At the very first, some don't like him. But, on the whole, he is a fabulous ski instructor who had a time passing his exam. Chilton was a tremendous help to the whole area; he became the backbone. He didn't have the lodge duties Jean had, and he became the

St. Bernard under construction, Hondo Lodge to right, 1958. COURTESY BLAKE FAMILY COLLECTION.

Looking down at old St. Bernard and Ski Valley. PHOTO BY DICK TAYLOR.

Papa and Dadou Mayer, Hotel Edelweiss dining room, March 1982. COURTESY BLAKE FAMILY COLLECTION.

instructor of the instructors. He's completely honest. He is chintzy in monetary things. He was generous with the musical thing, but he's a little Swiss, but I'm worse. Spending money is not a Swiss habit.

Chilton Anderson: I went to the bank to buy the ranch. As soon as I was able to get it paid off, I got out, and I've never done it again. I don't do things so I have to go into debt. Ernie was exactly the same way. No matter what the business, all the business people would say what's 7% interest? Just add that on to it. But I don't believe in that. So, I agreed with Ernie and maybe that's why we got along so well. He didn't like owing money, and I don't think he liked the growth. He didn't feel safe the last few years with the big expansion, or so many people skiing on the slopes. Which is why when I took the ticket off the tennis player, John Newcombe, for skiing out of control, both Ernie and Mickey thought this was great. That is when I was presented with a sheriff's badge and made honorary sheriff.

Ernie: Jean was just beginning to build the St. Bernard when Dadou and the Mayer family arrived. Dadou came in September of 1958, and then we fired him right away, and he spent a few years in Santa Fe, and in Red River, and then he came back to us. Dadou was a big addition, but we had troubles in the beginning.

Nicole "Mama" Mayer: When we arrived in Albuquerque I was looking for the town, and I could see only the flat thing; everywhere flat, and it was hot. Then we called Blake, and he said he was coming, but in one hour. There was a long road to come and pick us up. I said we'd go to see the town; I'd like to see Albuquerque, and we took a taxi. I told the driver to go to the cathedral because in Europe you first go to the cathedral of the place. He said he didn't know about a cathedral, but they had a principle church, or he could take us to Old Town. And for me, I thought it was not a town. We came back and waited. Everything was getting me at that moment. Blake came, and we took the car with him. He told me he was hungry and had some soup which surprised me in the middle of the day. I asked him, "Where are the Indians?" He said, "Over there," and that's when he told me to call him "Ernie."

Dadou Mayer: I'll remember that ride all of my life beause that was before radar and Ernie was speeding to get back, and I couldn't understand exactly what he was doing. He drove like a maniac. When we got to Taos there was no snow or nothing. I was disappointed, expecting a very big ski area. That was for me the start.

Mama Mayer: The first thing I wanted to know

was if we have a lot of things to do in the kitchen. Tom and Tomasita were there, and they gave to their dogs all of the leftovers from the dinner, and I couldn't understand how come. They would give meat prepared in a burgundy beef surrounded by a crown of rice, and people have very little, and they were giving that to the dogs! Again, surprising to me. I went to the back and looked, and I thought all those things in the bar, the glasses, were done in an electrical machine, and I had to wash my glass and things by hand; this was unbelievable for me. I understood then that we were still pioneers. Everything came very, very slowly for one month. It felt like digesting something.

There was not very much there. The old road was just a trail nearly. It was better than a trail really, but only a little. There were people coming to ski. I had seen Dave Polson, for example, and Ashley Pond and Al Rosen were coming. We had no telephone, no electricity.

Dadou Mayer: When I arrived here with my parents, we started right away working with the building that was in construction, the St. Bernard. At that time, I was carving out logs to make lamps, and we were sanding the beams, trying to get them smooth enough to paint. I was just continuing on something that was going on from the beginning in my family. We work all together; we're not paid, but just for room and board. So, we built the St. Bernard and finished it that year. We did get the snow pretty early, and I was very excited.

Ernie always liked competition. It was 1958, and I remember very well my first ski test because I had to show my ability as a skier for Ernie who was very doubtful. I remember that I didn't have my skis by then, and Ernie had given me a pair of those old army issue boards, hickory, white, wide boards that still had the little things on the tips, you know, and the old bindings. I did have my boots. He took us down on Al's Run which at that time was the narrowest thing. It was set up incredibly narrow, just for that Poma lift. I started making an ass of myself. I was falling all over the place; I couldn't ski those skis, and I had never seen that much powder. Ernie, with a little smirk on his face, was just sinking down in his old Swiss technique that worked in anything, anywhere.

So, I didn't make much of an impression. The next thing that happened is that I was told that my abilities were not up to what they expected, and they already had ski instructors. They had at that time Chilton, Jay Vaughn, and Georgia Hotton, so I was really low man on the totem pole. I was responsible for the upkeep of the slope, going packing and doing all that type of stuff until I kind of proved myself, until there was a need for me. That didn't really go very well with the little cocky Frenchman who came from the National French School teaching at the Club Med in Switzerland. I

Papa Mayer. Photo By Dave Marlow. Courtesy Blake Family Collection.

Papa and Mama Mayer. Photo By Ken Gallard, Courtesy Ilse Mayer.

Mama Mayer. Courtesy Ilse Mayer.

Dadou & Jean Mayer jumping in front of the St. Bernard. PHOTO BY WOLFGANG LERT, COURTESY BLAKE FAMILY COLLECTION.

Lunch at the St. Bernard, 1987. PHOTO BY RICKE/HULTS, COURTESY JEAN MAYER

thought I was hot stuff. I had a year of teaching experience behind me from teaching every day. So, I thought I should get what I had been promised. I told that to Jean right away, that I was not going to go up and pack snow for Ernie. I was hired to be a ski instructor, and that's what I was going to be. That was my first face-off with Ernie, and I was an eighteen-year-old coming from Europe, and I just told him, "No, Mr. Blake, I was not going to go up and pack," and that was it.

That same day, a very good friend of Jean's was there, Harvey Chalker, who at that time was manager of Santa Fe Ski Basin. He heard of that conversation, and he heard of me being upset. Two days later, he called Jean and told him that if I was interested, I could go up and teach for him in Santa Fe. He offered me a great salary and a place to stay. I had everything set up, and two days later, I was gone to Santa Fe to teach.

I stayed a year at the Santa Fe Ski Basin, and then I followed Buzz Bainbridge and taught a year in Red River. By then, I had become a fully certified ski instructor, one of the youngest ones in the country at that time. Ernie wrote me a letter saying Jean thought that I had proven my worth, that I was one of the top instructors in the country, and that he would be very willing to offer me the title of assistant director of the ski school if I wished to, if it was okay with Chilton and Jean.

My reply at that time was that I would be very happy to do that, but I would have to have some kind of incentive to come back to work at TSV, and that I was really interested in getting into it business-wise. Ernie saw that there was a possibility for the Twining Ski Corporation to sell a piece of land right there by the parking lot. It was kind of a bog. I was very interested, and I said, "Well, if I can buy this, that would definitely be an incentive for me to come back and start something." That's the way I came back to Taos Ski Valley.

Papa Mayer: Ernie and Dadou fought, because Dadou is not flat. He is more aggressive. Everything Jean and Dadou do is competition; even now with tennis, windsurfing, business. I don't know why. In my time, the competition was the Grand Marnier, you know. We finish a race, it was a very big banquet, *et à votre santé*.

Ernie: We didn't get along very well with the parents Mayer in the beginning. They did funny things; everybody ate together at one big table in the Hondo Lodge. They would serve steak to themselves, to Jean and Dadou and Tiky, their daughter, and they would serve sauerkraut and hot dogs to the Blakes and their gang. I love sauerkraut, but I didn't think this dual system was very good. That wasn't Jean's idea. Jean was great. Mama was a fabulous woman, but Papa was

a difficult man; I think the problem was with him.

Chilton Anderson: You know, Ernie could be hard to get along with, but so was Papa Mayer.

Jean Mayer: I would say for three or four years, Ernie abused us. My parents left and went to Red River. Life became so difficult for French people who were imported.

Mama Mayer: Papa and I left not because of Ernie. It was for Jean as it seemed important for him to be alone and to do what he wanted. Then we went over to Red River. It was so different.

Dadou Mayer: With my father and Ernie, I think there was a conflict of power and of interests. I think my father, who is extremely self-assertive and just as strong a character as Ernie, felt that he had to stand for our rights.

Mama Mayer: Jean told us to come because without us he couldn't have started the place without the money we bring. It was not a big amount, but just the amount necessary to be part of the Twining Ski Corporation.

Papa Mayer: When we came here, we thought we were a unique group. We decided to come through correspondence with Jean even though we had lost our money with the war. I was in the underground. We sold everything to come to Taos Ski Valley. Ernie thought I was only a cook. I told him I stopped in New York and had a letter from the minister of economic affairs in France explaining what I was going to do and that I was accredited by the consulate of France and everything; I explained that to him. I thought he was going to be happy, but he was jealous; I was too smart.

I was a much more experienced skier than he was, and he was jealous of that. He was afraid Papa Mayer was going to take his place. I say, "You don't pay me for a job. I come with my money." We invest everything we have in the Twining Ski Corporation. "If you want to order me around or something, then pay me." That was the beginning.

Mama Mayer: Blake was very strict. He was talking to us in a way that was difficult to stand sometimes. The deception for us was that Blake was rude because he thought we were cooks. We had started cooking because of the war. Charles had studied to be a lawyer, and he had been to the university, but the war cut everything. He was in the war, in military. I had four children, and I made him come back with my fourth child. We started a restaurant in Nice, because we couldn't give to eat to our children, and with a restaurant it was easier. We had special tickets to buy food.

Blake wrote Jean while he was in the U.S. Army and asked him to direct the ski school because he read everything about Garmisch where Jean was ski patrol and did very, very beautiful skiing. Jean was very liked

Jean Mayer serving dinner at the Hotel St. Bernard.
PHOTO BY KEN GALLARD.

Chef Claude Gohard of the Hotel St. Bernard.
PHOTO BY KEN GALLARD.

by everybody when he came here to Taos. We were in Nice when Jean called us to come quickly and bring money, that there was an opportunity here. Jean said it was marvelous; New Mexico was the best place in the world.

Ernie: When the Mayers came, they brought with them a very crazy chef named Yvon Silve, a real character. He was a wild man for the girls and hunting; he was always in trouble with the game and fish department because he had no allegiance to the seasons.

Mama Mayer: Jean was just finishing the St. Bernard Restaurant, and Yvon was the first chef that we bring. His father had a very good restaurant in the back of our club we had in Nice. His father could work only with champagne. Yvon was the old-fashioned man, the old-time man. Papa asked him to come, and he came something like two or three months after us. He had to make papers and such. But he was there for the first Christmas.

Yvon was a wonderful man. He cooked marvelously and was very funny. He was in trouble with the guests maybe a thousand times because he had his French humor. He was a good fisherman, a good hunter, and he was also very proud of his physical appearance. He was sure of himself and he thought every woman would love him. He is probably waiting marriage to some of them who are still here.

One day, around 11:30, we heard the noise of Yvon's boots on the trail, and he was coming running, "America, America!! This is America. Everything miracle." He came with buckets full of water, leaking, and full of fish. He went to the back porch, emptied the bucket, went again and did that twice. And when he came back, I said, "You have to take back all those fish back." He says, "Why? They were in a hole." "Yes," I said, "but it was the game and fish department. They bring this every week from the hatchery." You should have seen that poor Yvon going back with these buckets.

Yvon was very friendly with the game and fish department. He was going to hunt deer, and they told him, "Yvon, did you take a permit to shoot deer?" "Yes, yes, I have." "Okay, don't do it before the date, the opening of the season." We could see Yvon making a face long like that.

One night before the day of opening, he took Jean in the VW and went to catch his deer and came back with a deer. In the kitchen, it was very busy. Yvon was skinning it. He and Jean were walking and singing; it was a big feast; they were drinking. At that time, Papa and I were sleeping in the trailer by the restaurant. We went to bed and early in the morning, Yvon arrives with a big sheet, dirty, and full of blood telling me, "Mrs. Mayer, you have to hide me, fib for me. The game and fish are here and they are looking all over for the proof." I told him to put it in my bed. I had at the end of the trailer a big bed; we put it at my feet and covered all over me, and I was uncomfortable. You can imagine!

Later, somebody knock at the door, "Mrs. Mayer, are you here? Oh, excuse us." "Oh, please come in. I am in bed. I am a little tired." "Oh, don't move." I was not moving. "Well, we heard that Yvon had shot a deer and we are looking around, but don't worry. It is nothing. Sorry we disturb you." He opened the refrigerator and looked in—nothing. "You like it here? You are happy here?" he said. Then they left.

I know one more story which is better. Usually, Yvon went down to the Rio Grande to fish and this time he was with Buell Pattison. Buell went thirty yards from Yvon, and Pattison couldn't catch anything, but each time Yvon pulled the rod he had a fish. He had all the catch of the river. Then Pattison came and he said, "How do you do it? Tell me how." Yvon said, "Well, it's simple. You have your worm, put it on the hook, then you lick the worm with as much saliva as you can. Try it, you will see how good." Then I don't know how he showed it. But the fact is, poor Buell came back a little short time after vomiting, sick, sick and white like a cadaver.

Mama Mayer: From one surprise to another, we came to be American. I thought Ernie and I could have very good relation in the end. One day, when we were still in on the lodge when he look at me—I was at the bar and very proud of myself—he looked at me and he said, "We work well together." Ernie and I had a little point in common of pleasure and happiness. We had much pleasure to find in each other sometimes. I remember eight days before he died, I went to see him, and he said, "*Restez encore, restez avec moi;*" he acted with me a gentleman, always.

Papa Mayer: At the end, we were civil. I have nothing against him, but he could not support somebody like me.

Chilton Anderson: I remember Jean getting his citizenship. And it was the next year that his parents came over. Jean had just come back from Albuquerque livid. He had gone down to get his parents, and the guy down there, whatever department of state that was, and the guy said, "You damn Frenchmen. You come and get your citizenship, and then you bring the whole bloody family over." Jean was just furious. He'd worked hard; he'd been in the army and done this for his new country.

Ernie: We had trouble with the Mayers, but Jean is the one I'm really lucky to have found, the one that we owe things to; he has done many things for the area. After Al Rosen, Jean was most important.

Jean Mayer: One of the reasons that maybe my life has been so touched by Ernie is because, over the years, Ernie is the only one who has ever acknowledged my contribution. Not that you look for acknowledgment or anything, but as far as I'm concerned, he is the only one who saw that. The importance of my being here; of Jean being here.

Dadou Mayer. Photo By Ken Gallard.

Nobody else did because I was surrounded by people who were jealous.

Rhoda: Jean made a tremendous contribution. They were very different people, Jean and Ernest, but they both had that touch of making people feel special. Jean, even in the big business today, does that with his guests. Here they come, and it's not as if they were just somebody who were sleeping there and paying their lodging, but they are valued guests.

Dadou Mayer: I think there was always trouble between Ernie and Jean. I remember very well that first year when they punched each other out—it was always the challenge.

Jean Mayer: We fought, but that was a part of Ernie. It was a competition. I think when Ernie and I fought, when we had it out, then it was much easier. It was like dogs doing their little pecking order. You establish the situation. I never thought of it as the way he was brought up, but I just knew that it was something Ernie needed.

Ernie: The important fact with Jean is that he came and helped build this place when there was no money to be made and when it was really rough, as long as nearly thirty-five years ago, and I won't forget that regardless of what battles we may have had. It was our combined efforts to make Taos a very special place and a great deal of our success is due to Jean's efforts, his charisma and his exceptional abilities both as a hotel operator and as the brain and the heart of our ski school.

Jean Mayer: I did the work, dealing with the people, but it was Ernie who made this little valley world famous. I only dealt with the people when they came here, but he was able to get them to come here. That's the big difference. Now we still find ourselves the rinky-dink little ski area that has international status. And that's Ernie; that was originally his doing, and we have to follow through.

Chilton Anderson: The guests were well taken care of by Ernie, and by Jean with their European, continental manner. They were beautiful at that; they lived that way. That's the way they were brought up and that affected people. They were a fantastic combination.

Herman Kretschmer: Jean had an awful lot to do with what happened in Taos Ski Valley. I don't think Jean gets enough credit in this relationship; he was so close to Ernie. Jean, in his way, was as big a bullshitter as Ernie. They had a hate-love relationship for years. Jean made you feel, even more than Ernie, that you were the king. He was a consummate host.

Alan Crane: I think a lot of life is lucky; I think it was lucky that the Mayer family arrived, Papa and Mama had their lodge in Red River, and that Ernie and Jean and Dadou were here because they have played a major role in the building of Taos. Jean and Ernie had that certain something. How many people would keep coming to a crappy little place like this year after year where in the old days we'd run out of water in the middle of a shower and all of a sudden cold water would come out; the lights would go out because of the generator, no heat; the rooms are 6'x 8' and you trip over yourself coming and going with no closet to hang your clothes up in; not a phone, not a television in this day and age. But people came and that's to Jean's credit. I'd say there were some pretty wealthy people out there who in their wildest dreams wouldn't stay at a place like this who went away loving it.

People love Jean; you don't have a choice; you must love him. He comes, he smiles, he's a little human dynamo, and he's there for you. He's got the same dream and desire about this place. That food! It's so creative, not only these menus but the presentation. Jean comes out, and he is so proud of it all.

Jean Mayer: What made Ernie and my bond good together, and the bond with Al and Chilton, to some extent, was those people whose only motivation was Taos Ski Valley, the mountain resort. These other people, their motivation was their own personal standard and status, social behavior and pattern, money and business, recognition and acknowledgment. They thought of their own

business first. I never thought of the St. Bernard. For us, it was Taos Ski Valley, not Taos Ski Valley the corporation, but the mountain. That's what our thing was. That's why we were able to work on the road together, run the lifts together, do things with money coming in or not.

Max Killinger: Between Jean and Ernie there was something going on that was unbelievable. They were beyond friendship. There was a bond there that I experienced so many times that goes way beyond any kind of common business interest.

Dadou Mayer: Jean and Ernie loved and hated each other. They would always come to an agreement. It was very interesting. I think it was very very similar to a marriage, a really raucous marriage.

Papa Mayer: Jean is very complex, and even with all his different American women around him, Jean never missed serving a meal, not one dinner, because it is part of his life. It is not for the money.

Louie Bernal: Jean Mayer is a good man. He's been really good to us here in the parking lot. We are good friends. I think about that man a lot, I pray for that man, too. He's a very kind man. That's why the people come in. Whatever he does for the people, it come back on him and gives him more. He's a very strong man like Ernie.

Jean Mayer: When you remember, you try to remember the good things, but there were awful times at the beginning. Like when Ernie and I got into fights. He was just a rough, tough person to deal with, but I excused everything because of his vision, his almost blind dedication to Taos Ski Valley and everything that he had to deal with.

Dadou Mayer: I'm not one to rave about Ernie because I've had very difficult encounters all my life in Taos with Ernie. I think he was a great man, and I think his greatness was in his views of what could be done and his ways of doing it. It was very interesting because mine was not an arrangement with Ernie. From the beginning on, everything was set; the boundaries were set. I knew what I was supposed to do. He knew how he was supposed to handle things. I think that we probably wouldn't have survived very easily if it hadn't been for his friendship with Ilse, my wife. I think he had a very tender heart for Ilse, and with that, it kind of mellowed things out in many ways.

I never was a part of any of this game or of this combination or this arrangement. I was really a total foreigner to that whole thing. I was the young brother that was taking the overflow of Jean's business and under Jean's protection. Jean was the head of the family, and he definitely felt that it was his duty to take charge of making sure that the rest of the family was taken care of. So, just as much as Ernie was doing that in his family, I think Jean was doing that in his family, too. I felt that all along, and I was as much told that if I wanted to continue in what was going on, there were some rules I had to abide by. One of the rules was to get along with Ernie or things were not going to work for us.

Ernie had all types of power plays. I remember at one time I wanted to build a ski shop very much. I have a letter I have saved from Ernie saying, "If you build your ski shop, you can forget about getting any package deal through Taos Ski Valley, forget about any savings device that you could get." It would be in direct conflict with TSV. That was a continual thing that was taking place. There was always a conflict.

It took a tremendous amount of work for Ilse and me to get the Edelweiss to the stage where it is now, so that actually it would be accepted in Taos Ski Valley as one of the luxury places. Then we got accepted, and then Ernie started sending people over to us, and he started taking pride in what was happening. But that took an enormous amount of time.

Ilse Mayer: We started the Edelweiss in the winter of 1964. We had lots and lots of snow. We still hadn't finished the fireplace. We had to put the rocks up on the fireplace under terrible conditions. It was an experience I'll never forget. We barely had enough money to finish those two floors of hotel rooms and the snow came and the guests started dropping in, little by little. The real skiers were looking us up at that

Front of Hotel Edelweiss. PHOTO BY KEN GALLARD.

time. Whoever we could get, we let them stay and sometimes they had to help.

Dadou Mayer: The brilliance of Ernie was that even with his pride and with all the conflict that he had with me, he still saw in it the fact that there was something really attractive being built, and he was going to take advantage of it and use it. Even with all the conflict we had, he still was able to put that aside and say, "This is good for Taos Ski Valley; this is what we need." And he would help. We built that tennis court and some part of the tennis court is on Taos Ski Valley land; he let us use it all that time.

Ilse Mayer: Dadou was hardheaded, and he doesn't negotiate with anyone. He is not a man of talking or communication. If Dadou wanted something, he'd put it on the table, and if it was accepted, fine, and if it was not accepted, forget about it. Ernie was much the opposite. Ernie liked to talk about things often and didn't have an opportunity. I think the two characters really rubbed on each other and probably many other people had the same problem.

Jean always thought that he was a little bit better in communicating. He still is. Jean was the bigger negotiator with Ernie, and he played that part very well. Not only the Edelweiss and Dadou and I were following Jean, but the Thunderbird was also following and whoever else came along. I think everybody was afraid of talking with Ernie directly.

I loved the fact that Ernie needed the two Frenchmen with their education as ski instructors and as chefs de cuisine, and the two Frenchmen needed to find somebody like Ernie in order to develop their skills. They needed each other; I think Taos Ski Valley wouldn't have become anything without Jean and Dadou there, and Ernie knew that. It was such a match when it first started; a real lucky match.

Of course, you'd have to include Papa Mayer in there. He's the one who made the original connection to his sons and saw through all this chaos at that time. He saw how important it was that they would get there and stay there and make their lives there with Ernie. Papa is a very clear-sighted man, especially now. It was Papa's foresight. I think all throughout life he had a good deal to say, even if he was rejected by them.

In France, there is a saying that blood is thicker than water, and that family is very typical example to interpret that saying. It doesn't matter how much they fight each other or disagree; it always comes through that they are the family. That's also a very European system, and you cannot ignore it. If it ever came to a discrepancy between the two of them, there would be not only two Mayers but three Mayers against Ernie, no matter how much or how little Papa had to do at that point. Papa was the pusher. He pushed Jean in a certain direction, and I know he pushed us into buying

Hotel Edelweiss from beginners' slope. PHOTO BY KEN GALLARD, COURTESY ILSE MAYER.

Dadou & Ilse Mayer. COURTESY BLAKE FAMILY COLLECTION.

the original land to build the Edelweiss and pushed maybe even with Al Rosen making all these things happen. He pushed in the right directions.

We were just sort of tagging along all the time, Dadou and I, with whatever Jean would negotiate with Ernie. Jean needed us to fall back on oftentimes in order to pursue what he wanted to pursue. He was of great help in our career in the beginning. Al Rosen was more instrumental in what we have done with the Edelweiss than maybe Ernie at that point. He was wonderfully supporting to us. I can't say that often enough.

Ernie agreed with us coming into the valley, and he was in a way very happy that another European lodge owner would settle there. Then the third one was the Thunderbird, and again, Kaarlo Jokela, the owner, was European. Ernie was very proud of the fact that it was so European.

Dadou Mayer: Jean never really went against any of Ernie's moves. Ernie was the king, absolutely. Ernie for Jean was a kind of surrogate father. There was a real strong power that was overtaking, and Jean accepted. I never accepted that. I think really that my father felt that power, and there was a very strong jealousy instigated there between my father and Ernie because of the surrogate type of father attitude. Father was losing his grip and Ernie was gaining. It was a very strange reaction really. Jean was pulling himself away from his father, and yet still needed Ernie as some kind of a fatherly figure.

I think there were two different worlds. There was the world of Taos Ski Valley, and then there was the world of people who wanted to stay in Taos Ski Valley. So, there were two different entities really, struggling to survive with each other, yet against each other. There was Ernie and his family, and then the other families like the Mayer family and Chilton and the rest.

Ilse Mayer: With Jean's help and everybody behind him, Ernie made the Taos Ski Valley what it finally turned out to be. It was like the queen bee with all the little bee workers around him in a beehive: one main person, and all the others fell into place.

Harry Franzgen: When we talked at the meetings with Ernie, I always saw that Ernie and Jean had a very good male relationship, not just business. It was a good mutual respect; if Ernie listened to anybody, he listened to Jean. I think if I had been in Jean's position, I would have reacted the same way. To commune with Ernie the way that Jean communed with Ernie to get what I needed for my business, absolutely. You can't blame Jean. I also think that Ernie looked at some of us almost like sons and especially Jean.

You know, when we just met on a personal level, it was always okay. On a business level, I understood where he was coming from after a while. But he frustrated me because I must admit, in retrospect, I definitely was jealous about the relationship Jean and he had. Jean could do things and not get punished; I did. After a while, I understood that too.

Buell Pattison: Ernie didn't like people to compete against him when it came to business. He wanted that whole thing for himself, and he did not want anybody else to come around and give him any competition. When I built that building for Doug Terry that is now Terry Sports, he came and kept saying that I was stabbing him in the back. I told him I wasn't doing anything illegally; I was building a building and leasing it out. A person can do anything he wanted to do with it. It actually improved everything, and of course, he didn't like it when Dadou Mayer allowed a little ski shop to go in. He didn't like it when John Cottam came in and put in his ski shop. There was a lot of hard feelings between John Cottam and the Blakes.

Harry Franzgen: Ernie and I talked about life often and he said, "You don't know no different," and I called him a fascist and a dictator. With him being a Jew, I know what they went through over there, and I knew his thing in Switzerland where he couldn't be on the hockey team because of this; that hurt him. I said, "You know, Ernie, you're doing the same that those guys did to you." He knew that message very well,

and he used it to scare a lot of people. He told me, "I know I can't get anywhere with you," and that's right because I don't react to that. It went so far once, I said, "Ernie, look, if I'm such a thorn in your side, buy the lodge. If you want to control this piece of land, you have to buy it." Then he always backed off and got a little bit soft and, "Well, no, no, keep it." We had so many talks about some things that were so good, and then we had so many talks that were so hard; he made it so hard to be here. I always thought if we could all get together and pull on the same thing, we'd be so much better. But he never wanted that.

But Ernie was this kind of a man. He was a black and white man. There were no gray areas. Ernie once said, "The only way a ski area can be run is by a great dictatorship."

Section IV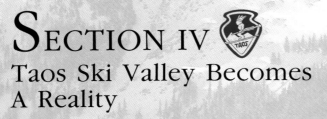
Taos Ski Valley Becomes A Reality

Ernie was tremendously fortunate to have hooked up with someone like Jean Mayer with similar drive and understanding. But Jean also turned out to be a true genius as far as ski technique was concerned. Jean was the innovator who kept the ski school at Taos Ski Valley in the forefront of skiing for over 30 years. Ernie attracted many such stars, including Max Killinger and Godie Scheutz who have been ski instructors in Taos for many years. And even if Ernie himself was not known for finesse with a class, the ski school was always his biggest passion.

Ernie was one of the first certified ski instructors in the United States (#5 was his pin number). The early ski instructors' exams were held at Arapahoe where all "the guys" got together at Max Dercum's Ski Tip Ranch. There were people like Max, Willy Schaeffler, George Engle, and Ernie; they were all involved in starting the Rocky Mountain Ski Instructors' Association. It was at one of these meetings that he met Godie Schuetz, a fellow Swiss, whom he lured to Taos as an instructor and restauranteur. Ernie knew Schaeffler before, in Garmisch, in 1945. Willy was responsible for getting Ernie the job as chief starter for the 1960 Olympic games in Squaw Valley.

It was tough going in the beginning of Taos Ski Valley, but Ernie and Jean created a civilized atmosphere in uncivilized surroundings. Ernie even used to close down the lifts for lunch. There was time for plenty of skiing, a rest was needed, and there were very few guests anyway, so at noon everything stopped. At lunch, Ernie used to tell stories and some of them were about the old gold mining days in the Twining valley. But in Ernie's case he was not looking for gold. Ernie's gold was his personality and that kept getting him the right connections at the right time.

With Ernie's European charm he captivated Steve Mitchell from Chicago who was a real gentleman. He was also a politician, the Democratic national chairman. He introduced Ernie to Chicago, the Harry Leonard ski shows, and the Santa Fe Railroad. It was the big ski shows back then that brought in the business and Ernie was at his best in front of an audience. His personality and charm were vital to the success of the Ski Valley. And it was one of those times in Chicago that he also met and persuaded Herman Kretchmer and Elisabeth Brownell that their futures lay in his Ski Valley. The Chicago connection suited Ernie's idea of a destination resort. He created the ski-week idea and people began arriving from Chicago by train.

CHAPTER 12
Ski School and Techniques of Skiing

Ernie: Jean created our ski school. This was the time of the big revolution when Kruckenhauser came with his Austrian method the winter of 1955-'56. There was a big fight going on in Europe when we went to Switzerland. Many resorts had two ski schools in red and in blue uniforms, respectively, fighting with each other. Some skied the Arlberg method with snowplow and stem turns with the weight way back, and some skied the Austrian method with their skis locked together, knees stuck one into the other and swooshing their skis from side to side with a mock folder position, the comma position, the reverse shoulder, great emphasis on side slope and so forth. I translated some of the material for *Ski Magazine* when I came back from Europe in the spring of 1956.

Friedl Pfeifer: We lived through all the techniques for skiing; that was the first miserable thing to go through. Every country had a different technique and every ski school, too. I made up a little story that, if Einstein hadn't shown us how to split the atom and Kruckenhauser hadn't shown us how to reverse shoulder ski, the world would be so much better off. Kruckenhauser sure hurt the beginner with the reverse shoulder theory. They were the guinea pigs.

Warren Miller: There was such an Austrian influence as opposed to Swiss. There was always that battle. One's doing the uphill skiing and one's doing the downhill. People don't realize, at the turn of the century, it was probably a two- to three-day trip from where Hannes Schneider lived in St. Anton to St. Moritz where Fred Iselin's father lived. Fred's father owned oil tankers, and he brought a Norwegian telemark instructor to St. Moritz, and as they got on steeper and steeper slopes, the telemark position gradually became contracted. At the same time, Hannes was inventing the downhill stem over in St. Anton. It's a bit of trivia that I've never seen documented, but it makes so much sense. There was absolutely no Swiss-Austrian intercourse then because the trains were steam and the tunnels were closed because of the avalanches. Friedl, Fred Iselin, Ernie, Jean Mayer, Alf Engen and Dave McCoy figured out how to bring the right combination of techniques to the public.

Ernie: When Jean arrived, he had already a little sheet with sketches showing that it was absurd to go for this composite thing, that it was the new thing, but that the extreme reverse shoulder was not functioning. This locking of the skis was wrong, we should not emphasize this effeminate, artificial hand position, but ski with our arms in normal position. I was shocked. I didn't think we could get away with that much arrogance to fight the God, the apostle of skiing. But Jean was consistently right. He was way ahead of everybody. He took over the ski school and did a fine job. That's when the Learn to Ski Week started to pay off because people then became interested in technique.

Jean Mayer: Ernie always had total faith in my vision in ski school; even if I made mistakes, he still gave me free rein to go in what direction I thought would be best. That does not quite exist anymore. Now I have to deal with all kinds of people who have totally different ideas.

Ernie: I have said it before, Jean is by far the most gifted skier and ski instructor I have met in exactly seventy years of skiing. . .and I have said it publicly time and time again.

Elisabeth Brownell: One time, Ernie was representing Head skis and I don't know what else they had at that time. He dictated a letter to me and

Ernie on his radio. PHOTO BY DAVE MARLOW, COURTESY BLAKE FAMILY COLLECTION.

Jean Mayer jumping. Courtesy Blake Family Collection.

said, "To all ski instructors: Every ski instructor has to ski on Head skis." So that was posted. The next day, everybody came on Head skis except Jean. He came on his Rossignols. Ernie saw that and didn't say a word. He came running back in and said, "Elisabeth, write a new notice. Every ski instructor has to ski on Head skis or Rossignols." He dictated it. He ordered it that they all can ski on Rossignols because he could not tell Jean not to ski on Rossignols, but Ernie had to be the one to make the rule.

Ernie: Jean knew what to do in order to sift through all the different techniques and find the most efficient ways to ski and teach. He worked very hard at figuring out what to do next. Back then it was very nationalistic; every country wanted their own technique.

I didn't want the Austrian type of mountain kid, big shot ski instructor, having nothing to talk about but skiing and sex and drinking. That's not what we wanted. The English girls used to marry their ski instructors who looked great in Austria where they were tanned and looked elegant, like great athletes, fabulous people. They took them to lunch, and after they married them, their fathers would give them

jobs in their stockbroker's firms or something. Then they looked ridiculous because they were all much shorter than the British and their good looks went with the suntan, and they looked pale from the lousy weather in London where you never see the sun. They lost all their glamour, and their accent which had sounded so sexy in St. Anton and Zurs and St. Christoph sounded ridiculous in London. You couldn't take them to a party. They were hopeless; they couldn't talk about anything but skiing. They thought it was a big thing to marry an Austrian ski instructor.

Friedl Pfeifer: Ernie's trouble was he was Swiss and German. The Americans are good sportsmen. They really are. I would say that the Americans are even better but not quite as clever as the Swiss are. The Americans, you can put them on top of the mountain, and this is not today, this was then, and they go straight down. That's all they know. They have tremendous accidents. The Americans have absolutely no fear whatsoever. I wouldn't call it reckless but they have a little bit too much guts. The Australians wanted to be taught from the bottom. Both nations are very easy to teach skiing to. The English are too technical. The French are the

116

Ernie Blake running Ski School from his command post on the beginners' hill. Courtesy Blake Family Collection.

Ernie Blake. Courtesy Blake Family Collection.

slowest. It was actually one man that got the French on the ski map—Emile Allais. I'm talking about tourists' skiing. The Austrians are, of course, way out in front.

Ernie: Producing racers was very difficult. Skiing was not a money-making proposition at that time, and to be a racer was to be like a ski bum. When things were beginning, there weren't many resorts in the Rocky Mountains. The only places in the United States that broke even or better were Berthoud Pass in Colorado, and Stowe, in Vermont. Our ski school is what held everything together; it was the strong point, and it must remain so.

Chilton Anderson: I think that Jean made the ski school. He was the star. He came over, and he was the one who knew the technical aspects. And when Dadou came, the two brothers looking alike and skiing the way they could, added great flavor to the show.

Max Dercum: Jean and Dadou are great. They started coming up here to our Ski Tip Ranch as examiners. They were instructors among some of the earlier people. Of course, Chilton Anderson, the guy who plays the cello and has that music school and raises Black Angus cows, he was a big help also.

Dadou Mayer: There is a very strong energy here in that whole image of the ski school. The guests keep coming back because they are getting something extra. It's partly the technical, but it's also renewed friendship that they go for. Every year they come back, not so much to really improve their technique, but to get updated on what is happening, socially as well as technically and with the whole world of skiing. It's the whole image that they are trying to update themselves with. So many of them have come for so many years that they are a part of Taos Ski Valley, and they relate to TSV as being part of it. They've grown with it. So, whatever is updated now, they feel that they want to know.

Ernie: The ski school is the thing that ties the whole village together; that's the key element, and the spirit it has created. That's the difference. Getting the recognition of being the number one ski school in the country in 1988 was a great achievement we owe to Jean and the other supervisors. It says a lot for the ski instructors, but it should not make us sit back and take it for granted. We now have to fight to remain number one; we have to keep the enthusiasm and the drive we have in the school and the quality of the lessons; they must remain top quality, and the classes must remain small.

Walter Widmer: The ski school was Ernie's baby; it was what created the spirit for Taos Ski Valley. It all started out to be kind of like a family. Ernie also felt that people had a better time skiing

Ski School line-up on Ernie's 70th birthday. PHOTO BY KEN GALLARD.

when they went to ski school. I'm very happy that it came out that Taos Ski Valley was the #1 ski school in the country before he died. Ernie was very proud of that #1 ranking, and then when it happened again in 1991 he would been even more proud that it is continuing to be the best.

Ernie could sometimes hardly walk down the stairs, but he was over there at the ski school with his skis on, every day, twice a day. He skied well, even though his knees were bad and he couldn't see well. He wouldn't go on the steeps anymore, but he still had that same style he always had. The day they took him to the hospital in an ambulance, he was at ski school that morning. You could say he was there to the very end.

Ernie: The cooperation in the Ski Valley is the fact that it's a village held together by a ski school program that encompasses virtually everybody who's up here. And the system makes it so attractive for people to come back, like the family-style eating where they meet new people from sophisticated groups that are not just crummy one-day, two-day skiers with lots of patches and pins on them. They are people who can do other things and talk about other things besides skiing.

We needed Learn to Ski Week. The mountain forced you into having people in ski school. It wasn't just that we wanted to make money out of it. We tell that to the local hotel people even now, that it's silly to have people not take ski school. Some of them are great skiers at home in Illinois or Wisconsin or Minneapolis or Boston, and when they come here, they are baffled by the tremendous mountain, and they would leave angry at us and not at themselves if we didn't force them to go into ski school. They learn so much because our ski school is built not as a business but as a service to the hotels and to the ski area to make people happy because they learn to handle our mountain. If they are good skiers, they learn entirely new things, thanks to Jean's ingenuity and always being two steps ahead of the PSIA (Professional Ski Instructors Association), which didn't exist back then. The ski school is the integral part of our ski area as it was in Aspen and Sun Valley with Friedl and Fred Iselin, and Alf in Alta, and the other great resorts. There is a friendship, a feeling of learning the mountain and being with other skiers; the camaraderie is the most important part.

Friedl Pfeifer: I was not interested in any big

Rudi Wyrsch with Kinderkafig, March 1976. PHOTO BY ERNIE BLAKE, COURTESY BLAKE FAMILY COLLECTION.

Theresa & Max Killinger. Courtesy The Killingers.

Max Killinger. Photo By Ken Gallard.

Theresa & Max Killinger. Courtesy The Killingers.

"That son-of-a-bitch announces to all the lodges and gets this tour up there, and then he just leaves everybody." People would follow Ernie anywhere; Ernie was like a pied piper. Many people followed him to Taos.

Theresa Killinger: The next year, we came back to stay, and I remember this was just one of Ernie's blows. We drove from Chicago and drove up the Ski Valley road in the late afternoon, and it had snowed and it was miserable. Halfway up, we meet Ernie coming down. He looks at us and he says, "What are you doing here?" We had just left our jobs and the apartment and had broken up our lives, and then he says, "What are you doing here?" I felt like crying!

Ernie was very hard with us. During that time I worked for the Edelweiss, but it was like, "What are you doing here? You don't belong here. You just happen to be along with Max." I couldn't even go on the lift; I would be shaking, and any second Ernie would be there, "Theresa!" I don't know what I always did; it was always something; either it was the lift ticket or it was the wrong time or something.

Max Killinger: That man gave me so much shit in the first two months when I was up here. I worked for my room and board. They had just put in that new sewer plant, and I was supposed to just check it out; it wasn't a big deal, okay? But he gave me so much shit that I went up to Mickey and said, "Listen, I cannot stand it anymore. I love it here, and I'm trying to do my best." But Ernie was just trying to test how far he could push me. After that, he never ever gave me any more shit because Mickey talked to him.

From that moment, he was very agreeable. I didn't go to Ernie; I went to Mickey because I had to do this sewer plant through Mickey. I had some really good jobs before I came to the Ski Valley, and I was always treated with respect. I wanted to be a ski instructor but not under those circumstances. It was just a game he played to find out how much he could push you. He did the same thing with our dog.

We brought our dog along when we first came to Taos. We stayed in that little chalet, the Chalet Alpina under the #1 lift, and the doghouse was right by the woodpile. It was our understanding that while the ski business was on, the dog was not supposed to hang around. We had him chained, but the moment the last people came down, I let the dog loose and he ran around. Almost invariably, every morning, Ernie said to me, "I'll have to shoot your dog because I saw him again last night shitting on my beginners' hill." That was one of his tortures he had for me. At that time, there was a restaurant next to the beginners' hill, and Ernie ate a lot over there, The Taos Ski and Cricket Club. One day, I came out of the St. Bernard going down to the Edelweiss, and I saw Ernie walking over there for dinner and my dog walking along with him and Ernie was petting him. Then when he came back out again, he brought out some scraps that he saved for my dog, so I knew bloody well that he wouldn't shoot him. Two years later, we wanted to go to Australia, and we said to Wendy that we would like to have somebody take care of our dog. Before we left, Ernie said, "You can leave your dog with me. I'll take care of it." The same dog that he wanted to shoot a year before.

Georgia Hotton: Ernie had his own style. He was crazy about animals and practical jokes said with a straight face; he made the most unbelievable believable. He always had some kind of strange animal around.

Ernie: We had this tame deer once that someone found, that thought I was its mother. It would nibble on me and follow me everywhere. It would make bleating sounds that sounded like a sheep and eat the papers that came out of the typewriter when I typed anything. It had a terrible stomach problem and couldn't keep any food down; Chilton, our resident rancher, knew the right mixture to get him on a proper diet.

The deer also went to the movies with us. I had the Porsche then, and it would stand on the rear seat which is very small and watch the movie intently, the outdoor movie. Once Mickey got out to get an ice cream cone, and the light went on, and you could see that the deer was standing looking over my shoulder looking at the movies.

Another time there was this famous British architect who taught at Georgetown University in Washington, D.C., having lunch with us in summer. There was a goat that Peter left that Jean Mayer adopted that used to relieve itself on the beds; it used to walk around on the balcony. The architect looked at it, he had a British accent and he sounded very affected as he said, "What is this?"

Peter Blake with pet deer "Chris," 1961.
Courtesy Blake Family Collection.

Peter Blake on Velvet. Courtesy Blake Family Collection.

I told him this was one of the chamois we imported from the original herd of chamois kept for Emperor Franz Josef of Austria near his castle in the Tyrol. He didn't say a word, he didn't excuse himself; he dropped his knife and fork and grabbed his camera. He ran out and took thirty-six shots of that damn old goat and showed it to his students a few weeks later as the descendant of the goat herd of Emperor Franz Josef.

Also, we had a Mexican raccoon-like animal, a coatimondi, named Little Joe; it was a small and very strange animal that was very attached to me. It would go everywhere with me. But, being that it's a tunnel-type of animal that lives in a hole, when it was time to

Godie Schuetz, veteran ski instructor.
COURTESY BLAKE FAMILY COLLECTION.

Henry Hornberger, Ski School Manager. PHOTO BY KEN GALLARD.

sleep, it would wind itself in the lining of my bed, and I was bare and froze to death while it was very comfortable. It was a strange animal.

Chilton Anderson: The ski school grew in the sixties and we got Max Killinger and Hardy Langer and so on. As long as Max has been here, he's a newcomer.

He's only been here twenty years now compared to my thirty-two and Jean's thirty-one, and Dadou's thirty and Godie's twenty-eight. But, nevertheless, it was that nucleus. And as we grew it became harder and harder to train 150 instructors the same as when it was small, but we continue to do well with it.

Somebody five or ten years ago said, "God, this is the oldest ski school that I've ever been to." That's true. You start out with Godie who is the oldest, I'm now the second oldest. Jean is no spring chicken and neither is Dadou. They are all in their fifties and older, and there's Max and Hardy and so on. Then you've got Keith, Rob, Derek and this new guy Stuart who's fifty. You've got Dr. Acos, Jim Burns, and the pilot Mack Brown. But this is old for ski instructors. When you've got a good percentage that are over forty, and we do, that makes a difference. When I'm in a hiring clinic, I ride the lift with everybody. And I ask the young guys, "What schooling have you had? College? How much? What did you take? What do you know? What are your interests? Any interest in art? In the Indians?" Not just that they are good skiers, but they've got to ride the lift for a week and talk to people and be able to talk about art, Indian culture; it's a whole experience, not just skiing.

Henry Hornberger: The ski school has to stay the strong point; that's the common thread for the lodges. That's what keeps the lodges tied into the Ski Valley. You don't have to buy a lift ticket: they're involved in the package deal. You're a special person when you take a ski week. You're in a class of six or seven people. You've got your own instructor for the week and you're off, hassle-free. That's why our ski week works. It works because it's there for the lodges and the convenience. We offer so many more services than any of the other areas and again, Ernie had forced these things on the lodges.

I had a guy call me the other day, a tour operator out of Toronto. He likes to bring groups to Taos. They come down here and ski their asses off, sit around and drink some cocktails, go to town and buy art and Indian things. What he was saying is that he's skied a lot and takes groups, and he likes to go to Europe because when he travels, he likes to go to areas where he feels like he's out of the Canada/United States culture; to be in a different country where people speak different languages, have different foods, experience new things. He can buy unique items. Taos fills all his needs right here in the United States. There's totally different architecture, different culture. He doesn't have the hassle to watch what he eats like in Mexico or a lot of places in Europe, or he doesn't have to pack toilet paper or learn to speak the language. And the weather is fantastic.

Elisabeth Brownell: The ski school created the

image of Taos Ski Valley—a world of its own. Now is the time where we really have to think to hold on to it. I don't know if Taos Ski Valley really understands that, if Mickey understands that. That is my big question. I think we all hope it will continue; it's what binds us and the skiers.

Herman Kretschmer: I personally thought Ernie was the world's worst ski instructor. Once I was out on the top of Powderhorn and Ernie came along with a class. Apparently there was a shortage of ski instructors at the time. These people were just so happy to have Ernie. There used to be a little knoll on top of Powderhorn; there was a ridge and then a fairly steep section that led off of it. He had them all standing on top of this hill, and he got down below and started talking. One of the things that he suggested was that they try and ski down to him. One guy started and bam, the next guy bam; I think there were ten people in that class and everyone of them crashed. It looked like his favorite expression: "Napoleon's retreat from Moscow." There were all these bodies on the snow, and he just scratched his head and couldn't quite figure out what happened except that none of them were able to do it. He finally got them down, and Ernie said, "Well, if nobody wants to go up, we'll just ski the beginners' hill. I like to give them a real experience." And so he did.

Max Killinger: Ernie used to take people down slopes that they had no business being on just to give them the experience and show them what skiing is all about. I think there were three instructors up there that sometimes came down with tears in their eyes; one was Ernie, one was Ed Pratt, and the other one was Franz Voller. Ed Pratt was great, as long as you realized that he was just hiding his clumsiness behind a golden heart. Sometimes he was grumpy to his students, and so was Chilton, and Ernie too in a way.

Franz Voller: One time, I had a student in my class, and she skied stiff; I mean stiff! I was standing up there on Powderhorn, and she came close by me and I said, "Bend your knee," and I whacked her with my ski pole. Three or four days later, Ernie and I met on top of the #2 chair, and Ernie turned to me and said, "Franz, please do not hit my guests."

Ed Pratt was a supervisor then, and he was out there teaching a lady how to do a snowplow. He said to keep the legs straight, and she kept closing her knees and just opening the lower legs. He got so frustrated that finally he yelled at her and said, "Goddamn it, open your legs. You're not going to lose the thing."

Fred Fair: I was back working for Ernie in the ski school on a part-time basis when I was fired for the second time. It was more like the second coming. It was a Saturday morning, and there was a good foot-and-a-half of fresh powder. Jean, Chilton, Dadou, Georgia, Ed were all there, and it was going to be one of those mornings. I'd try to get one of the other instructors to try and hold my group together, and I'd try and sneak another run on Al's; I'd already been warned about it, that you didn't do that. You should spend all your time with your class and behave in a responsible fashion. There I was sneaking on the lift and the chair had just left the platform. I was on the chair by myself, and I felt something like a heavy weight hanging from my skis. I looked down between my legs, and there looking up at me with this angry, contorted face was Ernie, hanging from my skis. About that time, somebody pushed the stop button and the lift stopped. We were high enough that Ernie was just dangling from my skis, and there were about thirty people hanging out watching because the ski school used to be right next to the lift. Ernie was hanging from my skis, and he hung there just long enough to realize it looked pretty ridiculous. He wasn't yelling at me or anything, and finally, he jumped off and then he stomped over to his office. I sat there feeling pretty foolish because people were still staring at me, and I'm thinking, he's going to come out of there with his rifle and blow me off the chair lift. He had the gun up there.

I decided to face him like a man on the ground, so I jumped off and shuffled over to the old office. I remember passing by all the people in ski school, everybody was still frozen and horrified. I walked up to the office door, and I was still in my skis, figuring if he came out with his gun, I'd try and stab him with my ski pole. He burst out of the door, and he had a check in his hand. He handed it to me; he managed to figure out what he owed me, he probably was going to fire me that day anyway, but he had it. He said, "From now on, you pay." He never said, "Get off my mountain," but from then on I had to pay.

Georgia Hotton: The best instructor at Taos was always the mountain itself. Taos is different because the whole area is different. The Indian culture, the Spanish culture, the Anglo culture and the interaction of these three cultures is important to the whole picture.

CHAPTER 13
Early Instructors' Exams and National Races

Ernie: Willy Schaeffler was the chief examiner when I took my instructor's exam which I never intended to take in the first place. I had to take it because Buzz Bainbridge was running the ski school in Santa Fe for me, but he wasn't willing to face the examiners in Colorado. So, I went up. I had no idea what it would entail, but I passed the exam. That was in May of 1951. Willy Schaeffler, George Engle of Winter Park, and Max Dercum were the examiners.

That first exam was very difficult to take. They insisted on us skiing through the forest through deep snow crust in May without stopping. That was Willy's idea. It was a question of stamina. I had bought new clothes, and I looked very elegant, and everything was in shreds when we finished. But it was fun. There was humor in it; there was not the beastly seriousness that we have now.

I first met Willy Schaeffler the day the war ended when I was the first American to go up the Zugspitze with a friend. We had arrived in Freising and went down to Garmisch in May of 1945 and took the train up to the Zugspitze. They asked us for tickets, and I told them in German that we were American and didn't need tickets. And I said it in a very Prussian military voice, and they snapped to attention. We rode up for nothing. That's why I watch my tickets; I know how it's done.

I met Willy while he was coaching a girl up on the top of the Zugspitze. He was bare-chested and yelling at this girl, Mary Fisher, who later became Mary Bogner. She was seventeen then, and she made out very well in the 1952 Olympics by winning both a silver and bronze medal. There was too much bitterness after the war to let the Germans compete in 1948. They let the Austrians compete, but not the Germans.

When Jean took the instructors' examination, he got into a terrible fight with Willy Schaeffler and Schaeffler beat him. Willy was the proponent of the Austrian school of Kruckenhauser. Jean told Willy that this locked position was nonsense. They wanted to flunk Jean; they didn't flunk him, but he didn't convince them. They didn't like his self-confidence, but he outskied all the other applicants except for Stein Eriksen. Willy Schaeffler and Stein Eriksen were the "godfathers" of the wedeln technique, and they didn't want any changes.

Mickey Blake: Willy's idea of an exam was not

Ernie on the Zugspitze. Courtesy Blake Family Collection.

Willy Schaeffler, Courtesy Colorado Ski Museum, Vail.

your teaching ability. My father was really into the teaching end of it. Willy was a year ahead of my father in terms of importance in the Ski Instructors' Association. He was kind of the ultimate he-man. Willy, at least according to the story he told us, served on the Russian front. He would tell us about packing newspaper and stuff into their boots to keep from getting frostbite. I saw him later, and it was in the last year of his life. He recognized me and couldn't have been more cordial; the one thing he had always insisted on was that we call him "coach," which I did automatically, and he appreciated that.

The Denver University Ski Team used to have to run around Washington Park in Denver, and he would hide in his car and watch us to make sure everybody was running. By the time we got back to DU, he would be there to criticize everybody's efforts. It reminded me of my father who used to climb up and check on the workmen, but his dogs always gave him away.

Max Dercum: Willy came to Arapahoe in 1948, and started working that summer clearing a little trail just above midway. It wasn't a major trail or anything. He had a horse, and he'd skid down these logs in what they called the Gluckenspeil Glades; he made quite a story about this. In 1948, Larry Jump offered Willy the ski school directorship at Arapahoe; he could own the ski school, and he also had this job as ski coach at DU. Willy and I were skiing on one early November day, and he asked me if I'd like to go and teach for him. As it turned out, he said he had to be at DU most of the time, and he couldn't be up at Arapahoe except on weekends. So, I was to take over and run this school for him in the middle of the week, which I did. I ran that ski school during the week and helped to supervise it on the weekends for twenty years. It turned into a hell of a good school.

We were training instructors at Arapahoe who eventually would go to Aspen, to Highlands, to Vail, to Copper Mountain. We had some of them that ended up down there in the Southwest. It was a well-known school, and of course we produced an awful lot of certified ski instructors because we had a lot of the exams here. At the same time, George Engle was doing very much the same thing over in the Winter Park area on that side of the mountain.

George Engle: Those first exams were something else. The first one we ran we organized in the spring of 1951. We had seventeen candidates, and we all stayed at Max Dercum's Ski Tip Ranch. The candidates were mixed in with the examiners, and we all ate together; we did it there for many years. After a while, it got so that there wasn't room for the candidates, just the examiners could stay at the lodge.

Max Dercum: We'd have fifteen or twenty of the examiners sit around there in this small room on their haunches on the floor and figure out who was passing

and who wasn't. Ernie was involved in that process many a time.

As ski instructors, Ernie and I also were involved early on in the certification program. I was certified in 1946 with the first group that ever was certified here in the Rocky Mountains. There were sixteen or eighteen of us at that time. Whenever we had a certification, Ernie would come up here because there wasn't anything going on down there in the Southwest at the time except for the T-bar at La Madera, in Albuquerque. That was when they had to drive around and come up from the east side through Denver. Ernie was a guest of ours on an annual basis.

Ernie: Everybody that was in the ski business came for that exam. That was the biggest exam the Rocky Mountain ski instructors had.

George Engle: We had trouble getting Aspen, Friedl and Fred into the association. Those guys had run ski schools longer than any one of us; they knew what it was all about, and they didn't need us. We needed them a lot worse than they needed us. And Willy would hear nothing; he wasn't about to do this, and quite a few of the others on the board at that time said, "We don't need Aspen; to heck with them." I finally talked to Friedl and to a few of the boys over there, and we agreed that we would go over there and run an examination in conjunction with them, with Friedl and Fred and their top boys.

We put together an examining board, and Friedl was with me when we ran that exam. We came to an understanding, and he liked the way I made turns and so forth and what I graded on, and Fred kind of went along with it too. Friedl decided that it was a good exam, and he could see where we were going. I tried to point out to him that if we all hung together, we had something really good going, and it could help the whole teaching industry. He finally went along and from then on they were part of the organization. That was a big opening right there; it made the difference.

Ernie: Another Swiss import that I met at one of the early certifications in Arapahoe was Godie Schuetz, he was great character. He now teaches for us in Taos and he owned the world famous Casa Cordova Restaurant that was very helpful to us in the beginning. Very elegant dining in a charming atmosphere.

I had met Godie at Arapahoe when I was running Santa Fe. We went there before and after the season because it had steep slopes. You got in shape and your timing got very good quickly because it was steep. We always stayed with Max Dercum at the Ski Tip Ranch, and that is where I first met Godie. It was a special friendship between those of us who were starting out in the ski business. I told Godie about the wonders of Taos, but he decided to outflank us and stake his fate on Red River. He followed Toni Woerndle to Red River.

The Dercums' Ski Tip Ranch, 1948. COURTESY MAX & EDNA DERCUM.

Participants at 1953 National Senior Championships at Arapahoe Basin, Colorado, including Ernie & Willy Schaeffler.
COURTESY MAX & EDNA DERCUM.

Godie Schuetz: I was in California at Sugar Bowl as sport's director before I came down to New Mexico in 1958. Ernie took me up in his Porsche, and the first man I met in Taos was Al Rosen. The first thing Al said was, "Ah, here's another crazy Swiss," or something, making sort of fun of the Swiss. Then Ernie and I drove up to the Ski Valley. Of course, it was the old dirt road. I was very impressed with the steepness of the mountain, Al's Run, Showdown, and was also impressed with the spartanic living conditions Ernie and Rhoda showed me. That was in the fall. Later on I said, "Okay, I'm coming out."

After a year in Red River with Toni Woerndle, I went to work with Ernie in 1961. There were just the five of us; Chilton, Georgia, Jean, Dadou, and me. Everything else is history; I've been here ever since.

Ernie was a big help to me at the Casa Cordova. He sent all the important people to eat there. Whenever there was a writer, and in these early days, they came all the time to this ski area to see this character Ernie, with all of his pros and cons, with his biting humor, Ernie would send them down to my restaurant for dinner.

Ernie: George Engle convinced the others that I should become the secretary of the examiner organization. We had many exams in Taos, and I was an examiner until 1970. In that year, Harry Franzgen was here for that exam. That was while he was still in Vail before he bought the Hondo Lodge.

Harry Franzgen: We came down here to do our certification. That's where I met Jean again, and Dadou was there. We sat here in the afternoon, and it started snowing and it piled up. Until then, we'd had nothing but school and demo and all this dry stuff. They said the next morning we had free skiing. Part of that at that time, you had to race a slalom. So, what did the Mayers do? They went up from the high traverse to Stauffenberg and set a slalom into West Basin, and that was our free skiing.

It was quite a group of big names who who were down here that year. Roger Staub was there, Art Furrer, Bill Duddy, Dick Peterson, Egon Zimmerman, Hermann Gollner who did the mobius flip, and Rudi Wyrsch who was a juggling clown. I used to come down to Taos because I thought that mountain was great compared to Vail.

Ernie: In 1958, we had the National Veterans' Grand Slalom here which was people over forty, and Rhoda won the ladies' division of that. She has a national medal. That was the only time she ever raced. We had the race course packed and set up on Longhorn, but we had an avalanche which wiped

Godie Schuetz. COURTESY BLAKE FAMILY COLLECTION.

Ernie & Godie Schuetz. COURTESY BLAKE FAMILY COLLECTION.

Godie Schuetz at the Casa Cordova Restaurant, March, 1975. COURTESY BLAKE FAMILY COLLECTION.

out the whole race course along with all the telephones Mickey had set up on the rescue sleds. We had two little cabins that served hot chocolate, and everything was wiped out by that avalanche. So we ran the race on Showdown and Snakedance, and Rhoda beat all the women by a fantastic distance.

Willy Schaeffler came here for those National Veterans' Races in 1958. The day before the race, or two days before when he arrived, he went up to the Poma lift which Lee Varoz, Sr. was running. Lee said, "Do you have a ticket, sir?" Willy looked him straight into his one eye with his two blue eyes and said, "No, I don't need a ticket. I'm a friend of Ernie's." And Lee looked at him and said, "Everybody is a friend of Ernie's. You still need a ticket." Willy was mad as hell. I told Willy, I said, "Willy, wouldn't you want your employees to be that way? That's the only way to be because how is he supposed to know you're a friend of mine?" Willy didn't see that at all.

Racing was important to me personally. I raced in all those Veterans' races in those days. I wanted relatively big races, because it wasn't such an expense as it is today. But we never had the ambition to attract the Olympics or anything like that or the World Cup today. Willy Schaeffler, being such a very close friend of mine, was interested in racing and producing young racers.

George Engle: It was one of those early certifications that Willy Schaeffler was going to go down to Taos and set the courses for one of our ski

Ernie at National Senior GS Championships, April 1955.
COURTESY BLAKE FAMILY COLLECTION.

Ernie at National Senior Championships, Arapahoe Basin, Colorado, April 1953. COURTESY BLAKE FAMILY COLLECTION.

Pete Seibert—National Veterans' Race. Rhoda in background, April 1958. COURTESY BLAKE FAMILY COLLECTION.

Rhoda Blake—National Veterans' Race, April 1958.
COURTESY BLAKE FAMILY COLLECTION.

instructors' exams. Then Willy had something else come up, and he couldn't make it in time to set the course. I didn't know this. I drove into the parking lot at Taos which was right at the foot of the mountain, just to the side of Ernie's house and shop.

Ernie came out to meet me. I said, "Ernie, is that where the downhill's going to be?" He shook his head, "Yes, that's it." I looked both directions, and I climbed in my car and turned on the key and was going to back out and he said, "No, no, you can't go." "Well, I'm sure not going to run a downhill on that thing." I really had him going. I looked at that hill and thought, "My God!" He said, "No you can't go. Willy can't make it so you have to set the courses. Choose the terrain and set the downhill."

Taos was amazing then with the steepness of that mountain. There was nothing there then. I told him somebody had to give me a tour of this area to let me make a choice. As it turned out, there wasn't much of a choice. The only place I could put the race was on Porcupine. You couldn't run it anyplace else. The thing that really got me was that after I had planned where the race course would go, Dadou and Jean insisted that it had to end up in front of their lodge. That forced me to take it down that cat walk; there was a bad turn there. I said, "No. There is no way that anybody can carry that kind of speed and make that turn." Guys were trying to carry too much speed into the turn, and we piled a lot of guys up in that thing. It worked all right, but it sure ran a lot of guys off the road.

Ernie loved to race; he was very competitive, and Willy was the same way and loved to compete. Ernie and Willy were great friends. They were both involved in the 1960 Olympics in Squaw Valley.

Ernie: I got the job of being chief starter for the 1960 Olympics from Willy Schaeffler. I told him that I wasn't interested. He told me, "Ernie, it's your duty as a new citizen, and you're the only son-of-a-bitch who can be mean in four languages."

Vera Bloch: When Ernest was a starter at the Olympics, he was on television; that was when they first had down jackets which were very puffy. We said, "There's Ernie, there's Ernie." My mother said, "That's not Ernie; he's too fat."

Ernie: I had terrible trouble with one Turk who didn't speak any language that I spoke. Usually, people spoke either French or German or Italian or English, one of the four. With him, nothing worked. When they said seven or whatever, he just took off and got disqualified. So for the giant slalom, I told him through an interpreter, "I'm going to have my hand on your shoulder; I'm going to grab you tightly. Don't go before I let you go." Well, I counted seven, six, five, four and wump, he took off with me on him; the two of us went down the course.

It was great fun actually. I had to go the year before where I made another faux pas. We had a party early

for the Olympic starters. There were so many officials, I told Willy their Olympic races were just in the way, that we actually should hold the Olympics just for the officials and forget about the bothersome races and competitors. That got me a lot of laughs. The U.S. Team had too many officials and too few racers and no discipline. Al Rosen was along as a doctor for the cross-country skiing. The Olympics should have never been involved in politics. Boycotting the Olympics is ridiculous because sports should never become involved.

Linda Meyers: I raced in the Squaw Valley Olympics in 1960. Ernie was the starter for the Women's Downhill. He was a real character. He was always very jovial, and he made everybody feel good at the start.

Friedl Pfeifer: We cannot compare racing today because America is the least advantaged ski-racing nation because it's so far away and so complicated to get somebody discovered. In Aspen, I'm trying to discover somebody and then go with them, you see, but it's so huge. The interest to have racers isn't there. We have some fabulous skiers, but they have to do it all on their own.

Linda Meyers: If our racers don't fit the mold that the United States Ski Team wants, it's going to be a tough go for them.

Dave McCoy: I had fourteen or so, plus or minus, on the U.S. Team at one time. I'd have gone to be coach of the U.S. Team, but I wasn't good with being out front with other people. Bob Beattie did such a good job of raising the funds and getting the kids out in front of all of the industries. That wasn't my way.

I don't think we put the proper faith in our athletes. I don't think we give them the time that it needs. We all know that skills come with repeated effort and knowledge of where they are going. We are inclined to always take the up-and-coming newcomer, and in that way, we restrict ourselves for the knowledgeable, and the mature athlete never happens in the United States.

Linda Meyers (Tikalsky) racing at Winter Park National Championships, 1964. COURTESY LINDA MEYERS.

Mammoth Mt. owner, Dave McCoy. PHOTO BY TOM JOHNSTON, COURTESY MAMMOTH MT.

McCoy Family. PHOTO BY TOM JOHNSON, COURTESY MAMMOTH MT.

We hurt them too young because we push them too hard. If we would protect the young and put them in the categories that they really want to be in and then train them in a broader field, we would have a much much better chance. But it wouldn't be instantaneous. The young that are coming up today are so pushed forward that they don't have an idol in front of them; somebody that they're shooting for.

Look at Corey and Alf Engen, they did such a great job for Idaho and Utah. There are a lot of good people out there that have done a lot of good things for kids, and they saw them just eaten up by the national program.

When you deal with kids, you ought to figure

you're dealing with a real intelligent group that only wants to be treated justly. If you can make things understandable, justify them, how they can progress, then they can really go. I don't manage; I coach. The kids taught me a lot.

Friedl Pfeifer: Racing has always been very important to the economy of skiing. When Henri Duvillard won the Olympics, it made a 28% difference in imports for France and the Austrians got really worried about it. So obviously, you made an effort to get champions. Look at Czechoslovakia and its tennis players. They discovered Ivan Lendl and they supported him all the way to the top. And skiing is the same way.

The Mahre brothers were naturals. They went out on their own. They had no training in any way but their own, but they got away with it because they won; that's what mattered. You can be an individual but you must win.

Dave McCoy: The Mahres were by far the best thing that happened for us, but they didn't seem to think that they had the right help from the team and the coaches. And, not trying to put anything down on the Mahres, but they were so busy always improving themselves that they didn't necessarily hand it down to others. I think if one of those boys was to go back and say, "I'm willing to coach," they could really handle it. They would see what they did and instill that into the nation. Nothing is any good if it isn't nationwide.

Jean-Claude Killy was another one that I got really close to because of what I did for the kids here. When we were training, he would sit and watch for hours. He really has great respect for Gary, my son. Gary is a super, super skier, even today. He won all those races, but he wouldn't go on the team because of the politics. Gary just wouldn't participate under the leadership that was provided then, and my daughter Candy wouldn't either, and Candy is as good a girl skier as I've ever seen in my life. When Gary said he wouldn't go, Penny and Pancho were just kids playing out here in the snow, and they came to me and said, "Dad, we'll race in the Olympics; we'll do it." And they both did it. But I was never disappointed in Gary, no not at all. I respect everybody's personal approach to their own life.

Alf Engen: In racing everyone had their tricks. Mathias Zdarsky skied before the First World War against the Danish in the late 1800s. They did stem turns and snowplows, and they had real long poles. But, as I say, take nothing away from Zdarsky, take nothing away from Schneider; they all made an improvement. I can remember so many of them— Emile Allais, Schneider, Eriksen, Killy. They all had a trick. They skied at the top of their heads, and they were never afraid of falling. You can't be afraid of

Dadou & Jean Mayer racing. Photo By Ken Gallard.

falling. Then the others would learn that trick and then have to come up with one of their own. That's how they learned.

Friedl Pfeifer: I was seven years on what they called the "A" team, the national team in Austria. I only remember vaguely, twice, that I went to the early fall practice. I did it on my own. That's the basic way. You make it on your own; they can't drum it into you. Up to a point you can get help, but it has to be a natural thing.

Even competitive skiing has taken the romance out of it. In 1927 or 1928, skiing was only a few years old; we had many more people watching competitive skiing than they do now. Nobody is interested because there is no excitement anymore. It's all a crazy mess. The modern slalom is disgusting. It was to show the public what skiers could do, and now it's nothing but trying to keep up with the world. Amateur racing is ridiculous and always was. Amateur racing was created by the English because that's the way you sorted out the rich and the poor. It's totally ridiculous, particularly in this day and age when a football player is a millionaire the day he signs a contract. In skiing, we go around with a hat and collect the money so we can send the boy to the Olympics in this country.

I started the first pro tour; I'm going to start another. I'm not going to do it amateur but professionally. It's going to be invitational, senior skiing with skiing and slalom. I quit racing. You can't teach and race. You can't do both, and I was running a ski school.

Alf Engen: In Norway, there were two brothers that I particularly fought all my life in ski jumping who were some of the best and were in the Olympics. I should have been in them, but I got branded as a professional so I couldn't go to Garmisch for the 1936 Olympics. I got on the *Wheaties* ad. I had been reinstated as an amateur but somehow, for some reason, there was a *Wheaties* ad

Jean Mayer running gates. Photo By Ken Gallard.

Dadou Mayer pro-racing. Photo By Ken Gallard.

133

still lingering in there, so they turned me pro while I was on the boat. In 1936, I was national champion here in both ski jumping and cross-country. Ernie couldn't go to the 1936 Olympics either, for different reasons. He would have gone for ice hockey. So, I didn't make the Olympics in 1936. Birger Ruud won it. I would have out-jumped him by quite a bit. I could have won the gold medal, but still, as it is, I probably have more trophies than anyone in the world.

In my lifetime, I can only remember four times I didn't get a prize; I fell. Only four times. I was the strongest athlete. When I went into competition, I didn't think there was anybody there that was going to beat me. They might beat me once, but not the next time because by then I had that learned. Whoever was the best, I'd hunt them up because that's how I learned.

I even tied for the Harriman Cup. In 1947, I coached the Sun Valley Racing team which became the Olympic team in 1948. My captain was Barney McLean. There was one day we skied for the Sun Valley diamond. I told Barney that I thought it was a fast enough day, and we could make the diamond. You couldn't make the diamond if it was a slow day. So, we went for it, and one day we both won the diamond. Barney ran it in 2:48 flat, and I ran it in 2:48 and 1/8th, so you see how close we were.

Ernie: I set a new record in the Golden Sun Race in Sun Valley back in 1941. I was racing for the Swiss Ski Club of New York. I remember the time was under two minutes. I think my time was about 1:57.

Alf Engen: The U.S. Olympic team doesn't believe in themselves. When you are in competition you have to have that; now I have had two careers. I had the racing/ski jumping career, and I was really tough because I believed in myself and I did my homework. But I had no room for any people; I couldn't let my personality flow. But now that I'm a teacher, I tell my students to let it flow.

Godie Schuetz: I won the National Individual Championship for the Grand Marnier Chef's Race three years ago at Taos. People ask me how I do it; you have to pace yourself, and you have to do things in moderation. You don't get into lethargy; you don't just sit still. I'm willing to learn even today. I don't say "I've been doing it this way all along." Even today, some of the basic skiing hasn't changed, let's face it. You still have to put on two skis. We are better skiers today because physically, people are in better shape; to say nothing of the new equipment. You stand on skis, you do something, and they turn. They didn't used to do that years ago. You had to do something extreme with your body. Not today, now you just go for a ride. You still have two poles, you have to bend your ankles and knees some, and balance, a little courage.

Ernie's original Instructor's Certification Pin, #5.
PHOTO BY KEN GALLARD.

CHAPTER 14
The Chicago Connection

Ernie: In the beginning, even though it was a tremendous struggle, we weren't really looking actively for financial help. The only financial parties that came in early were Chilton Anderson's mother (for $5,000) and Dr. Ash Pond, on Al Rosen's suggestion. Five thousand dollars was a lot of money; now it sounds like nothing. In return, they got paid a dividend. I think $168.00 was what each got out of it.

Some of our best support and business came from the Chicago area. It was the summer of 1958 when I met Steve Mitchell. He was a big shot in the Democratic party and had been the Democratic national chairman during the first of the Stevenson campaigns. He was the father of Tony Mitchell who has been with us for most of the years.

Steve Mitchell asked me if we did any business in Chicago, and I said we hadn't yet. He asked me if I'd be willing to go to Chicago and speak to a meeting he would call of all the newspaper, railroad and the airline people. I said I would be delighted to. So, he arranged that, and we also rented space at the first ski show in Chicago given by Harry Leonard, a charming organizer. We stayed in the Hotel Maryland, a dreadful hotel.

I gave that show of slides and movies at the Chicago Athletic Club in a very elegant place at a luncheon party Steve Mitchell organized for me. He was very worried I wouldn't know what to say, but I knew what to say.

As a result of that Chicago meeting, and the relationship with Steve Mitchell, we ended up with a tie-up with the Santa Fe Railroad which gave us weekly business automatically. By the time Jean got rolling, which was the second winter he was here, better than 40% of our guests were here on a weekly basis from Chicago by railroad.

In a year, we became civilized under the guidance of the Santa Fe Railroad people who helped us tremendously. They taught us how to package, and we had folders for package deals earlier than anybody in this vicinity or in Colorado. We were far ahead of anybody in the business end. The Santa Fe Railroad had a man by the name of Amos Stromm who was the motor behind that. They had these tall, white-powdered-faced old ladies selling skiing, but we had them coached so that they could talk convincingly. They sold a lot of ski packages; all of it was Learn To Ski Better Week at rural prices. The dormitory in the Hondo cost you less than $100 for a week of skiing,

twenty-one meals, seven ski lessons, seven days of lift use, and roundtrip transportation from Raton.

A whole bunch of Chicago clubs, including one black club, came to ski in Taos and loved the hostels. That group came for many years regularly, once or twice every winter. Then businessmen started coming, and that carries over to today except that at that time, it was half our total business. Over 43% was from Chicago and suburbs, as opposed to only about 7% now.

Tony Mitchell: My father was very taken with Ernie and thought he was a farsighted and courageous person to undertake this idea of a ski area and he thought it was something that I would be interested in. In the fall of 1958, Ernie came to Chicago and did a couple of promotions. My father had good contacts

Ernie Blake at Chicago ski show.
<small>COURTESY BLAKE FAMILY COLLECTION.</small>

with the news media in Chicago, largely with the *Tribune*. Ernie came and did his wonderful show with his movies.

My father was the prime mover in helping arrange the shows and some publicity. It started to go reasonably well, and Ernie said that maybe I could help him with some shows, or some contacts; Harry Leonard was one of the guys. In those days, things went as slowly as molasses in January, and I could go in and light fires and try and move things ahead. But going into the Santa Fe Railroad offices in the fifties was like going into most other offices in the forties.

My father, in a number of areas, had a very good eye for people. Ernie was thoroughly charming. He was a handsome and energetic man. I think probably an awful lot of Americans are suckers for accents which suggest romance and danger. This was a man who was going to make some things happen. My father had a house in Ranchos de Taos, so we knew Twining before we knew Ernie; we fished there but really hadn't thought about the skiing. Ernie was a thoroughly engaging conversationalist and raconteur. He was also very intelligent. These were important attributes for a place that we were a part of.

After the beginning of the 1960s, you were supposed to make money with real estate plays in the ski business, not by running a ski area. I don't think people had any idea what the Blakes, and I broaden this because it involves the whole family, have done in terms of plugging every penny back into the Ski Valley.

Ernie: The Santa Fe Railroad was our lifesaver. From Chicago, there was this wonderful sleeper train that left at 6:30 Friday night, got you to Raton, New Mexico at 11:00 the next morning; it was excellent and the food was very good. It was a delightful experience. At Raton, the two Indians, Paul and Louie Bernal, picked you up and then later, John Lackey became a very reliable supplier of transportation.

Herman Kretschmer: When you rode the old Santa Fe out from Chicago to Raton, it was a fantastic experience. We got off the train and Paul Bernal met us. From the very moment that we got off of that train, both Jeannie and I were absolutely fascinated with the country; unbelievable palisades. First the prairie and then palisades, then the mountains; it was a spectacular drive. It was incredible. We went through Cimarron and past the area around Eagle Nest down through the Moreno Valley over Palo Flechado Pass and down into Taos Canyon, and then it opens up into the Taos Valley and up again to Twining; there aren't many trips as exceptional as that. The Taos valley and that whole area is one of those special places in the world.

Louie Bernal: That's when I met "The Man." That's when I met Ernie. From then on I began helping him. There weren't too many buildings here at

that time. I was working for the government. When I retired from the government, just fifteen years ago, I came up to see him, and he remembered who I am, and he told me about this job here. He said, "Louie, any time when you want to come to work here, just come and see me." So I came up, and he put me to work here in the parking lot, and I'm still here.

One time, Ernie had somebody from over there in Germany taking photographs and pictures of Ernie and me in here, showing the people which way to go with him standing there and talking to me. That was a great thing what happened to me. Later on I heard that a guy used to work up here who used to be a ski instructor, and he went over there in Switzerland. Then he came back and he told me, "Louie Bernal, I know this guy, and you are a movie star like over there with you and Ernie in those pictures." All the people want to know who that Indian guy was who worked at Taos Ski Valley. Then later on, other people came by, and they wanted to take pictures in the village and talk to me about the Indian village down there at the Pueblo. And, of course, I told everything.

Herman Kretschmer: Two things started the ski thing in Chicago, which was a big ski town as Ernie later discovered. The beginning of the ski season was led off by two events. One was Warren Miller's annual trip to town to show his movie of that year, and the other was the Harry Leonard Ski Show. Everybody who skied any place at that time went to the Harry Leonard Ski Show.

Ernie: In 1960 I met Herman Kretschmer at the Chicago ski show. I had Dadou with me. It was just after the election of John Kennedy for president. We went to Chicago, and we met Tomayoshi Fusho in Chicago, who had written us fabulous letters of application for the employment as a ski patrolman, affecting this perfect typing, and when I met him in Chicago, he didn't speak a word of English. He could say, "Mommy," and you didn't know what he meant.

Louie Bernal & Ernie. Courtesy Blake Family Collection.

Taos Pueblo pow-wow dancer. PHOTO BY KEN GALLARD.

Tomayoshi was our first paid patrolman and shoveler of bumps.

Herman Kretschmer: Ernie and I met at the Chicago ski show, in the fall of 1960, and that was a day that changed my life. I was on top of a primitive ski deck that Stein Eriksen was later to appear on. It was one of these things with carpet, and then we put dance floor wax on top of the carpet, and these people did their thing on it. We were tacking down the carpet, and all of a sudden, Harry Leonard said, "Oh my God, there's Ernie." We looked down, and there was this fellow who was just red as hell; I later discovered that he probably doctored his complexion a little bit at that time, because one of the things he always did before he went to Chicago was to make sure he had that good outdoor look. There was Ernie wearing a gray Persian lamb hat, the kind of thing the ski patrol wore, with two guys behind him. One was Dadou who at that time spoke with a very strong accent, and the other was a Japanese guy who's name was Tomayoshi. Everybody sort of stood up and took notice; I'd never heard of Ernie Blake before.

We spent the whole ski show working, either taking tickets or doing something, and I got to know Ernie pretty well. Jeannie and I had breakfast with him one morning, and we were so enchanted with Ernie and the idea of Taos; I didn't care what it was. At the time, I barely knew where New Mexico was. I knew it was in the United States, and that's about it.

It was at that first ski show in Chicago that we picked up a couple of other characters that showed up at Taos Ski Valley and are still there. One of them was Steve White, who Ernie hired, without asking Jean. He decided Jean could use a fellow who played the guitar. Ernie also decided he needed a secretary, and Elisabeth Schlegl showed up. He hired her right on the spot. These people have been there ever since. Elisabeth is now a hotel tycoon in Taos Ski Valley and married to "Cecil B." Brownell.

Elisabeth Brownell: I met Ernie in Chicago at the ski fair. It must have been September, at the old Morgan Hotel. My first contact was Herman Kretschmer who told me Ernie needed a secretary; he didn't have anybody. So, I came back in the afternoon, I met Ernie and he promised me the sky. He said, "You can type and you speak two languages," (I speak three) "and you take shorthand?" I said "Yes." "And you know how to ski?" I said, "Yes," but I'd never taught before. He said, "If you can ski, you know more than most people, and besides, don't lose your accent." Which since that day I haven't.

When Ernie hired me, he had written me a letter confirming because I said, "I can't believe all the things you are saying, that all this should be true." He said, "We have beautiful sunshine, deep powder," and "You can buy Head skis for $45." I'll never forget that because I didn't have any money to buy good skis. I

had some hickory skis which were fairly good at that time and had the cable bindings I started out with. Then he said, "We can't pay you much, but we have excellent food." I said, "How much can you pay?" "One hundred twenty-five per month, but you have room and board free." So, he confirmed all that in writing by return mail. It was almost immediate.

Ernie picked me up at the bus station in Albuquerque. It was in the evening, and he had a gun in the back of the car, and in the middle of the canyon, he stopped because he saw an animal. He stopped the car, and got his gun; like the Wild West I thought I was coming to with that dirt road and gun. He just stopped and got out with the gun and looked around. He didn't see it anymore.

When I arrived on the mountain the first morning, I was looking for Ernie and somebody said he was on Snakedance. So I came down Snakedance, and he looked at me and said, "Aren't you afraid?" I said, "Of what?" He always introduced me as a German immigrant. And at other times, he said, "Well, I taught her German."

I was born and grew up in Munich and I thought before I'd settle down, I'd like to see the United States. I decided on the German consulate in Chicago and worked there a year-and-a-half, and then I thought if I went back to Germany, I want to work in a ski area.

I had skied in Europe, mostly hiking because I didn't have the money to pay for a lift ticket. So, we hiked; I belonged to an alpine club. I shared so much in common with Ernie because he also hiked in the mountains with skins. That was the atmosphere which Jean started here at Taos Ski Valley. That's how it was in Europe. We put that together here and up to this day, we still have it. That's what our real atmosphere is and what the people appreciate.

Herman Kretschmer: During that ski show we got to know Ernie and talk to him and were fascinated by this guy and the stories he told. We were all staying at the Knickerbocker Hotel in Chicago that time. He cast his spell on everyone. Ernie was a little bit like the pied piper. He certainly was the pied piper in Taos because I wasn't the first guy who followed him. Ernie had a way of attracting people to his kingdom. Jeannie and I both decided that we were going to go skiing in Taos; to hell with the rest of the club.

Our ski club had originally planned on going to Europe. The travel agent didn't respond the way he should, so we said, let's try this Taos place. Getting reservations in Taos in those days was almost impossible. There was no telephone up there; Chilton Anderson had the phone at that time. I tried to do it through a travel agent, and the travel agent said, no, they're all booked up. I wanted to go very badly, so I called out there, and I got Chilton. He

Taos Pueblo in winter. Courtesy Blake Family Collection.

said if I didn't have to come on a weekend, they could take us on a Monday.

When we arrived the magic started all over again. Ernie created snow for us with an unbelievable snowstorm the next day; it was just great and the first time I'd ever skied in powder snow. I had a chance to get downtown and see a little of the town and got to see Ernie again and was fascinated by this guy. We decided we were going to move out to Taos if we possibly could. By the time we got home, almost before I had a chance to check in to see if the kids were okay, I went to the real estate office and put the house up for sale. That June, which would have been the summer of 1961, we arrived in Taos, and I hadn't the slightest idea what I was going to do.

Max Killinger: Ernie had a tremendously powerful personality, and he was a very well educated man. In a way, he was a gentleman from the old school, the epitome of a gentleman. Since he had this powerful personality, it was almost like he could get a lot of good people, like Herman, to congregate around him. He was always able to get top-notch people for a song because they felt he had something going that was almost worth the cost of being there. And you never felt you did it for him. It was always a feeling that you

did it for a cause, for the cause of the Ski Valley, which in the beginning definitely was him.

Herman Kretschmer: Ernie had said, "Come on out," and he would say this to almost anybody. "Come out, we'll find something for you to do." So, I ended up becoming a transportation service from Albuquerque to Taos Ski Valley. I made three round trips one day at $15 per round trip, and I thought, life is too short for this.

I also took over the telephone from Chilton. Ernie figured he'd had it for two or three years. So, the first year I was out there, I took over the reservation thing, and that's how I ultimately got into reservations and marketing at Taos Ski Valley. Ernie decided that I probably had some friends in Chicago, and he hated to travel. He hated to be away from Taos Ski Valley. I started making trips first to the Chicago Ski Show with him. Ernie was the greatest marketing genius that ever hit the ski business. Bob Parker in Vail has the reputation of being the marketing genius in the ski business, but actually it was Ernie.

Ernie made people feel special, even if it was for only that one meeting when they happened to arrive, or when their children were introduced to him or whatever; and that was a great gift. It was the same gift, in my opinion, that helped him get the publicity that attracted people.

Ernie and I had taken the train to Chicago to work the ski show. That was the first year I was working for Ernie and I realized I was involved with a real character. We entered the Morrison Hotel and we were sitting in a bar area while we were waiting for Harry Leonard. We noticed a guy who had been sitting there for a while. Ernie was wearing that Persian lamb hat and obviously spoke with an accent, which I am convinced he cultivated because the longer I knew him, it never got any better.

Ernie: For the ski show in Chicago, I wore a German army fur coat and a fur felt hat of baby lambskin, a Russian-type hat, with a big Taos pin that Al Rosen always wanted with a skiing Indian on it. The man at the bar pointed at me and said, very unsteadily, some remark to Herman.

Herman Kretschmer: This guy was about half-crocked. I remember Ernie's eyes and how stern he could look. This guy whispered to me, "Is your friend from Russia?" And Ernie turned around and looked at this guy and fixed him with these blue eyes of his and said, "I am the consul general of the Soviet Union in Chicago, and I believe what you said was disparaging, and you have insulted me. This is the type of thing that could create a major incident." That guy was so scared, he got up and took off. He was afraid somebody was going to ask his address. Ernie was absolutely flabbergasted. He didn't realize he could be so effective. I said, "You should have been an actor." That was the first adventure we had, and there were many of them, and a lot of them involved ski shows.

Monica Brown: Herman, myself and Ernie were creating a new brochure for Taos Ski Valley, and Ernie said, "What can we do to enhance Taos Ski Valley and put it in our little brochure? What do we offer people? And in the summer? Let's start a tour guide down to the Rio Grande. And Herman, why don't you become the tour guide?" Herman Kretschmer, the famous historian—and then it starts. There was a U-boat commander, and he was very famous; he sank a lot of boats, and he would always come to our little valley, "Okay," Ernie said. "U-boat Commander Kretschmer, that's not enough. Let's make Herman a baron, not a baron but a Baron von Kretschmer," Ernie said. I explained to Ernie it's either a baron or a von Kretschmer, both don't exist, but he put it in the brochure anyway.

So, when he went to Europe, all his classmates asked him, "Ernie, what are you doing these days?" He just handed them this brochure, and they looked at one another and said, "Wait a minute. Something isn't right." And then Wendy said, "But Daddy, you made him a baron." Those people were not ready to listen to a word he was saying anymore. That was when he

Herman Kretschmer & Ernie. Courtesy Jeanie Kretschmer.

went to Germany. So much for Herman, the baron.

Herman Kretschmer: We were a great team for quite a while, for about ten years. Our final breakup came from the sum of his tyrannical things. The last year, I had some problems with him. I don't even think of the problems, because if it's possible for one man to love another without any sexual connotation at all, I loved Ernie. I make no bones about it. Other than a couple members of my family, there's nobody in the world that I loved more.

Ernie: Chicago was a great social event. All the high society came, and you met some very amusing people. It's not that way anymore at all. It's a miserable deal now. Alan Crane was one of those that helped a great deal in the beginning and has been a friend throughout.

Alan Crane: A lot of people have brains, and a lot of people have guts but lack the energy to make it all happen. Ernie made it happen even against God knows what. There's nothing between zero and a hundred with that man. He either admired you or loved you, or you were of no use to him at all.

Whenever Ernie had a problem, he went to all of his friends to write their congressmen: we need a road, we need electricity, we need phone lines, and if on the company stationery enough senators and congressmen

The Streaker. COURTESY TOM BROWNELL.

Ernie & Alan Crane. COURTESY ALAN CRANE.

Alan Crane. COURTESY ALAN CRANE.

got letters saying that you'd love to come to Taos but you can't because there's no way you can be out of touch with your office or things like that, then we might get those things.

It was in the early sixties, or whenever "streaking" was in, and Ernie and I were riding up the lift together in Kachina, and down underneath the lift, right at the top in the basin comes a naked girl with a figure—shit—and two naked guys following her, and skiing behind them is a third guy carrying their clothes; you know, they had these snap-off shirts with pants, and he's carrying all the clothes. Here they come right down the face of the mountain. Ernie got on his radio and said that there were two guys and a girl streaking down Kachina Basin, and he is angry that someone would defile his mountain. He says, "You catch those two guys and throw them the hell off this mountain, and give that girl a season pass."

Another time we were out here one spring and our group had the whole Alpenhof at the St. Bernard. We had every room in the place, and we had a couple of rooms in the A-frames besides. We brought with us tons of booze and salami and cheeses and things for the afternoon. We'd sit on the steps of the Alpenhof and carve up the salami and the cheeses, and all the help knew that we were there, and they'd come over and we had wine and whiskey and beer. One day this was a happening, one of those things when half the valley's help was over there. We got them all drunk and word got around to Ernie that we were having a big party and getting his help drunk. Ernie came storming over screaming, "Here we are, my best friends in the whole valley getting all my goddamn help drunk." Okay, we quit that.

The next night, my daughter Jennifer and Steve Crown were sitting in the john of one of the A-frames and the rest of the kids, by this time, they're older like sixteen, eighteen, nineteen years old, rolling joints and half the adults and most of the kids are sitting in there and smoking and laughing and Ernie hears about this. He comes over there, and Bob Haas puts his arm around Ernie and says, "Goddamn it, Ernie, quit your screaming and yelling and smoke one." Ernie wouldn't do that, but it broke him up.

Bob Haas was in the advertising business and did all the brochures for Ernie in the beginning and didn't charge Ernie anything except for the actual printing costs. Bob was the exact opposite of Ernie. Both were exceedingly bright, but where Ernie was proper, Bob was a wild ass. You maybe would not think that they'd get along, but they loved each other.

Bud Crary: That Alan Crane, he was a dandy guy. He was the only one Ernie would let come back in the ski shop. He'd bring his kids and their friends down for two weeks and buy them skis, boots and poles and charge them. One time, he owed $8,000 for skis and

Vee Troy & Joe LeBlanc, backgound, & Laura & Mike Kaplan at the St. Bernard chalets. PHOTO BY KEN GALLARD.

stuff for a bunch of kids. The Crane Carton Company; he owned it, and it made money. If he was up on the mountain, he'd come and check in the ski shop sometimes, and if we were behind, he'd come in there and help out until we got caught up. Ernie would see him back there working and he'd say, "Why aren't you up there skiing?" "I've got to help these boys out; they're behind." Alan would also help Rhoda in the ski shop when they needed help.

Alan Crane: I used to love to work in the ski shop with those guys back in the early days when they didn't have enough money to hire people. I used to go down there every night to that ski shop and mount bindings. It was wonderful. That was a major part of my life there.

When we first came to the St. Bernard, there were no keys to the rooms. I used to come at Christmastime with the family. We knew we were coming back for Washington or Lincoln's birthday, and we'd take our skis, stick them in the snow out there, and they'd be standing there when we got back two months later. In what other place in the world could you do that? I used to tend bar for Jean at night so he could go a little early. I'd ask, "What do you want me to do with the money?" He'd say, "Put it in the cash register and close the door." Anybody could come, open the thing and take out a thousand dollars. In those days, that was a big pot of money. It was still there the next morning.

SECTION V
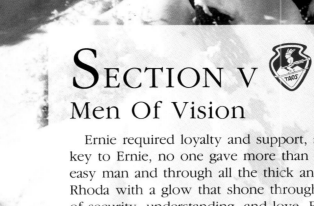
Men Of Vision

Ernie required loyalty and support, and of those that were key to Ernie, no one gave more than Rhoda. Ernie was not an easy man and through all the thick and thin, there was always Rhoda with a glow that shone through and gave Ernie a sense of security, understanding, and love. Ernie and Rhoda were a great team. It took both of them, and after a few years they were beginning to see that their idea of a destination resort was now a possibility. The volunteer ski patrol was becoming more professional, and avalanche control was becoming an important ingredient in maintaining the safety of the mountain. And Georgia Hotton came as Ernie's children's tutor, soon rising to become assistant manager of everything. She was tough as nails, very able, and would have made a great dictator, but there is never room for two.

Men who have vision are wonderfully different. They come from all kinds of different backgrounds, like school dropout Dave McCoy of Mammoth and Ernie of Taos with his privileged private Swiss schooling. Dave McCoy was the only other person to start, build, and still own a major ski area, and he began with even less than Ernie. They stayed in touch over the years and traded ideas. Their approach to the mountain and the skier was about the same, yet no two people were more different than Ernie and Dave McCoy. And you can be sure that Gary McCoy never "punched out" Dave as Mickey Blake did Ernie.

As skiing grew as a sport, the competition for skiers became more intense. Where Ernie had been concentrating on the Chicago market, he soon saw a need to get back into the Texas area which he had cultivated in his early years in Santa Fe. Ernie and Buzz Bainbridge of Santa Fe were both tremendous public relations people who worked together and against each other to promote their separate areas to the Texans. Ernie was the acknowledged genius of public relations, and one of his public relations coups was his famous martini trees.

No matter how much of a challenge and how much fun the old Poma was, it was becoming very dangerous, so out of necessity, the first chair lift was installed in 1960. This was about the same time that Ed Pratt was being wooed by Ernie to buy the Hondo Lodge. As unlikely as it was, "Big Daddy" Pratt and his wife Phyllis both quit the army and came to Taos Ski Valley to "retire" as hotel owners. Ernie made Ed and Jean Mayer custodians of the old generator. Neither one was mechanical and the lights were always going on and off, but in typical Taos make-do fashion they convinced the guests that candlelight was more romantic anyway.

CHAPTER 15
Loyal Supporters Shape the Ski Valley

Ernie: Rhoda and I, we were co-conspirators. Taos Ski Valley succeeded because she was with me. Rhoda was very enthusiastic. She thought this idea of a ski area was a good one, this crazy idea which couldn't make money. There were only three areas that did better than break even in those days. They were Aspen, Berthoud Pass, and Stowe. So, there wasn't a chance to make money here that we could see for a long, long time to come, if ever. We didn't have a large fortune.

Pete Totemoff: If Ernie hadn't had Rhoda, I don't think he would have made a success of it. To me, she was always the power behind the throne. If Ernie made a decision, he sort of looked at her to see whether she'd nod or shake her head. She never said anything, but it was very obvious to me that he couldn't do a whole hell of a lot without her approval. Ernie was lucky to marry a strong woman. I don't think he had half her strength. She was tough, smart, and she knew where she was going; she knew what she wanted. Rhoda made it go, as far as I'm concerned. If I saw something in the area that wasn't right, I'd make a suggestion to Ernie or Mickey, and they would do nothing. I'd make a suggestion to Rhoda, and it got done. She trusted me on a lot of that stuff. She never questioned the fact that I was bullshitting. I wouldn't say anything unless I knew it was either hazardous or should be done.

Georgia Hotton: It was early on, perhaps the second or third year of Taos Ski Valley's operation when Ernie gave me one of the nicest compliments that I've ever had as an employee on any job. Ernie said, "If it hadn't been for you and Rhoda, I would have given up." So, he was willing to give us the credit that I guess we deserved, especially Rhoda. I very strongly believe that without Rhoda's contributions, Taos Ski Valley never would have made it.

Walter Widmer: Ernie and Rhoda were a very good combination. When dividing up the chores in the early days, Ernie claimed he didn't know how to use a hammer. Anything that had to be fixed, painted or put together, it was Rhoda. On the other hand, Rhoda never wrote a letter. After Ernie's death, she got so many letters, and she answered every one of them. She would get up at four o'clock in the morning and write practically all day. That was something incredible because Rhoda never wrote. It was always Ernie's thing. Ernie would write and handle the finances and things like that. Anything manual, Rhoda did it. I'm sure Ernie

could have done it, but he just established early on that it would be very dangerous for him to pick up a hammer.

Mama Mayer: Rhoda put up with a lot. Rhoda accepted everything. She wanted him to be there, near her. If Ernie had gone away, she would have been lost completely. She was looking for Ernie like you would look for a glass of wine or something exciting. I don't know if she had everything she wanted, but she did everything to be sure that he would not go anywhere. She was a wife extraordinary. She knew what he liked. She is very strong. If it had not been for that love of Ernie, she could have done something other very well. She was brilliant and elegant. Rhoda was loved like a woman wants love. Ernie was in bed with her in the night.

Monica Brown: Rhoda was Ernie's strength, absolutely. She backed him in everything, and she was not in any way domineering. She was there for him and the valley. She was never a nagging woman and never a problem for him. I don't know how much Ernie needed a woman, but he certainly needed

Rhoda Blake. COURTESY BLAKE FAMILY COLLECTION

Ernie & Rhoda. PHOTO BY WOLFGANG LERT, COURTESY BLAKE FAMILY COLLECTION.

Ernie & Rhoda in their apartment. PHOTO BY KEN GALLARD.

someone at home. I think in seeing him later and looking back, Ernie needed the family, and Rhoda took care of the family.

Rhoda's pride was the sport shop, and when the shop got enlarged, we would make do with boards and put a few nicks in there to make them look like old boards. Ernie didn't have much sense for that. He only cared it went up and fast, and then we would be there and doing certain things, and he would say, "Is it not getting ready? How long is it going to take?" We would say, "We are Taos artists, don't rush us." It was all done by hand. We were carpenters, we were salespeople, we were ski instructors, we were nurses, we listened to the pain and problems of the people. We were everything to everyone. But everybody was everything to everyone, and that was the wonderful feeling.

Tony Mitchell: Rhoda was very quiet, but she was always there. I don't think for a minute that Ernie didn't always ask for and count her vote.

Alan Crane: Rhoda is a very strong lady, very strong, and dedicated. Totally dedicated and emotionally tied to a project such as building Taos. Ernie looked at this mountain as his mountain. His pride, which was immense, was in this mountain. Luckily Rhoda was strong because after all, Ernie was

the Blake publicity man and Ernie was the mountain, and all the articles—Ernie, Ernie, Ernie—you know how hard that has to be on a woman if she herself doesn't have great dignity and a great sense of self-worth? Rhoda had that self-worth; she was magnificent.

Rhoda played a major role in shoring up Ernie when he got the blues. We all get our fears that maybe we're not going to make it. The cash flow was practically non-existent, and how do you keep hacking and building with limited funds and limited access to major money? Ernie didn't have a wealth of friends who could say, "Here's a hundred thousand; when you make it, give it back to me." So, under those conditions, it was tough. Back in the early days, Rhoda was always there, always at his side.

Bob Brierley: I have to take my hat off to Rhoda, because Ernie would ask somebody down to their place, and Rhoda didn't know anything about it. She would be gracious and go along. Rhoda was the balance wheel.

Bud Crary: Oh, Rhoda is a dandy, you bet, she's a dandy.

Henry Hornberger: Ernie would never argue with a decision that Rhoda would make. Rhoda was the one who hired me; Ernie wouldn't. When he first met me he said, "No, I don't need you and you need a haircut, your hair's too long, you look like a hippie; you're too young to work here." And then Rhoda hired me. They were building lift #4, and she had all this carpentry-type work that she needed done in her shop and all the people were helping on the lift. In those days, that was the project of the season, and it took the entire crew. Ernie wandered in one day, "What are you doing here?" I said, "Rhoda hired me." That was the end of it; he didn't go and say, "Bullshit, Rhoda." It was fine.

Victor Frohlich: Rhoda was always behind the scenes. If Rhoda said, "I want that," it was done.

Ilse Mayer: It was a hard life for Rhoda and Ernie. Ernie listening to Rhoda, and Rhoda putting in her little grain of pepper or salt or sugar, it came so that the two of them really were a strong bond; Ernest's strength and her support.

Ernie: Rhoda and I did it together; we were foolish as all hell to go into the ski business. We went into it open-eyed; I didn't realize how big it would get and how much the financial involvement would grow. But I knew that you made money on beginners and intermediates, not on expert skiers. And I knew I was going to get away from the Santa Fe syndrome which was that people would come to Santa Fe, and they'd ski a weekend with us. They'd take lessons, and they'd end up learning to do snowplow turns to the left, to the right; then they felt they were perfect. They would tell us that now, thanks to our efforts, they were ready to go to Aspen and to Sun Valley for a week of skiing. That made me mad. I wanted to build an area that they wouldn't be able to handle after two days of weekend ski instruction. I wanted Taos Ski Valley to be a destination resort right away. That was very clear in my mind. Also because it was so steep, consequently people had to stay a week to get anything out of it and be in ski school.

Friedl Pfeifer: At Sun Valley and Aspen that's what we all wanted was a destination resort. Averell Harriman put it the right way once. We became good friends, but we were both quite outspoken about everything. One time I made a little remark that, "You shouldn't have built so close to Hollywood because that's all the people you're going to get," I said it as a joke. And Harriman said, "The Hollywood people are fabulous to have; they come for a week or two, and then they go home, but they at least come for a week, not a few days."

Chilton Anderson: It was a skiers' ski area for those people who didn't want to go to an Aspen, or later Vail, but who liked the atmosphere of Taos. It was more than just Ernie and Jean at that point; Dadou, Godie, Kaarlo, myself, we were with the guests. It was because everybody was a part of everything. The

people who came early in the season went up and packed, and somehow they thought that was fun. They were in on something that was special. If it was bad weather, we were all there together; we didn't leave the guests to go sit at the bar. We enjoyed playing bridge with them or whatever. We don't do that now.

When the instructors used to sweep the trails at four o'clock, we would sometimes pick out one exceptional person in our class or the kids and reward them by taking them on sweep; that was a big deal for the guests, and they loved it. Even if there was a family of five and you could only take one of the five, the others were pleased for that one member who was invited to go and sweep at 4:00—wow! "And where did you go?" "We swept White Feather and got to ski down and pick up this person, and Chilton took that guy down on his back," or whatever. Well, these were neat things, and people still remember them.

Ernie: We had a red flag mounted on a flag pole on top of the ski shop where part of the Hondo is now. We locked the door and had a sign which said, "Raise red flag if you need assistance." If we skied down and saw the red flag up we would go and help. The first one who came down would sell tickets or rent them skis or whatever they needed.

Early on we established the habit of closing down all operations for lunch. The lunchtime break was a good idea because it forced people to come in. Their lunch was included in their package anyway; they'd paid for it. We made them take it because with the Poma lift and then so few skiers, they got an enormous amount of skiing in, and they broke their legs if they didn't get a break at midday. In 1975, when the highway was built, you couldn't do that anymore because people who did not stay on the Learn to Ski Better Week at one of the lodges, who only had one or two days of skiing and paid for a daily ticket, wanted every minute of it. They didn't feel that the lunchtime break was for them.

Walter Ruegg: I enjoy thinking of the old days. I knew it would get big, but I'm glad it didn't get big too fast. Now, I think back to the good old days when everybody was eating at the St. Bernard including the lift operators. Ernie shut the lift down for an hour. At lunch, Ernie would tell little stories and charm the guests.

Herman Kretschmer: Ernie used to have great fun with people, especially at lunch and dinner when we ate with all the guests. He was a great practical joker. One thing that just bothered the hell out of Ernie was women who put their hair in metal curlers. Well, some gal showed up at dinner with a head full of this business, and he looked at her as only he could do and hollered, "YOU!" and pointed, "At last we have found you." And this gal thought, what in the world is this? And he said, "The Federal Aviation

Authority has called us up here (we didn't even have a phone up here) and indicated that there was a disturbance in the Van Allen Belt." I'm sure he knew what the Van Allen Belt was, but I didn't. "It's creating a major problem for airplanes flying over. I know what that disturbance is because by triangulation, they brought it in to Taos Ski Valley, and it is those things on your hair." Needless to say, we never saw "those things" on her hair again. It bothered the hell out of him, and he had no remorse at all. He really embarrassed that poor woman.

Ernie: In the early years, we were our own ski patrol; Jean Dadou, Rhoda and I; everybody joined in as ski patrol. And the sweep was done by the ski instructors. Al Rosen was the big organizer of the patrol. Clark Funk was on the ski patrol back then and Kristina Wilson. Al would throw them a first aid book and say, "Now you're ski patrol." Bob Brierley was the head of the Texas patrol. He was a good friend throughout the years and always came for breakfast. Bob was a great help with the Kandahar condominiums when we first got started. He didn't ski at first, but he learned.

Bob Brierley: Ernie always said, "Skiing must be fun." Taos is a different place, because Ernie wanted it that way. I was lucky to be able to be his friend. Ernie and I were best of friends for most of the years this place was growing. He'd fire me, but he wouldn't let me leave.

Walter Widmer: Brierley was part of the Amarillo Ski Club; they came almost every weekend, and would do the voluntary ski patrol. They would wear leather chaps, and six guns and cowboy hats, and the skiers used to say, "How come these ski patrol are wearing guns?" We'd say, "Well, it's a long way to the hospital from here. If somebody's in too much pain, we just shoot them, to get them out of their misery. And we leave them here in the snow until springtime."

Our first ski patrolman was Yung Cho, the Korean, who was the first Korean ever to be in the Olympics in alpine skiing. The Koreans had been good skaters, but they never had any alpine skiers. So, he came here to be on the ski patrol and he was here quite a few years.

Georgia Hotton: In the early days, the ski patrol was extremely well-organized, even though it was a volunteer ski patrol. Al Rosen was on that ski patrol along with Dr. Pond as well as a number of skiers from Los Alamos. There were times, though, when Rhoda and I were the only ones there who could bring a sled down. While we had both assisted with sleds, we were very glad that we never had to bring somebody on a sled down Snakedance.

Once I volunteered when the ski patrol was just starting to be a paid ski patrol. They were practicing bringing a sled down Snakedance. Malcolm Brown was trying to design some sleds for us that would work. This was before we had the Akjas and some of the

Bob Brierley playing cricket. COURTESY BOB BRIERLEY.

Alyda Blake & Bob Brierley. PHOTO BY ERNIE BLAKE, COURTESY BLAKE FAMILY COLLECTION.

more sophisticated rescue sleds. It was basically a toboggan with a Stoke's litter, a frame, a mesh litter on top of the toboggan and a chain under the front of the toboggan. If you lifted up on the handles attached to the toboggan, the chain would come off and the sled would go; if you came down on the handles, the chain would dig into the snow and the sled should slow down. It had two ropes off the back.

We needed somebody to ride and these guys were practicing on Snakedance. There were two people on the back, each hanging onto a rope, and one person on the front. I was lying on my back in the sled, and I had a pair of ski boots that had clips in them; they had laces up in the back; they were Heierlings from

Early Taos Ski Patrol: Ernie, Rhoda, Al Rosen, Clark Funk, Chilton Anderson, Georgia Hotton, Brooke Cottam & Jerry Laughlin.
<small>Courtesy Myrtle Rosen.</small>

Switzerland. I was riding down this hill on my back very fast and smoothly, and I heard, "Georgia, jump out, jump out." Well, I realized at this point that the two guys on the back had fallen off, and what they should have done even though they had fallen, they should have hung onto the ropes so that their bodies would act as some sort of a drag, but not only had they fallen, they had let go of the ropes. It was only when I got to the bottom that I realized that the person yelling, "Jump out" was the guy still on the front of the sled. He wasn't at all sure he could bring it to a stop. We would have crashed right into the St. Bernard. At any rate, I was glad I had not tried to jump out because when I did try to get out after the sled had stopped, the hooks on my laces on the back of the boots were caught. So, if I had tried to jump, I would have been caught and dragged. Next time, for practice, they could put a log in that thing or sand bags or something.

Chilton Anderson: I remember once on Chicken Alley we were doing toboggan training. Somehow, I was supposed to bring Myrt Rosen down, and I was in the front, and whoever was on back let go, so I let go, and Myrt bombed off down the hill in the toboggan by her lonesome for a while, until it flipped her over or else she bailed out.

Rhoda: When you think of what the ski patrol was

like then! Anybody who was there took a sled down. They had a great system. You'd get a Texan up there who couldn't ski, and they'd say they were hurt but you knew damn well they weren't hurt. So, taking them down, the patrol never missed a mogul, and if there weren't any, they dropped the sled a few times. But you know, despite the fact that the patrol really gave people who weren't hurt a bronc ride, I've also seen them come down holding the sled in the air so that they wouldn't risk a bump.

Once, Ernest and Walter were taking the litter down, and Ernest came down pretty fast with a sled with Walter on the back and snow was flying in his face. He couldn't see where he was going. They hit a bump and pretty soon Ernest felt this thing wasn't handling the way it should. He turned around, and there were Walter's gloves sitting on these two little handles; that's all there were, just the two gloves.

Ernie: Today our ski patrol is as good as any in the world; like the ski school, we have the best in the country. They do a great job at controlling the mountain and avalanche areas. They are very professional. They do a magnificent job keeping the mountain open. They are a breed unto themselves. In the early years, skiers were more self-sufficient; today we must be very careful. Our patrol does a fabulous job and they are essential to our mountain. When Kevin

Phil Sanchez & Yung Cho. Courtesy Blake Family Collection.

Beardsley came, or really when Pierre Landry arrived, we were just becoming a professional patrol. Before that it was John Koch, Yung Cho, Pat Imeson, and the ski instructors.

Kevin Beardsley: Pierre Landry is probably responsible, more than anyone, for professionalizing the patrol. He brought not only some experience, but he also brought a tremendous concern and desire and pride with him that connected the patrol to the mountain. And that really started what has turned into the most independent department the Ski Valley has.

The patrol has tried to remain isolated, tried to keep its own agenda and program going. The mountain is really something that the patrol has considered as theirs. Before that, it was the instructors and all the friends and wonderful people that did everything. They packed, they patrolled, they swept, and fixed the chair lifts. They did everything. But in 1974, the Ski Valley hired George Hatch for snow grooming and things took off. Part of the ski patrol's responsibility then was relieved because the grooming gradually became so good that it really made it easier for us. Grooming used to be done with shovels and skis.

Chilton Anderson: To get rid of moguls, we used to shovel, which is what we tried to do with the

Korean, Yung Cho. I mean, one mogul every half-hour doesn't get you very far. The ski school all packed and shoveled. Then you'd go by Yung Cho and he'd say, "Stop, stop. You pack, I beer." He'd buy a pitcher of beer for the class if they'd pack it once.

Ernie: Shoveling and packing were our snow maintenance. It wasn't until 1970 that we used mechanical equipment to pack and groom our slopes. When the winter started, we all packed. Rhoda and I did that until maybe ten years ago. It was a tradition, something we always did, something that I always thought was good for the valley; it bound us together and was good fun.

Jean was always great. He was always there for those things. Ed Pratt was there, but he usually had some pain very soon. He was always sensitive; he wasn't lazy. He always had something wrong with him. The instructors, other lodge owners like Victor Frohlich and some of the real skiers from town helped, too.

Walter Widmer: Ernie and Rhoda only packed together; they never skied together. They never would ski when we needed packing. You know, we used to side-step that mountain. I side-stepped it more than I skied it. We all packed; it was part of the spirit.

Rhoda: When the first snows came, we'd say, "Great! Let's pack and get ready to open." We ran the lifts ourselves and did everything ourselves. We were here anyway, so it didn't make any difference. In the early days, when we didn't have a paid ski patrol and before opening, all the lodge owners would come and we'd all pack together. The spirit was different then: we're going to open, we want everybody to like it, let's all go and help!

Max Dercum: If you had a slope, we packed the slope. If somebody made a hole, a sitzmark, we were educating those people to fill their holes up. If you stood in line on a rope tow, you stood in line; you didn't barge up to the front of it. People nowadays don't seem to realize there was a long cultural educational process in how to become a skier. What do you do? You go out there and help clear the trail, help string the rope and pack and all the rest of it.

Jean Mayer: We had the spirit always; we did a lot without snowmaking, and we always came out all right. Now we have snowmaking but when it snows we still must help the mountain. It is nature and that is the mountain. When nature is there and helps you and you don't jump in and work with it, if we don't, then there is something lacking.

Let's get the instructors and go and pack snow and get our mountain ready. Let's do it as we used to do it twenty-five years ago. You don't do it for money. You do it because it's your livelihood; it's your life, your enjoyment, your fun. We don't expect money, now they all expect money. They go pack for a while, "Do I get paid?" Those letters that Ernie sent me said you may get $250 at the end of the season. I came, and we did it. We were doing it because it was a challenge, not for money.

Ernie: Today we still must pack some of our trails, but the packing machine changed things. Skiing became a different sport. Steve Bradley, who was another good friend of mine from the pre-war days, was the real inventor of the snow packing machine. He was the manager of Winter Park. We visited with him when we started working in Santa Fe and learned a lot from him. Steve Bradley was one of several brothers, the heirs to the Crane fortune.

Bradley already had a roller in 1950 that looked like a tennis court roller made out of lightweight wood. We had one here once. His employees took it up on the T-bar and then skied down with it. If they fell down, it went over them and cut them into little ribbons. He also had a giant machine that looked like a tank in a metal workshop in Hot Sulfur Springs, Colorado that he took me to look at with all sorts of gadgets. It had sheep's feet, those funny metal extrusions to pack snow and break up surfaces. It had rippers, and it had plows and everything on it; a giant machine that he probably financed out of his own pocket.

George Engle: If it weren't for Steve Bradley and that innovation, skiing would not be what it is today. That changed the ski world. To prove it to people, one

Jade Jahrmarkt, Jeff Johnson, Steve Kinslow, Charlie Raskovics—shovelers at St. Bernard. PHOTO BY KEN GALLARD.

time we did it with the ski patrol boys; I think we had four machines at that time. This was in the mid-fifties. We took the machines and did half of "Bash" and left the other half bumpy. We then took pictures of it with people skiing on it. There wasn't anybody in the bumps. All the people were skiing on the packed slope. It was just like night and day; you could just see it.

Ernie: We started packing our mountain with machinery in 1970. I didn't think Bradley's machine applied to us until 1970 when my son Mickey forced me to pay for the first one. Today, the bulk of our slopes are being packed, and now we have to tackle the grades and make sure they don't get too dangerous by packing them because, like on Al's Run, no bumps could be disastrous; if people fell, they would just slide all the way down. The moguls have some value in keeping people from sliding down too far.

John Koch: You look at people today and talk about shoveling moguls, and you get a completely blank look. They have absolutely no idea what you're talking about. Now I look at what's driving around twenty years later: $150,000-$160,000 a piece, and they are beautiful. And the heaters work!

One New Year's Eve, I was up pushing snow with the old Sno-Cat down into that narrow path on the catwalk. The reason we were pushing snow is we hadn't had any, and there were snow fences in there, and that night was a complete blizzard and the only way to see was to have the door open. When I got out in the morning, my left foot was frozen; God, it was fun. That's the way it was. Now I look back on it, it was awfully nice of Ernie to build me a ski area where we could go up and play. I just never thought about it at that level. One thing about Ernie. He may not have cared too much for some of our shenanigans, but he let it go as long as the work was getting done. I still pick up rocks on the slopes when I see them because of all that damn packing and grooming we did by hand; it was great.

Kevin Beardsley: Koch was a madman in those days. I didn't know him well and I had only met Ernie two or three times that first winter. He was pretty aloof and he was "The General." One night I was walking up the old steps behind his house with the ski shop and his apartment, and I came around the deck, going to the St. Bernard, and here are two guys who I didn't know at that time who turned out to be Bill Whaley and John Koch. They were on the deck and had one of these short wooden benches, and they were bashing it up into the deck above and screaming at Ernie, swearing at him to come out; they wanted raises and were all pissed off. So, Ernie ran out onto his deck with this big German rifle and started screaming back at them, telling them he was going to shoot them if they didn't leave him alone.

Koch was a wild man, insane. The next year after

Pierre Landry driving Sno-Cat. COURTESY BLAKE FAMILY COLLECTION.

Sno-Cats grooming Kachina Basin at sunrise.
PHOTO BY KEN GALLARD.

Claude Gobard & Kevin Beardsley in Patrol headquarters, March 1978. COURTESY BLAKE FAMILY COLLECTION.

Pierre Landry got hurt, I took over the ski patrol, and Ernie actually came to me and said, "If Mr. Koch ever wants a job, you hire him; you make room." I couldn't believe it. Ernie and he had some kind of understanding. From then on, for years, I saw the way Ernie could see so much more in people and understand and connect better with different people. Ernie saw something much more in Koch, obviously.

John Koch and Pierre Landry and Deming Gustafson formed the nucleus of a working ski patrol. We worked our butts off constantly, and we loved it. That first year I came to Taos was probably the start of the professionalism and the really excellent ski patrol. You got guys in their twenties who worked ten to twelve hours, killing themselves all day long, and then we would party until midnight every night and be back at it the next day. Ernie knew that very well and put up with it and with us. I think he took a lot of pride in the patrol, even though he never showed it. We knew that he cared.

My first year here, the ski patrol room was that little shack with no electricity, no stove, just one cot, and a little chair. You'd bring your sled down there and wait until somebody went to the hotel and borrowed a car and drove the injured skier to town. We would have people literally hopping or crawling down the steps to get to that little shack while they'd get "Big Daddy" (Ed Pratt) at the Hondo to call us. They'd knock on his window and have him call the patrol; "I think I broke my leg. I was on Rubezahl, but I'm here at the bottom now." They would come in with dislocated shoulders and ski all the way down to the bottom and then call for us.

There is such a big attitude change now in terms of skiers. People then were responsible for themselves. They took it upon themselves to have fun and to take the chances. When they got hurt, they were either embarrassed, in pain or mad, but never at us or the mountain. Skiing and the risks were something they loved and understood, and they knew what they were

John Koch. COURTESY JOHN KOCH.

getting into and were willing to take the chance. We never had the attitude that skiing should be restricted or cautious; skiing is up here to do as you will, as long as you don't endanger somebody else. Speed was only controlled on the beginners' hill or the cat walks.

From 1970 on we became a very tight professional unit that had a huge amount of pride in how we packed and how we maintained the trails. There were five or six of us then. Some of the areas that we had to work on, that Ernie insisted on opening, scared me to death, but I was ignorant. For a couple years, we watched Ernie and some of the others totally ignoring any of the common instincts of safety and just going into all of those very steep areas and up on the ridge. It wasn't until about 1972-'73 when we started to press the point of avalanche control. We had arguments and run-ins with Ernie. He would tell Walter Widmer to call us and tell us which trails to open, and that didn't fit; it didn't work, not because of pride or our personality, but because we knew what we were doing and safety was far more on our minds than on theirs.

Walter Widmer: Pete Totemoff used to come up to Taos Ski Valley a lot in those early days and he and Ernie used to knock avalanches down by skiing and jumping up and down, hoping they would go, not the safest way of doing it. But we also shook them down with dynamite. Ernie always had these stacks of dynamite under his bed. Then he would put it together with caps in a capsule and put it in little cigar boxes. We'd take the whole thing up on the ridge and light it and throw it in there.

Once Ernie and I were going up the lift; it was about 1960. On my lap, I had the rucksack full of these boxes with this dynamite charge. Ernie always used to say "When I die, I would like to die in an explosion; it's the fastest way. You won't even know what happened." And here I had this rucksack right on my lap. I said, "Of course, if that thing should go off now, I would be quite dead too," and Ernie said, "A good way to go, but my God, it would tear down the lift at the same time! What would Rhoda do without the lift?" But that was typical of Ernie.

Ernie: The people who are experts on avalanches are all dead. There are no experts. Avalanches are tricky, there was no rule on them early on; we tried not to be stupid and to be careful. Today our patrol knows much more and they are very professional.

John Koch: Ernie loved to blow things up. He had me send away for this blasting handbook, in those days you didn't have to go through any federal nonsense to get it. There was an explosive outlet place in Albuquerque, and Ernie sent me down there to buy dynamite.

Ernie designed what we called a platter charge—

Early snow grooming equipment at Santa Fe. COURTESY KINGSBURY PITCHER.

Chat Campbell preparing to throw explosives.
PHOTO BY KEN GALLARD.

Ernie at the helm of one of his Sno-Cats.
PHOTO BY KEN GALLARD, COURTESY BLAKE FAMILY·COLLECTION.

shaped like a dinner plate—and I'd read all the literature on them. The theory was you were going to get rid of all the monster rocks up in the West Basin. Once Ernie was working on a trail, and he had some stuff up there he wanted to get rid of and one rock that kept bugging us right down on the lower catwalk. I can't remember how many windows he took out. It was a fearsome bang.

I didn't really know anything about dynamite; I learned on the job. When I came to Taos Ski Valley, I thought I was going to learn everything about dynamite and avalanches, but nobody knew anything. We were doing as good down there reading the book and using our heads as anybody else in the country at the time. There was a guy named Pat working there and he and I couldn't go anywhere without something happening, some adventure. One day after the lift had closed, Ernie was going to put on one of those giant demonstrations of dynamiting avalanches. Ernie, Pat, myself and a couple other people sat there and cheerfully laced all the dynamite together and stuck the cap in it and pulled the fuse. Pat threw it as far as he could, it landed in a damn tree branch and came back and landed about twenty feet from us. Everybody else got out of there, and he and I were laughing so hard, we couldn't stand it, and all we could do was bury ourselves in the snow. Fortunately, it didn't slide.

The advantage of not knowing anything about it and not having some whiz-bang trying to tell me about it was great. Reading the books, reading the literature tells you what to do, what not to do. The reason it's written is that it makes sense. I still have all my fingers and toes.

Kevin Beardsley: Koch had done some dynamite work and avalanche control, but it was in its infancy. John, like Ernie, liked messing with dynamite. That first year I helped them, I went up with Koch on the ridge on the West Basin route. He had bombs stuffed into his parka with all the fuses sticking out of his coat front. He'd pull one of these igniters and light it; then he'd sit there laughing and talking to me while the fuse was burning. Then he'd pull out a bomb, and it would be the wrong one, and he'd joke about it.

Ernie: Koch was crazy; I liked Koch. He loved dynamite, and he hated billboards, and sometimes he was a little out of control; he did not like discipline, but Koch knew how to work, but I fired him many times.

John Koch: I would like to get back to Taos sometime. I'm trying to think of how I could get down there just early enough, before anybody knew I was there, and knock down a couple of billboards and see if anybody started getting nervous. Everybody talks about billboards and how awful they

look. Jim Wagner was begging me to take him with us, and he went once. We went to the K.O.A.; we were going to hit the K.O.A. sign, and I explained how we did it—cut through the back side and leave just enough so that it's standing and the wind would get it. So we were cutting away and cutting away, and this car came down the road. Instead of just dropping so they couldn't see him, he started tying his shoe, standing in the middle of the road tying his shoe. I always knew that if I got busted, and I kept thinking the cops had to know because everybody else in town knew who was doing it, that somehow in my post office box would be my fine money or my bail money, whatever from "the friends of Taos." The only thing I missed moving up to Aspen is that they don't have any billboards.

Kevin Beardsley: From the early seventies on, we did a tremendous job of avalanche control. Safety became very important. We built the #4 chair lift in the summer of 1971, and when that all opened up right underneath the face of Kachina, that was the first time that massive control was important. Fortunately, in the spring of 1970, there had been a very large avalanche, and the whole face of Kachina came down, right down into the notch of Rubezahl Gully, leaving stacks of trees, showing what could

Avalanche on Kachina Peak. PHOTO BY KEN GALLARD.

Ski Patrol on Kachina Peak, 1989. Photo By Ken Gallard.

Ski Patrol on morning bombing route, Taos Ski Valley. PHOTO BY KEN GALLARD.

happen. It let them know that they were building a chair lift directly in the path of a twenty- or thirty-year avalanche path. It was a major one as evidenced by the trees that were not there, making it a natural basin.

We brought in a couple of the most respected national experts, and Pierre and I took them around for days, and we located several potential sites for a military weapon like a 105mm recoil which we ended up with to control Kachina. It's the only thing that has kept the Kachina lift standing and that terrain safe.

In the old days, they used a lot of dynamite, and it was obvious that snow and ice don't respond to slow speed, slow explosives like dynamite as well as they do to sharp, very fast, high velocity explosives. When you take a stump out of the ground, you want dynamite under it because there's a lot of push there. On the other hand, if you just want to break material, crack the rock like in hard rock mining, they use very fast explosives. Snow and ice are essentially more like hard rock in reaction, because there is so much air volume in the snow that any push, any gas formation in there is just absorbed. But if you get a very strong shock wave, it runs

through that air mass in the snow and loosens at the same time millions of crystals; the crystal bonds that you have between the snow can be compromised over a huge area if the shock wave is fast enough. Once you've done that and you've basically rattled some crystals or gotten the shock wave through the snow pack, if it's got a tendency to move or slide, it will slide. Dynamite would only blow a huge hole in the snow.

In the early eighties we had Dick Lunceford, an avalanche expert, as director. He was followed by Sylvia Lamson who was one of the very first female patrollers and was as good or better than anybody I ever worked with. Then in about 1984, Jim Lee was made director. He's an excellent man. It's big business; the concerns have shifted full spectrum now to where avalanche control, avalanche safety, rescue dog program and the Avalauncher and the bombing and so on is a major operation.

The Ridge now is essentially open terrain all the time. It's tremendous, both a great experience for the skiers and a tremendous asset. It's also safer and better in the long run. The grooming and the snowmaking now, all of these things have advanced to where Taos is right up there. Taos is in the 21st century in terms of ski area operations now. The patrol up there today is some thirty-five people that are amazing. They are so good; it's truly impressive. I believe the Taos Ski Patrol, if they aren't the best in the country, they're tied.

Georgia Hotton: Taos Ski Valley, unlike the other major ski resorts, was done with a whole lot of imagination, a whole lot of hard work and a whole lot of contribution on the parts of individuals, including guests who came to ski.

When the lifts would break down, I'd go in on Sunday afternoon and say, "Hey, if we want to ski some more this afternoon, I need some help." Guests would volunteer to help put the bull wheel cable back on the first lift. It was incredible the things we did with relatively little money and just a whole lot of hard work and a whole lot of volunteer help. That was very important at Taos.

We didn't have the money to go in and bulldoze and change the shape of the mountain, to go in and cut trees down massively and create incredible wind or erosion problems that some of the other resorts had. We had to do everything on a smaller, more human scale, if you will, and that made Taos always a more interesting resort to ski. Every one of the runs at Taos has its own distinctive flavor; every one has its own challenges.

Ernie: Georgia Hotton came in 1958, either just before or just after Jean. She had been a school teacher and was very enthusiastic about skiing. Georgia's specialty was that she was going to outdo all of the men at everything. She came down Al's Run with her class; it was the second day they were on skis. They had to show that they had learned everything by the second day. Georgia did a great job for us.

Georgia Hotton: Ernie, in quite recent years, commented what a great ski instructor I had been. I think I was a fairly good ski instructor for two reasons; one, I had been such an impossibly slow learner myself, and two, I had learned under incredible conditions; when I learned to ski, we skied through the woods, and rarely skied on packed slopes. So, I was forced to learn to handle all different kinds of snow as well as occasional challenging meetings with trees. I would often get the class from ripe beginner within a week to coming down Al's Run.

Herman Kretschmer: Georgia was the school teacher to the Blake children before she became the bookkeeper and ski instructor, et al. Georgia did a lot of detailed work. Ernie hated to mess around with stuff like that. She was a lot nicer than a lot of people thought she was. I think Ernie admired her toughness, and Ernie needed a good, loyal helper,

and she was that. She was a jack-of-all-trades: ski school, she ran the shop, she sold tickets. She was his original "right-hand man." She was powerful because Ernie liked her. If he liked you, he would do almost anything for you.

Chilton Anderson: Georgia had power, and she was tremendously loyal.

Harry Franzgen: Georgia either liked you or she hated you. If she hated you, there was nothing you could do.

Rhoda: Georgia never had a tremendous sense of humor. She did come out with a great remark once. She lived in our trailer for a while, and Chilton used to come up, and sometimes he would stay here and sometimes he'd stay in the trailer. Finally she threw him out. She said, "If I'm going to get the name, I want the game."

Georgia Hotton: When I first started at Taos Ski Valley, I was hired to be a tutor for the three Blake children. Peter was in second grade, Wendy was in fourth grade and Mickey was in ninth grade. Because the road could not be kept open on a regular basis in the wintertime, they were not going to be able to get to the regular school, so we used the Calvert system of private teaching.

Once there were some people up there visiting Ernie in the summertime, and they said to him, "How do you get your kids to school and how do you get your kids educated?" He said with a straight face, "I believe in the Bible, and we just use the Bible and I read to them." He could say things that were out of this world nonsense in such a convincing manner that people accepted it.

I was a pacifist at that time. I really didn't want to pay any taxes to the government for war-type things, and so the easiest way to avoid paying taxes was not to earn very much. I literally started out at Taos Ski Valley working for $50 per month plus room and board.

The Blakes accepted me as a part of the family. It worked out very well for me; if they were going to go skiing up in Aspen, I went along and had a great time. It was the Blakes' generosity that made it possible for me to do the things I did. I think I was earning my way, but I was earning my way in a way that I had chosen. It was exciting to be involved in Taos Ski Valley from day one because I had a chance to learn the development of a whole ski resort, to participate in it, and to learn from doing it, too. That's made it possible for me in more recent years to be a very successful teacher of resort management.

It wasn't long before Ernie said to me, "Come on, we're going up." I was still quite a novice at skiing at this point. Ernie said we were going to ride the new Poma lift up and go over and check on the crew that were cutting trees. Most of the crew at that time were from the Pueblo; they were cutting trees with

Georgia Hotton on the river. COURTESY BLAKE FAMILY COLLECTION.

Yolanda Blake, Mickey Blake, Eric Gros & Wendy Blake at the Mine Slide Cabin. Courtesy Blake Family Collection.

St. Bernard Bar. Tom Camero, Pierre Landry, Albert Deveaux, Mickey Blake, Yolanda Blake, & Reggie Becker. Courtesy Blake Family Collection.

chain saws on Snakedance. Ernie got to the top of the lift with no problem. I fell off about 100 yards below the top, and he said something about, "Where are you?" And I said, "I'll get there, go ahead." I continued to climb up on foot and then went across on skis over to where the crew was cutting. We got over there and Ernie said, "I have to go to town for some errands. Will you please tell these guys which trees to cut."

Another time I was taking a ski class up the mountain on that Poma lift. We got about halfway up when the cable had too much sag in it, and I had to put my best student in the class in charge and told them to go down the road. I took my skis off and climbed on up to the top because I knew what was wrong. The counter weight was floating on the snow and therefore not exerting enough tension, and I was the staff up on the mountain that day. So, I had to climb up to fix it. We didn't have any vehicles that would go up the mountain in those times. If we needed to get to the top of the mountain, we either had to get on the lift or we had to climb up. So, I climbed halfway up the mountain in fairly deep snow that day, and when I got up there, I shoveled out the counter weight so that the lift would run. In those days, you also have to remember we didn't have the walkie-talkie radios. Everybody takes it for granted today; it was fun in those early days because you learned how to do it the hard way. But, you learned that it could be done.

My job evolved over a period of time and eventually Ernie said, give yourself any title you want that will work for you wherever you need it: marketing director, manager, he didn't care. In fact, when I was working full-time at the ski area before I finally left, my real title was that of assistant manager. It was an enviable position for me in a lot of ways because I backed up Mickey in terms of operations. If Mickey was not there, then in a sense, I was in charge of everything that was happening on the mountain. It was not difficult because Mickey had it extremely well organized. I backed up Ernie on marketing. I did the books, and I did a whole lot of the PR. It's a strange thing to say, but I suppose I could run the mountain better than Ernie could run it, and I could run PR better than Mickey. So, in a sense, by backing up each of them, I was in a position where I learned a whole lot. I had the respect of the operations crew, and I had the respect of the Blakes.

CHAPTER 16
Men With A Vision

Ernie: During these early years we grew very slowly. The Thunderbird Lodge had been built by Buell Pattison who wanted to get into the ski business. It was a dangerous situation because he had a giant water heating furnace that had no safety valve that would have blown up sooner or later. We also had electricity made by Buell with a homemade water turbine which was something that didn't work very well.

Buell Pattison: Dad always wanted to generate his own electricity by using water power. He tried two or three different things, and eventually we put a twelve-inch water line down from the old beaver ponds which is a half-mile above the village of Twining up the Lake Fork stream. We tore the beaver pond out and put a dam across it with a twelve-inch water pipeline and brought it down to right beside the Thunderbird Lodge.

Mickey Blake: The opening of that contraption was quite something. Orville waved the flag, Buell was halfway up the hill, and there was a cousin whose name was Buck who was at the head gate. He opened the head gate and the water flowed down the line. It was the 25th of January, and it was twenty-five below zero; the wheel didn't turn at all when the water hit the wheel. It went straight up in the air and froze. This created a giant ice sculpture. Finally, in the springtime, the thing unfroze and started to turn.

The power was never constant; you could never get a constant flow. The lights would go bright and dim and bright and dim, and they could never get the cycles right, and they had the greatest array of ancient electrical equipment they'd gotten from everywhere.

Kaarlo Jokela: The generator didn't work too good. That was O.E. Pattison's invention. He was a sharp cookie though. They tell me that he had the first rubber tires on a tractor in the state of New Mexico, and he made them himself, if you can believe that. Orville built that generator out of all kinds of different

stuff. He went and he got some material from a fish hatchery someplace, and he got a lot of it from army surplus. This was long after the war. Then they went to Mexico, and they bought that tremendous steel pipe. That thing never ran full blast. The problem was, you really needed the electricity in the winter months, and that's when the snow melt is the lowest and everything is frozen, so there was not much water. That first year we got an electric grill, we'd turn the grill on. And the lights would go off. The icebox was fluctuating and you never knew in the middle of the night what would happen, and I was no engineer.

Buell Pattison: Dad and I built the original part of the Thunderbird in 1959. It took about three years to finish. It was a stone-faced building, but we built the walls from logs. We cut our own timber. My dad had

The old Thunderbird Lodge. COURTESY PATTISON FAMILY COLLECTION.

bought an old saw mill and rebuilt it and had it situated up there where we could mill our own lumber. I was planning on running it but by the time it was all done, my kids were starting to get of school age, and the road was so tough that we had to move out of Twining down into Taos. It just didn't pan out to do it that way, so we ended up selling it.

Ernie: Those first few years the Thunderbird was minimally run by Buell. Buell was not suited to running a ski lodge, and with small children it was not easy in those days. So Jean brought in his army friend, Kaarlo Jokela, who leased it from the Pattisons, and made it a better operation.

Kaarlo Jokela: Jean and I were in the service together. We were in Germany in Garmisch-Partenkirchen and happened to be in the army ski patrol back in 1955-'56. I'm from Finland. I put in four years in the American air force, and I was stationed in Europe where I met Jean.

I used the Thunderbird basically at the beginning as Jean's overflow. There weren't any other hotels there except the Hondo Lodge and the St. Bernard. We went to work, kept the lodge going and stayed there for six years. It had a flat roof on it; it was a three-story building, but it hadn't been painted and the furniture wasn't there. It was pretty crude. This was before telephones; there was no electricity. We were generating our own electricity with the generator O.E. Pattison manufactured; it was all very primitive.

We did everything. There weren't that many people there. It was fun in a way, but it was kind of rough, too. You had to make it in four months for the whole year; that was the roughest part. The first year we were there, I was able to get the Peace Corps to come from the University of New Mexico. They were going to go to the D. H. Lawrence Ranch, and I found out the ranch wouldn't be ready, so I wrote them a letter and invited them here. They just had their 30th reunion.

Ernie: The Thunderbird was very crudely built and very spartan, but in those days so was everything else. Buell was very funny about certain things. The whole family was strong into religion, but they interpreted their beliefs in a rather unique way. I enjoyed O. E. Pattison; he was a real individual.

Rhoda: We did a funny thing with Buell years ago; it wasn't nice, but it was very funny because they were so contradictory in what they believed. Years ago Herman Kretschmer wrote that famous letter to Buell, knowing their prejudices that contradicted their religious beliefs. In the early years when they had the Thunderbird, he wrote a letter from the Negro Junior League; the sponsors were Eleanor Roosevelt, etc. He got this all printed up on some special stationery and wrote this fictitious letter from a group of blacks who wanted to come here; a great flowery letter and between the lines, not only were they black, but they were also nudists. This was sent off; they offered to rent the entire Thunderbird Lodge for two months. We were on pins and needles waiting for an answer because we could just see the Pattisons torn between their greed and their prejudice. But nothing happened. For years nothing happened. Only a few years ago, Buell off-handedly one day said to Ernest, "You know, years back we got a letter that almost tore the family

apart." It was exactly as we had predicted.

Georgia Hotton: Ernie's letters were gems, and they were originals, typed on his typewriter with his unique hunt and peck system of typing. He'd watch his favorite soap operas on TV and type. In his own style, he'd write letters to people that were unforgettable. They were prompt, and so the guests came. We were sitting around at dinner, and we were asking one of our first guests how come he had happened to come to Taos Ski Valley, and he said, "Well, because you answered my letter so promptly."

Elisabeth Brownell: Ernie was hardworking. When I came over at 8:00, he had been up at 6:00 and had typed letters already. And he answered every one of them. He was very fast with two fingers. He just wrote the way he thought and the way he spoke. He was always very personal. Ernie took such good care of people, and I think that was his strong point. Anyone who wanted to meet Ernie could call him up and say, "I'd like to meet you," and he received them with open arms; he listened; he was interested where that person came from and what his name was. He remembered the names. If somebody wrote him a letter, he answered every single letter. When I first came here the mail was the main communication. Ernie wanted me to answer every request for information with a personal letter which he signed. He never gave me a day off; we worked seven days a week.

John Koch: I can still see Ernie walking out of his office; he had his office back in the far corner behind the bedroom. He had his exercycle set up and a punching bag in the corner, and he stood there for, I swear, five minutes looking back and forth between the exercycle and the punching bag; he shoved his little hat back, walked over and smacked the shit out of the punching bag and went back to work; I loved it. That just about sums him up.

Monica Brown: I stayed down in Santa Fe at Ernie's house and sometimes he was there in between trips to Europe and Texas. The first month in the house, I thought I was dreaming because here he is typing, the TV going, the radio going, the typewriter going. I asked how he could listen to all this and he says, "If you don't listen to *All in the Family,* you are missing out. on life." He runs to the garage to the punching ball, and he runs from the garage like a maniac into the swimming pool, and he swims, and then he sits again on the typewriter. I'm watching this and ask, "What are you doing?"

Ernie used to write letters in the winter and he would say, "Okay, letter to the editor." We were writing that there were people from Europe coming to Taos Ski Valley having a wonderful time. He wrote letters to the editor, to himself, about what a great time the people had or what a bad time they had or whatever story he wanted to come out with. He

Ernie in his apartment. Courtesy Blake Family Collection.

Blake living quarters/office. Courtesy Pattison Family Collection.

handed me the letter with the envelope and he said, "Now you have your sister there, you have your mother there and so-and-so in Vienna. I want you to send them these letters and have them mail them to the magazines." Then he would go to the punching ball. Then we would ship the letters off, or I would go on vacation to Europe and take them, and they would come up in some magazine: "Boy, the Forest Service really ought to do something about this. I love the experience of skiing in Taos," and it was signed so-and-so from Switzerland or so-and-so, Munich. It was wonderful.

Walter Widmer: Ernie was a pioneer in how to get tremendous publicity with very little money. I remember in the beginning when he had so little, the way Ernie was able to promote Taos, writing letters to the editor from *Ski* or *Skiing Magazine* or any other. He would write, "I enjoyed your article about Aspen. I used to ski there, but I have now found a place which is so much better. Great mountain and wonderful European food and so on . . ." Then he would sign some name of someone in Chicago. He'd get someone in Chicago to mail it.

Rhoda: One of the techniques was he would start a discussion with himself and then somebody would send a letter, and then he'd answer it, and the whole time you're having a discussion with yourself about

how good Taos was. Gisela Lowenburg was one of the pen names. She appeared in all the publications. Of course it was Ernest at both ends. He had the art of publicity down pat.

Ernie: Freedom of the press allows you to lie about anything.

Tony Mitchell: One of Ernie's great remarks was, "We have plenty of Scotch and sex when we don't have snow."

Georgia Hotton: Ernie was super excellent at public relations. It was a matter of timing; it was a matter of originality; it was a matter of cleverness in the way he put words together. His facility with language certainly helped, but it was also being on top of what everybody else had said, so that he could say something that was original.

For a number of years, I probably had more ski pointers in *Ski Magazine* than anybody else, with the possible exception of Willy Schaeffler, and I was just an ordinary ski instructor and Willy was a big honcho, head of the U.S. Ski Team and so forth. It was fun because I had read all the ski pointers, and I knew what was going on, and I could always send in some little gimmick thing like don't wear your straps over your wrists when you ride on a lift and things like that nobody else had said yet. I'd get paid $25 for it, and Taos Ski Valley would get a mention. You learned tricks like that from Ernie. He was that good.

I remember once he was very upset about a woman reporter having left TSV out of a major story, and Ernie felt that Taos deserved to be included. We were working with an advertising agency at the time, and Ernie wanted to send a bitter letter to her, but the advertising agent convinced him that it would be smarter to send her a dozen roses to remind her that Taos Ski Valley still existed and, fortunately, the advertising agent's way prevailed. She got a dozen roses, and I think we got some pretty good publicity out of her down the line. Ernie and Rhoda were very generous to media people. I remember Paul Harvey coming and being quite impressed. Alex Katz from the *Chicago Sun Times* was also always terribly impressed with Ernie and with the skiing at Taos Ski Valley and the hospitality that the Blakes would offer them when they came.

Wolfie Lert: Two important things that I admired about Ernie, first of all, he could put in one lift and get the majority of usable terrain out of just that one lift. The other thing was he'd do something that cost him virtually nothing and get nationwide publicity. Like those damn martini trees, a brilliant idea. It cost him a few bucks for booze.

Ernie: The martini trees started because of a person that at the time I had no sympathy for at all.

Now that I can't see, I sympathize only too well. It was March 13, 1959 when I was skiing with a lady by the name of Mitchell who had fifteen-year-old twin sons, so she was a mature lady. She was a great skier, technically perfect, but when the sun went down, she was terrible. She couldn't move, which was essential to her skiing.

I had no understanding for that like I have today. But in those days, I was less forgiving; I told Mickey who happened to come by, "Get the hell down to Mommy and have her mix a batch of martinis and bring them up; don't spill any." And it was like a miracle. One sip and she skied like a goddess. It was great. So, we felt we had made a great medical invention, and they still exist today.

Warren Miller: I would guess that when he hid the martini on the hill, he always knew where to get one for himself, too, and he never told anybody about that.

Linda Meyers: One of the first things I had to do for the insurance company I worked for was to inquire about the martini trees at Taos. The liability problems were just starting, and they were getting worse and worse. The company thought it was really going to be a problem. I said, "Okay, but I'm not going to be the person who is going to tell Ernie he can't have his martini trees." I arrived at Taos, and I didn't even have to say anything. Ernie was ready to show me the martini trees. So, away we went, and Ernie got the martinis out and set it all up, and some of the people followed him and watched what he was doing. That wasn't going to cause any problems. There's no adversarial relationship connected to that martini tree, and that was what was going to prevent it from ever being a problem.

Georgia Hotton: Ernie took the martini tree idea, and he got more mileage out of that little idea than anybody else has out of any ski gimmick I can possibly think of.

Rhoda: We all knew skiing; we all knew each other. Back then you didn't take it seriously because it wasn't big business. You weren't contending with 400 employees. It was a big family, and it extended to other ski areas as well. There was a camaraderie that doesn't exist today.

Ernie: We did it because skiing was our life and because of the type of life that skiing provided; it was because we loved to ski and live in the mountains; that was our life. It was the same for the others and there weren't many then. Money wasn't a consideration because you couldn't make any.

Dave McCoy is the only other person that has built a family-owned ski area with Mammoth Mountain in California. He started with even less money than we did. It's still owned by the family,

Rhoda with pouron for martini tree. PHOTO BY DICK TAYLOR.

Martini pouron. PHOTO BY DAVE MARLOWE, COURTESY BLAKE FAMILY COLLECTION.

Mammoth Mt., California. Photo By Tom Johnston, Courtesy Mammoth Mt.

and he is still quite active. He does a magnificent job caring for the skier. We were always watching each other, we stayed in touch, but we all had our own areas to operate. So we didn't see as much of each other as we would have liked.

Wolfie Lert: I think Dave McCoy is the American counterpart to, let's say, the European, German/Swiss Ernie. And McCoy didn't have some of the advantages of social background and backing that Ernie had. But at the same time, he had that same kind of determination and the same approach of doing something for the skiers. He made a mountain for skiers, not just for socialites or for fancy people.

Warren Miller: When Dave McCoy was trying to get started he wanted to buy a rope tow to put in McGee Creek in 1937, and he tried to borrow the money on his motorcycle at the bank, $85, and they wouldn't loan it to him. The secretary said, "If you don't loan it to him, I'm going to quit." So, they loaned it to him, and she married him and that's history.

Dave McCoy: That's about the size of it. I had lots of luck through my life in that way. It's been nip and tuck all my life. At twelve years old, my folks started to separate, and at thirteen, I was on my own. There

was no monetary support whatsoever and a lot was expected in return for labor performed and yard work. If I wanted a dime, I had to go earn it. I was up in Washington where I didn't really like it. I loved the outdoors, but I loved the sun also, and the mountains.

I wasn't a college boy or anything like that. Once you learn about people and learn not to prejudge people and give them time, there's so much in life to be learned that you don't learn in school. That's the way I feel about being in Mammoth because, when I was twelve years old, I had the feeling that this was where I wanted to be. My mother brought me over from Pacific Coast to visit a friend in Independence, and I saw the eastern Sierra and the white snow on it in the summertime like July-August; and I loved seeing that. Right at that time, I started to inquire what kind of work there was to do here, and how people lived and what they did.

I feel like I was just kind of dangled from a string and brought along but never got a formal education. And every time I needed someone to do specific jobs, they've been delivered to me. It still happens, even today. The right person comes along, grabs a hold and does the thing and makes this organization just blossom, and I see it growing.

One of the things Ernie and I talked about prior to him going down to Taos and developing was that owning a ski area was enough, don't worry about the land development. And another thing was not to get excited and get too big too quick, where you would have other people dictating how and what you would be doing.

Everybody said the only way you can have a ski area is take the money from the development of the land, but that showed me real shortsightedness because the ski area is the one thing that is lasting. And developers don't really last in a given area; they have to move to keep growing. We're lucky here in that we have a developer that has stayed with the community; Tom Dempsey has done a truly good job.

Wolfie Lert: Today an Ernie Blake or a Dave McCoy couldn't make it because today you have to have a-half-a-million-dollar environmental impact statement before you ever put the first rope tow on the hill. This business of starting small and building something out of your personality like Ernie did, like Dave did, it's no longer possible, unfortunately.

Dave McCoy: I think the areas try to make artificial fun out of it instead of just letting it be. At Mammoth, a guy can ski in Levis, he can ski in his $3,000 ski outfit, or he can come with lace boots and twenty-year-old pants. Everybody feels comfortable because the town is that kind of a town. It's spread out; it's spacious.

I have stayed here seven days a week, and I have never let the ski area give me an opportunity to be away from it. That's what happens so much to growing businesses. The founder, the developer, somewhere along the line gives himself the freedom to get away from whatever he's doing and puts it into the hands of other people, and once it's in the guidance of other people, that's the direction it's going to take. When you're driving a team of horses, you don't drop the reins and walk off and let them keep moving. You gently keep them on the track, but you let them do the work. And there are a lot of things left here to do. I feel I have another lifetime ahead of me if I can accomplish it, and if not, then it will be clear enough that somebody else can do it.

I'm a great believer in faith—faith in all things. I am grateful every time I have an answer. I'm really grateful for some days' great awakenings. When the time is right, and the vision comes, then you do it.

Linda Meyers: The thing that is incredible to me is, although Dave McCoy, Ernie, Pete Seibert and Friedl Pfeifer weren't in the same places ever very often, they had a tremendous amount of respect for what each other was doing. I knew that because Dave would talk about what was going on here in Taos and what was going on in Aspen with Red

Rowland and Pete Seibert in Vail. Even though they were in competition with each other, they still had a tremendous amount of respect for one another.

Gary McCoy runs that mountain the way his father would like it to run. It may not be the way he thinks it ought to run himself, but you'll hear him say, "This is the way Dad wants it." Somebody on the board said, "Well, we don't really owe that skier anything." Gary said, "Wow! We owe that skier a lot. I don't care what anybody else does but this is the way we're going to do it at Mammoth because this is the way Dad wants it done."

Dave & Roma McCoy. Photo By Tom Johnston, Courtesy Mammoth Mt.

Warren Miller. Photo By Scott Martin.

Old rope tow at Mammoth. COURTESY MAMMOTH MT.

Dave McCoy: Gary's been here ever since the beginning of time, so he knows what it's all about. We work really well as a team.

Linda Meyers: The history of American skiing is with these guys. They are the only ones with the story. The new skier looks for it, but it isn't there. I guess what those old guys all had in common was they all had a vision, and they all sort of created their visions in different ways. I would hope that the vision doesn't get lost in all the growth. That's why it's really nice to have Taos just the size it is. The other thing is, Ernie didn't build Taos to make money and become a millionaire. He built Taos because he loved his mountain and the skiing. And that's why Dave built Mammoth.

Warren Miller: As far as Ernie is concerned, and Dave McCoy, Pete Seibert, Friedl Pfeifer, Alf Engen, Fred Iselin, Ed Scott, those guys are the legends; how can you say enough about those guys?

Dave McCoy: It took us all. Everybody did their thing in their way in their place. We talk about Warren Miller; look at how he was the ambassador for everybody. All of us. He really brought skiing to the people through his ski movies.

Tony Mitchell: Ernie conveyed the quality of Taos. It was single-mindedness. I think a lot of the success in Taos Ski Valley has been due to the dedication of the individuals involved. There was really no other show close by; there wasn't much distraction in those early years. Taos Ski Valley was at the end of a ten-mile, one-lane dirt road with no phone and no electricity, and there was virtually nothing to do but to think skiing or to actually ski, with no other diversion possible.

CHAPTER 17
Competition Among the Pioneers

Ernie: There was great competition for the Texas market with Buzz Bainbridge who was running Santa Fe Ski Basin. He was my ski school director in Santa Fe when I was there, and then he took it over. We traveled all over Texas and Oklahoma developing interest. In those days, most of the ski areas that are famous today didn't exist yet.

The only major areas were Sun Valley and Aspen which opened in 1947. Sun Valley had opened in 1936. There were Stowe, Santa Fe, and Glenwood Springs which I ran for two winters when I was living in Santa Fe, which gave me the opportunity to find Taos. Mammoth was getting going, but there wasn't much.

Bob Brierley: Ernie and Buzz were both fighting for the Texas market. Ernie had Chicago, and the Santa Fe Railroad was beginning to work, but Texas was a very valuable market; there was a great struggle for that market between Ernie and Buzz.

Ernie: Buzz was a good friend and a good adversary. His family was in show business or something like that. I fought hard against Buzz in Santa Fe in the beginning years. There was so little business and we were trying hard to get the same people. Texas was the closest market so we campaigned throughout, going to Dallas, Amarillo, Lubbock.

Herman Kretschmer: When we traveled over the country Ernie would always carry a box full of brochures in the back of the car. We'd get some place in the middle of Texas, and there on the stand would be something advertising Mammoth Cave, Kentucky; he'd pull that out and stick his own brochures in. Everywhere he went, the trail was marked with Taos Ski Valley brochures which was a very effective way to do it.

Buzz Bainbridge: We used to fight, oh, how we used to go after each other. Ernie was the long-range thinker. I suppose there was a little feeling about my coming here and taking over his job when he went up to Taos. He was going after the Chicago market, and I wanted instant success and was going back for the Texas market, which he didn't really want at first. He wanted the Chicago skiers because of the train, and he wanted the international set. He was happy with the Texans later on, but in the beginning, he wanted Chicago, long-term people, which was right. He was thinking far ahead of us. All I wanted to do was get bodies on that ski lift and make money. But, he was in

there for the long haul, and he was smarter.

Ernie: We had a pretty good following in Texas from the days in Santa Fe; the six winters in Santa Fe had made me well-known in Texas. We used to travel around, first by automobile, and then the last two years by plane with my projector and skis. It was an interesting time and a tremendous way to promote. We were like a traveling gypsy show.

There are some great Texas stories. I like the story about Rhoda's student, who told Rhoda, "I'm ready for the parallel class now; I have mastered the snow shooter." That's typical Texan.

Keith Byers: The Bubba Story: Ernie was standing out there at 2:00 for afternoon ski school line-up, and he had elected himself to be the guy who stands in the middle of the gate which is not a ski width's wide; you can side slip through, but it's pretty narrow. Ernie is standing in the middle of this gate, and there is this one guy who obviously should not even have skis on who is not going to say a word. Ernie is waiting for him to declare himself. The guy starts sliding like a dog

New Mexico Ski Team including John Brennand, John Kinsolving, John Dendahl, Jim Jordan, Mary Lind & Buzz Bainbridge, coach. COURTESY BUZZ BAINBRIDGE.

on ice, and Ernie is going, "Don't you slide towards me," not saying it out loud, but out loud saying, "Go slowly, go slowly." The guy doesn't know slow from fast and is totally out of his element. He finally gets himself sort of dug in somehow, and he's saying, "Give me a break; cut me some slack, Bubba, cut me some slack!" Ernie didn't say anything but just sort of moved aside. He was a big guy—football material, like a linebacker; a Texas boy. It was like, "Who the hell is Ernie Blake anyhow? Give me a break; cut me some slack, Bubba, cut me some slack!"

Ernie: I enjoy the Texans. I wouldn't want to run the other type of New Mexico area which is all Texans; that would be too much. I used to get letters from them saying, "Will you please send us two ski poles to put in our club room? Some people in this area can't believe that you have snow in Taos."

Buzz Bainbridge: Skiing was in my blood. I was the captain of the Minnesota Ski Team. I was the Central United States slalom champion which didn't mean a thing. My family were show people. We had the theater in Minneapolis. My father was the mayor of Minneapolis.

After I got out of the navy, I went over to Northland Skis, and the old man hired me to go down and buy hickory in Alabama. I didn't know a thing about buying hickory. Just before I was to leave, Ambrose Lund, the son who really ran everything at that point said, "No, you're going to go out West and open the territory up again for us."

Lund sent me out West in my little Ford with the bald tires, and my wife and I came out. We went all over the West, to every ski area in the western United States. I rode the old boat tow at Aspen, sold skis to Elmer's Pool Hall and Crested Butte, all the way to Dillon, Montana. I gave away hundreds of skis, authentic Alf Engen skis. That made me very popular.

We traveled around all that spring, and we said, "Oh boy, Santa Fe, this is where we are going to live." We went back to Minnesota. I ran an ad in *Western Skiing* magazine. Bob Nordhaus answered it and said he had a job for me if I wanted it, opening up this little rope tow area between Tesuque and Hyde Park. We sold our house in Minneapolis and came out here, moved into Bishop's Lodge as their resident ski instructor, a nifty deal.

Nordhaus brought me out here, God love him. Nordhaus hired me to run Hyde Park; $200 a month and half the profits. The next year, he moved me down to run the big one, La Madera in Albuquerque. They had a big T-bar that was 4,600 feet long, the biggest lift in the state at that time.

I never did a thing to help Ernie in Taos. No, not a thing. I was in Santa Fe then. Every minute that he

Buzz & Jean Bainbridge. Courtesy Buzz Bainbridge.

Ernie with cowboy hat. Courtesy Blake Family Collection.

was tied up there, I was trying to get his business away from him down here. I did everything I could to thwart him. I was over there promoting those Texans and flying Texas flags.

I was better at PR with the Texans, but Ernie was better at PR with the international set. We traveled together; we'd go over and promote in Texas, and God, it was discouraging. We'd go to the Amarillo Ski Club or the Midland Ski Club, the Dallas Ski Club, and I'd get up and break my butt to give a good presentation. Ernie would get up and say, "I do not speak very well" and everybody would cheer and holler, and I would think, "What's the use?" He had a great wit.

We drove all over Texas together and that was something you would never forget if you ever drove with Ernie. Ernie drove like a maniac. He had that little Volkswagen, and we'd be jammed in there with our slide shows and our style shows and all this stuff, all the way from here to Dallas and Amarillo. All the way he would say, "What's this dumb son-of-a-bitch doing, look at that jerk there . . .," gesticulating out the window with his fists, yelling in Swiss.

Pete Totemoff: He'd drive you nuts if you let him. I rode with him to Ogden, Utah once, and that's a long way; that's 700 miles. He'd go like hell, and then he'd let up on the accelerator, then go like hell again, and then let up. All day long, it just got to you after a while. I don't know where the hell he learned to drive, but it must have been on a race track.

Herman Kretschmer: He was the most fantastic driver I've ever known. He would tailgate unbelievably with his Porsche, and then he would rush right out with a semi-truck coming right at you and cut the other driver off and keep going, anywhere from 90-100 mph. When you were driving with Ernie down to Texas, no matter how far it was, you damn well better be prepared to eat something in the car; and God help you if you had to pee.

Walter Widmer: I never thought he would die of pneumonia. I was almost sure he was going to die in a car. He would pass where he couldn't see. I'd ask Ernie, "What's the hurry to get there?" He'd say, "Well, I just can't help myself. It's my genes."

Bud Crary: Oh, Ernie was a crazy driver! There was one time we had to go to Breckenridge; I went with him then, but I wouldn't go with him anymore. He'd come by my house when we lived in a trailer in town. He'd say, "I'll be there at 8:00." I'd say, "Well, come a little early, and we'll eat breakfast; Tacky will cook us something." He'd come at 7:30 so we could leave at 8:00. So he'd came, and she had bacon and eggs ready when he got there at 7:30. We ate and we took off.

We went over the gorge, and then he put it in overdrive; he could go up to 140. That thing would

run, and oh man, I was sitting there with my butt sewed to the seat. He got going up a hill and a policeman went by and Ernie just went faster. We'd meet somebody on one of those curves, there was ice and snow on the road, snowpacked. We wound up in the bar ditch next to a barbed wire fence two or three times before we got on the road going up to Alamosa. It's a pretty straight road but icy, snowpacked all the way and just driving like a drunk. Some of those curves, he'd corner them where he couldn't see what's coming, and that's what scared me. He'd have to wheel over and fly around, and then he'd cuss them for being there. We left my house at 8:00, and we set down in Breckenridge Park at 11:00 drinking coffee. Ernie drove like an idiot, and he couldn't see fifty feet ahead of him.

George Engle: Ernie would drive up from Taos and arrive so he would get there in time for our pre-exam meetings at 8:00 in the morning. The first time I went down for an exam in Taos, I asked Ernie, "How long does it take to drive?" He said, "About four-and-a-half hours." And I didn't think anything about it. So, that day I thought I'd go early and ski in the afternoon. I left about 7:00 in the morning, and I got in there late in the afternoon. I told Ernie when I got there, "Ernie it took a day to get here. You told me it would take four-and-a-half hours. How fast do you drive?" He said, "I never go over 135 mph." He was driving that Porsche at the time. I don't even have a car that will go that fast, and normally, it takes about eight or nine hours to drive down.

Pete Totemoff: Ernie could not drive a car; he was a terrible pilot. I don't know how he flew airplanes or drove a car; he had no feeling for that.

Ernie: I enjoy driving, and I used to enjoy flying; it's a fantastic sensation, doing it yourself. I don't like flying in small airplanes with other people, but I don't like to drive with other people either.

I hired Fred Fair to be our charter pilot in the early times. He didn't need to make money so I could never find him when I needed him. He is a tremendous mountain flyer and an excellent skier in powder snow, but he is totally unreliable and sometimes he skis where he is not supposed to. I hired him but quickly fired him. He didn't want to work; he wanted to ski, he knew nothing of discipline.

Pete Seibert: I flew one time with a guy out of Taos, Fred Fair, and on the way back, he said, "There's one thing we have to do." He took me down the canyon, and we flew under the Rio Grande Gorge Bridge. That was a great thing.

Mickey Blake: I used to worry with Fred there was going to be a collision one of these days. Because the Air National Guard always comes up, and if you've ever noticed, Fred normally flew down the canyon, and they're just not expecting anybody to be in that valley. At the speeds that they're traveling, I think you could have a whopper of a collision. When we were moving those lift towers with that helicopter, I called them and said, "We're moving the towers with the helicopter today. Let's try not to have a helicopter/A-7 collision."

Elisabeth Brownell: I think the minute Ernie felt people were dependent on him, he became mean. But independent people like Fred Fair were different. Once Fred had lunch with Ernie who had some writers here. I was just walking by there and I overheard Fred say, "Well, this year I didn't buy a season lift pass; I just buy a daily ticket when I ski because when they take my ticket away, it's only for the day." Ernie did not know what to say.

Fred Fair: The first time I was in Taos was in January of 1959; I was coming up from Mexico where I was going to school, and I had a wonderful day skiing Al's Run with that little short Frenchman, what's his name. We'd ride the Poma lift up, and in order to ski down, there was so much snow that you had to put your skis on the Poma track at that steep top, pick up speed, float out into the powder, and before you drown, just stop on Al's. You'd come back to the Poma track and do the same thing. That's how we skied Al's for an entire day—just the two of us. There were no such things as bumps. A week after the storms, you still didn't have bumps.

During that week Ernie and I were skiing down Al's, and he said, "Where are you from?" I said I was in graduate school. He said, "Well, you should come back and teach here." So, six months later, I wrote him a letter and said I was a bilingual ski instructor, and so he said, "Well, we have a bilingual ski program." So, I was appointed director of the bilingual ski program.

Ernie picked me up in his Porsche, and he bought me lunch at the Lotaburger. That was the level of eating. Ernie was never big into eating. Of course, if he went to one of the lodges up there, they'd serve him the best; but on his own, Ernie was not highly motivated to eat well. So, I was never wined and dined, but it was what he did.

As an employee, I was instructed to continue south to Mexico on a strategic errand to the Mexico City Ski Club and to find out where the lift was that was supposed to go up on the Nevada de Teluca Mountain that had apparently been shipped to Veracruz twenty years before and had never been erected. I was supposed to find out where all this equipment was so he could buy it, and also to take the old Ski Valley logo down there and get a jeweler to make up pins using the logo: the old pin with the Indian skiing down.

I went to Mexico City, bought an airplane en route,

had a great trip down there, came back just before Thanksgiving and was "the ski instructor" from the time they opened at Thanksgiving until about the 18th of December. There were only three or four people a day at the very most who would come into the ski school during that slow month. I lived up there in that shack, the Chalet Alpina. We would eat in the Hondo. We were staff and I had my jacket; I had everything but a salary. I wasn't tacky enough to address my salary. I just knew he was going to come through. After all, I was the director of the bilingual ski program! Around the 18th of December, he handed me my check for the preceding months and my room and board had been deducted off the net, or off the take-home, and there was no take-home pay. That first winter I also started doing charters, grossly illegal charters. Ernie, once again, promised me that the world would open with a need for charter flights for Taos Ski Valley. He was always into promoting something for Taos.

Ernie could never intimidate me; I never let him. I was independent financially. I didn't have a lodge there, because back in those days, if you were at Taos Ski Valley with property, you depended on Ernie. I was the only one except for Chilton who was never beholden. He felt that he had a proprietary right to everybody's wealth up there. It's a perfect example of medieval feudalism because he felt everybody held property at his whim, and in a sense they did. Ernie was Old World charm and American con.

Ernie: In about 1962 or 1963, Herman and I drove Mickey's Volvo to Midland and Odessa. We were going to a meeting which the Midland Ski Club had agreed would be very brief, and we were promised that we would be put on first. We drank martinis because they offered me martinis, and I drank them very happily. So, when they were finally through with their other business and let me give my show, I told them it was silly for them to come to Taos because we had an IQ test for our skiers because it was a difficult mountain and few of them would pass it. That brought lots of laughter; they loved it; they came here. One football player was mad and wanted to beat me, but I didn't realize it. Herman was very worried about that, and I didn't catch on.

The Texans loved that kind of thing. I told them we had a rule to permit no one with an IQ of less than fifty-five on our slopes. And I made a remark that the ski swap items were wasteful, that most items were antiquated and not worth selling; but that some of them should be selected out because they were so antique that the British Museum would pay a fortune for them.

Herman Kretschmer: There was a guy by the

name of Bernie Bracker who was the weatherman on one of the TV stations down in El Paso. Ernie liked to go down there because we would make booze runs. In those days, you could get a gallon of Oso Negro cheap, and that was the main supply for those martinis that Rhoda used to hide in the snow in winter. We would go down in the summer or fall on these barnstorming trips.

One day we were down there, and we pulled into this motel, and Ernie was always kidding the check-in people. That year, in the ski shop, there were a whole bunch of black T-shirts with white collars and things that looked like a clerical collar. Each of us was wearing one. We went to check in, and the girl looked up and asked, "Are you people priests or pastors?" Ernie said, "Well, yes. Do you have clergymen's rates?" She said, "Oh, yes, we do." He says, "I'm Father Blake, and this is my associate, Father Kretschmer." We signed up and everything was great, and we actually signed as a Reverend Dr. Blake and Deacon Kretschmer or something like that and thought no more about it.

We went in and did a television show with Bernie Bracker. Then after kind of a wild time in El Paso and Juarez, we ended up in the middle of the bull ring in Juarez. Bernie Bracker was bombed out of his mind and was playing bull. He was the bull and Ernie was the matador, and I was going "Olé, olé," just the three of us except for the night watchman. Whoever he was ultimately heard all this commotion and came out and finally threw us out in a nice way; he thought we were nuts.

When it came time to check out, the gal said, "Father Blake, did you have a successful revival?" Ernie said, "Oh, yes, yes, we converted lots and lots of souls." At that exact moment on the TV set behind her was a rerun of the program that we had done with Bernie Bracker the night before talking about skiing. Fortunately, she didn't see it. We did get the reduced rates.

One day, on one of our trips to somewhere, Ernie said to me, "Do you realize today is Hindenburg's birthday?" and he proceeded to explain its significance to him. He said, "Well, today is von Hindenburg's birthday. It represents the anniversary of the one and only time that I was ever approached by a homosexual." He hastened to tell me that he was so embarrassed that he didn't belt the guy or anything, he just walked away. It was the one and only time.

Kingsbury Pitcher: Ernie, Buzz, Bob Nordhaus, Ben Abruzzo and myself were all very compatible, very friendly. We used to have joint marketing, and Ernie would usually lead the pack because he was the guy that had the most ideas. We couldn't work with him too well because he was looking at different markets. Ernie was looking at the global market, and we were

Fred Fair. COURTESY FRED FAIR.

Ernie & Buzz Bainbridge. COURTESY BUZZ BAINBRIDGE.

merely trying to get them to come from Texas. There was a lot of back and forth.

Darcy Brown: Ernie and Bob Parker at Vail were marketing geniuses of the ski industry, but they had entirely different approaches to marketing. They had entirely different personalities, too. Bob Parker's marketing approach was much more conventional than Ernie's. Ernie took great pride in the fact that the front of his mountain was so steep. I think he kind of approached people the same way as when people go to Aspen. They all want to say they skied Aspen Mountain, but they'd be better off at Snowmass or Buttermilk. The idea of telling people that this mountain is too tough for them makes them want to try it. I think that really explains a lot of Ernie's early success. He used that steepness as sort of a challenge.

George Engle: Our marketing at Winter Park was local/regional. Ernie was looking to the international set and the elite skiers who were looking for a particular experience, and Bob Parker was looking for yet another or a more inclusive group to draw from. He wanted everyone at Vail; I don't think Ernie felt that way. Taos is a different mountain entirely.

Buzz Bainbridge: How do you think Ernie got all that publicity? He was the smart guy. A travel agent would come out here, or an airline guy, and Ernie would break his butt to be good to them. They would repay him. Look at *Ski* and *Skiing* magazines and all of his buddies there. He'd get more publicity for that little area; it was a little dinky ski area, and he would get more publicity for that area than Vail or Aspen would get, and they were spending $50,000 a year on space. He wasn't spending $5,000. And it would kill me when he didn't have any snow, and he told everybody not to come, and they came anyway.

Rhoda: Ernie had this unique ability of saying the truth; he would do this with snow conditions. He'd say that the snow conditions were terrible, but somehow he conveyed the idea that, hey, it's really worthwhile coming anyway! I don't know how he did it, but he could always make it sound much better than it was while using the words that were absolutely true. He would do it in such a way that people think well they just had to come; it couldn't be that bad.

Buzz Bainbridge: He had a big hole up there that he used to measure snow in. I was out there on the flat of the hill, honestly, and Ernie was standing at that five-foot hole saying 80" of snow. Ernie and I used to fight; oh my God, we used to fight over snow reports!

The funny thing is that we really hacked at each other those first few years, and then I went to Aspen and of course we became real good friends. After that we had the "Ski the Rockies" group where we met once a month together, and then we really got close. Ernie always said that I taught him everything he knew, and I also said Ernie taught me everything I knew, so we had a mutual admiration society.

Pete Totemoff: Ernie always said that Buzz Bainbridge had messed with so many different ski areas like Santa Fe, Red River, Flagstaff, Aspen, that Ernie made the remark one day, "If Buzz ever shows up, we'd better hire him to protect ourselves."

Ernie's big strong point was to make anything work; he was one of the best marketing men next to Buzz in the state, in the whole United States. To make any ski area go, regardless if you've got the best ski area in the world, if you don't have good marketing people, you're dead; maybe not dead, but you're not going to make it very well.

Bob Nordhaus: Oh, gosh darn, Ernie did a fantastic job. He had so much charisma. He just attracted skiers from all over. Taos Ski Valley is an outstanding place. With Ernie, there was a mystique about the difficulty of Taos. That was something that always appeals to good skiers. You know, Al's Run was supposed to be the toughest hill in the country, and what was that sign? *Achtung?* The steepness definitely worked to his advantage. There were people who said, "I want to ski Taos because it's tough. None of this easy stuff."

Walter Ruegg: We worked harder then; it was different. Today, if people had to work that hard, they either couldn't hack it or they wouldn't want to do it.

Ernie himself worked hard. That's why you could work for a guy like that. If he worked hard himself, he could demand that of us. Ernie never really wanted a chair lift; he liked things to be rugged. Like the big Poma—he liked that lift.

Ernie: The big Poma lift was the toughest Poma lift in the world, I am sure, which kept the beginners off the hill anyway. We produced the most vertical feet skied in the world with our marathon. I did fifty-two runs when I was fifty-two years old, 86,000 feet. It was a great race. Jean did even better; over 100,000 feet. It took real endurance.

Georgia Hotton: Ernie got a whole lot of mileage on the fact that Taos had more vertical feet of skiing than anywhere else in the world. I don't think anybody ever beat that challenge in terms of other ski resorts because very few ski resorts had a Poma lift that would go up that far, that fast. So, it was virtually impossible for the others to beat us on that one.

Ernie had this contest; I skied eleven runs by about 1:00 in the afternoon, and I couldn't even move anymore. I was so tense at that point, I couldn't even let go of my ski poles. I quit, but Ernie and Jean and Paco Santistevan were among the ones that went on and on and on. It was a very intense competition. It was with these special events that Ernie got us some exciting national publicity.

Elisabeth Brownell: I had signed up for that marathon race. There were twenty people, and I was worried about Georgia Hotton because she was a ski instructor, and she was a strong skier. I had no idea how many runs I could do. So, we started out, and I have a competitive spirit. Ernie was in that race. At noontime, somebody said Georgia had dropped out, and that gave me an extra boost. I continued until 4:00, and there were only very few left out of the twenty. Then I thought, I'm not exhausted; I might as well go up on sweep. I made forty-five runs. Ernie was fifty-two years old and I couldn't beat him. The others said, "It was a good thing you didn't beat Ernie because he would have fired you."

CHAPTER 18
A Melding of Characters

Ernie: The first chair came in 1961, and we opened up the 15th of January, 1962. I had not been in favor of a chair lift. I preferred the Poma which was much more difficult; it kept the poor skiers off the mountain.

Georgia Hotton: The big Poma lift was called the automatically ejecting lift. If you couldn't ride up it, and a lot of people fell off riding up, the chances are you weren't going to be able to ski down anyhow.

Rhoda: Can you imagine being a beginner and coming off the beginner hill and going up that Poma, and then you fall on Al's? You've got to come down Al's as your first run. I can remember following a beginner class up, going to the top and picking up all the beginners who had fallen on Al's and getting them off the mountain. If you did not ride with someone that was heavy on that Poma, there were close to fifty feet where you never touched the ground. Then we built the ramp, but even that didn't do it if you were riding alone.

Pete Seibert: I remember riding up the lift with Ernie. It was after the chair had been put in. While we were riding up, somebody was entangled in the Poma. Ernie was looking across and yelling from the lift at them, saying he should set up an I.Q. testing office down at the bottom of the valley and unless they qualify physically and mentally, then he said he's not going to let them in here. It was a treacherous lift. Ernie was like the bartender or restaurant owner that insulted people and they loved it.

Georgia Hotton: I remember the day Ernie fell so badly. I think it was the day he decided he should look into a chair lift. One day, Ernie and Pete Totemoff were doing some repair work on the ski track itself; it was somewhat icy, it was early in the season, and they were shoveling snow onto the route that the skiers would be going up while riding the Poma. They were on foot. They had gone up with their skis and then had left their skis up a ways and were using shovels to shovel snow onto the track. All of a sudden, Ernie lost his footing, and Andres, one of our lift operators, was at the bottom of the lift, and he said he thought Ernie might have been going 35 mph when he crashed into the trees. He lost his footing and slid down that icy slope.

Now, guests had fallen off the lift from time to time and slid down that slope and slid into the trees and fortunately none of them were very seriously hurt. But Ernie had sort of pooh-poohed that, saying they

couldn't have skied down that anyhow, so that's okay. But, when he slid into the trees that particular day, he was quite seriously hurt, something like breaking all the blood vessels in his thigh. He was in a lot of pain; he hit the trees hard. I remember sitting at the dinner table with him that night and his saying, "I guess maybe it's time to consider a chair lift." He really did not want to go to chair lifts. Ernie realized that you could get hurt, and maybe a chair lift was going to be necessary to get people up that mountain.

Mickey Blake: In the the fall of 1961, we built chair lift #1 and that's when Walter Ruegg came. The story is he came in the box with the lift. It's not true that Walter was unpacked with the lift.

Walter Ruegg: Not too many people know it, but they used to call me Rubezahl when I was here the first year. They called me that because Rubezahl was sort of a big giant who walked around the forests in Germany. He had a tree for a walking stick. When I came here at first, I was pretty strong, and that's what they called me. And when they cut Rubezahl, I think it was named after me.

I was born in Switzerland, in the Zurich Oberland. I worked for Stadeli Lifts there. The first chair lift in Taos was actually the first chair lift Stadeli ever built. We had lifts that could be converted; in the winter, it was a T-bar, and in the summer it was a chair lift but you sat sideways in the chair. But this was the first real chair lift. I built all the lifts except for the Poma and the new Quad. But I did all the other ones and Kachina, too, in 1971.

Ernie: The lifts were diesel. The #1 chair, the old Super Chief, had a Cummins 170-horsepower engine. It is now the standby engine, and the main engine is an electric one. The engineer for that lift was Ilse Mayer's brother, Alfred Gulz, who came as a salesman for Stadeli. Taos Ski Valley had the first Stadeli chair lift ever built. They had sold some T-bars in Oregon, Mt. Bachelor, but they had never built a chair lift in this country. Gulz had designed the lift, and he came four years later. He said that nobody will ever have any fun with that lift; you're wasting your money. Well, I'm not a man who listens easily to other people as I've proven with my insanity.

Rhoda: In order to get the foundations for the #1 lift filled with concrete, we put hooks on the Poma and mixed the cement at the base. Then buckets were filled with cement and went up on the Poma instead of platters. They grabbed them off at the top and dumped them.

Hauling cement for new chair on old Poma lift. COURTESY ERNIE BLAKE COLLECTION.

Walter Ruegg: When the lift came, we got it together in pretty good time. I think the whole lift with all the material, everything, was $52,000. That maybe didn't include the engine; but the cable and towers and bull wheel. The new quad cost close to a million dollars. Since Ernie bought the first lift from Stadeli, they had a contract that if Ernie wasn't happy with the lift, Stadeli would come the next year and tear it down at his own expense and give him his money back. That was a pretty good guarantee and Ernie was happy with it.

Matter of fact, one day Stadeli came to me in the shop and asked what kind of a deal I made with Ernie. I said I didn't know of any deals. He said that Ernie was going to send me $500; "What was that for?" Well, I guess he said if the lift runs good the rest of the season, he was going to send me some money. So, he was pretty happy with it.

I got the chair lift finished, and the first time I started it up, the cable came off and fell. In those times there were practically no machines at all. There were a couple of Indians, and the first Spanish guys, Lee Varoz, Sr. and Andres Montoya, Phil Sanchez and a few other guys. We took pieces of tower up in the old jeep and then bolted them together.

Walter Ruegg splicing cable. COURTESY ERNIE BLAKE COLLECTION.

I'm not an engineer in the true sense; I don't have any big degree or anything like that. I had been a mechanic for four years over in Switzerland which was more like a machinist. You just slowly get into it; you can't go to school and learn how to build a chair lift. Before I came here, I knew I had to splice the cables, and they sent me to the factory for four weeks to learn. I had a little black book and took notes and made some drawings, and when I started to splice the cable, I would read the book again. They've been kidding me about that for years and years. Walter Widmer helped too. That splice lasted twenty-six years.

Ernie: Walter Widmer came in November of 1961 because he was a friend of the Weber boys, two brothers, one of whom is the one who sold me the first Stadeli, and later the Pullman/Barry lift. Walter had been in this country as a pastry chef and a general chef at the Greenbriar Hotel in White Sulphur Springs. It's a famous hotel in the southeast where the Duke of Windsor stayed. Later he was at The Breakers in Palm Beach.

Walter wanted to get into the hotel business, and we got to an agreement; I told him there was little money in it, but it might be a good investment for him to take over the Hondo. He was the perfect guy. We thought of him as buying the Hondo Lodge, but it ended up that he took over the ticket sales and has handled them ever since. He's done a terrific job and been a great friend. Walter has very few shortcomings because unlike most other Swiss, he has a good sense of humor; and he cooked kidneys for me. No one else would eat them.

Walter Widmer: Ernie loved kidneys; he loved liver too, but more than anything else, he liked kidneys. Nobody here would eat kidneys. I would cook them for him. When we made that tour through Europe with Mickey and his kids, at every stop I would start checking the restaurants around the hotel; we had to have kidneys on the menu. It was a kidney tour of Europe.

Ernie loved eggs too. I did a funny thing to Ernie with a goose egg I got from Claude Gohard, chef at the Hotel St. Bernard, from down on his farm. He has all kinds of animals; he had goats and geese, rabbits and chickens. I always had breakfast with Ernie and Rhoda. Ernie was not the world's greatest cook, but he thought he was the only one who knew how to boil eggs exactly right. So, he always cooked a soft boiled egg in the morning.

Claude had given me a goose egg, and they are very big. So, I soft boiled that up at my house until it was just about cooked. When Ernie would hear me coming up the steps, he would turn on the water to boil the eggs. He did that and then went to the bathroom. I

took one of the eggs out and put the goose egg in there. He came in, turned the thing off, and took the cover off the pot. He didn't say anything; he just kept looking. Of course his eyesight was not very good. So, he threw out the water and here were these two little eggs and one huge egg. He kept looking and picked it up. He said, "It's not possible." Somehow in his mind, he thought that one egg had just swelled up. But he kept saying, "That's not possible." Then I told him what I'd done, and he ate the whole thing.

Papa Mayer: Walter Widmer was Ernie's best friend.

Monica Brown: Walter would tell Ernie when he thought something was "bullshit;" he did that all the time to Ernie. But Ernie would take it from Walter. He wouldn't take it from anybody else. Things would be steaming, there would be explosions in that little room and Walter would come in the door, and he would not say a word, and then he would say something and everybody would laugh.

Walter could tell Ernie off in a humorous way. Often times, even when Rhoda could not get to Ernie, Rhoda would get to Ernie through Walter. He could do no wrong. They were both Swiss. They understood the language. There comes also Fred Iselin in there, the third one in the group. There was something within themselves; they knew what they were talking about. They could make you feel like a million bucks, and they could make you feel like you were under the ground. They had the power to do that and don't ask me how, but that's the way it was.

Tom Brownell: Walter Widmer, I think, was the closest to Ernie, but still there was a cellophane barrier of employee/employer where he wouldn't talk about personal finances and things. Ernie saw the changes coming and knew it a little better than Walter, the coming of his time. Walter is still very European. One of our staff sent money ahead of time for a lift ticket to beat the discount period. I took it over to Walter and asked for a receipt, and there was the old European way with the book, the writing out of each one and a stamp that said Taos Ski Valley, Inc. There were no numbers or anything. Just a very deliberate, old Swiss way, and of course, that's all gone. It's all computerized now.

Walter Widmer: Ernie and I always have been very good friends, kind of almost like a brother relationship, me being the younger brother, of course. He was not an easy person to get along with. But somehow, we hit it off right from the beginning.

Ernie wrote me and said he had a very small place up there, and it was not much, and, "We don't make any money. We have a lot of fun." He said, "I need somebody to take over a small hotel for me," and asked if I was interested in checking it out. I had heard of New Mexico, and the thought was kind of intriguing to me. What the hell? I'll go and spend one winter out there, why not? That's how I came.

When I arrived, Jean still had the lease on the Hondo Lodge, so I started work for Ernie and Rhoda. In those days, that old building, Ernie's old home, and the other half was the office, a rental shop, software, hardware, and all tickets. Everything was in the other half of that building.

When you came in the door to Ernie's office, he had a cabinet there like a high filing cabinet with a pullout thing for his typewriter. He would be sitting there behind that thing. Every person that came in had to come in through that door, so he got a draft every time a person came in. So, the greeting at Taos Ski Valley was "Close the goddamn door!" Ernie didn't like anything which was not orderly, yet he wasn't a very orderly person.

Elisabeth Brownell: When I arrived, I said to Ernie, "Are you moving?" And he said, "No, it looks like that all the time." The first little office I had was in a little trailer. The first year it was right behind the door. Everybody who came in brought a whiff of cold air. My fingers froze. I had to wait for the sun to warm up the typewriter because there was no heat in that area. That was a little cubbyhole.

I lived in the Chalet Alpina, right underneath the lift with six other guys and a girl. I stayed underneath the roof in the loft. Walter Widmer slept right under me, and there were those cracks, and he snored.

Ilse Mayer: Walter Widmer and I arrived at the same instant in the parking lot of the Hondo Lodge in 1961. Jean had just made the second story above the dining room on the St. Bernard that year, so the original dining room and the second story with the hotel rooms were there. The original old hunting lodge, the Hondo Lodge, was there with a big recreational room in the middle and the huge fireplace.

My ambition was to learn how to ski. I think it was Chilton who took me out the first time. Ernie had assigned Chilton to me, of all people. My equipment was so funny. I had to ask somebody, either Dadou or Chilton, to help me and to show me how to put those skis on.

I met Dadou that first winter. He was first working as an instructor, a ski patrolman, the maintenance crew and bartending at the St. Bernard and waiting tables and whatever. Everybody had to do everything. Dadou had no interest in getting involved with anyone at that time. He told me that first thing. I said fine, I don't need anyone. I am just here for a few months, and then I'm going back to Austria. Well, things happened, and it didn't work that way. I got more and more involved with the St. Bernard and with Dadou, and we got involved rather than with Ernie's ski lift.

Ernie wanted me to be an instructor, and I told Ernie I do not know how to ski very well. He said I

Max Killinger & Walter Ruegg at Rhoda's shop, February 1970. Courtesy Ernie Blake Collection.

would be a good instructor within a week, with my accent and whatever; coming from Austria, it didn't matter how I skied. "You will be an instructor," he said. He really tried to make that decision for me. My whole thirty years in Taos, I never taught. I told him that I wouldn't stay if I had to be an instructor. I wanted to have another job just because I was very practical minded. I told him if he couldn't find me another job, I wasn't going to come. "Don't worry," he said, "I will find you something else." He sure did; we had the Edelweiss for more than twenty-five years.

I'll never regret that we got the Edelweiss now. It's so much a part of my life, and I cannot understand that it won't be part of my children's life. This is going to be real hard in my head, but that's how it is. People say that I should be happy I can get rid of it now, and in a way I am, but there is so much attached to it.

Ilse Mayer: No electricity, no telephone, no T.V., no road, no communication, nothing. We had an old generator; that's all we had. We had to keep it alive every time it snowed real hard; we'd have to go and fix it at 2:00 in the morning with six feet of snow to wade through right out of your bed. It was hard. The shoveling was so super primitive, a real contrast to Vienna. And Ernie was right in there; it was just as primitive for him. He lived under the same conditions, and Rhoda and the kids.

Ernie: With the generator, we made the great error of putting Jean in charge as mechanic. That's something he failed completely. Mechanical equipment is something he's no genius at. He did everything else fabulously, but not this. We had lots of expense in fixing the engines; bearings burned out and no fuel. Diesel engines should never run dry; that's disastrous.

Walter Widmer: Ernie liked to joke about Jean's responsibilities on the generator. It was Jean's job; he had to take care of it. It was a building with kind of slits; there were openings between the thing, so the snow would be drifting in. Sometimes that generator was standing in two feet of snow. The thing is, the generator didn't work very well. It usually kicked out and then we were back to candlelight. We didn't get electricity until about 1963 or 1964 maybe. The telephone came the same time, almost ten years from the start.

Mickey Blake: The lights used to go off at 9:00 at night, and they would turn that thing off. There was nothing wrong with the generator, but the way they had it set up was really a crazy thing. That may be how I got into the electrician business. I wired all that stuff. Kit Carson Electric Company didn't come until 1963. I can remember Ernie Santistevan and those guys building that line. Why we always build everything in winter, I'll never know. But they built that line in the

Hondo Lodge. PHOTO BY DICK TAYLOR.

Ed & Phyllis Pratt. PHOTO BY DICK TAYLOR.

middle of winter up to the Ski Valley, and that's the line we use today.

Ed Pratt: The big thing was we didn't have electricity. The only electricity we had was an old 175-horsepower generator that was housed in sort of a log lean-to down a little bit between the two lodges and a little bit lower. That supplied the electricity for the two lodges and Ernie's place. The lights would go up and down constantly like an elevator depending on how the generator ran. There would be nights that thing would go down so low, and I'd hit the back door, and Jean would come out the back door of the St. Bernard, and we'd meet at that damn place and start throwing oil in there. It drank oil like you would drink water.

The generator broke down in the summer of 1962 when Jean was building onto the A-frames, and we were remodeling the Hondo Lodge. We had to have the engine pulled out and brought to Albuquerque for overhaul which took six weeks. Jean was cooking for all the workers on both jobs. It was all done by lanterns. We'd eat before it got too damn dark so you could see what you were eating. We used lanterns to get around and went to bed early. That was the best summer of all, without any electricity.

Judy Anderson: We picked Taos Ski Valley, partly because they advertised candlelight dinners, and we thought that was very romantic. After we got here, we realized it was because the generator kept going out. I came on a ski week with a friend of mine. We were going to Sipapu, Santa Fe, and I forget what other brochures we had. That was in February, 1958. The Hondo was the only thing there. We came for a week's vacation to go skiing, and then I went home and gave three weeks' notice on my job and came back to work.

I was a ski bum, which meant I tended bar, I did some cooking, we did some cleaning; anything that needed to be done, we did. It was just from March to the end of the season. I got paid about $56 for the season plus room and board.

Ernie: Ed Pratt came and bought the Hondo Lodge in 1961. I met Ed at the Chicago Ski Show around 1958 and he brought his club, the Allouettes, out two or three times. Then he decided to retire from the army and bought the Hondo Lodge in 1961, which pleased Al Rosen and me greatly.

The summer of 1959, Jean added the eight rooms on top of the restaurant of the St. Bernard. Then he bought the land for himself and ultimately separated himself from the Hondo Lodge. Then we leased the Hondo Lodge to Ed Pratt who then bought it from the Twining Ski Corporation who had managed it very well.

Ed and his wife Phyllis were both master sergeants and together they had a tremendous pension. Ed was

Rhoda & Walter Widmer. COURTESY ERNIE BLAKE COLLECTION.

very military, and by that time, I had enough army life behind me that I wasn't anxious to hear a sergeant's voice; now I think that was a great error. He ran a first-class operation. He had no salesmanship and not much ski charm for his guests, but he was precise and honest; when they made out a bill for a guest, there were no errors. Ed used to like to help Myrt Rosen, and later Rhoda, in the ski shop to fit girls into their ski pants. That was a weakness of his.

Walter Widmer: I never got into the hotel business. Ed Pratt took over the Hondo Lodge, and I hired a Swiss Chef for him named Albert Trutmann, but he didn't get the visa in time, so we had to hire a local fellow by the name of Al Summers. He was a good chef, but he was very slow. He also had been shell-shocked or something in the war, and he was on some kind of medication which they sent him automatically from the Veterans' Administration; they never took him off it. He drank too, maybe. Anyway he couldn't handle breakfast. He was good at getting everything prepared, and then you just served it out for lunchtime or dinnertime. But breakfast where you do everything a la carte, when you order, he was sunk then. So I used to cook breakfast at the Hondo Lodge in the morning.

Walter Widmer, April 1969. COURTESY ERNIE BLAKE COLLECTION.

Then I would go to the ticket office and open that up. The guests used to come in the kitchen and say, "I want more eggs—two blindfold or three sunny side up." Then I would come over here. Then they said, "Oh, I thought I saw you over in the kitchen in the Hondo Lodge." And I would say, "That's my twin brother; he works over there." Sometimes Ed would come running over about 10-11:00; he'd say, "Well, Al's drunk." So, I would close the ticket office, and I'd go over there and put something on for lunch.

Ed Pratt: Walter gave me an awful lot of help the first year cooking. He was the one who got all of my chefs except for Al. He had carte blanche as to what to offer them salary-wise. As I look back on it, it was peanuts. I paid them a thousand a month which was a fortune in Switzerland, and room and board went with it.

Theresa Killinger: The Hondo Lodge was a gorgeous lodge; so very clean. We were at Christmas at the Hondo our first time here in 1965. It was decorated and it was heavenly, and the two of them, Ed and Phyllis, welcomed each guest and you were seated. It was a celebration. The Pratts had class.

Max Killinger: They were very straight, like in a bull's-eye straight, and some of them like Bill Whaley and John Koch couldn't stand it, so they always tried to needle them. They had a following of guests who loved to come back year after year. If you came in the lodge with your ski boots on and you weren't supposed to, he pulled you out; I mean it was clean in there and everybody had to do it. You couldn't help it when the two of them spent forty-three years in the army together; it forms one's character.

Ed Pratt: I've heard Ernie tell the story of my woodshed a thousand times. It was the first year I had the Hondo after we rebuilt it. I had a little shed in the back of the Hondo that we used as a storage shed. I built a log wall back in there, a retaining wall, to hold the dirt back, and that's where I had my split wood for the fireplace. We would split those logs and line them up. I happened to be looking out the window one early October, and as Ernie walked by, he saluted it. He said, "That Pratt's so military, hell, I can't even go by that woodpile out there without stopping and saluting those goddamn logs; every one is lined up like a bunch of troops."

John Koch: It was as if "Big Daddy" (Ed Pratt) used to nail the woodpile together. I couldn't walk by it and keep a straight face.

Chilton Anderson: "Big Daddy" would do anything for anybody. He had his problems. He didn't know how to run a lodge, and he ran it like a military company, but he'd do anything for

Lisa Harner, Phyllis Pratt, Walter Ruegg, Franz Voller, April 1970. COURTESY BLAKE FAMILY COLLECTION.

Ed Pratt, 1970. COURTESY ERNIE BLAKE COLLECTION.

anybody. Phyllis used to blow a whistle at 5:00—everybody out! Everybody had to get out because they were going to set up the tables for dinner. Ernie ran a strict ship, but he didn't run it quite the way you would run something in the army. "Big Daddy" and Phyllis sure did.

Bob Brierley: I remember the first time that my nephew George came, and I took him to the Hondo Lodge. Ed was giving a party for someone, and I happened to be with Ernie and he says, "Why don't you come on over and go to Ed's; we're having a party." I said, "I'd like to, but I've got this shirttail nephew of mine." He says, "Oh, bring him along." We go on over there, and "Big Daddy" is behind the bar with his apron on, and here comes Ernie and me, and then he looked at George, and he knew darn well he hadn't invited George. We went up to the bar. Ernie orders whatever. George says, "I'll have a dry sherry, if you don't mind." "Big Daddy" puts his cloth down and says, "What?" "A dry sherry." He said, "Young fellow, we don't serve dry sherry except to women and these fancy fellows that walk like this." He said, "Well then, I'll have a whiskey and water."

Ed was funny though. He told us that we were the only persons that he would let take a dog in there. This was our first, Freckles, a cocker spaniel. We'd go in there, and even she felt the sergeant major bit because she'd go in there with all the people eating, and she'd just look. Then she'd trot across and turn down and go to her room. She never went inside. "Big Daddy" was a typical sergeant major: straight as an arrow, a very honorable man.

Rhoda: The first years, the two sergeants ran it like an army camp. I smoked even then, and the minute you put your cigarette out, the ashtray was whisked away from you, and a new one put in its place. They softened a little with time.

Ed Pratt: Most of my military learning never did leave me and hasn't left me to this day, but it took me over a year or so until I began to lose the spit-and-polish image. Ernie used to say, "Hell, you can eat off of Pratt's floor in the dining room." I just like things clean.

When I first came out there was nothing for me to do, and I was at most a rank beginning skier. So Ernie made me take lessons; it was my pleasure to take private ski lessons from three people for thirty days. At the end of thirty days, I had learned to ski reasonably well. My three instructors were Ernie, Jean Mayer and Chilton Anderson. One of them had me every afternoon. If I wanted to take a day off and sleep, no way, let's go. I knew from military experience that when you're told to do something and you're on somebody's payroll, you better do it.

I spent the next thirty days learning the techniques of skiing and teaching, and then on the 2nd day of February of 1962, at ski school one morning, I wasn't there. All of a sudden, I heard my name called, and I stepped outside and said, "Did somebody call me?" Ernie says, "Where are your skis?" "Right here." "Well, here's your class." That was my first introduction to ski teaching.

That first morning was a fiasco. I had a beginners' class and they got going in all directions, and I didn't know how to stop them. Finally about halfway through, I used my military experience and said, "Everybody just stop where the hell you are. Nobody move from this point on unless I tell you to. I don't care what direction you're standing, you stand there until I tell you to move." By the time class was over, I had them pretty well straightened out. It was an experience I'll never forget, but a great one. It led to a lot happier times and some super years of teaching a lot of great people. I taught Patrice Munsel, the famous singer. I became a supervisor and for a while Ernie called me his assistant director, but he called a lot of people that.

When I first got there that first summer after the snow melted, I had a chance to really look around. I didn't really have a picture of what the Hondo Lodge looked like without snow. I'd seen it as a visitor but this was the first time seeing it as an owner. What I saw scared me. The old Hondo and the St. Bernard with eight rooms on top, that's all that there was. When I saw that with all the snow gone, I said, "What did I buy?" I wanted to tear that thing down and start all over but I couldn't. The only thing to do was just to go in and remodel it which we did that first summer, and many summers after. At that time, we proceeded to literally tear it apart. We gutted the inside and got it ready for the opening of 1962. We spent a lot of money making a lot of changes to try to make the old log cabin into a livable ski lodge.

The water system came from about 1,000 feet southeast out of the side of the mountain. In mid-October, we started getting a little worried back in those early years, because before the snows came, that water would freeze since it was not protected. Jean and I would spend all night building fires along that water pipe to keep it from freezing, or if it had already frozen, to thaw it. Some mornings, you would look in the mirror and you'd say, "Who's that person?" because you were all soot-faced and dirty and hungry, cold and sleepy. Year after year, we kept it going.

I learned the hotel business, I learned the ski business from the ground up, and when I say from the ground up, I mean it literally. I went into it with absolutely no knowledge of even being able to ski. I had no knowledge of teaching; no knowledge of what a ski lodge should be like. But fortunate for me and those involved at that time, it was such a difficult situation, such a remote area, so few people you might say, that mistakes that we made were not as noticeable as they would have been in a developed area as you would find today. In fact, some of the mistakes I made, if I made the same mistakes today I'd have been broke the first year, out on my ear. But back in those days, you could make mistakes and get away with them. And you learned from your mistakes.

I guess maybe I was the one person in the top eight or ten people in the Ski Valley who had no experience whatsoever, unlike Jean and Dadou, being members of the French National Jr. Racing Team, and Ernie with his years and years of experience, Chilton Anderson having the experience he had as a teacher and a skier. Here I came along from the flatlands, and I was thrown in with lions, and I've had to look from all sides to make sure that I didn't get clawed to death.

Fortunately, like in the Bible where the lions and the lambs can lie together without eating the other up, that was the way I felt. We were able to hit it off reasonably. If there were any problems, I just said fine; you've got more experience than I. We'll go your way until it doesn't work, and then we'll go my way. That's the way I tried to operate the lodge when I took it over.

I used to tell my staff, this is the way we're going to do it. Now if you can show me somewhere down the line you've got a better way, then we'll change. Until you show me, then we'll operate my way because I'm the guy who has to bear the brunt of any mistakes that are made. If I'm going to lose, it's going to be my mistake, not yours. That's the philosophy I tried to bring with me when I went into the hotel business. And those were some of the happiest years of my life; difficult years, yes, but happy.

Section VI

The Valley Grows: Past, Present & Future

In 1965 Ernie expanded Taos Ski Valley with the #2 lift which gave access to the top of the mountain (elevation 11,860 feet). This meant that now we could ski The Ridge and all the way down the back of the mountain, down a six-mile run called Rubezahl. Now Taos was getting the long runs like Europe had, and Ernie liked that.

Changes were happening very rapidly; the Santa Fe Railroad was fast becoming Amtrak and the airlines were becoming the preferred mode of transportation to ski the West. So Ernie and his colleagues started "Ski The Rockies" and got involved with airline promotions. Growth problems started to emerge and one that seemed to catch all expanding areas was a sewage problem. Taos Ski Valley was no exception; they had their own "hot springs." Some monstrous fights took place until a solution was found.

More lodges were needed, and some people came with money, and some came only with their skills, their hard work, and the gift of bullshit. Victor Frolich built the Innsbrook Lodge with Ernie's help and as Victor and Ernie used to say, "everything is possible in America." Ed Pratt was forced to sell the Hondo Lodge because of illness and Harry Franzgen came from Vail and bought it. We called him "Harry Hondo"; it seemed that everyone who owned the Hondo Lodge got a nickname. Kaarlo Jokela was forced to sell the Thunderbird Lodge to his partners Tom and Elisabeth Brownell. Even if "everything was possible in America," there were still many difficulties. The lodge owners were independent folks who looked out for themselves. They all had their own quirks, but when anyone was in need or in trouble, they would all throw away their jealousies and pull together.

It was the same for Ernie and his son Mickey. Mickey was beginning to make more and more of the decisions. Succession is not easy, but, incredibly, they got through the fistfight stage, and Mickey's skills became a great complement to his father's. They ended as good friends.

When Ernie opened the Kachina Basin area he had found the moderate terrain he was always searching for. He finally could make the intermediate skiers happy. As the area grew, Taos was no longer such a well-kept secret and the need for controlling growth increased. Quality instead of quantity became the cry. Ernie was only looking for enough skiers to make his area successful; he never wanted large crowds. Controlling growth is a universal problem.

Ernie knew his dream was almost over, but he had faith that Taos Ski Valley would survive the pains of growth under Mickey's rule. He hoped that Jean and Mickey would see eye-to-eye for the good of the ski valley, to maintain the right spirit. Ernie always wanted a destination resort, not one for day skiers, but he knew that that was breaking down, making a new huge day skiers' building a necessity. And debt, for the first time, was a great worry.

Ernie knew that "the steeps" and the uniqueness of Taos would keep his area different, no matter what. His eyes would twinkle when he read the articles about how steep and tough his mountain was. Getting the number-one rating for the ski school was most important because Ernie believed that to enjoy Taos, to get the flavor of what he dreamed, skiers must be in ski school, they must be here for a week, they must enjoy the mountain, and keep their goddamn skis off the fence.

CHAPTER 19
Demands of Growth

Ernie: In 1965 we expanded to the top of the mountain with the #2 chair to an elevation of 11,819. It had the same capacity as our #1 lift, 615 skiers per hour. Then we started opening up towards Kachina Peak. We had already spotted it on the photo map, and we had skied from Kachina several times. Going to the top of the mountain gave us our first run down the back side called Rubezahl; it was six miles long. But our first ten years we were down on the lower mountain.

Governor Campbell came on Thanksgiving Day to open the new #2 lift, but he had to go to a funeral first. He arrived in a black city suit and black necktie, and, I am sure, no heavy underwear. It seemed like always when we built a lift, there was lots of snow and this day was no exception. The governor insisted on going up there; he didn't want to back out, so he went up in the bitter cold and nearly froze to death.

Mickey took him up in the Kristi Kat. It had a Porsche engine and was a strange vehicle that could be tilted. You could go over steep side hills; you could traverse them with it which you can't with others. When they crossed the traverse where it intersects between upper and lower Powderhorn, it started slipping off. We had no snow maintenance machines yet. I still think of Governor Campbell because I can still see them sliding off the mountain. But, they made it somehow. I was worried about Mickey first, then Campbell second, then my $6,000 Kristi Kat third. He withstood the cold; he didn't catch pneumonia as he should have by rights. Campbell was a wonderful governor.

The Santa Fe Railroad was a tremendous amount of help to us in our beginning years, but quickly it was apparent the airlines were going to become the major factor. The airlines were not really in the ski business yet to any marked degree. That was still a new idea. But when the Santa Fe Railroad became federalized, became Amtrak, John Reed, the president, warned us that the railways would collapse, and I didn't think he could possibly be right; he was absolutely right. We had lost much of the Chicago market to United and Continental Airlines who ran special packages to Colorado. We couldn't compete with that.

The airlines took over. From 1968 on, we joined the new organization to market skiing in conjunction with the airlines. Taos was one of the founding members of "Ski the Rockies." Bob Parker of Vail was a key

person. The organization was a fabulous organization which now, through the sabotage of one of the Steamboat Springs personalities who felt that they weren't getting enough publicity out of it, broke apart. Now it's a small organization. All that's left in it are Aspen Highlands, Telluride, Big Sky, Snowbird, Jackson Hole, and Chris Stagg from Taos.

Buzz Bainbridge: When we started "Ski the Rockies" about 1967-68, Bob Parker and I started to work together with Vail and Aspen. People used to try and work us against each other. I'd call Parker, and he'd call me. He'd say, "Did you promise so-and-so this or that?" I'd say, "Bullshit." We got so we'd call each other and compare notes, and then we started going to the ski shows together. Western Airlines didn't hurt. They kind of helped us get organized. We had a group that they flew around the country to all their stations. Then United started working with us, and TWA, Continental and Frontier. They all were coming to our meetings and saying, "Here, we'll donate $100,000 to your budget." We had a big kitty that we used to fight Europe.

Early "Ski the Rockies" advertisement. Courtesy Buzz Bainbridge.

We had thirteen guys that met; Ernie was one of them. We met once a month and plotted against the the big boys. We just started to kill Europe. I remember a travel agent boss that said, "You know, before you guys got the business, I used to do twenty-five charters a year to Europe and three to the Rockies. Now we've just reversed it." It was because we had all these good heads, working our butts off, putting our dollars together. We got the business turned around. We had Sun Valley to Taos. We had every major ski area in there. We sure had a lot of fun.

In the good old days, everybody who was in "Ski The Rockies," or half to three-fourths of the guys in the ski business, had been in the 10th Mountain Division during World War II. The 10th Mountain was where most of those guys got the love of skiing and decided they wanted to make a life out of it. Unfortunately, now it seems like there are more comptrollers and big businesses running ski areas than there are 10th Mountain guys.

Ernie: We were at this time a true destination resort on the same scale as Aspen, only smaller. We were beginning to get some of the same problems other areas were getting because of growth. Our sewer problems became a real controversy in the valley. It was what all ski areas were experiencing: growth and the opposition to that growth.

Herman Kretschmer: It was very primitive in those days. The sewer system was what Ernie referred to as the "hot springs" down on the bottom of the beginners' hill; people believed it. They had to because they'd get down there, and the stench from that thing was unbelievable. He would say that is our hot springs, and he would point to the Hondo River which was going by, and he said the hot springs feed into the river. That was a terrible thing. And at about that same time, Jean Mayer had his dump outside of the building.

Godie Schuetz: We must face it. We all knew. There was real negligence on the part of the whole Ski Valley, not just Ernie. It was everybody, all the sewage went right in there, and they neglected it for many, many years.

For instance, who took care of the first bitty-bitty sewer plant? Who checked it out three times a week? It was Max Killinger, he was a ski instructor not a sewer person. It was really bad. So the people down valley had a legitimate complaint. I addressed that problem when I was on the board. I said to Ernie, "Look, you know as well as I know that the Ski Valley is at fault because it was a great negligent thing."

I told Ernie we could have gotten that sewer plant built with federal and state money, and the Ski Valley would have had a bond of maybe $300,000-400,000. And they turned it down. They wanted to do it their

way just because they didn't think it would be right for the people down valley to have access to our records and a moratorium that we couldn't expand another building for three more years. As it turned out, they didn't do anything for three or four more years anyway. And now we are stuck with this expensive sewer plant and the whole works.

Buell Pattison: Certainly there was trouble with the sewer. As soon as we knew the sewer was going in there we organized the first Water and Sanitation Association, which was unfortunate for me—I became the president. Money was loaned from the Farmer's Home Administration to build the first plant. They required that the plant be built for that need of that day, not for any growth. So, from the first day that plant was finished, it was already too small.

Harry Franzgen: We Germans don't like to be pushed. We react a lot better if somebody is diplomatic or controls us. It's sort of an egotistical way of wanting to be accepted for what one is. If you begged Ernie for something, that was okay. But, if you told him something was necessary, logical or not, he wouldn't do it because he felt pushed. I think that's why he played so much local politics on the sewer thing. But there was no way anybody would tell Ernie how he could do his area.

Ernie liked to manipulate. He was a crafty and shrewd businessman, and he liked to get something for nothing. He tried to manipulate the various segments in this community, in this county, to the point where he could save face and say, "Nobody told me what to do, but I got it accomplished and made everybody else pay for it." And he couldn't with this one. I think he resented the fact that someone said you need to do this, and you're going to pay for it. Ernie was not greedy, just stubborn.

Max Killinger: Hardy Langer had been here for years and was a good instructor. Ernie saw Hardy at one of the sewer meetings once, and Hardy clapped when somebody said something Ernie didn't like, but that was actually right to say, and Ernie wouldn't hire him back the next year.

Tom Brownell: The Water and Sewer Association several years ago became the powerful force in the valley; no question, they were and are the force to reckon with. They control things now. That's what Ernie worried about, and it happened. But it was all of our faults; we should have done better together. Incorporation would have been a plus. Ernie wanted nothing to do with it. He didn't want to turn Taos Ski Valley into an Aspen and have some hippie as a mayor. So the water and sewer now have control of the roads. They can tax us; they can tell us if we can or can't build. They really became very powerful.

Tony Mitchell: I don't think there was ever a time when there was not a desire and a good faith effort to

Backside, Kachina Basin. PHOTO BY ULLI SEER, COURTESY BLAKE FAMILY COLLECTION.

Front side, Taos Ski Valley. PHOTO BY ULLI SEER, COURTESY BLAKE FAMILY COLLECTION.

Rubezahl Run to Kachina Basin area. Courtesy Blake Family Collection.

solve the sewer problems. Getting power up there was not easy. Getting electricity was a difficult challenge. Getting the phone was almost as difficult. Getting sewage and getting that handled was tough. We didn't have big money available to us. This was a sweat equity operation. We didn't have the money to get the planners to say, "Now you put in the infrastructure."

In my view, it came as a shock to all of us, particularly the vehemence and the ugliness of the meeting in the Arroyo Seco school. That was about the growth of the Ski Valley, and for the first time we talked about it. They shook a bottle of dirty water and said, "How would you like to drink this, Ernie?" Ernie wasn't afraid, he wasn't a person who got afraid. He was offended, and he was surprised, and hurt.

It was at that point we began to recognize the issue was not only correcting the sewer, but it was growth, if you will, in the context of wealthier people. It was not the loyal opposition, and they consistently proved that when they blocked our efforts to try and solve our problems. Al Rosen stood up for us and said how important cooperation was. The opposition did everything they could to stop that.

Ernie's enthusiasm was infectious, if you were inclined. If you were a no-growther like Larry Frank,

then none of that appeals. In my view, Frank has not been the loyal opposition or an honest opponent. We should have been working together. We should have been on the same side to correct the problem. The fact was that they did not want to see that sewage problem eliminated and they are mad about it now that it's gone. We thought we were committed to the right things and have tried to do things the right way.

Tony Mitchell: The only way we finally got a sewer plant built was when the Taos Ski Valley community decided to dig down and pay for it themselves, because they couldn't wait. We were polluting, and we knew the pollution had to stop. They stopped our federal money, so we had to do it ourselves, out of our own pocket.

West Basin. Photo By Ken Gallard.

Ernie skiing in West Basin. Photo By Ken Gallard.

CHAPTER 20
Anything is Possible in America

Ernie: This whole valley was made possible because we had a tremendous group of lodge owners who were always part of the ski school and the glue that held Taos Ski Valley together. Victor Frohlich was another Swiss that we imported. He built the Innsbruck Lodge in 1967. He did very well for us and was a hard worker. He had bad luck and broke his leg many times; he was not the champion skier as he had indicated in his letter to us. Victor was one of those who proved that anything was possible in America using bullshit, hard work, and skill.

Victor Frohlich: I immigrated to Canada in 1956, and played professional soccer for Edmonton for four years, but I always wanted to come to the States. I didn't want to go back to Switzerland because it was so much better here in America; the opportunities were better, life was so much easier and so much freer.

I got a chance to come to America and play soccer for the Pistols in Los Angeles; I was later drafted into the U.S. Army. After two years, it was time to get out of the army, I read the ski magazines, and there was a beautiful write-up about Taos Ski Valley. I had skied at Davos when I was a little kid. We had a little club type of thing; all the soccer players came together, and we had a picnic up in the mountains in the wintertime and we did some races like the Nastar. It wasn't a downhill, it wasn't a slalom, it was a combination, and I won that thing. So, when I wrote my letters to the ski areas, I wrote down that in 1953, I won the National and Regional Championship. I had one letter for ten ski areas. I put all my soccer and swimming stuff in. It sounded like I was in the Olympics. I got letters from Vail and Mammoth and Squaw Valley and all over the place. Most of them were looking for instructors, and "This is our salary structure, and we'd like to have you, and those are the dates we have the clinics, so let us know if you'd like to come."

Then there was Ernie's letter, a classic one. He wrote, "We would love to have you; you'd be an asset. By the way, we have one Swiss here already who is a ski instructor (which was Godie at that time), and this guy makes $1,800/month. If you have a good character, you can make a fortune at this place; if you have a good accent, that helps, too." And he said, "We are very small, just building up, and we're looking for people to build hotels." So, I said, "That's the place."

Ernie picked me up in his Porsche. He was talking to me, reading the book coming up from Santa Fe,

driving and talking to me at the same time, and reading, driving like a madman. He hadn't asked much about anything. And we came up and the road was a dirt road, and we ran into Kretschmer and Monica, and he introduced me, he said, "This is the guy we talked about,"—champion skier and everything.

I moved into the Chalet Alpina. They were just finishing up the downstairs of the ski shop. They had just moved out everything from the old house. The St. Bernard was here and the Thunderbird and The Hondo Lodge. Dadou was just building the Edelweiss. Ernie said to come down for dinner. We ate at his place, so I went down for dinner, and he said, "When you come down tomorrow, you report to Rhoda."

So, I came down into the old ski shop the next morning and there was Rhoda, and I said, "I'm supposed to do some work here." She said, "Well, Ernie wants a little counter here and one of those little benches in there." So, I went down and got all the lumber and mind you, Ernie knew right away I was bullshitting. I went and bought a book about carpentry. I was there about half a day, I had to see

Victor Frohlich. COURTESY VICTOR FROHLICH.

what boards to buy; I had no idea. I had to go through that book first. So I got lumber and all that stuff and brought it all up to the valley. I really was dragging my ass because I needed another evening to really study that book. I started making some plans in the evening and I did the whole thing. I put a burnt finish on it, and Rhoda thought I was wonderful. It worked out good, better than I had anticipated.

Then the first winter, we went skiing before we opened up, and they had just gotten the new #1 chair lift, and I was scared shitless. Ernie said, "Let's go up and survey a little up there." So, we went up the lift, just me and Ernie and Hans Rieger, and there was fresh snow, and I had never skied fresh snow in all my life. In packed snow, it was no problem, but in fresh powder, I had no idea how to turn or anything. So, they were standing there and decided to ski down and I let them go. And Ernie looked around and said it didn't look like I could ski that stuff. So, finally, I got a little of the feeling and made a few turns here and there, but I was wondering what Ernie was thinking when he saw me those first few wipeouts. It was very funny. After that Ernie put me to work in the ski shop. He would call me out for skiing whenever it wasn't busy. I started to ski better and he began giving me the beginners because by that time he had figured out I wasn't any hot-shot skier.

At that time in America, you could just say, "I am a carpenter," or "I am a plumber," and nobody asked you for any papers. You went to your job and either you did it or you didn't. It was just the idea that you could say, "I can do this," and they gave you a chance to prove yourself. You couldn't do that in Europe. I figured I had enough guts, I can bullshit, I can do anything I want to. Ernie knew I worked hard, he had a good feeling about me, but I'll tell you, I never asked how many hours I worked; I just did my job if it had to be done and I'd work until ten o'clock at night. There were no questions asked; I just did it. That, I think, he appreciated more than anything else.

My first pay check was $100; Ernie gave me the check. In the army, you made $180/month and that was tax free. Here I made $100. I never asked, "How much am I going to make?" Ernie never promised anything. So, when he gave me my check I looked at it and I sort of joked that I should have stayed in the army. Ernie said, "What do you mean?" I said, "Well, they promised me this and that." And he said, "I think they must have made a mistake." He took it back again, and I got a check for $250 after that.

After the first year I told Ernie I would love to get some land. So he sold me a half-acre but there was a stipulation that said I had to build within one year or lose it. I said shit, somehow I'll get the money. I went down here to the bank and said I'd like to build a lodge up there on half this land, and they just looked

at me and said, "What do you have for collateral?" I had this half-acre of land up there. They said I needed a little more than that for a loan. I went to Ernie and said I'd gone to the bank and they just laughed at me. He said, "Just see what you can do, and if you have any problems, just let me know."

I went to California then and worked two jobs. I worked one job as a draftsman and one job as a pastry chef; I made good money. While I was in Los Angeles, I talked to a friend, Franz Voller, and I said I might build a hotel in Taos. He said maybe he could come up with $10,000-$15,000, and if I had maybe about $5,000-$6,000 we should get a loan. I went back to Taos in November and again went back for a loan, and they said no. Now Ernie could see I really was hustling, and he said, "I'll tell you what I'll do. I'll loan you $60,000 to build the place, and then you just pay me back." I thought I was in heaven. So, I built the place.

Franz Voller: Victor built the Innsbruck Lodge, and we came up in 1966 and brought a whole bunch of commercial kitchen equipment which we found in a place in L.A. that was going out of business. Then when we came here, we had to sleep on the floor because there was no furniture. We cooked on the bathroom heater. We took it out of the wall, set it on a couple of concrete blocks and cooked out meals in there for quite a while until we got furniture. The first year we almost went broke; we had hardly any guests. Victor and I got a lot of skiing in.

Victor Frohlich: I went to Ernie any time I needed some money to pay the contractor, and he made a check out. We had no paper, no agreement of any kind except a mutual agreement. We shook hands. When the building was finished, we had an open house and invited everyone. At dinnertime Ernie said, "I think maybe we should sit down and write up a contract." I had no idea on the interest. So, Ernie wrote up the contract, and it was four-and-a-half percent interest and to pay it over fifteen years, and that was it. When you think about that!

You just don't find people like Ernie, it's impossible. So trustworthy, and when people tell me Ernie was an asshole and rude, they didn't know him. I think he was the fairest guy of anybody that I ever knew, if you did your job. If you were a screw off, he hated you. I think any businessman should be that way.

Franz Voller: Before I came to Taos I was a machine builder and die maker. I was building machines and from 1966 until 1972, Theresa and I went back every summer to L.A. and got our jobs back to make some money. We didn't make any here. We still don't. Now we've learned how to do it without money. There was a guy named Mr. Green in a little supermarket called the Mariposa where Terry Sports is now right beside Michael's Kitchen, down in

Thunderbird Lodge & Chalet. PHOTO BY LARRY CASE, COURTESY OF THE BROWNELLS.

Taos. He trusted us and he gave us credit because we didn't have enough money to buy food.

The first time Ernie took us up to see if we could ski because he wanted us to be instructors, and I was skiing down with reverse shoulder and everything and Ernie yelled at me, he said, "Hey, Franz, we know you're from Austria. You don't have to show us." Ernie, he always gave people a chance. He gave us the chance to start something. We came with very little.

Ernie: Another lodge owner who was important to

our success was Elisabeth Brownell who had been my secretary in the early years. She then ran off and married Tom Brownell who had an interest in the Thunderbird Lodge with Kaarlo Jokela at the time. She stayed away from the valley and had her children, but she came back to take over the management of the Thunderbird around 1970. Elisabeth is very able.

Elisabeth Brownell: When we bought the Thunderbird Lodge, it was far removed from everything; it was way over on the other side of the valley at that time. The action was only at the St. Bernard. It was German determination why we succeeded. Now we have the best view in the valley. Far enough away, yet close enough. Everybody laughed about us taking that dump over.

Working for Ernie in the beginning years was fun; coming back to try and put the Thunderbird in order was real hard work. That was the winter of 1970-71, the worst winter we ever had. We had only a few guests. We had a crazy chef, we had bad morale among the staff, we had a fire, and we had frozen water pipes.

Tom Brownell: We hired the Swiss girl named Terry Nippesen. She was a tall, glamorous, Swiss—kind of a Zsa Zsa on wheels. She was well-trained, so we got her to run the lodge which lasted only until January.

Elisabeth Brownell: I had to fire that Swiss girl; she was a very pretty girl and the crazy French chef who liked to throw knives made advances to her and I guess she didn't like it. So they fought all the time. Then the chef said, "Either she goes, or I go." I couldn't do without a chef, so I had to fire her and take over the lodge.

Ernie was a big help to me. He gave me confidence. One time I went to ask Ernie for advice; that one time changed me forever. I went to Ernie and I said, "How do I do this? I have an employee who doesn't know a thing. He was supposed to take care of reservations, and he came from a hotel school, and he is not worth anything; he's awful." Ernie said, "You look him cold in the eye and tell him, you are fired." So, I went back, and I looked him cold in the eye and said, "You are fired." After that year, I felt nothing could shake me anymore. I became so strong.

Tom Brownell: I met Elisabeth when I came out on vacation. I hadn't skied in thirteen years. It was in March of 1963, and Elisabeth was working for Ernie; it was her first year. There were no paved roads. There was glorious snow. They put me in a class with Godie who looked the same as he does now. After one day, he bounced me up to Dadou's class. There were no phones, so Kaarlo who owned the lodge drove me down, and I told the office I was staying another week.

Elisabeth worked in Chicago in the summer at the German consulate. I came back the next year to the Ski Valley and produced *Cry Desire,* the movie, in January, and the following year I got involved in the lodge. Kaarlo was ready to quit. His gross for a year would have been about $33,000 and his payments to the Pattisons were about $14,000. Then, of course, he had to pay Ernie. He was pretty down. So, I invested, and we became a corporation 50/50 with Kaarlo continuing to run it for about a year or two. Elisabeth

and I were married in 1966 in Germany. Karlo called me in Chicago and wanted to know if I could buy him out. So I did, and we had some managers for a couple of years that didn't work out.

Ilse Mayer: Elisabeth really was into running the place and decided to move here. Tom was able to do his business from anywhere in the world so he came along. She started out ten years later than we all did and look where she is now. She's done a really good job. I am proud of her, and she deserves it. The Thunderbird was a hard place to buy into with so many things a mess. Elisabeth was smart enough to be friends with both Jean and us, and we sent people over to her in those first years. We really supported the Thunderbird.

Elisabeth Brownell: Ernie would come over and help with the guests; he was great at making them feel good even if the pipes were frozen or the snow wasn't great. He said, "I know the snow is bad, but you have good food, and you will have a great time."

Kaarlo Jokela: Ernie would go from one place to another like a general just looking around and checking it all out, entertaining people, rubbing elbows. He would wear his little Prussian things, those little jackets and stuff like that, special ties.

Elisabeth Brownell: When our guests come to the Thunderbird Lodge, we do many things to entertain them. We hire a magician, we hire belly dancers, we have a band, we have the Legends of Jazz in January, and we have "pimp and whore" parties. It's a round experience. You have to offer many things, not just take their money; we offer something and we care about them. This is what Ernie did, and that's what we're trying to do. That's what Jean does at the St. Bernard. So many of the new ones do not understand what is necessary for the guests.

Tom Brownell: I started the Jazz Legends on a quirk. I love jazz. I took piano as a kid, and in high school I took jazz piano for about three-and-a-half years. I had to work at it. I'd play here and there a little bit, but never seriously. It was just for fun.

I had heard Ralph Sutton on record, and I had read that he lived in Bailey, Colorado which isn't too far away from here. At that time he was playing in New York, and I was in New York often with clients. I dropped in one night and saw him and asked if he'd be interested in coming down and he said, "Sure." That started it. He and his wife Sunny came down; Sunny had Sunny's Nightclub in Aspen years ago.

We hit it off, and he introduced me to the other people. Over the years, I'd called other musicians and they'd hang up on me, wanting to know how much money? But now, like Kenny Davern, and most of them say they will gig, which is very complimentary. We bring the wives, the food is good, and the audiences are great. The valley is hooked on it now.

Jazz Legends at the Thunderbird, Milt Hilton. Photo By Ken Gallard.

It started out as "Jazz Legends" in 1980, but now I'm getting some young guys. We've had about thirty different top musicians over the years. For example, on piano, Ralph Sutton, Monty Alexander, Ross Tompkins, Ray Bryant, Eddie Higgins. On bass, Ray Brown, Milt Hinton, Brian Torff, Phil Flanigan. On guitar, Barney Kessel and Herb Ellis. On drums, Gus Johnson, Butch Miles and Jake Hanna. On saxophone, Flip Phillips, Buddy Tate, Jim Galloway, Scott Hamilton and Eric Schneider. Trumpets, Conte Candoli, Warren Vache. Clarinet, Kenny Davern. Trombone, Carl Fontana. There are a few others I've forgotten. There were some big catches in there like Ray Brown and Milt Hinton, and of course Gus Johnson. Gus was the first one to ski. Ernie was always very supportive of the jazz. He let them ski and do this and that.

I did things behind the scenes that nobody knew about. Like the advertising and brochure work which I did for years with Ernie at no cost. I was a management consultant, but he thought I was in advertising, which I wasn't. I never really convinced him otherwise. We started doing those early ads, and my art director of the firm, Louann Jordan, did the original aerial map. She did it and was on my payroll, but Ernie gave her a letter which gave her a lifetime pass, which had to be rare. Then she did the second one and updated it. It's quite big and very accurate with every tree.

Elisabeth Brownell: Jean is excellent with what he helped Ernie create; he has been number one for so long. And at that time, we were at the bottom; now we are equal or better. As far as the quality is concerned, Jean knows. He doesn't come over, and we don't go over there. He loves the jazz, but he does not come. I think it's very painful for him to see our success because he was like Ernie. He never liked any competition.

One time Jean said to me, when the Thunderbird Lodge was still looking unfinished, "You know, the Thunderbird Lodge looks like a woman with mascara." Like an old woman with makeup, he said. I never forgot that. It sort of hurt me, but I was thinking, we just keep on working away and improving every year, and now I would like to say that to him about the St. Bernard. When I have the right moment, I'm going to say it to him. We are very close in a way. We go that far back. He was so nice to me when I was just working for Ernie.

Jean knows me and I know him. There is no barrier in between other than the competition in the winter which is healthy. He always gave me good advice. Jean could always maintain the continuity at the St. Bernard no matter which girl he was with or without. The guests hardly noticed that a new woman showed up. He never missed serving a meal or telling a story.

Ernie: Harry Franzgen came and took over the

Elisabeth & Tom Brownell. COURTESY OF THE BROWNELLS.

Brooke & Harry Franzgen. PHOTO BY R. ROWEN, COURTESY THE FRANZGENS.

Hondo not too long after Ed Pratt. We call him Harry Hondo; he came here from Vail. He has always been difficult. He didn't want our ski week package; he would rather sell his rooms by the night and that has always been a sore point with us. I should have bought the Hondo Lodge, but now it's too much money. Harry was very charming at times, and then he would change. Harry and I have had our troubles; maybe we knew each other too well.

Harry Franzgen: I met Ernie in Vail. Ernie used to come to Vail then because they started the Big Six, and he would come for meetings. Ernie and Kretschmer were interested in the central reservation system that

Thunderbird picnic in Kachina Basin. PHOTO BY KEN GALLARD.

my wife Brooke had started, the Vail Resort Association. I had my night club, the New Gnu, so we of course met Ernie all the time when he came up there. I knew about Taos because we made the certification there.

After Vail had kind of grown and suddenly developed, I got disenchanted, and I wanted to go somewhere else. I had a friend who owned the La Fonda in Santa Fe, and I went down to him to see what was going on in the hotel business down there. On the way back up, I thought I might as well say hello to Ernie. It was summer so I cruised in and in typical Ernie fashion, he says, "How have you been? I've had the troops out looking for you. I understand you're not in Vail." I told him we were looking. He said, "I have the lodge you can buy," and that was the Hondo Lodge. The price was a bit too much for me. I went back to Vail and Ernie called and said he had a guy who has all the money. He wants to buy the lodge, but he needs somebody who knows food and beverage. That was Dave and Judy Buck. We made some sort of deal in October, very late.

I came because of Ernie.

Tom Brownell: There's a lot of jealousy in the valley with all these different nationalities, French,

Austrian, German, Swiss or whatever else we have around here. It's been a mystery to me because I grew up differently. I had American business experience. Now the Scandinavians, fine; a handshake with Kaarlo or Mogens Hansen, it's golden. Unfortunately it's not with the others. I've almost given up. I've quit going out of my way. There's no rebound.

Elisabeth Brownell: Even with all of our jealousies and extreme competitiveness, we bonded together, and that bond really made the Ski Valley. We all contributed. We copied from one another and figured things out as we went along and helped one another.

Ed Pratt: Sometimes I used to sit and think, "What am I doing here?" I'm killing myself, working eighteen or twenty hours a day getting very little sleep, just trying to keep ends going. I'd sit down sometimes after being very frustrated over something and say, "Why did I leave retirement to come into something like this?" You never give up. When you wake up the next morning, you always feel better, a new day. After you live together with people as we did up there and live so close, you get used to these little idiosyncrasies. You worked and you melted together as a unit. If somebody needed help, you did what you could. We had to work together.

I recall some years later, 1967 or 1968 when Jean's A-frames caught fire when he had the music school going, and we had some guests staying at the Hondo at that time. I was in bed and all of a sudden, there's a knock at the door—fire! Of course in the Ski Valley, that word is one you didn't want to hear. I jumped out of bed and threw my pants on. I went out that back door, and I had a couple of two-and-a-half-gallon buckets sitting next to the back door for some reason. I grabbed those two buckets. It was like walking into a deep freeze. Jean had put a ladder up in the back of the A-frames that faced the Hondo. Somebody was living up there and evidently a cigarette had gotten in a mattress. All the music students, the girls in nightgowns and guys with shorts on, everybody was pitching in. They were carrying every kind of a container from the kitchen that would hold water.

Jean, being a little fellow, was standing at the top of the ladder, and I was standing just below him and passing buckets up to him and he was throwing it in the window, but half of it was going in the window and the other half was coming down on us. So, I was soaking wet. After about an hour, we were so cold and numb and couldn't feel anymore. About this time the fire department got there and did a tremendous job.

When it was all over, Jean fed the whole crew. Man, I mean there was the fire department, the people working, pouring coffee down us, eggs and bacon and everything that went with it. All of a sudden, it became a fun time. We're beginning to thaw out, beginning to feel our toes again and realized we were able to save everything except just the one room because of the bucket brigade we had.

Elisabeth Brownell: All the lodges tried to help each other; even though we had our differences. I remember once we were supposed to have a chicken dinner, and we didn't get the delivery. So I called Jean, and he had some steaks in the freezer. He defrosted them and he pre-grilled them already so we would not have to because the time was short to get them for dinner. He gave us the steaks which later we paid back, but still, he was ready to help out.

Kaarlo Jokela: We had those meetings for advertising and such and to get something together was not easy at all. We knew that we had to pull together, but at the same time, we were competing against one another.

Ernie: Mickey was always involved from the very start; he was eleven years old when we started, well actually December of 1955, and he was driving our Sno-Cat. We had a Tucker Sno-Cat then with skis that were steerable. He drove that up with twenty to twenty-five SMU kids during the Christmas vacation

Ernie & Mickey Blake, June 1970. Courtesy Blake Family Collection.

Mickey Blake. Photo By Ernie Blake; Courtesy Blake Family Collection.

in 1955. He drove it up the Burroughs' path and turned it around. After they had turned around, they came down this trail which was very steep to them.

Mickey went to Denver University and showed his ski qualities. He was invited to be on the university team by Willy Schaeffler, who was coach for Denver University and a part of the U.S. Ski Team; that would have been great for Mickey, racing, slalom and downhill, but he didn't do it. DU was on the quarterly system, so he took the winter quarter off and went to the university in the summer and helped us with the ski area in winter.

Mickey made the decisions. The Poma lift, taking it out, was Mickey's decision, not mine. That's the first time actually. So, 1974 on you can say he had surely been making the key decisions more than I. We took it step by step, very slowly, painfully, not always smooth. Step by step, I have taken my hands off the thing and let Mickey run it. With Mickey and me, it came very slowly; it was done perfectly actually. Of course, it's difficult being father and son; the perfect relationship doesn't exist yet.

Monica Brown: It's the old European way. The oldest one gets everything, and he tells the rest of the family what's going to happen. But, if the father happens to live long enough, the oldest son can be sixty and still have nothing to say. But when the oldest son gets the fortune or the business, he is then supposed to take care of the other siblings; that is also the old European way.

If it was hard for Mickey and Ernie, it was many times harder for Peter (Blake) with Ernie. To be the youngest son, to have all the expectations and never to fulfill them. Peter was more with Rhoda than with Ernie. Mickey was the eldest son after all, and Ernie lived by that ethic.

Bud Crary: Mickey is first-class. I've seen him and old Ernie just stand up and fight like old dogs, oh man. Hurt each other! You go in to stop them and both of them say, "Back up, this is nothing to do with you." Both of them would have black eyes. Boy, I mean they was hitting; like they meant everything. One of them would hit just as hard as the other one. I never would have thought of hitting my father, no way. Mickey's got a hotter temper than Ernie, to me at least.

Dadou Mayer: When I came back to work at Taos Ski Valley, it was early on. I remember Mickey actually going to fists with his father for a happening that was between Ernie and me, and getting a bloody nose, or giving a bloody nose to his father. He was really upset with the way Ernie was treating me and with some of the injustice that had been done, and they had an actual fight.

Chilton Anderson: Ernie needed to be physical; that's what Jean says. Jean and Ernie got along a lot better after he knocked Ernie down. Maybe it was the German upbringing, but Ernie needed to be tough.

Walter Ruegg: Ernie was a tough man. I remember one time, Ernie with a guest fighting. They had some fight I think that started because of Ernie's dog, and then eventually, they were rolling around on the floor and had a fist fight. Then Ernie told him not to come back anymore. Today, the man would have taken Ernie to court. Mickey and Ernie both had real hot tempers. Basically, they got along pretty good, so it's just one of those things. They'd just let off some steam and keep on going.

Jean Mayer: At Al Rosen's once, they had a party and Ernie had it out with Ben Harker right there on the floor, fists and everything. We were really surprised because it was a real brawl. And Al Rosen, it didn't bother him at all. I guess he was used to it by then.

Kevin Beardsley: After 1974, Ernie kind of withdrew from direct involvement with operations. He retreated into marketing and PR and the ski school, which he did until the very last. As Mickey grew into it, he began to take over, in some cases by default where Mickey's knowledge and incredible ability filled a gap with the mechanics and the lifts. Those were things Ernie was very happy to see him move into, I'm sure.

There were a few things they butted heads on, and they had a couple of knock down fights. The emotion that would bring you to that, through the care, the concern, the love that can get you that mad and can break through the politeness, that's why people like John Koch and Mickey and others were respected by Ernie far more than any of us ever realized. It was a hard thing to watch, but I never felt bad about it for them. Mickey and Ernie were doing a thing that they had to do to work something out.

Ernie relaxed his grip on the mountain and on the patrol after that. It was more like little run-ins, or we'd talk and ski around or he'd scream at us on the radio, but it wasn't the constant meetings and the involvement that he had before that. Mickey took over that, in many ways for the better.

It's never been a company operation; it's been a family operation. Mickey would say over and over, "Look, the mountain is yours. We want it to function that way; the patrol needs to feel that." Ernie would never have said that; the mountain was his, and we thought it was his. There was a tremendous loyalty there.

There was nothing better than having Ernie come up with a VIP and ask us where there was a good trail we had just packed. When we had a trail ready to go, it was ready, and when they came back and complimented us on it, we felt good for a week. It happened rarely, but it happened enough. After 1973-74, it didn't happen; Mickey wasn't that kind of a person.

Tony Mitchell: Ernie was very comfortable with

Mickey's succession. He would, in one sense, deny the relevance of a more modern view, which was coming from Mickey or Chris. But Ernie was always testing. And yet not always; on some things it was, "That will not be as long as I'm around."

Louie Bernal: Mickey is a lot different from his dad. You know, when I go home, I do my thing and I pray. I pray down to my house early in the morning. I use charcoal that I burn, and I think about this man Ernie that he's gone, but I think about his family like Mickey, and he's got a big job here. Everything we got here belongs to him. And I can imagine that man what kind of mind he have. And I know that Mickey knows whatever he got here in this Ski Valley, he knows exactly what's taking place. He knows what's going on, who dented the shovel and all that. He knows.

Tony Mitchell: I think Ernie had trouble letting go. Taos Ski Valley, other than his family, was the major thing of his life. That was what he was—Taos Ski Valley. So, do you stop? You are a living legend. Do you say, end of living legend, I've retired? That's hard. Ernie appreciated and respected the dedication that Mickey gave and the energy that he put in. You know, Mickey served his time over and over.

Walter Ruegg: Mickey maybe knows more technically than Ernie does, but he is not as good at public relations. Ernie was good with everybody. And, of course, at that time, it was a lot easier. I mean, Ernie had a lot easier job than what Mickey has today with five hundred employees. It seems like Chris Stagg every once in a while doesn't agree with Mickey, but overall they get along real good. I don't think that there are too many other big companies with this many employees where you can just walk in the head man's office and talk with him.

Mickey Blake: I didn't have control back in 1972, but basically I started doing more of a manager's role in 1972. We tried to divide up the responsibilities. Mine was more mechanical and operational, and my father's was more promotional plus the added thing of ski school. I knew more about the daily operation. People didn't realize that my father wasn't really that involved in the operation for many years. My father was certainly the spirit of Taos Ski Valley as Jean is in many ways today.

Harry Franzgen: On the bottom line, Ernie was in control. I say this because a couple of times when we had something business-wise, and I went to him kind of easy and he said, "Well, Mickey is running it right now, and you really should go to Mickey." And I kind of said, "Come on, Ernie, don't bullshit me." He would kind of smirk and pick up the phone or send a letter over or whatever was necessary because I knew he was still in charge. He wouldn't let go, even though he said it.

Ernie: It will take Jean and Mickey together to preserve Taos Ski Valley the way I would like to see it.

Jean has the sense of the mountain, and Mickey will acquire that. Mickey knows the operations of the mountain better than I ever did.

Henry Hornberger: I think Mickey's right on track. I just hope that Jean and Mickey can develop the same mutual respect that Ernie and Jean had. Mickey is hard with people in the wrong way, like Ernie was sometimes. He'll blow up at them, yell and abuse the shit out of them, but Mickey can't say, "No, I'm not going to lend you any more money, or I'm not going to bail you out on your next DWI." Ernie could never say that either.

Kaarlo Jokela: Mickey was a wonderful person growing up, rather shy and reserved, but then again, when you have a person like Ernie for a parent, then the kids have a hard time. I always thought that Mickey was very sharp.

Jean Mayer: What's difficult right now is that Mickey doesn't understand the mountain; he does not love the mountain the way we did or do, but he might learn to. Well, finally now, probably, Mickey will grow to be more like Ernie. The only thing that's lacking is the essence of what Ernie had because Mickey does not have enough of the mountain. Mickey is more into the mechanical part like Sno-Cats, trucks and all those things that Ernie never was.

Mickey Blake: When I'm an old man in thirty years, I would like to see Taos Ski Valley run by somebody other than me, hopefully my kids. Then I could pursue my history interests. I'm more into history now than archeology. Some say it's hereditary.

Ernie: The controversy about Taos Ski Valley, its growth and the Kachina Village bothered me greatly. People had so much anger! We thought we were doing great things for a hard-to-reach area that was dead in winter for all practical purposes. Everyone agrees now that a 4,000-bed Kachina Village up there would would have been too much. But, you have to keep in mind that in the early days there were no hotels in Taos except the La Fonda, the Sagebrush, and the Taos Inn.

Buell Pattison: Ernie started talking about Kachina early on, around 1968. Ernie and Tony Mitchell came over and talked to us about mainly putting in the Kachina lift. He always wanted to put the base of the lift on his own land or on private land instead of the Forest Service land. So, we made an agreement with him that said the Blakes would do a certain amount of ski development in that area, and the Pattisons would build or cause a village to be built with commercial and residential sites. Neither side has kept their total agreement.

Part of the agreement said that if the Forest Service disallowed certain things that made the agreement impossible or did not approve the village to go into effect or the whole ski area up in that Kachina area,

Dana Brienza, Mike Kaplan & Ed Baca hiking the Ridge to Kachina Peak. PHOTO BY KEN GALLARD.

then it was pretty much null and void. Well, the Forest Service did not stop the lift from being put in, but they stopped us from putting the road in that we felt we needed on Forest Service land. That's still a problem.

Ernie: The Kachina lift was put up in 1971; it was the first time we went with something other then Stadeli. I left Stadeli because he was a little bit of a chiseler in financial deals, and I went to a subsidiary of Pullman/Barry which had developed a new lift by a Swiss engineer, a Mr. Hunziker. He bid on the lift at a price that was much too low, and wanted to build it himself. He was very angry at me when I accepted that bid. They lost a lot of money on it which is unfortunate. It was also unfortunate that he was killed in an airplane accident on the way out here later on. The Kachina Lift opened up the 6th of January, in 1972.

Chilton Anderson: Ernie got so mad with some of us; Jean and I thought it was foolish to spend all that money on one big Kachina chair lift when you could go back up there and put two or three Poma lifts in different places. I called it "Ernie's white elephant," and it made him so mad. Certainly Ernie proved all of us wrong; by putting the Kachina lift in, he opened up

a great deal of intermediate skiing and made it skiable for all the Texans to ski where they liked to go.

Pete Totemoff: Rhoda really liked the Kachina area. So did I, especially in the back bowl. As far as determining a good amount of snow and quality skiing, Taos turned out to be the best snow in New Mexico.

Bob Nordhaus: Ernie picked an outstanding location for a ski area—good snow and very difficult terrain and he developed it very well. He found out later that the mountain was too steep for the average person. He had to have easy terrain. You know, Al's Run with the moguls is pretty tough. Then he built Kachina Basin. Then all of these hotshot skiers would say, "Well, I skied Taos." They'd go up there and ski Kachina. It was the mystique. They skied Taos—but only Kachina.

200

Dana Brienza & Johanna Woll hiking to Kachina Peak. Photo By Ken Gallard.

Jean Mayer, Mark Wilson, and Steve Tichnor on Reforma. Photo By Ken Gallard.

CHAPTER 21
Controlling Growth

Ernie: The paving of the road was a blessing that we owe to Al Rosen and his great political skills, but it was also the beginning of changes which we did not foresee; we became accessible. In 1971, the road was paved by the state and federal authorities on the basis of 20% state money and 80% federal money. They started on that giant project which cost a million and forty-seven thousand dollars, which was a lot of money then. That money has been paid back to state and federal authorities many times over in sales taxes they get from here. In the fall of 1972, the road was completed.

Ed Pratt: The road changed it; no question. I got the feeling at times that we were getting away from what we were in the beginning, but I also felt it was inevitable that progress had to be made. There had to be a certain amount of change, but I always felt that was up to the people dealing with the public like the lodge owners, Ernie and his staff, the people who really made day-to-day contact. It was our·job to make the guests feel welcome, make them feel a part of the whole setup while it was still expanding.

You can't turn things around. That's hard to do when people can say, "Well, it used to be we could sit down and have a drink and look out the window and see nothing but trees. Now you look out the window and you see buildings and buildings."

The only way that valley could have ever stayed the way it was, was if the owner was one person who had millions and millions of dollars and said, "I don't want to change it, and I don't need to make any money; this is my private ski area. Those I let in, that's it." That's the only way.

Chilton Anderson: Certainly the building of the road was the turnaround of the Ski Valley. It surprised everyone how much all of a sudden people would drive that twenty miles up to the ski area to go skiing. I think Taos Ski Valley is now maybe beyond the legacy Ernie would have liked to have left, because it's gotten out of hand. In my mind, his original intent was a family ski area to support his family, to supply excellent skiing for his family and for people who loved to ski, for those true aficionados.

For a time after the road was paved, it didn't seem so bad. It wasn't until maybe ten years ago that change was noticeable; it's hard to say how long because all these things keep moving, and you almost don't see it. I go up to the ski area, and I think, "Wow, isn't this neat; look how they groomed off the top of this knoll. That makes this run a lot better. Wow, isn't that a nice run," and so on. You see these things, and you think it's nice. Then you begin to get more and more people, and you begin to have all of the problems that all the other ski areas have with the uninitiated, with the people who don't know any better, who speed out of control. Really, the ones who are out of control are those who think they know how to ski but don't. They are intermediates. When we built the road we became more accessible to the general public instead of the aficionado. It became easier to get here. Then it grew, and they were afraid to cut it off; they were afraid to make people mad. There comes a point where the quality plays an important part. How many can you handle and keep the quality?

Economics don't have to be the decisive factor. I think that it is like anything else. It could be like my ranch where I raise Angus cattle. Fifteen years ago, I suddenly thought, "Gee, what I maybe ought to do is buy some more land down in Mora." Then I went around the very southern part of Colorado and found some places and talked to people there. You could do this and triple the herd. And then I ended up saying, "Shoot, why?" You triple the herd, you quadruple your problems. You quintuple your expenses. Can you make it all back? You have to hire more people. The hassle is a lot greater. Why not just spend a little bit more money and improve what I've got here so that I can carry more animals on the land I've got and forget all of that?

I think that same thing was true with Taos Ski Valley. Another simple example was Victor Frohlich and Frolic Ski Wear. One time, a couple years after he started and things were going reasonably well, he went off to a show, and he came back and said it was great. He could sell two or three thousand suits, where he had only been selling eight hundred to a thousand. I asked what he was going to do. Well, that's the problem. "If I'm going to do two thousand ski suits, then I have to have a warehouse, I have to get a computer, I have to get a couple more people to work at it with me. I have to pay them. And then, I couldn't do it with two thousand; I'd have to have five thousand, or whatever. Then, can I sell five thousand? I know I could sell two thousand." The end result is, "No," it's not worth it.

Look at the Taos School of Music which has been going almost as long as Taos Ski Valley, thirty years now. Over the years, there has been a great deal of pressure to enlarge. More people want to come, and there's this sort of thing, "Oh, you only accept nineteen students? Gee, when are you going to get bigger?" Well, all of a sudden, maybe that pressure goes to your head and you think, you know, maybe we should. But if nineteen is a good balance, then we'll double. We'll make thirty-eight. All right, but it loses some of its quality.

I look at Taos Ski Valley the same way. More people want to come; gee, we can't tell them they can't come. Therefore, we have to put in another lift. Uh, oh! Too many people on the mountain, so we have to cut another trail. Uh, oh! We need another lift now to serve all these people.

Chilton Anderson: We originated the Taos School of Music in 1962. A group of us got together weekly and played all kinds of strange music. In the group were violinist Ken Schanewerk, head of the violin department of Texas Christian University; clarinetist Bob Parr, who was also a composer; Bob Ray, a Taos artist who played the flute; and Bill Letcher who played trumpet and myself on the cello. At one point Ken said it would be fun to have something musical in the summertime in Taos, a school of chamber music, perhaps. Thirty years ago, there were no chamber music summer programs or camps. The Aspen Music Festival was going at the time, but primarily for orchestra, and later solo work and opera.

So with very little idea as to what we were getting ourselves into, we founded the Taos School of Music in 1963. Because of my perceived business acumen, I was volunteered to be the director. The first faculty included Ken on violin, John Goldmark, piano, pianist at the Mannes College of Music who later became president of that school, and Harvey Wolf, cello, who was recommended by Klaus Adam, of the Juilliard quartet.

Where were we to do this? There was only one place that would work, which was the Hotel St. Bernard in the Ski Valley. I talked to Jean Mayer who said that that would be great because he needed something to do in the summertime. He was running training sessions for the Peace Corps at that time. We mimeographed material, sent it around and then told the faculty they had to bring students. We had quite an odd group the first year!

We quickly realized that we should have only string players and pianists and not get involved with other instruments because the altitude (9,000 feet) was too hard for wind players. The magic number of students was set at nineteen—eight violinists, four violists, five cellists and two pianists. We like being small. The disadvantage of all of the large summer festivals is that the students get very little personal attention. With us,

Taos School of Music, Dan Avshalomov with students. PHOTO BY KEN GALLARD.

Taos School of Music, Bob McDonald with student in the St. Bernard. PHOTO BY KEN GALLARD.

they get coaching everyday, eat with the faculty and really get to know them. We not only wanted to stay small, but also this combination of instruments covered the vast majority of string chamber music, piano trios and quartets written.

We began slowly, with a small group of students for a four-week session. Years later, we expanded the summer sessions to eight weeks and set the concerts at eight for the students and five for the faculty. Our resident quartet now is the renowned American String Quartet, and Robert McDonald, pianist, who is recital partner of Isaac Stern and other noted musicians. The student body is picked from the top students of music schools throughout the country and abroad. Our graduates are principals or members of every major orchestra in this country and others throughout the world. The school has become known for the high caliber of the students it graduates, and many of the top teachers in the country recommend the Taos School of Music to their students. It's been gratifying to see the success and recognition of the school and the achievements of its alumni over these thirty years.

Chilton Anderson: The one big thing that Chris Stagg and Mickey see is we do not have any first-class lodging. If we had that then it ceases to be that nice family ski area; you're adding more people. To me, those two concepts oppose each other. The hotel and what we want for a hotel versus what Ernie wanted in having Jean and Dadou and the others, keeping the Ski Valley with a family atmosphere.

I can remember a woman coming down from Aspen. She was in my class; about the second or third day, I said, "Let's go up after lunch and make a run." We came back in, and she said, "Well, how much does that cost?" It took me by amazement. She'd come from Aspen and everything costs. She thought I was hustling her, I guess. It kind of made me mad. I was just being friendly.

Max Dercum: The atmosphere is what is so important. It's what they all want. They all want that ambiance. Taos has it. Pete Seibert and Ernie always wanted us to come to their area and make a place like the Ski Tip Ranch. They knew the kind of place we ran and the real charm we created. I hewed every one of the beams in our lodge. I had to go out in the woods and cut them and haul them in. I cleared trails by hand and picked all these rocks off the mountain by hand. Ernie always picked up rocks; we all picked up rocks. It isn't like it was; it won't ever be like that again. We were all pioneers, the whole lot of us; we

New Taos base lodge under construction, Fall 1989. COURTESY MICKEY BLAKE

did it for the way of life, not the money.

Tony Mitchell: Taos Ski Valley is the only ski area that has a limit of 4,800 skiers per day. This is based on our sewage capacity. We didn't want any limit. I think it's inappropriate to limit for a couple of crowded days out of a year as though it were a criminal act. The objective is to have the flexibility of the market. We have pretty good judgment of how to run a ski area and about what that monster carries. It's wrong to have an artificial number imposed.

Taos County needs the economic stimulus that our Ski Valley provides. The trickle-down effect is enormous, and Ernie always appreciated the local economy; it has been a major concern to him. He had no trouble with the native people and very few problems with the Hispanics. The Indians have not been upset by Taos Ski Valley; the Pueblo has not been an issue. We've had very good relations with them.

Art Pfister: I think the best number for Taos is around 4,000. On a normal day at Aspen it's between 3,000-4,000. Now between Christmas and the first of January, it'll be over 5,000. When they built the gondola, they said a lot of people would ride down. Anybody who spends $40 a day for a ticket isn't going to ride down. Except now, I was mistaken about that because now the locals ride down because they are terrified. Hell, you can get killed on that mountain. People who used to ski all day and are in good shape, young guys, they're sitting in a restaurant now at 1:00 finished for the day. That gondola takes them up in fourteen minutes, and they get so damn much skiing that they quit. With the tourists, it's helped the economy of the town. They shop in the afternoon now. High speed lifts are great. Someday Taos will probably have a high speed quad. Pressure dictates it.

Rhoda: People have trouble understanding that we put everything back into the mountain. Now, with all this big borrowing of money for the day skiers lodge, it makes it a different business. Ernest hated to be in debt. That's what people don't realize. They see all of us sitting up here counting our millions, not putting it back into the mountain as we always have. Before, the area was all of ours; it doesn't seem that way now.

Ernie: The size of the new base lodge scares me; I never would have conceived of it. But, the size is right because of Mickey's theory, and he's right, that everything we've ever built is too small by the time it was finished.

Kingsbury Pitcher: The size of Santa Fe got to be out of control. I wasn't having any fun running it anymore. I'd come home and the pressure was such that I didn't even want to talk, and one day my wife Jane said, "Why are you doing this?" I began to think, and Jane is a very smart lady; she functions as the president of these companies, and she could see the

Max Dercum. COURTESY COLORADO SKI MUSEUM, VAIL.

pressure. "You're going to stumble around in Santa Fe until you die; is that your idea of fun?" And you can't answer that. You go home and don't even want to talk about it.

Now I'm at Wolf Creek, and you go up to Wolf Creek, and it's all peace and quiet, very nice tourists; 60% of the people at Wolf Creek don't ski anywhere else. It's like an old-time ski area. The ski school at Wolf Creek leaves their skis out all winter, just stuck in the snow next to the ski school side. In Aspen in the early 1950s, we left skis everywhere.

Friedl Pfeifer: Well, the times, of course, have changed. The masses changed; the increase in the population on the slopes changed. Mass tourism in general is about the ugliest thing that we have created. You go to a beach and see the masses; it's awful and unbelievable. When we used to go out in the morning we would look forward to skiing and teaching in fresh snow, it was there all day and tomorrow too; now the new snow is only there a short time with all the skiers. They ski it down in half-an-hour. The worst change was the amount of equipment that you need to groom the trails; another one of the romances was the mogul skiing, and now there are no more moguls. Actually, it's good because the moguls were changed by the technique. The technique doesn't make a turn anymore. Most skiers don't even know the real pleasure of skiing, to make consecutive turns, on a rhythm kind of a thing. I can't get anyplace with the Aspen Ski Corporation; they like me to blabber for a while but they won't do anything. It takes a little guts to do it. Ernie had guts.

Henry Hornberger: I think we're fortunate in having people that are very concerned as Ernie was for the Ski Valley's growth. Mickey has a very good idea of the direction in which the Ski Valley should continue to go, in a vein that Ernie would have wanted. Jean's philosophy is right on in that direction, and Chilton is very much so too. In little ways, you can look at it and say, "Oh, this is a bunch of old farts resistant to change," but that's not it at all. They are a little resistant to change and not just because of age.

It's like I say, "I'll sign the petition for the airport, but there's a part of me that's not for it." Part of me says, "Do we really want the airport?" With Jackson Hole, you say, "Catch a plane from Chicago and by noon you're there; check in and go ski for the afternoon." We all know what the benefits are. But we know it changed Jackson Hole too. I'm not sure it would give us that much growth. There's a part of me that says, "No, I don't want Taos to grow," and yet I do want Taos to grow because I think what's going on is making the people a little less poor, and it affects us all. The change that is happening is a drastic one. You don't go back on that kind of change.

Louie Bernal: What the Indian is afraid of, the airport expansion, is that we got the Indian religious right in the village, and so a jet comes over and it's going to disturb all the things what we are doing. I don't know what the Pueblo governor is really saying. A year ago, they said the governor and his staff were all for it. Last year, they said they're not for it, so I don't know what.

This last year in August when everybody went to Blue Lake walking, there was a plane flying very low, and I wouldn't be surprised they were taking shots of people there. They wrote to that Senator Domenici and all those senators over there but they said they didn't have no reply. Everything is modern now. We should go back about fifty years.

Henry Hornberger: When you're out there selling Taos, we attract a certain type of clientele. Other ski areas are up there to try to target 100% of the skier market; for us being a destination resort that we are, even if we have an airport right here, it's still not going to be that easy to get to. The type of mountain that we have and the reputation that we have, which I hope doesn't change dramatically, because that's the unique aspect, limits the number of people who come to Taos.

It's just the reluctance to change, and that's where Ernie was afraid of the new building. I think that's where he was afraid of the quads because those changes were changes that made you say, "Wait a minute; are we moving too fast? Is this treadmill starting to move me, or am I moving it?"

Maybe it's a good thing that Mickey's now at the helm, because it is a different generation. I feel real confident that Mickey is not the sort of person that moves irrationally and too quickly; he's not a corporation per se. He is his father's son in so many ways. I think he still has a lot of faith in Rhoda to give him some direction.

Mickey Blake: The changes are easier for me to see in Aspen than in Taos. I had been going to Aspen since either 1951 or 1952. Then I went to high school in Carbondale, Colorado starting in 1958, so I had the chance to know Aspen pretty well. After that I went back every three or four years, and I saw the change more distinctly than you did here which was over a continuous period of time. The change here has been incredible to go back to what Taos was like when we were kids. I remember we didn't have any telephones in Twining for years, or electricity. I remember getting the first dial phone, but it didn't work; you still picked it up to get an operator.

The core of our business is the weekly skier; it's what's important, if we can maintain that by working with Taos proper, and I think we can. The weekly skier is what will keep Taos what we had intended it to be: a destination resort. It's getting tougher and tougher. The whole change has been the other way. If I could, I'd go back to the situation that we had in years gone by when it was mostly just a small crowd on the weekend. You had mostly ski-weekers. But, how can you go back to that? People's time is too short now.

Otto Lang: I think that we have sort of reached a platform now. Many people have become discouraged with downhill skiing. Many people are scared to get on the slopes and get hurt by the other skiers. There are too many out-of-control skiers who don't understand the rules, the etiquette. And for the average family, it's too expensive—the equipment and the lift and everything. Many people are doing cross-country skiing like in the old days which is so much simpler and less expensive.

Max Dercum: I think there's a lot of education that ought to take place on how people could really enjoy skiing. Unfortunately it has turned into an amusement park situation. You buy your ticket, and then you get the thrill.

Wolfie Lert: The ski business is basically stagnant and has been for several years for sure, partly because of weather conditions, but I think partly because of the economics. Who can afford to go skiing today? It's crazy. We are holding a price line of what we have, for example, sweaters. We have no Meister sweater in this next year that is over $100. Everything is under $100, every sweater in this line. Why? Because people do look at prices. It's very nice to get a $1,600 Bogner suit. After all, I also used to be the Bogner salesman. Peter Fischer, my partner, is the Bogner rep for the Rockies and does a wonderful job. But, for the average

person today, especially with children, skiing is expensive. And everybody bitches about the lift price, but the lift price is the least thing. Everything around it is even more costly like the rooms, the food, the clothes.

That's one of the things I love about Taos. If you stay at one of their lodges and eat the food there, you don't have to worry about making a reservation and standing in line for an hour to be allowed to eat at a restaurant that's usually not very good. If you want to go pub crawling at night, you haven't got many choices, but you can to a degree. There was always something going on at the St. Bernard or the Thunderbird. I'm the original ski-to-the-door-of-where-I-stay type. If I want to see the culture in town, I'd rather drive down to town and go to dinner, see the Indian dances, but then come back up, the next morning fall out of bed onto my skis and be on the slope. Everyone can't stay at the valley or it would be ruined. The demanding skiing at Taos will always make it special along with the inaccessibility and the ambiance.

Louie Bernal: Taos would not be what it is today without Mr. Blake. I think a God give him strength to go on. Look at all of Taos. What would that have been today if it weren't for Ernie Blake? It would have been nothing but a ghost town. In the summer, we have a lot of tourists at the Pueblo, but if it wasn't for Mr. Blake and the Ski Valley, it would never have been like it is today.

Friedl Pfeifer: God will take care of places like Taos and Aspen. It's amazing, in Aspen we nearly got snowed under by the hippie era, when the slopes looked much more like a rodeo than a ski slope. We outlived the hippies, and then came the drug center of America in Aspen for distribution. We outlived that one. Then came the money, and that's the worst. I don't know what will happen.

Joern Gerdts: Taos Ski Valley can never change too drastically because it's at the end of a narrow valley. It's even more narrow than Telluride. Telluride has the great advantage because you have the narrow valley with the old town, and the big development is going on the other side. You have a mountain range that is quite unlike any other ski resort. The old valley doesn't have much room so that will keep its atmosphere. The Telluride valley is so narrow and so small that they could never develop a place like Aspen itself. And they put really strong limitations on size of buildings and how many units are allowed in the whole valley. They will weaken when the pressure gets strong and they need money.

Ernie: I don't see any large areas being built anymore; no more Vails or that kind of thing. Vail was a unique situation, and Aspen is its own special place. Now it will be more important to be different and use

Telluride today. PHOTO BY BILL ELLZEY.

Bob Mahoney & Cecil Goldsworthy pulled by car.
Telluride Main Street. COURTESY BILL MAHONEY, SR.

Undeveloped Vail valley. COURTESY VAIL ASSOCIATES.

Modern-day Vail. PHOTO BY JACK AFFLECK, COURTESY VAIL ASSOCIATES.

those differences to our advantage. It costs a monstrous amount of money to get a new area going today, too many outrageous regulations.

Friedl Pfeifer: I see maybe a few more ski areas in Colorado. It has to be in Colorado because of the snow. California has terrible snow problems. Idaho has nothing but snow problems. Colorado is just right. You have to cooperate with nature; you can't beat it. Eastern skiing will always be there. The best in New Mexico is taken; Ernie got that.

Darcy Brown: In the future, I see relatively few new ski resorts being built; I'm sure of that. It just costs too much, and there's too much red tape to tangle with now. Everybody says skiing is expensive. But, I've taken up golf in my old age, and golf is a damn sight more expensive. You go to Cypress Point in California now and pay $150 green fees.

Max Dercum: We used to do it with hard work and good sense. It isn't done that way anymore. Now you have millions, and they want you to take ten years sitting there with the plans. You keep pumping this money in, one study leading to another study, and pretty soon everybody is broke. That's the reason a number of the major potential areas have never come through. The areas that will probably continue to develop are already in. They have the organization, the money, the expansion and the potential, and the public is already conditioned to going to those places. We were very fortunate to get Keystone in when we did. My plans and the Forest Service approval all came through in nice order. We promised them good environmental protection and did it without going through ten years of paperwork.

Howard Head: Whether things have gotten out of control, I don't know; about growth, I don't care. It's not in my thinking. There's an expression from Marlowe, in 1600. He and an old friend were sitting around the fire discussing old times, and one of them said, "Do you remember Sally?" And he said, "Ah, twas then another land and long ago. Besides, the wench is dead." That's the way I feel about a company; I move on.

Warren Miller: You can't stop growth. What are you going to do? Close the road and get sued? Where do you draw the line? After I get there? I spent my whole life trying to convince people that they don't belong in square rooms because their bodies are round, and to get out there and enjoy the freedom that this sport has to offer.

I used to surf in Malibu; a crowded day would be the second auto with boards in it. And when you saw a car go by with boards, you knew who they were. It was almost the same with skiers. With skiing, I can't predict where it's headed. I can say, however, that I think skiing and windsurfing are the two most freedom-oriented sports there are in the world. I don't care when you started skiing, you can remember your first day, your first turn, the clouds.

I ran into a lady who was eighty-four, and her grandchildren gave her a Learn to Ski Week for a birthday present. She was up there for the first time in her life, rode up in the gondola and was skiing in China Bowl at Vail. That flat hill up there at three mph was extreme skiing for her. You don't have to do all this crazy ''rad'' stuff to enjoy skiing.

Why should I shut the door? On the one hand, Ernie wanted to limit it to whatever he wanted as his little piece of paradise. When people discover paradise, they tell a friend. Ninety-five percent of the skiers have heard from a friend. How many people see an ad in a magazine and then decide to take up skiing? Not many, no. Ninety-five percent of the people who ski are brought here by a friend. My wife owns Ski Rack Sports in Seattle, and she says it takes five trips to the mountains to make a skier, or one trip to one of my movies and one trip to the mountains. Then they're hooked.

Pete Seibert: Skiing is probably going to continue to grow, but to grow as a recreation. People don't get into it for the same reason that we got into it. We got into it for a sport more than anything else. Now people get into it because it's the thing to do, or to say you own property in an important place, and by coincidence you may ski.

Philosophically, the thing has changed. Unfortunately, we have not really picked up on the European idea where a lot of them go skiing and they ski for part of the day and then picnic the rest of the day, just for the sake of enjoying the outing. Our whole lift ticket system is designed against it. Over there, they encourage it. It's the experience; that's what it's all about anyhow.

Alf Engen: Skiing has been so good to me that I would want to see the whole of America on skis because then there wouldn't be so much talk about war and things like that. We would be a healthier nation, and get away from the dope and drinking. I look forward to tomorrow because I think tomorrow will be a better day than I had today, and this is the best day in my life.

Dave McCoy: Today is the best. Look what we're missing. Look at the wonderful facilities, look how the slope is groomed, look at the equipment, look at the people that are out there enjoying it. It's a greater scope of people. Even the handicapped people can get great enjoyment. The guy that is pent up behind his desk and has to be so formal and so right when he meets his clientele can come here, and he can wear the loudest clothes, and he can go out there and hoot and holler, and ski and fall down on the darn snow and roll around a little bit and enjoy it. It allows everybody an individual

expression, which you cannot do when you're wrapped up in your own business; with skiing you just have fun.

To be able to ski and to be lucky enough to be in the mountains—it's a regeneration, it's the revitalization we need. If you sit and meditate, you stagnate, but if you get out and move and create flow and use energy, it's cleansing. It clears the mind, it clears the body, and without a real good, healthy, strong body, you can't have a real alert working mind. There is great strength in the mountains; Ernie knew it and used it.

Henry Hornberger: It's the mountain that I think is the reason we were all attracted to Taos in the first place, and I think it became a common thread for us all. The mountain is what gives us life and energy. I don't mean livelihood; I mean, that's where we draw our energy from.

The only thing that scares me is that some of the people who have gotten into high positions don't even like to ski that much. It would be a lot more pleasant having someone else around you that's into skiing. They just don't understand; there's snow on the ground, and I want to make turns. You start talking about hiking up, and the comment is, ''Why the hell would they want to hike up?'' If you don't understand that, you'll never enjoy skiing. It makes me sad to see those people, the mountain doesn't give them any energy or give them any purpose. They don't come in after a day of skiing and go, ''Wow, man, that was it!''

Friedl Pfeifer: I was not interested in any big money. I was interested in a big ski school and teaching the sensations of skiing, of turning, of speed flowing down the mountain. Like Fred Iselin used to say, ''Ski like a bird and caress the mountain like you would a woman's breasts.'' The Japanese are doing what everyone thinks is a good job. You can't knock it. They're doing a good job. Breckenridge is better than it ever was. The employees are very happy. Some people say the Japanese are going to buy America because they couldn't get it with their guns. So they'll buy it.

Darcy Brown: I am sorry to see the Aspen Ski Corporation being dismantled the way it is. First they sold our interest in Spain, then they sold the two areas in Canada, and then they sold Breckenridge. The only thing left of Aspen now are the three ski areas in Aspen. They were far on their way to making the biggest ski operation in the world ten years ago.

I don't like the Japanese coming into our country and buying up ski areas, but I am prejudiced. I spent two years in the South Pacific, and I don't like the Japs. Big money is changing things. Sixty-five million dollars for Breckenridge is pretty damn good. But I hate to see it happen.

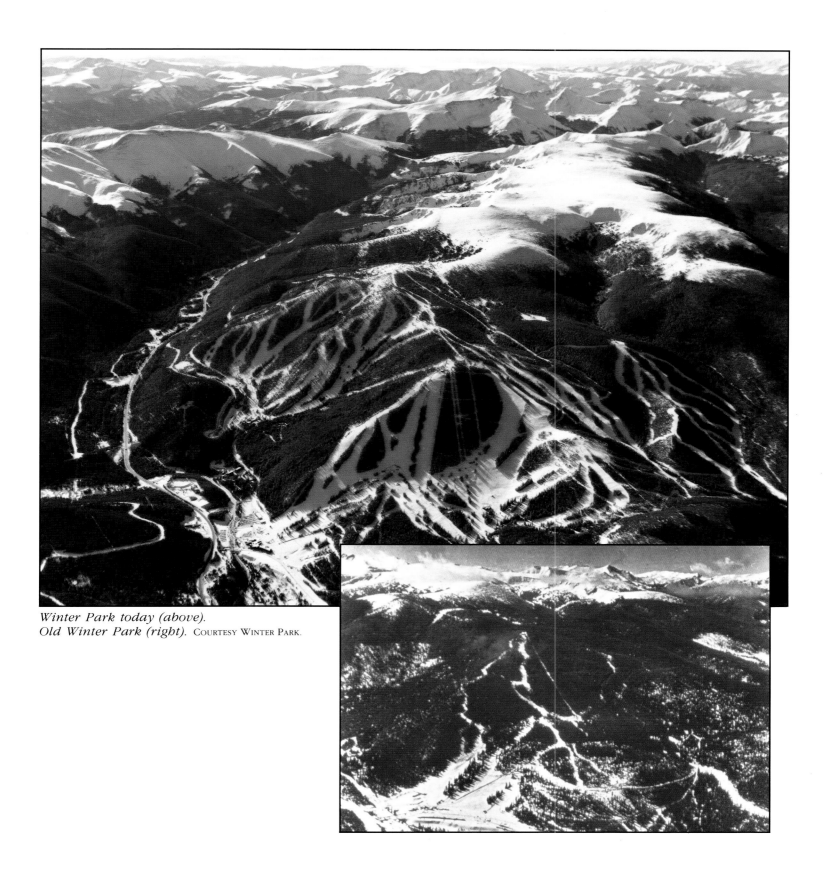

Winter Park today (above).
Old Winter Park (right). Courtesy Winter Park.

Pete Totemoff: Now big money is in this town of good old Santa Fe, squeezing out the poor old Hispanics, just like any other place. It's crazy. You know what irritates me most about this town? They honk at you when you're driving. Ralston Purina and the Japanese are the numbers people that are now running ski areas, not the people who have it in their blood.

Art Pfister: Taos must stay in the family, the same with Mammoth and Dave McCoy; that's the way I feel. Ernie and I would talk about that. We sold Aspen to 20th Century Fox. The only way you get your money out of a company today is to sell it, if you're interested in making money. You can't just sit there and run it and make money because you keep plowing it back in, and no matter how big it gets, you still are plowing it back in. So if you really want money, you have to sell it. That's why there are so many acquisitions.

Chilton Anderson: It all goes back, maybe to the road, maybe to the idea that we have to get bigger and better. And when we get better, that's fine, if you just change for better.

Henry Hornberger: I know Ernie wasn't interested in growth for growth's sake, but growth for the sake of offering a better quality product. There's a lot of talk about getting a luxury hotel at the Ski Valley. That would be another scary change. I don't think a bad change, but a scary change, because that would really change the clientele. The type of people that now don't come here because they need that sort of thing would begin to come. Those that are happy to stay at the St. Bernard in a little old room are wonderful people because of that.

Ernie preferred the style of hotel that's here, the lodge style hotel or the European type of scene. He liked the small, intimate village setting where you could walk everywhere you wanted to go; it was convenient and catered to the guests.

Ernie was a man who, when guests came to his house, he served them. Service was a very key issue with him. It wasn't beneath him. It is the same with our ski school; we serve the customer, and we say to the customer whatever it is they want to hear that makes them happy, whether it's true or not. That's where Jean is brilliant. That service is something that we have to offer. Where else but Taos do you check in, go up to breakfast, and they deliver your ski week tickets? Those are the little things. You lose that if you have to go down and stand in a big line for someone to give it to you.

Rhoda: For Ernest the change became very difficult the last few years. Ernest hated the idea of going into debt, and for the first time, we were going into debt for the new base lodge. This was against his upbringing and everything he'd ever done. But there was no way you could finance something of that size out of earnings. Change was a gradual thing. In fact, Ernest objected to the new base lodge while all of the rest of us thought it was essential because you couldn't go on with the crowded situation we had. Of course, he was less aware of it because when did he ever go down into the base lodge?

With age, Ernest became less flexible, and I felt sorry for him because very often in board meetings, he would be overruled. After all those years, what he said went unnoticed.

CHAPTER 22
What the Future Brings

Ernie: Taos has always been a unique ski area and a different experience. The steep mountain made it so, and the ski school, and the ambiance that we all created. And now we have excellent intermediate skiing although we have never been known for that.

Friedl Pfeifer: Taos must remain different; the steep skiing Ernie crowed about was his best asset. It must try and keep the jet airplanes out. They changed Jackson Hole and Aspen. Taos must stay unique because there aren't many places that can be different. Ernie knew that.

Kingsbury Pitcher: To survive, Taos must continue to capitalize on its differences and I think they should have fewer people. Maybe the answer for a place like Taos would be to be more like Deer Valley where they really charge you, and change the ticket structure to eliminate the day skiers by limiting it to three-day passes. Or, you could buy a ticket and ski one day, but it'll cost you. That will cut out the riffraff quickly. But Taos has a problem with being on Forest Service land, because of the laws on equal opportunity. That's why they can do it at Deer Valley; it's all private land.

We're going to be faced with it at Wolf Creek because sooner or later we'll get that village built which will change the whole character of the place. Wolf Creek was the first and only ski area in the United States that was able to buy its own base area from the Forest Service.

Art Pfister: Taos has great snowmaking now. I don't think there's any ski area in the world today that has any business that doesn't need snowmaking, even if it snowed every day, because they wear out the bottom and it melts off a little faster. You need it on the bottom. That's what's wrong with Snowmass. They can't make quite enough snow because they don't have enough water.

Water usage will be the determining factor in all these ski areas. In the *Rocky Mountain News,* it said that skiing and the ranchers and the rivers are at odds with each other because snowmaking is taking so much of the water out of the river in the winter when trout and vegetation need it the most. The old view was that when you take out water for snowmaking, it goes back in gradually, and it's better in the spring and summer. But now, like at Keystone where they have seventeen million dollars worth of snowmaking equipment, they are just about emptying that stream

there in the winter. We don't have that problem in Aspen, but I can see where that could happen at Taos, too, very quickly. That was our main concern when we started snowmaking; how much water we could take.

Louie Bernal: The most important thing here is the snow. That's what we pray for when we go to the Indian things. We pray to have some good snow, and in springtime, the water go down along the stream and then rain in summer time. We depend on God, you know, when we pray for this. It helps everybody and not just only us.

When Ernie had troubles with the weather, he would come talk to me. Sometimes I saw Ernie afraid about the weather. Especially when we need snow, he'd come down just to talk about the weather. We'd talk and laugh too, and predict. We don't go by TV. One time he came down as I was watching and sure enough we got a little snow. He said he knows about the mountain, but not that.

Ernie: Our expansion will be minimal from here on out. There's not much room for any major runs. There's one big run next to Al's that we could cut through the land that we own with the Burroughs. It could be a great run, as good as Al's and Snakedance; maybe we'll call it "Ernie's." It would start at the top of Al's and come down through the aspen trees that come all the way down to the return trail. You can see a very good outline of it and the slope from the trail going up to Bull-of-the-Woods.

But there will be no major growth. The growth we can advance to is a refinement more than any growth in numbers, and the using of the not completely used seasons, like from Thanksgiving to Christmas. This could be a peak season which is usually very good in New Mexico. The Thunderbird and the St. Bernard, the Hondo Lodge, the Innsbruck, everybody is going to ultimately rebuild more luxurious accommodations because everything built here in the beginning was pretty spartan.

The fact that skiers stay in the town of Taos has also worked to make more short-term skiers, which is not good from the point of view that they don't take lessons. When they don't take lessons, they leave Taos dissatisfied. They think Taos is a tough mountain. It is. People ski too fast, and it's a place where you should be in a ski school more than any other place. Jean has worked on that very efficiently by providing the best ski classes any place in this country.

We still want to remain a destination resort. The day

"Don't Panic" sign. PHOTO BY KEN GALLARD.

skier I accepted because they bring money. But the people we like, the people we enjoy, stay up here. We are slowly convincing the Taos people to sell the week and ski school, the Taos experience. We're getting there now, but it's a slow process because most lodges are short-sighted sons-of-bitches who want to sell rooms.

Chris Stagg: Admittedly, in our marketing and sales efforts, we have stopped selling the idea of staying seven nights with meals and ski school in the Ski Valley. But we've done it because there isn't any availability. Most of the places in the valley are full from December until April.

Taos has always been known for its combination of great skiing, good snow, a great mountain, the ambiance. Remember, you're talking 1955 when it started. There weren't many ski resorts, first of all, in the western United States. Vail wasn't there, Copper Mountain, Keystone, Breckenridge. You had Sun Valley, Alta, Aspen, Arapahoe and Taos. When it started, Taos may not have been one of the biggest, but it was right up there in that league.

Then in the early 1960s, we started to have big ski development. Taos had a reputation at that point, and we were ahead of the game. Any place in the West has

a charisma about it for the guys in the Midwest or the East. Taos had its niche. It had good skiing, it had good snow, and it was a great place for a certain type of vacation.

Fred Fair said when he first came here, he was here a whole week, and there weren't enough people to ski off the powder. That group of people, that niche in the market, has moved off into the helicopters. Low volume, high price. The lodges are nice but nothing to write home about, but an elite corps of people; fantastic skiing, best skiing in the world, hot stuff. Little groups of ten with a guide off skiing for the week. That's just not an area that we have the option of moving into. None of the resorts have this. Actually I think we still get more than our share of those skiers, of the guys that like helicopters and adventure skiing.

Mickey Blake: The steeps have always been a great attraction at Taos. Once Warren Miller came to do one of his shows in the old Enos Garcia gym in Taos. He came up the next morning, and I was to greet him. He wasn't sure he was going to stay until he took one look at Al's Run. Then he told his wife, yeah, they were staying.

Chris Stagg: The mountain is our biggest asset, its steepness, our expert terrain, our adventure skiing;

Scott Kennett in Fifth Chute. PHOTO BY KEN GALLARD.

that's the one aspect that we've got that works. We are one of only four ski areas in the country that are telling you they're the best for experts. And our ski school is again #1 in the country by the October, 1991 *Ski* survey. That's the second time we've gotten that ranking, and we are very proud of that. There are four hundred other ski areas saying that they're the best for the intermediate. Why try to take away your natural asset and convince people that they should be over here? If we were trying to build another Vail, then it might be a problem, but with the number of skier days we're doing, we can live quite handsomely off the people that go to Vail and say it's too boring. That's more our niche.

Chris Stagg: The people who work here at the valley are even more important now that Ernie is gone. It used to be when you went to Taos Ski Valley, all three hundred people in the ski area knew Ernie Blake; they knew the guy that owned the place. That's like going to a restaurant and having the owner come and greet you for dinner and buy you a bottle of wine. That's part of the reason you wanted to come back. When you're beginning to grow like we are now, you are on a different scale. And then the people who work for you have to fill in that personal role. That's where the ski school is very important, the lodge owners, the lift operators, the guys who park the car, everyone.

Everybody has different views of the ski business. From our point of view, we've got eighty percent of our business that is not staying in one of the hotels or condos in the valley. They don't have a place to go to the bathroom or change their boots or get out of the weather, so we've built a much nicer day lodge to take care of the majority of the business.

I think the Ski Valley could help in being the force to pull things together and make things work for the future, but we don't have that subtle charisma that Ernie did. You'd have to sit them down and say this is the way it is. The problem in the last five or ten years has been that there's been more and more friction between all the different factions especially the Ski Valley and the lodge owners. Ernie held it together, but there was a lot of resentment about Ernie doing that.

I think the lodge owners probably don't like us having a restaurant in the new building. But the St. Bernard is always packed, and if I want to take somebody to lunch, I can't. If you do want to have Jean's guest food, the line at the sandwich counter is around and out the door. The burger deck is packed; you can't get a seat at a table by yourself. Yet, I don't think they understood our position about the overflow.

Dave McCoy: I never believed in competing with

the community. That was one of the big things that Ernie and I talked about prior to him going down there and developing Taos. And one of the other things was not to get excited and to get too big too quick where you might have other people dictating how and what you would be doing.

Tony Mitchell: The valley certainly has a different appearance than it had years ago. Some of it had to happen. There's no way around that. I don't know how it will be twenty years from now. Somebody young like Chris Stagg is probably what is thought to be necessary. I think that Mickey's attitude has gotten better. I think it's a continuing agenda to make Taos Ski Valley better for the skier like Ernie always wanted. By that I mean we need discussion and debate because having gone to Vail for the first time in seventeen years last February, there is simply no way that Taos Ski Valley can or should try to emulate that.

It took a lot of different people to make Taos Ski Valley what it is. Ernie was the king, along with Jean, Dadou, "Big Daddy," Herman, Kaarlo, the Brownells, the ski school; it took all of these people and that kind of commitment. It's the question, whether when those people are gone, will it continue in that same way? I'd like to think it will. In Taos we are blessed by our physical limitations. I think that the hodgepodge of styles and things that we have is pretty tolerable.

Ernie: We need new lifts because I don't like lift lines. I don't like it for myself. I don't go to a restaurant if I have to wait long, or a theater. Ultimately, all the lifts will be replaced. But the existing lifts are not that outdated because we were lucky by putting them so steeply that we actually get a faster climb than you do in most of the high-speed lifts built in Colorado. You have to get people up fast so they don't get cold. We don't have the same cold they have in Colorado, Wyoming, and so forth, but it's still the thing you want to avoid. You want short lift lines, and you want the people skiing between lifts.

I would never put a lift up to Kachina Peak, but that's left to the next generation. It would give us the three-thousand-vertical-feet differential which is a mythical figure of achievement for a climber. Mickey has to decide that. We have a lift line laid out. I laid out a lift line for a Poma lift actually, a drag lift, but I think now I like for skiers to hike the ridge. It makes it more of a mountaineering experience, what skiing used to be and still should be. I wouldn't put a lift there.

The good skiers are the ones who know the literature, and who are aware of Taos and who automatically go into ski school here and take very little selling. Europeans don't like to have a crowded ski school. We don't have large classes, and we teach them things that will give them the opportunity to improve their style.

Installation of top terminal for new quad, Fall 1989.
COURTESY MICKEY BLAKE.

Helicopter transporting cement for new quad lift towers, Fall 1989. COURTESY MICKEY BLAKE.

Wendy (Blake) Stagg, Keith, Chris & Erin Stagg. PHOTO BY KEN GALLARD.

We should have a guide service like they have in Europe, an in-between class, between private lessons and ski school. A little less teaching and a little more adventure. At the right hour and the right place, they could ski over the summit without the threat of getting lost, and they get the camaraderie that is what skiing is about.

Barbara Ferries was here after lunch today; she was Chuck Ferries's sister. They were both tremendous racers in the 1960s. She thought the article on Taos in *Outside Magazine* was tremendous. *(Ed. Note: See Appendix C for a copy of this article.)* We always get these stories that are terrible for our publicity. It wasn't a good story from our business point of view, it was disastrous. All this talk about steepness, it discourages people too much and those stories attract the weirdo skiers. Sure, I built Taos Ski Valley with the idea it was steep and rugged, and it is a difficult place to get to and that makes it more charming. But we needed intermediate skiing; that we didn't know at first. But now I'm pleased Taos is being recognized and known for its steepness; it helped us in the end.

John Koch: I remember talking to Ernie about cutting easier trails, before we got Rubezahl finished, and I kept saying "No, no, no; none of this intermediate bullshit. Keep the tradition. Stand apart." And he'd say, "Yeah, but look at Vail and look what they're skiing on and they're making money. I'm tired of not making money."

Ernie: To ski the steeps in the early years was much easier; there were no moguls. The snow was soft then; now, there is no need for the old signs for "fill your sitzmarks." Before the war, there were never any moguls, and I didn't even know the term—*bukelpiste* —is the German term for it.

I have a funny story from *The Aspen Flyer,* March 19, 1955 about sitzmarks. It says, *The skiing is unbelievably good. New snow, fine sun and all the trimmings. But, withal, today's skiing may have its little tragedies. For instance, if you make 1,978 sitzmarks on your way down the mountain, it'll be too bad. If you don't fill the depressions up before leaving the vicinity, it'll be worse. That is to say it's unfortunate to fall, but it's villainous to leave such a yawning pit behind for someone else to ski into and maybe disappear forever. We know of one man who chortled at such advice and belligerently left an unfilled sitzmark. On his next run, he skied into that very same pockmark and broke his leg. And he deserved it. So, replace your divots, that's all.* Now we have Donny Campbell, "Cat Daddy," and with all the packing equipment and snowmaking there aren't sitzmarks.

I think we will have a lot of Germans and British coming here if things go the way I think. The romantic appeal of the Southwest and the publicity we've had in books and magazines helps. Even the name "Taos"

Annual Ernie Blake fireworks. PHOTO BY KEN GALLARD.

Torchlight parade for Ernie's birthday. PHOTO BY KEN GALLARD.

adds something to the appeal. Taos Ski Valley must remain fun and it must remain an adventure. We must always make it better, not bigger.

Mickey Blake: You can't keep building. We keep trying to improve our equipment, and I think that's essential. We can still do a quality job on a small scale and go our own way.

Alf Engen: We are doing the same thing in Alta that Taos and Ernie are trying to do. We are not trying to make it big. We are trying to make it better. We have to cut a little more room for them to ski. They say they'll cut out that tree over there and a little bit over there and make a bigger opening. You have to make it look natural.

Jean Mayer: In order to maintain the charm and charisma—that's what it is, charisma—it's got to be felt from the heart. When people talk to you about ski areas in the U.S. today, what is the key word for the development of ski areas? It's real estate, it's condominiums, it's building up houses and things like that. They don't talk about the skiing experience, the camaraderie. It's turned around the other way now. And that's what's wrong.

Ernie was never thinking of the money coming into Taos Ski Valley; he was thinking of the mountain. There is the key; that's where we had a common goal. But it's a growing pain, and that growth has to be channeled properly. Mickey totally agrees with me that the idea of service for people is most important here. We must not put priorities on keeping up with the Joneses, being like the other ski areas. We must have the guts enough to be different and to be individualistic. I can foresee so many problems.

Papa Mayer: The people are not the same in skiing as it used to be. Now it's a hungry businessman who invests but doesn't ski. They must love to ski; they should love the mountains. Jean's life is Taos Ski Valley, not money. Ernie has been educated, he has traveled and everything, yet from the moment he moved from Santa Fe to Taos, nothing else was of interest to him except that all the world should know about Taos Ski Valley.

Jean Mayer: Society has lost the sense of value, the real basic sense of value. That's why Ernie and I were good, because Ernie and I understood the very fundamental basic sense of value. That's what I mean when I say the mountain, that it's been worth it, and that's it. And the value of the effort, and the reward is within the effort itself; not the reward from financial gain.

Ernie brought the people here. We were important to bring them back, but Ernie would get them here. Once they were here, then it was up to us. But, still, he was very good in making a story from nothing

and feeding the people with stories and things, and just keeping after them over the years. That's why you had a resort like Taos. It became famous. Even years ago, they were comparing us with Sun Valley. Well shoot, there was no way you could compare it. They all say the mountain is great. Now, we find ourselves—I mean it's going to change—but we still find ourselves the rinky-dink little ski area that has international status. And that's Ernie; that was originally his doing, and we have to follow through.

Ernie had class. He had heart also. Class and heart, and he was able to charm people; he had a lot of charm somehow. Lots of women would fall in love with him; his eyes, you know, would twinkle. In his own way, he was able to be very attractive to people in general. Attractive in such a way where the men would not feel threatened, and the women loved him. That's the kind of stuff they don't talk about, but that's some of the real Ernie.

He had class because he was able to be friendly with all kinds of different people. It's like that piece from Rudyard Kipling: *"He who can walk with kings and not lose their common touch."* That he was able to do. He had respect from his workers, the Spanish, the Indians. He had connections all throughout the United States. People with lots of money would come to Ernie because he could talk to them on any level with all his stories.

Harry Franzgen: Ernie had the touch, it's so true. My grandfather once told me, "Some people you're going to meet in your life, you don't even want to waste the effort even knowing them." And Ernie didn't have that philosophy at all. If a dishwasher would come over and ask for a free pass, he would talk to the kid and get a kick out of it, especially if he got good PR out of it.

Chris Stagg: Ernie made the decisions from the start; we were lucky that he did, and we miss it now. Beyond the fact that Ernie was a master of publicity and of charisma, with his sense of history, Ernie was the man that did it. There's a mystique; this is the guy who did it, he's the celebrity. Taos has that with Ernie. You're always going to be Ernie's son or Ernie's family, but you won't have the guy who started it and developed it. You lose some of that celebrity status.

Henry Hornberger: The biggest change is that we don't have Ernie to make the decisions; Chris hit that one on the head even last year; Chris and I agree. Chris does the marketing, and I do the ski school. We used to go to Ernie and say, "Okay, Ernie, how about this; why don't we try this or let's do this?" and we'd go out and do it. Maybe it was right, maybe wrong; it didn't matter, but we always had Ernie, and whatever decision was made, "Ernie said so."

Tony Mitchell: We talk about his charm, but it was

Ernie with admirer, 70th birthday. PHOTO BY KEN GALLARD.

Ernie's ability in a crisis. He would be a good guy to have your back to if you were in trouble. While he moaned and whined in a crisis, he was at his best; he was at his most innovative, and those are all skills that are really valuable. When you got nervous, Ernie was not. When the issue was joined, he was a competitor and a fighter, a survivor and a success. When I would be concerned about bad news, Ernie would take it well. When we had a problem, Ernie was there and took it well and participated. That was leadership.

Henry Hornberger: Because Ernie had such an incredible confidence in himself, everything that he said exuded that confidence. It was either there was some shit under there, so it's no good, or there's no shit under there, so go for it. There wasn't a question in his mind; it was yes or no.

Before Ernie died, everyone ever hired had been interviewed by him. Somebody had to be way off base for Ernie not to hire them, you know, like in food services or some of those other areas.

But in the ski school, because that was his baby, we'd go through the whole hiring clinic process. We make our decisions like we always did, but now when we make our decisions, we have to live by them. In the old days we didn't have the final check, Ernie did. So we'd say, "Okay, we think you're a wonderful person, now go talk to Ernie," and Ernie just had the amazing ability to bring something out. They wouldn't say anything on the employment application, and somebody would then come back to me and say, "Oh, I need a previous injury report." Ernie would say, "No, we can't hire them; he's had operations on both his knees, and he's injured his back," and you go, "Huh?" Or he'd go, "Oh, no, he has a horrible driving record." I sat through dozens and dozens of interviews with Ernie, and it was really difficult to not jump in there and start to talk because he would just stop a sentence and sit there and stare at the person. The person would start to scratch. Ernie didn't ask a question; he'd just stare at nothing. The person could get up and leave if they wanted to, or they'd have to think of something bad to say—like my father is an alcoholic and so am I, but I'll never drink again and on and on. And holy cow, "Ernie, how did you do that?"

He would make statements about history or tell stories when you first met him that made you want to get to know him better; to stick around and say, "Boy, that was really interesting; this guy must have more interesting things." He would make statements which would crack me up, because he was so wrong on dates so often. He would go, "1944, Wednesday at two o'clock, the bombers came in and I was on the toilet." Nobody would ever possibly dispute the

time. Or he would say, "And so-and-so was retreating out of the outskirts of Frankfurt with his army which is ten battalions on," and he would name a date. My dad was also quite a historian, and when he visited he would say, "Huh? That wasn't the date," but nobody would ever dispute Ernie. That was hilarious.

Part of the intrigue was that, boy, this man knows a lot of stuff. I think that's what allowed him to sell Taos originally to people in Texas, to come here to ski. He never hesitated if somebody said, "Is Taos a good ski area?" "No, it's the best ski area." "What kind of snow do you have?" "We have light, dry snow, and the sun shines everyday." It's not like he believed it, but don't even think of questioning him because that's the way it was. And if you questioned him, it would be basically like saying, "You're a liar." Ernie, with his charisma, did not allow anybody to ever question that in him. When was the last time you heard somebody say, "Wait a minute, Ernie. I'm not real sure that that's true."

Harry Franzgen: What Ernie respected, I think, was education and wit. If you could show him a little bit of that and not fall into all his traps that he set for everybody, and if you showed a good sense of humor and a certain toughness, he admired you; he wouldn't shrug you off.

Tony Mitchell: Ernie did so many things, but one of his great skills that has always amazed me was how he brought people into an issue and drew from them their thoughts; in many ways it flattered people and appealed to their ego. But he could do things his way and not offend them. That wasn't hypocritical in my view. He was finding out what people thought; he was giving a piece of Taos Ski Valley. He sure let you participate, but Ernie was in control.

Georgia Hotton: Ernie was legendary from day one. He worked so hard and worked so long with so little financial backing. He made things work where others would have given up. But, again, we all believed in the idea, perhaps as much as he did at times. Ernie had tremendous family support. Mickey did a whole lot very early on, and Peter and Wendy did their share, too, when they could.

Chris Stagg: The European background of the people at the Ski Valley means a great deal. In the early days, Europe was the place to go. The Rockies didn't really count. Ernie brought a big slice of Europe to his ski area and down to the town of Taos. We're a different type area, and we're glad of it. Ernie was glad of it, too.

Elisabeth Brownell: The old school came through. He was of the old school, and there aren't many like that with the upbringing he had at school in Switzerland. It's nice; always the ladies first, and he was most charming when he was your guest. Ernie came and visited in Chicago, and in the morning when he was leaving, he had his linen and everything folded and handed it to me. I said, "Ernie, you don't have to do that." "Well," he said, "this is my upbringing." And he was most gracious as a guest. He was the old school gentleman when he was at your house; we had him often here for dinners, and at the Thunderbird with the guests, he sat in the middle with everybody around him. He mesmerized people.

Ed Pratt: Ernie's legacy to this world is that Ski Valley. I think his whole life, from the time that he came to this country, was spent making his dream take shape. He and Pete Totemoff found this place from the air; I think that's when the light flashed on. Later on, when they went into the Ski Valley on the ground, then the light burned brightly. From that day until the day he died, he was always pushing for completion of the dream. Now, whether the dream ever had an ending where he was concerned, I don't know. I don't think so. I think he was always looking to make it better—not bigger, but better.

Ernie was a man who had a vision. He knew what he wanted, and he didn't leave stones unturned to get it. I'm not saying from a standpoint of greed. I'm talking about painting the picture of making things happen: the vision that he had for that valley when he first found it to what it is today, which when he passed away still had not been completed. It had come a long way from his first dream of what he saw. Ernie would not sell his soul to get what he was after. He was a man who wanted beautiful things for people, but was not in the race horse time of getting it. He was willing to wait, to build slowly and try not to make too many mistakes. It had to be done slowly. This was his basic philosophy. I don't think in any time in his life that he ever had a thought of making money. Sure, knowing Ernie and knowing who he was, he didn't want to lose, but he could wait to reach his goal with maybe the pot of gold down the line.

Alan Crane: Taos Ski Valley was put together like an opera; a common theme that you come back to again and again is Ernie's dream. It moved everybody; it drove everybody. Ernie was so intensely proud of his mountain being special. I told him, there is no place in the world, and I've been to Europe and most major ski areas, but there is no place that has this personality and that came from one man's dream.

Can the dream keep going? God, I hope so. For sure the crowds have increased. It's the old-timers who make it different. Elisabeth, like Jean and Dadou, has the most loyal following; people who stay at the Thunderbird love Elisabeth. If Elisabeth stays, and Jean and Dadou stay, and Mickey and Chris and the old instructors like Max and Chilton, then it will work. Also the people who have been around for years in the lodges like Evan Blish and Phyllis Wilson. Of course Mickey has the controlling stock; Ernie did that. It is the old way. It's the most pragmatic way. You can't run anything from the grave.

Joern Gerdts: It's getting so hard to find an area that is not modernized with skyscrapers. But I think places like Taos will be more and more in demand because you can't find places anymore that are unique with that atmosphere. Very few places have it; it's something to preserve.

Linda Meyers: I keep telling Mickey that there is a mystique about Taos that is incredible. I'm not quite sure what it is, and he always laughs at me. But there is a mystique that's there that Ernie built, and maybe it was Ernie himself. I knew the feeling about Taos long before I ever came here. I had a feeling about Taos. Was it the steepness? I don't know if it was that. Was it the snow? I don't know if it was that. It had to be a combination of all those things that Ernie put together.

I don't know how or if that special feeling can keep going, but I think it can. I think we can give that person out there today some of that magic.

Jean Mayer. PHOTO BY KEN GALLARD.

Sometimes when I think about that, I think, gosh that's crazy. How do I give some guy I met from Philadelphia today some of the mystique? Mickey and I saw him first run in the morning, and he said, "This is fantastic!" So, somehow, he'd captured some of it.

Rhoda: None of the early people really went into this as a business. It was the way we wanted to live. We went into it as a way of life. We liked living in the mountains, and all we required was sustenance and a roof over our heads. We never anticipated it really being a big business. To Ernest, home was in the mountains. When we moved West, friends thought we were crazy, and then about ten or fifteen years later, they were all sorry they hadn't moved out of New York and done something different.

Walter Widmer: Ernie lived to ski. After all, when he started to ski it was over seventy years ago since his mother forced him to ski. He was one of the pioneers of skiing. When he began skiing in Switzerland, it was still in its infancy. He was in on the beginning of skiing both in Europe and in America. There are not too many like him around anymore.

Bob Brierley: There's a great amount of love that's still around that's gone into this mountain. Ernie chose people who loved the mountain the way he did, and they really didn't want anything out of it except to be part of a group and to belong and to ski our mountain. It's still our mountain. It's still a personal preserve practically for just about everybody that's here.

Darcy Brown: Taos Ski Valley has a much more intimate feeling than you get at the typical ski resort. There was always a personal touch there.

Wolfie Lert: Ernie carefully nurtured his persona of the tough old man of the mountain, which he was, but he helped it along with all his different hats and all of those things. He was quite aware, I think, of what he was doing and how he was building this reputation of throwing people off the hill and saying the wrong thing and inciting people and all of that kind of thing.

If only Mickey can carry on in the old way to a certain degree. He's just as unpleasant on the hill to some people as Ernie was, so that's okay. Being tough with the public is nice. I think that's a great thing. They get so coddled and so over demanding, and if there's a little rock or a tree somewhere, they sue. The hell with them. I think Ernie was right; he said, "Look, it's a sport that has its risks, and we make it not easy on everybody, and you take it as it comes." Mickey has certainly inherited some of it, and more and more as he gets older. He reminds me more and more of Ernie. I hope he and Jean can be close. Ernie wanted that.

Buzz Bainbridge: Some good years; lots of fun. It was fun to stop in there in the winter or summertime or anytime and say "hi" and go up and sit in the little apartment, have a drink, go over the years, brag to each other, look over old photographs. That was a tough act to follow. Ernie was the best. He made that little valley world famous.

John Koch: I guess what I mainly got out of Ernie and his Ski Valley was, "You gotta smile and you gotta have adventure." In the early days there was a whole herd of us living under lovely conditions. It was hard and wild, but that's what we did if we wanted to ski back then, we had smiles on our faces at the end of the day, and we had adventure.

There were times we would get snow, and it was the joy of being there then without the crowds of people that made it. We'd get all the guys together; we'd get our avalanches done in the morning, and the instructors would get done with their classes, and the Mayers would come, and we'd just ski; we'd start on one side back over in West Basin and just work our way across the mountain. It was a pretty awesome way to live, but that's what we did. I was skiing all day and getting paid for it; not much, but I was getting paid for it, and I was doing something that was making people have a good time.

Lee Varoz, Sr.: Ernie, he really loved the mountains too; more than anything, he loved the mountains. The last time I saw Ernie was that year before he died. He came over here, and he spend maybe about four hours over here with me. We sat here and looked at the mountains. It was my birthday, my 80th birthday. Ernie gave me a beautiful cowboy hat which I still have. I wouldn't get rid of that hat for nothing.

Louie Bernal: Ernie believed in the nature of God, this mountain. He spent half of his life right here in this valley. He told me one time, "Louie, you know, I love this mountain. Every time I think about you guys up at Blue Lake, I think Blue Lake is one of the most important things because it's a sacred place for you Indians."

Ernie, he lived up here in the mountains, you know, and that give him his strength. There is somebody around up here that take care of his life; there is something up here in this mountain that nobody knows. Mr. Blake, he was a strong man. I think he got that from this mountain.

Howard Head: I'd like to say that the difference between Ernie and everybody else in his class is like this: there was Sigi Engl who ran Sun Valley, but who had nothing to do with the spirit of the founding of it. There were Friedl Pfeifer and Fred Iselin who ran Aspen and Sun Valley before that, but they just helped run Aspen; they didn't build Aspen. There was Pete Seibert who, in a sense, did build Vail, but he left Vail. That separates him out. There is only one man in the

The Blake family today: Peter Blake, Chris Stagg, Mickey Blake, Wendy Stagg & Rhoda Blake. PHOTO BY KEN GALLARD.

world that I know who built an area. It happens to be Taos. The man's name is Ernie Blake. It's Ernie's spirit that makes this place, not the place that makes Ernie.

Warren Miller: To be a pioneer in anything is not an ego problem. The pioneers had very strong egos, but at the same time, I always use the analogy that pioneers have always dug with their ass full of arrows. That's the way it is. Ernie hung around long enough to get rid of the arrows and build a great legacy for the American skier.

Jean Mayer: Ernie never cared for money or things that were fancy. The old Poma lift that used to pick people up was a way to get up, but certainly not a comfortable, easy way. There was always a feeling of an achievement for everybody who came to ski or came to share with us; it was more of an adventure. Now the model of the ski area throughout the Rockies and everywhere is: make it as nice, as comfortable, as luxurious, as easy as possible for the public.

I don't think that the mountains should be tame; I don't think the mountains are meant to be that way, and I think that's what we understood. There's no better time to get out on our mountain than when there's a big storm, when everybody needs to be sheltered inside and stand by the fireplace and drink. That's when it's best for us to get out and enjoy nature. It's like being at sea in a storm. That's when the elements talk to you, when you feel it.

That's the way Taos Ski Valley was; it was always in a storm, in a challenge situation. That's what Ernie really did. He always enjoyed a good fight, and that's what it was; the fight was continual, against the elements. Everyday it was a new fight, a new challenge. There was never a winner in the fight. That's why it was good, and that's what I liked, and that's what Ernie liked.

I think that nowadays man is trying to be a winner, trying to control the mountain, to shape it, to mold it, to tame it. It's like you take a wild animal, and you make it totally domesticated. I feel we don't want our mountain domesticated. We want to keep it wild.

I am more aware now, after Ernie's passing and realizing all the changes, of what I've been able to share with Ernie for thirty years. What I can appreciate more now is his human side and his idea to really get the public; Ernie wanted to get everybody to share his association with the mountain, with the snow, with skiing as a winter sport. It was not so much Ernie the skier; that was not it. It was Ernie who loved the mountain and loved to bring people to his mountain, the tough mountain with its challenge.

Epilogue

On January 21, 1989, at 12:30 p.m., thousands paid tribute to the memory of the man who founded Taos Ski Valley some thirty-three years ago. From Kirtland Air Force Base, two New Mexico National Guard Fighter Jets, led by Ernie's long-time friend Captain Mike Rice and followed by Sandia ski patrolman Captain Dave Walker, took off on their mission. The two jets streaked across northern New Mexico, carrying the ashen remains of Ernie Blake for one last flight over the mountains he loved so dearly, flying over Sandia, Santa Fe Ski Basin, Angel Fire, Rio Costilla, Red River and finally thundering up Taos Ski Valley. They made first one pass over The Valley, glided over the top of The Ridge, turned sharply above the Valdez Rim and finally headed up Taos Ski Valley once again for Ernie's last run. Over the jet's radio, Captain Mike Rice spoke professionally to the ground crew, "Ready to jettison Ernie's ashes approximately over the top of the #5 Lift." But as the jets dipped their wings and rolled in the deep blue New Mexico sky scattering Ernie's remains, in a different voice filled with a mixture of deep respect and love, Mike added a final, "Goodbye, old friend." The Taos Ski Patrol gave honor to their general's passing with a 21-gun salute from Highline Ridge, the guns being replaced more fittingly by 21 avalanche hand charges which resounded from mountain to mountain shattering the respectful hush of the valley below, echoing in the hearts of all who looked on. All took their special places to pay homage befitting a man who not only founded a magnificent ski area now rated in the top ten in the world, but who also created a winter economy for the once small village of Taos. Rhoda Blake, his wife, stood up above Zagava corner. Mickey, his eldest son, stood on the specially made platform below Lift #3 with Mayor Jeantete and other town dignitaries. At 12:30 p.m. the lift operators stopped all lifts out of respectful mourning for their loss. Simultaneously, other ski areas like Santa Fe and Rio Costilla shut down their lifts to pay their respects to this unforgettable man who was one of the first great pioneers of skiing in America.

Ernie Blake on his 70th birthday. PHOTO BY KEN GALLARD.

APPENDIX A
Cast of Characters

ANDERSON, CHILTON & JUDY: Chilton is one of the first ski instructors and supervisor of the ski school. Raises registered Angus cattle. Founder of the Taos School of Music. Judy is one of Taos's first "ski bums," and a community volunteer.

BAINBRIDGE, BUZZ: Involved with ski areas such as La Madera, Santa Fe, Red River, Flagstaff, Jackson Hole and Buttermilk at Aspen. Public relations genius. With Ernie, helped create "Ski the Rockies" and "Ski New Mexico."

BEARDSLEY, KEVIN: For many years in charge of the Taos Ski Valley Ski Patrol, which is one of the best in the country, if not the best.

BERNAL, LOUIE: "Chief of the parking lot." Taos Pueblo leader.

BLAKE, ERNIE:* Creator/owner of the Taos Ski Valley and main subject of this book.

BLAKE, MICKEY: Owner of TSV. Ernie's and Rhoda's oldest son. Mechanical genius and radio "nut." Father of four of the grandchildren.

BLAKE, RHODA: Mrs. Ernest Blake. Baroness of the Ski Valley. Namesake of Rhoda's Restaurant and Rhoda's Revenge.

BLOCH, VERA: Ernie's youngest sister from New York City (via Germany, Switzerland and England).

BRIERLEY, BOB: Old friend and longtime investor. Built the Kandahar. Ran the Texas Ski Patrol.

BROWN, DARCY: Aspen pioneer. For years headed the Aspen Ski Corporation.

BROWN, MONICA (Schultz-Lidl): One of the first Bogner models. Ex-wife of ski film producer Roger Brown.

BROWNELL, ELISABETH & TOM: Owners of the Thunderbird Lodge. Elisabeth was Ernie's first secretary and champion chef ski racer. Tom brings jazz greats to TSV in January.

BRYAN, TONY: Ex-Taos ski instructor. Now number one Vail ski instructor.

BYERS, KEITH: TSV ski instructor.

CRANE, ALAN: One of TSV's first guests. Missed only one year in thirty-three. One of early Chicago crowd.

CRARY, BUD: A hell of a cat driver. Cut first roads on the mountain, then ran first ski and rental shop at TSV.

DERCUM, MAX: Built the Ski Tip Ranch near Arapahoe in Colorado. Created Keystone. Ski pioneer and racer. Wife, Edna, still winning international races at age 77. Third husband and wife to make the Ski Hall of Fame.

ENGEN, ALF: Norwegian/American. Built some of the early runs at Sun Valley with Friedl Pfeiffer. Was 50 years director of Alta Ski School. Famous ski racer, jumper and teacher of kids. The only four-way champion to emerge in any country. When he went to a race, he never thought he'd be beaten, and he was only beaten twice.

ENGLE, GEORGE: First ski patrolman at Winter Park in Colorado. Ran the ski school, was the accountant and has managed the area for years. One of the founders of the Rocky Mountain Ski Association with Ernie.

FAIR, FRED: Powder hound and fearless pilot. Perpetrator of many wild stories.

FRANZGEN, HARRY: Past owner of the Hondo Lodge, and before that, the New Gnu in Vail. Known as "Hondo Harry." Sold the Hondo to Mary Madden in fall 1992.

FROHLICH, VICTOR: A fellow Swiss who believed as Ernie did that America had great opportunities and very few restrictions. Owned the Innsbruck Lodge and managed the Kandahar.

GALANKA, ALICE: TSV ski instructor.

GERDTS, JOERN: *Life Magazine* photographer. Involved with Snowmass, early Vail and Telluride. Longtime friend of Ernie's.

HEAD, HOWARD:* A true genius and legend of skiing. Invented the Head Ski and the wide-bodied Prince Tennis Racket, revolutionizing both sports.

HOOPER, ROBERT: Associate Professor of Geology, University of South Florida at Tampa.

HORNBERGER, HENRY: Past manager of Taos Ski School, now director of Aspen Ski School. Originally from Canada.

HOTTON, GEORGIA: Educator of the Blake children and unforgettable early ski instructor. A jack-of-all-trades.

JOKELA, KAARLO: A Finn and friend of Jean Mayer. Owned the Thunderbird Lodge in the beginning years.

KILLINGER, MAX & THERESA: Max is a smiling and popular ski instructor, also manager of Taos Ski School. Theresa has done a little of everything at TSV. Avid windsurfers.

KOCH, JOHN: One of the first paid ski patrol. Now resides in Aspen.

KRETSCHMER, HERMAN:* Right up there with Ernie and Buzz Bainbridge as PR impresario. Storyteller supreme. Helped create Ernie's legend. Wife, Jeannie, taught skiing.

LANG, OTTO: Ski instructor for Hannes Schneider Ski School in St. Anton. Ran Sun Valley Ski School for years. Started Mt. Rainier Ski Area in Washington. Movie director. One of the first to see TSV with Ernie.

LERT, WOLFGANG: Partner of Hagemeister/Lert, San Francisco, importers of Bogner and other ski fashions. Ski friend of Ernie's, and one of the first to see TSV with Ernie.

MCCOY, DAVE: Owner and creator of Mammoth Mt. in California. Father of Olympic racers. Coach of women's junior ski teams. Veteran of thirty years of ski racing. Besides Ernie, the only other person to have a family-owned major ski area in the country.

MAYER, CHARLES & NICOLE (Papa & Mama): Father and mother of the Mayer brothers, Jean and Dadou. Helped to build the Hotel St. Bernard.

MAYER, DADOU: French ski racer with charm and style. Famous women's classes. Creator of the Hotel Edelweiss with its European ambiance.

MAYER, JEAN: Besides Ernie, the person most important to the

226

development of the Taos Ski Valley. Technical Director Ski School, coveted #1 ski class. Hotel St. Bernard creator and host *par excellence.*

MAYER, ILSE: Austrian creator and co-owner of the Hotel Edelweiss. Ski racer and mother of three.

MEYERS, LINDA (Tikalsky): Olympic racer and friend of Ernie's. National United States Downhill Champion 1957, Women's Combined Champion 1959, 1962.

MILLER, WARREN: The U.S.A.'s most famous ski movie mogul, out of Vail.

MITCHELL, TONY: TSV's attorney and board member from day one.

NEEDHAM, DICK: Editor, *Ski Magazine.*

NORDHAUS, BOB: Started first New Mexico ski area in 1936 near Albuquerque, retiring in 1977. Gave Pete Totemoff and Buzz Bainbridge their first jobs in skiing. A champion racer, still racing at 80 +. Built Albuquerque's Sandia Tram—a real pioneer.

PATTISON, BUELL: Along with his father, built the original Thunderbird Lodge. One of the largest land holders in the Taos Ski Valley area; negotiated various land deals with Ernie.

PFEIFER, FRIEDL: Started Sun Valley with Averell Harriman in the thirties. 10th Mountain Division in World War II. Started Aspen in 1945 and ran the ski school. Director of Aspen Ski Corporation. Started Buttermilk at Aspen. Famous ski pioneer.

PFISTER, ART: Director Aspen Ski Corporation and TSV Ski Corporation.

PITCHER, KINGSBURY: "Pitch." Around in the early days of Santa Fe Ski Basin with Ernie. Before World War II, the only American ski instructor in Sun Valley with Friedl Pfeifer. Helped develop Snowmass with Bill Janss and built Ruidoso Ski Area in New Mexico with R. O. Anderson. Owned Santa Fe Ski Basin and now owns Wolf Creek Ski Area in Colorado.

PRATT, ED: "Big Daddy." Early owner with wife Phyllis* of the Hondo Lodge which they ran for many years after they "retired" from the U.S. Army following twenty years service.

ROSEN, MYRT: Dr. Al Rosen's* wife. Owner of the first ski shop in the Taos Ski Valley.

RUEGG, WALTER: "Black Walter" or "Rubezahl." Built all chair lifts in the Taos Ski Valley. Another Swiss.

SCHUETZ, GODIE: Swiss restauranteur (Casa Cordova). Ski instructor and champion ski racer at 70 + years of age.

SEIBERT, PETE: Founder of Vail and Beaver Creek Ski Areas. Formerly manager of Loveland. In 10th Mountain Division in World War II. Former Aspen ski instructor.

STAGG, CHRIS: Director of marketing and supervisor of the ski school for TSV. Wendy Blake's husband and father of two of the grandchildren.

TOTEMOFF, PETE: * Aleut Indian from Alaska. First person to look at TSV with Ernie. Did everything. Installed chair lifts, was ski instructor, employed by the Forest Service and was a champion Senior Racer. Great friend of Ernie's.

VAROZ, LEE (Sr.): * First lift operator. As Lee said, "Ernie trusted me with everything. I had the keys to everything. I was one of Ernie's best friends."

VOLLER, FRANZ & THERESA: Austrian owners of the Innsbruck Lodge.

WIDMER, WALTER: One of Ernie's best friends and confidants. Ernie and Rhoda's "breakfast club." Head of ticket office until retirement in 1991.

*Deceased.

APPENDIX B
Taos Ski Valley Trails

as told by Ernie Blake

EARLIEST RUNS AND LOWER FRONT

AL'S RUN: Named for Al Rosen, the famous Taos surgeon politically instrumental in getting the Ski Valley off the ground. He skied with an oxygen mask and tank for twenty years until his death in 1982.

CHICKEN ALLEY: Shortcut around Snakedance. Self-described.

DON'T TELL: George Hatch, mountain manager, gave the name to this run next to Tell Glade.

EDELWEISS: The edelweiss is the hard-to-get flower of the Alps; it is the distinctive flower all over the Alps.

FIRLEFANZ: "Firlefanz" is a German term for something extra, like silver threads on a Christmas tree.

HANNES SCHNEIDER: Hannes came over here in December of 1938, after having been arrested by the Germans after they took over Austria. He was locked up in a concentration camp where he was bought free by Harvey Gibson, a New York banker. Gibson came from North Conway, New Hampshire. He had Schneider organize a ski school there, run by his star teachers from St. Anton who he had sent over here. He invented the Learn to Ski Week. A colorful man, he was a wise-guy who had black curly hair and very dark skin, much more Italian looking than Austrian. He skied at great speeds and was a great natural jumper, jumping off cliffs and over houses. He was the first one who put to use the ideas of Mathias Zdarsky, who had published a manual on skiing in 1897. He did it in practical terms and made the elegant stem christie from what was a clumsy snowplow turn. Schneider returned to Austria in 1955 and died there at the age of sixty-five.

INFERNO: Named after the famous race, still run yearly, started by the Ski Club of Great Britain and the Kandahar Club in Murren, Switzerland. It is an old race, and one of the longest, most vertically differential runs in the world.

JEAN'S GLADE: For Jean Mayer.

LONGHORN: Texas cattle. First run from the top. Avalanches easily.

PORCUPINE: That animal in the tree.

POWDERHORN: The device you carried your gunpowder in.

PSYCHO PATH: A path for "psychos." Named by Wolfie Lert.

RHODA'S REVENGE: Chilton Anderson: "Rhoda's Revenge" came about because when we'd go off the top of Al's Run to sweep, or just go up and make a run in powder, Rhoda would disappear, and then, all of a sudden, she would be with us again. We'd ask, "How and where the hell did you come from?" And she'd just sort of smile sweetly, and we'd go and ski down. It wasn't until a long time later that we realized that Rhoda had found this little cut-off so she didn't have to ski the first steep part of Al's.

SHOWDOWN: An army term, or gunfighter term.

SNAKEDANCE: Named by Wolfie Lert for the Hopi dancers.

SPENCER'S BOWL: For E.J. Spencer, my favorite English teacher and coach from my school, in the Engadine, Switzerland.

STRAWBERRY HILL: Called Beginner's Meadow, Idiotenhuegel. Lots of wild strawberries in the summer.

TELL GLADE: Named for William Tell, the crossbow-shooting marksman, who is also the liberating Swiss hero of the Rossini/Schiller opera.

WHITE FEATHER: Historically, a white feather was the symbol of cowards during the Boer War. In England, gentlemen who didn't volunteer for the queen's army in this fight were considered cowards and were sent white feathers by their girl acquaintances. So that's this easy run that we built.

1965 — RUNS FROM THE TOP

BAMBI: "Bambi" goes back to the Disney movie, as the timid one. It's for slow skiers.

BLITZ: This is the German term for lightning. A steep run which unfortunately sometimes avalanches.

BONANZA: A bonanza.

CASTOR & POLLUX: These twins of Greek and Roman mythology gave their names to the bright stars in the constellation Gemini. They also gave their names to two rock passages in Murren; we knew that from the Ski Club of Great Britain. Now they are two side-by-side double black diamond trails here in Taos.

DEREK'S PULLOUT: Named for Derek Hale, a patrolman here in the 1970s. Better swimmer than skier and represented Puerto Rico in the Pan-American games. The spot above the turn between Bambi and Zagava gratefully utilized by all novices.

HONEYSUCKLE: Named for the flower.

LORELEI: Lorelei is the blond German siren who combs her hair in the sun, sitting on a tall rock in the Rhine River singing songs that lured the poor German fishermen in their rickety fishing boats to their deaths in the whirlpools of the river. "Lorelei" here is the same thing; it is like a beautiful woman who is very admired but who is dangerous. There's a giant rock field on the right with narrow spots likened to a woman's figure.

MUCHO GUSTO: Named in honor of our Mexican friends.

REFORMA: Reforma refers to the Mexico City boulevard that honors Benito Juarez and the law and order he brought to the Mexican people with the Revolution.

SIR ARNOLD LUNN: A British skier largely responsible for making skiing a competitive sport and who set the first slalom course in 1922. He organized the first Kandahar Race in St. Anton, Austria, in 1928, and the first FIS Alpine World Championships at Murren, Switzerland. Through his efforts, slalom skiing was recognized in the 1936 Olympics.

WERNER CHUTE: For Werner Duettra, caught in a slide in 1971.

WINSTON: A double black diamond for the World War II giant.

YUNG CHO: One of the first paid ski patrolmen. He was the first Korean Olympic skier, and here he shoveled bumps.

ZAGAVA: John Zagava was the partner of Harker in the original Hondo Lodge in 1946, nine years before we got here and walked about with Pete Totemoff.

BACKSIDE — KACHINA BASIN

EASY TRIP: Named by Georgia Hotton in 1971.

EL FUNKO: Named for a local businessman who was not an especially gifted skier and may well have fainted at his first sight of this cliff-like run.

HUNZIKER BOWL: My favorite run, never to have a lift. Named for Paul Hunziker, the Swiss engineer who designed the first Kachina lift and who was killed in an airplane accident on the way to inspect the lift.

JAPANESE FLAG: One of the

many flags at the Ski Valley; this one used to survey the Kachina lift area.

KACHINA BASIN: Named for one of the deified ancestral spirits believed among the Hopi and other Pueblo Indians to visit the pueblos at intervals.

LONE STAR: Named in honor of the Texas flag.

MAXIE'S: For the late, great New Mexican balloonist, Maxie Anderson, who made the first Atlantic crossing in a balloon.

PAPA & BABY BEAR: Two of three original trails together on Kachina. "Mama" is now part of another trail.

PATTON: "Patton" is in honor of my commanding general, George Patton. He was the greatest American leader of the war, an American general who had balls, which most of them didn't. He didn't give his troops time to recover and the chance to reorganize; he followed up completely regardless of the exhaustion of his troops. It seemed inhuman to us at the time, and we were very bitter about it, but it was very wise. I think the role he played as the brutal, loud-mouthed general who tried to speak like a low-class soldier was a fake.

RUBEZAHL: Rubezahl is a red-haired, one-eyed East German giant who takes money from the rich bankers and manufacturers of textiles and gives it to the poor working charcoal burners and weavers, a schnitzelized Robin Hood. The first and longest run all the way down the backside.

SHALAKO: Named for Indian dancers celebrating a Zuni mystical being of extraordinary stature.

STREETCAR: Named by Tony Mitchell in 1971.

TOTEMOFF: "Totemoff" is named after Pete Totemoff, an Aleut Indian from Alaska, who worked with Buzz Bainbridge at Santa Fe. He was with me when we first looked at Taos Ski Valley from the air and on the ground. He was a great skier and became a great veteran ski racer later.

WALKYRIES: From Norse mythology: the Walkyries were the wood nymphs who tended the battle-slain warriors and led them to Norse heaven—Valhalla. This is a trail which disappears into the trees. "Walkyries" is a great run if you hit it after a powder snow; otherwise, there is knee-bashing through the trees.

WINKELRIED: A Swiss who led farmers with no breastplates, nothing, just knives and axes in 1386 to murder the Austrian army. He martyred himself against a wall of lances so his compatriots could be victorious.

THE RIDGE

FABIAN: "Fabian" was named for Fabian von Schlaberndorff, a technician, who plotted to kill Hitler. He was not military. He put a bomb on Hitler's plane disguised as two bottles of Cointreau. Fabian was ultimately captured and tortured monstrously by the gestapo who were sure he had something to do with the scheme. He denied everything; he didn't give them any names. He came out a wreck, but he recovered and became a Supreme Court justice. He wrote a book, *They Almost Killed Hitler* which had arrived already in bookstores in 1946.

HIDALGO: Named for the Mexican martyr and patriot-priest who perished in his attempt to bring about Mexican Independence in 1810.

JUAREZ: The notably honest and gifted pure-blooded Indian from the extreme south who brought justice and recognition to the Indians and mixed-blood populations of Mexico.

NIÑOS HEROES: Young Mexican cadets who all died in defense of Chapultepec Castle during the Mexican-American conflict of 1846.

OSTER: "Oster" was a German colonel, later general, who was the second man in the German Military Intelligence Service. He realized what Hitler stood for early on and sabotaged the German war effort by warning the Danes that the Germans were planning to attack on the 10th of May, 1940. They didn't believe him because he had several times before told them that the attack was coming, and they thought he was a fake sent by the Germans to deceive them. Oster was executed just at the end of the war by Hitler's men.

SPITFIRE: Named for the German World War II fighter plane.

STAUFFENBERG: "Stauffenberg" was the general who was nearly successful in placing a bomb, 2.2 pounds of high explosive, more powerful than dynamite, in Hitler's bunker. It was the 20th of July, 1944, but unfortunately, that day Hitler's meeting was not underground, but in the barracks above ground which blew apart with the explosion but didn't kill Hitler. It burned him, his clothes and his eyebrows, and his eardrums were pierced. His hair was singed, and his clothes were just gone, but he was not seriously wounded. Hitler was able to speak that night on the radio and stop the resulting uprising. Everybody, including the police, had been arrested, and not a shot was fired, to my knowledge. After midnight, the victors had to turn around and let the people go. Actually, there was not much revenge on the ones who had done the arresting because most had been taken by surprise and not resisted, and they were happy to forget. Stauffenberg was shot by a firing squad. He was 38 years old. He was very bright and came from a very distinguished and impressive Southern German Catholic family.

TRESCKOW: Another supreme patriot who conspired to eliminate Hitler.

ZDARSKY: The Austrian engineer, Mathias Zdarsky, born in 1856, who wrote the first really useful ski manual in 1897. He contributed the snowplow and the rudiments of the stem turn, and he was one of the first to go to a metal binding with toe iron and a device that permitted tightening.

NO WIMPS

THE STEEPS

Taos, Jackson Hole, Telluride:
If you want to relax, go somewhere else

BY PETER SHELTON

When Jean Mayer and I came upon her at the top of Stauffenberg, she was plastered against the side of the hill, clutching the snow with every fiber, as if by osmosis she might become part of the mountain and not have to face the inevitable: that down was the only way out.

"Oh, God. I'm so afraid. Do you see my friend? Is he all right? Oh, God." I peered into the narrow shoehorn gully and saw first a ski, then a little farther down a pole, then another ski and the other pole. And way down, about 400 vertical feet below, where the chute opened to become part of the West Basin, a tiny figure in a blue ski suit stumbled back uphill toward the wreckage.

"Oh, God, what am I gonna do? Don't touch me! Is this the only way down? Some people told us there was a big opening farther out the traverse." In fact, she had found it, the biggest opening, the widest and easiest of 20-odd skiable slashes down the West Basin Ridge at Taos. Ernie Blake, the area's Swiss-German founder, named it

Stauffenberg, for one of the three conspirators who tied a bomb under Hitler's table in 1944. Ernie, now 75, is fascinated with martyrs.

There are four ridges at Taos (the others are Kachina, Tresckow, and Highline) that together form the area's cornice-scalloped skyline. There are easy ways off this backbone to the more reasonable basins below, but they are not the reason you come here.

The chutes at Taos are a litmus test for good skiers. Survive these runs and you can legitimately call yourself a good skier. Ski them well, with élan, and you are in the hero range. Underestimate the extreme steepness, however, or the tubular claustrophobia of a 15-foot-wide slot through the trees, and you yourself are a candidate for martyrdom.

Taos does everything it can to discourage inexperienced skiers from trying the ridges. The start of the High Traverse, which takes you out to Stauffenberg, bristles with signs, including one that says: STEEP SLOPES ARE SLIPPERY. YOU MUST KNOW

HOW TO SELF ARREST AND PREVENT INJURY TO YOURSELF AND OTHERS.

For chunks of every winter the ridges aren't open because of avalanche danger. The ski patrol records between 300 and 600 slides within the area boundaries each year. When Rod Newcomb of the American Avalanche Institute first saw the weak, continental snowpack and radically steep pitches at Taos, back in the fifties, he reportedly said: "Why in the world did the Forest Service ever let you put a ski area here?!"

But when conditions are stable and the patrol has done its work and the ridges (and the myriad lines pouring off them) are open to the public, Taos is some kind of heaven. The steep is a magnet, an addiction. The body is lighter, the mind more purely focused when gravity works uninterrupted by horizontal planes of earth. And people come back year after year after year.

Jean Mayer came in 1957, fresh from the French national team, and hasn't budged. He skis every day, a tiny diamond

earring flashing from his left lobe. He is the proprietor of the Hotel St. Bernard, and some of his employees have been in the valley for 15 years, men and women who should know better. Some have made a religion of walking the 3,000 vertical feet to the top of Kachina Peak on mornings when the patrol is not likely to allow access from the lifts. Patrolmen call them the Rad Dogs.

Ask Ernie Blake about the stunning steepness and its appropriateness for the general skiing public, and he will tell you through a wry, tight smile, "It was a miscalculation. I assumed, after the boom of the 1950s, that people were looking for steeper and steeper slopes to test themselves." Most people weren't, but Ernie went with what he had and what he loved. It happened to work out. "I can't ski the steeps anymore," he says, an athletes's bitterness toward the temporal body shading his words, "...which I built for my pleasure."

Ski here and you feel a change; the mountain has raised the level of your game.

Or reduced it to shambles. Despite Jean Mayer's insistence that the woman on the hill relax and stand on her skis, that everything was going to be fine, she managed to go only a few inches into the couloir. Suddenly she was down and sliding. It was quickly apparent that the term "self arrest" was not in her ski vocabulary and that she was in for the full ride. Mayer took off like an ambulance-chasing dog. I couldn't watch, so I eased in and began collecting stray gear.

By the time I reached the little human cluster at the bottom (it took awhile; the intensity of the pitch and my added appendages reduced my technique to a timid survival stem), our lady was sitting up, the color back in her cheeks and then some. Incredibly, she was unhurt. Mayer was admonishing her to stick to the easier trails, read the signs, assess her ability, and so on. She wasn't listening. She was suffused with a deep radiance: one part shock, one part gratitude, and two parts sheer, freaking exhilaration.

It takes a rare combination of human and nonhuman factors to create such a severe situation. Most ski areas—most mountains —simply don't have the raw physical gifts. Some areas have

Dana Brienza & Doug DeCoursey on Hidalgo, Wheeler Peak in background. PHOTO BY KEN GALLARD.

pockets of steep, but pretend (or wish) they didn't. Most skiers today can't handle extreme terrain and/or wild snow conditions. And given the legal climate, the ski-area-as-amusement-park majority would rather their clientele didn't find themselves on that particular adventure ride.

There are exceptions, places with the natural talent and the enlightened attitude to prepare and promote the steeps. Jackson Hole, Wyoming, is one of the best. There is so much terrain (the mountain is 4,100 feet tall by three miles wide) that the patrol can rotate open areas, like crops, to give dangerous steep zones a rest.

Squaw Valley, despite its urban California ambiance, has some radically steep skiing. Scott Schmidt made his name (and a lot of oohs and aahs at Warren Miller screenings) jumping off Squaw's cliffs. And KT-22 is sufficiently titled to have required the owner's wife, years ago, to make 22 kick turns down its face to safety.

Telluride, Colorado, is a mountain blessed or cursed, depending on your aptitude, with a full quilt of tight evergreens. To know Telluride, to do it justice, is to become a shadow creature, a needle threading the spaces in the unforgiving, powder-laden woods.

Skiing this stuff requires commitment. You must be dedicated to becoming an expert skier. As Mayer says, "It takes condition, technique, and attitude—a kind of aggressiveness. You must have a very strong commitment to the outside ski." This is the ski that turns you, checks your speed, keeps you from slipping helplessly off the pitch. It's also the ski you lean away from when you are afraid. The movements, Mayer is saying, need to be automatic and fail-safe.

To achieve this kind of mastery in the no-fall zone takes time and mileage. There are no shortcuts. Ski school can help, especially at a place like Taos,

where good skiers come to take the next step up. But make sure you are assigned an experienced teacher. If he or she takes you directly to the steepest shot on the mountain, you've been had. Learning can't see its way through the fog of stress.

You need to love funky snow. It's an acquired taste, like caviar; there will be no grooming machines up here. There will be wind crusts, sun crusts, death cookies, sastrugi, ice moguls, avalanche debris, and various grades of corn and powder.

You need no-fault equipment. Top of the line. Tuned. No rentals. It's got to be yours, you have to feel intimate with it. You have to know your binding isn't going to release in the middle of a Hail Mary turn. You have to know your edges will hold on frozen ball bearings.

The commitment comes down, ultimately, to the moment. If you don't feel the seriousness at the top of Stauffenberg or Terminator, you are dangerously relaxed. Ken

Gallard, a 15-year Taos veteran, stops at the top of every chute and repeats his checklist mantra: "OK, adjust goggles, check pole straps, check ballsack, pole plant, pole plant, get it right..." Get it right now, in your head, because when you're slipping toward your first edgeset it's too late. "Get it right the first time, 'cause there ain't nowhere to bail out."

Then, when everything is ready, when all the pieces are in place, then you drop into a magic hollow, a place where rhythm replaces fear, where the feel of snow underfoot displaces style and technique in the conscious mind, where the steepness itself, the free-falling between turns, makes it all so blessedly, exquisitely easy.

[This article appeared in *Outside Magazine,* November 1988.]

APPENDIX D
A Winter in the Rocky Mountains

by André Roch, 1937

On the 10th day of our journey from Geneva via Paris, Cherbourg, New York, Chicago, Denver and Glenwood Springs we rolled right through the heart of the Rocky Mountains. Another few miles, and we'll be in Aspen, Colorado. The night is black as ink, our car shoots at high speed over the distance, our headlights silhouette a group of deer—another halt: Tom loads his rifle, Bill lifts it, aims and shoots. One deer is hurt, the rest jump the barbed wire fence and tear off into the night. Blood traces over the fence into the meadows. We try to hide the blood as best we can; fines for hunting out of season are high. One o'clock in the morning we drive into Aspen. The first impression is sad: the town is empty and dead, there is no snow, but an icy December wind drives dust through the streets.

Aspen was born nearly 60 years ago. The first trappers and miners arrived from the South, always fighting Indians, via Ashcroft or through Leadville and Independence Pass. They found lead, zinc and silver so that Aspen soon developed into a splendid location. In no time at all the town was built and soon it counted 12,000 inhabitants. It was here in Aspen that the richest silver mines of the United States were exploited. Of this boom period, the most magnificent stories are told of Aspen. Unlike the shady characters so common on the trails to gold or oil, the migrants who built Aspen remained remarkably honest. Money flowed easily and the bars, dancehalls and vaudevilles flourished. There was even an opera house where Sarah Bernhardt came to collect her share of the boom. The inhabitants of "Main Street" had their carriage, their own driver.

Then, at a given moment, the price of silver dropped and there was a terrible crisis; mines were abandoned, mine-owners fled and the miners themselves wandered off to Cripple Creek, where gold had been found. Today there are only 700 residents left in Aspen and the majority of buildings are in disrepair or ruined; many can be bought for $30 or thereabouts.

The town looks depressing, especially so in winter. In summer, the lush vegetation hides the ruins. But among the many ruins, there are still some palaces which have been maintained, mute proof of the glamor of bygone days. Some mines are in operation too, but to reopen those that were abandoned would require vast sums—and the value of their production would be questionable at present. There are, however, those old miners and prospectors who cannot overcome their mining-fever, who still hunt and dig for rich veins, big strikes. Usually they are quite penniless, but if by some misfortune they can dig up some dollars, they invariably waste them on new tunnels which usually run into thin veins or none at all.

Dr. Langes and I had left Europe in order to explore the Rocky Mountains to find the most valuable locations to ski. But when we were briefed, we found that actually our job was of quite a different nature. The location had already been selected—and we were instructed to verify its excellence, to check on terrain and climate to be sure this location permitted the launching of a big resort.

Unfortunately some serious errors had been committed before our arrival, and this complicated our work. Try to imagine a valley much like the upper part of the Valais. In all this land, there is only one town, Aspen, which would be located like Viege (Visp), with the one difference that Aspen lies at 2,400 meters. The highest mountains, just as in the Valais, rise above 4,000 meters and are located in the more southern chain. The whole country is completely wild. Old paths which led to mines or forest service trails are the only means of access to the interior of these several valleys. About 6 miles from Aspen, along the banks of Castle Creek, a splendid hotel called the "Highland Bavarian Lodge" was being built.

The group which invited us to the United States had formed a corporation in order to launch a major winter resort. Unfortunately, the location for the Highland Bavarian Lodge had been selected in summer. The majority of the slopes on which the winter vacationists were to ski faced South or West—and as we found during the ensuing winter, these slopes can never be skied at this latitude, which is the same as Sicily's. Even after the heaviest snowfalls, the strong sun and the dry air combines to let the snow vanish in a flash. On the other hand, snow accumulated steadily on the North and East facing slopes and stayed light and powdery from December to March. At the Bavarian Highland Lodge, the slopes were so steep that the danger of avalanches did not permit us to carry on any skiing. If you can visualize that the forests reach to 11,500 feet, that above the treeline the snow is continually blasted by west winds, and that the slopes below, with their steep cliffs and deep gullies, look much like the valley of St. Nicholas in the valley of Zermatt—you will understand that we were not exactly in a skiers' paradise and that we did not look forward with enthusiasm to the winter we were to spend here. Worst of all, the corporation had already launched a full-scale advertising campaign, and guests from Boston, Philadelphia, New York and Chicago were planning to spend their vacations at the Highland Bavarian Lodge and even planned to ski there.

To compound misery, the snows did not arrive all through the month of December and whenever we strapped on our skis, it was most damaging to their running surfaces because of the many treetrunks and rocks. We always returned dejected, promising ourselves that we would not venture forth again until real snow had fallen. However, we never could stand inactivity very long and soon we were out again hopefully searching for better slopes. The last day of December, we left to investigate a valley North of Aspen which we thought might carry some promise. We travelled by car on the road to Independence Pass, to the entrance of "Lost Man Valley", which we climbed and then proceeded along a side-branch which through Hunter Creek led us to a point above Independence Pass. This valley returns to Aspen, it is certainly 15 miles long; after the first, rather steep drops, it enters the forest where the fresh snow was very deep. Our return trip was strenuous. Night caught us when we were still 6 miles from Aspen. We were at the bottom of a gully, the sides of which were vertical. Only the reflections of light from the frozen river permitted us to advance—hampered by giant boulders and fallen trees. When it became quite impossible to progress any further, we built a campsite. We started several large fires and were soon engulfed by clouds of smoke. One o'clock in the morning, the moon broke through and gave us enough light to proceed on our difficult march. A coyote tried to scare us with his piercing shrieks and howls which echoed from the surrounding cliffs. Finally, quite exhausted, we drifted back into Aspen at 5 a.m. in time to wish everyone a happy New Year.

Early in January, the lodge was sufficiently completed for us to live there. From there, our excursions were limited to tour Richmond Hill in all directions. Richmond Hill is a small mountain facing the lodge. From it, a splendid view can be enjoyed—but for skiing it carries little promise. Its slopes are either too steep, or exposed to too much sun, or covered by dense forests or else battered by strong winds. The best slopes are certainly those running down into Aspen. But even there, the lower slopes are endangered by avalanches.

Ashcroft is located at 11 miles from Aspen, at 2,800 meters, on top of Castle Creek. The first miners arrived here from the South by crossing Taylor Pass, 3,600 m. Large mines were started, one of them the "Montezuma" at 3,800 m., from where the ore was lowered by cablecars to the mills, which were operated by hydroelectric power. At one time, Ashcroft had over 8,000 inhabitants who drifted by and by to Aspen, when richer lodges were found in that location. Nowadays there are only a dozen ruins left at Ashcroft and only one single inhabitant. As early as December, we came by to Ashcroft and two things impressed us: firstly, Ashcroft is the center of a natural bowl surrounded by high peaks, most of them reaching above 4,000 m. Secondly, in this vast bowl the east and north facing slopes appeared well-suited for skiing. The other directions are too steep or too wooded. During the month of January we had the opportunity to explore the slopes dropping East from Hayden Peak. The first stops were painful—frequently we lost our path in the dense forests and sometimes the hidden trees became a serious obstacle to the skier.

On the 15th of January, I left alone from Ashcroft, planning to climb Hayden Peak—about 4,000 m. high. It was a fine day, but towards noon, a strong wind came up and carried the snow into fantastic, turbulent shapes—leaving bare rock ledges. With luck I never lost the trail to American Lake; above, I came out into the open slopes. I climbed on over the bed of a former glacier, of which only the moraines are left, to arrive in a vast basin. I took off my skis and hid them in the snow so they wouldn't be carried off by the wind. On the ridge, the wind was so powerful that breathing became difficult. Without further troubles, I reached the peak by following this ridge—only to find that the real Hayden Peak was still more than half a mile away and that the ridge would be rough to follow. As it was 2 p.m. I had to turn around. I had a magnificent view of Conundrum Valley and in the distance many of Colorado's famous 4,000 m. peaks: Snowmass Peak, Maroon Bells, Pyramid Peak, Castle and Cathedral Peaks. I named my location "Ski-Hayden"—it is over 4,000 m. high. I climbed down rapidly and soon found my tracks in a small gully which we had explored a couple of days earlier. After this first success, we rarely had the time to explore any further: guests followed each other in rapid succession at the lodge and we had to act as guides for them. Though we knew very little about the region, we did have a few skiable slopes for them to use. On our trips we often ran across deer, skiing down noiselessly, it was possible to overtake them and ski right into the middle of their group. Coyotes were shy, one saw them only rarely. We were told that there are moose around as well as mountain lions, but we never met any. Once we saw a wolf from far away and another time a group of 4 mountain sheep.

The month of May is best suited for ski-mountaineering. The snow softens in the bright sun, but as there is fresh powder nearly every day, conditions were superb. Dr. Langes climbed one peak North of Hayden Peak which he called "Frida Peak."

A few days later, Billy Fiske, Dr. Langes and I climbed Hayden Peak; it was easily

the most magnificent ski trip of the winter. The weather was fine, a foot of fresh powder covered the country. The dark blue shadows of the spruce and the sun dancing through the aspens made our climb an enchanting experience. Above the trees, the wide open slopes in which our tracks looked minute, offered the promise of superb skiing. We left our skis on a secondary ridge which we then followed with some difficulty to the peak. The view was quite overwhelming and I recorded it by panoramic pictures. The slopes leading down to Ashcroft can be compared with the best of the Parsenn. Immense "schusses" where your face freezes in the wind and clouds of powdersnow rise behind you, making the skier seem like a rocket shooting along the ground. Hardly at the end of one schuss, we started into the next one, cheered by the fabulous skiing. Lower down we crossed a small forest, then we came to steep slopes which forced us to descend in short turns at the bottom of a gully. We returned to Ashcroft in less than 20 minutes—however we were still 6 miles from the lodge, luckily the road drops for most of the way. After our first ascent of Hayden, I returned there three times: once with skiers and instructors from the East; Messrs. Otto Schniebs, Florian Maemmerle, Heinrich Schoinsbach, Bill Blanchard and Romison; another time with the best skiers from Denver, Thor Groswold, Frank Ashley; and finally with Aspen skiers Fred and Frank Willoughby and forester Clarence Collins. Each time, we felt the same enthusiasm, as no one had ever seen more splendid skiing country before.

After Hayden Peak, I climbed alone to the summit of the highest peak of the region, Castle Peak, at 4,300 m. The climb was more demanding than Hayden Peak, but even more rewarding. The descent was again a series of basins and steps, one more rewarding than the next. We had climbed up via Pine Creek and Cathedral Lake and skied down by the abandoned Montezuma mines. After all these trips, I felt that I knew the region well enough to establish a list of all ski-tours possible. There we had the basic facts and valuable indications as to the value of the region as a potential ski-center. But were there not, near Aspen, other slopes suitable for skiing which might at one time or another compete with our projected development? In order to answer this question, we began to explore the regions around Independence Pass as that road became usable again. In this way we discovered Green Mountain, which has splendid slopes but not enough vertical drop. We also climbed to Lost Man Lake to explore Lost Man Valley, where a 6 mile long valley drops rather mildly to offer an amusing trip. Finally, the first day Independence Pass opened, Frank Willoughby and I took off in order to climb Mt. Elbert, 4,400 m., highest peak in Colorado. We left Aspen at 2 a.m. and

reached the pass in total darkness. Trenches 6 meters deep had been cut to open the road through the beds of numerous avalanches. We dropped down on the far side of the pass until Monitor Gulch; as we had never seen Mt. Elbert from near, we did not know yet from which side to attack it, though from studying the map, we had planned a tentative route. When we reached Monitor Gulch, we found that snows had melted too much to use our skis and we left them in the car. We climbed at first on a good path, which we had found quite by accident. Higher up, we crossed bare meadows, sparsely vegetated—then fields of hard snow which led us to the ridge, from where we can see the peak. This is a giant mountain easy to climb from any side. After only 4 & 1/2 hours we are on the top, surprised at the effortless success. A few days earlier, I had suffered from stomach troubles, which prevented me from enjoying fully this magnificent tour. We had a splendid and far-reaching view. In the southeast, one can recognize Pikes Peak through the fog, most famed mountain in Colorado— and to the southwest the familiar mountains of Aspen, which are barely recognizable from this side. We take our usual panoramic views for our records and then descend again. To speed matters, we slide down vast snowfields, often sinking in to above our waists. Finally we find our car and return to Aspen; tired and content I return to my bed to continue taking care of my health.

We have climbed many peaks, but still this is only a small fraction of the peaks in Colorado, which cover a much vaster region even than the Alps. Nonetheless, as a result of our many explorations, some valuable conclusions can be drawn:

The east-chain of the Rockies does not receive enough snow to permit establishment of a winter resort.

The west-chain is too low to offer good locations. Remains only the central chain of the Rockies. Aspen would constitute an ideal center to open the magnificent Ashcroft region, which once developed, would be a resort without any competition. Probably one could find other, equally splendid locations as Ashcroft in Colorado. However, the great obstacle in most cases is the fact that the valley-floor rises to above 3,000 meters— as the peaks barely surpass 4,000 meters this usually offers too little vertical differential. Another important point is exposure of the slopes; much more important here than in the Alps, because of the geographic location. West slopes are continuously swept by strong winds; south-exposure slopes receive too much sun and are usually bare of snow. Remain only the north- and east-facing slopes, which are heavily covered with powdersnow, sometimes too deep for comfort, for 4 months of the year.

Once the location had been firmly established, we devised a development of the ski resort as per the instructions received from the corporation. First of all, the road to Ashcroft must be totally rebuilt and in some part relocated to evade avalanche danger. At Ashcroft, hotels capable of accommodating up to 2,000 skiers—minimum necessary to make a cable car feasible—must be built. Besides the hotels, a Swiss village is projected with all the shops, cafes and offices found in a good winter resort. A lift is planned on a ridge facing exactly north. On the northwest slope of the hill will be the beginners' slopes and slalom glades. On the north- and east-facing slopes two or three jumping hills will be built, also a skeleton run and a sled-course for children. The lift in this way will serve various purposes. Besides the lift, the cable car of over 1,000-meter vertical rise will open unsurpassably beautiful slopes. The first (intermediate) station, 600 meters above the valley floor, will open up 4 different slopes of differing demands. The top station, 1,000 meters above the valley floor, will open up a much vaster region and 8 different runs. Moreover, a variety of tours and of variation to these runs will be available, maybe 15 all in all.

The upper terminal, at 3,800 m. elevation, will be quipped with another hotel which will offer spring and summer skiing. A special automobile service should be established to bring home skiers who used the long runs, not ending at the lodge. The most important runs will have a vertical drop of 1,600 m. over a distance of 2.5 to 5 miles. The ski tours feasible from Ashcroft have been explored by us and number more than 35. Keeping in mind that the country is beautiful in summer too, with fishing, horseback riding and camping available, many plains-inhabitants will search out this country in summer. Add to this the deer-hunt in fall, it is easy to see that America could find here a resort that would in no way be inferior to anything in the Alps.

But, let us not worry—the more Americans will enjoy skiing, the more they will want to visit our alpine ski resorts. All we must do is to receive them well.

Ernie Blake skiing into Kachina Basin, January 1972. PHOTO BY WOLFGANG LERT, COURTESY BLAKE FAMILY COLLECTION.